Key Urban Housing of the Twentieth Century

Plans, Sections and Elevations

Hilary French

Key Urban Housing of the Twentieth Century

Plans, Sections and Elevations

Hilary French

Laurence King Publishing

Published in 2008 by Laurence King Publishing Ltd
361–373 City Road
London
EC1V 1LR
Tel: +44 (0)20 7841 6900
Fax: +44 (0)20 7841 6910
e-mail: enquiries@laurenceking.co.uk
www.laurenceking.co.uk

This book was produced by Laurence King Publishing Ltd, London

A catalogue record for this book is available from the British Library

ISBN-13: 978 1 85669 564 0

Printed in China

Designed by Anita Ruddell
Drawings by Hilary French, Samson Adjei, Yan Ki Lee, Gregory Gibbon
Picture research by Claire Gouldstone and Cecilia Mackay

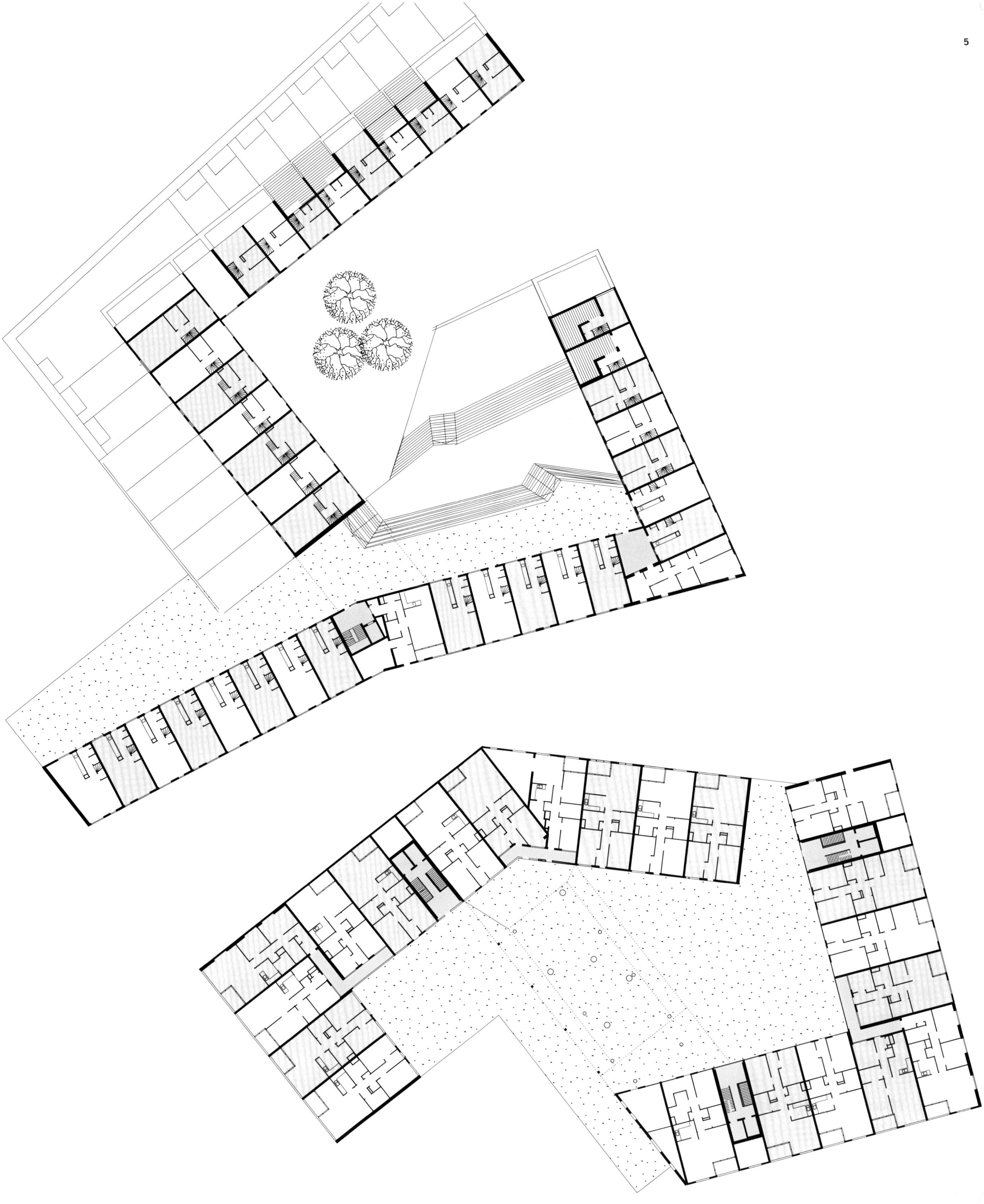

Contents

Introduction

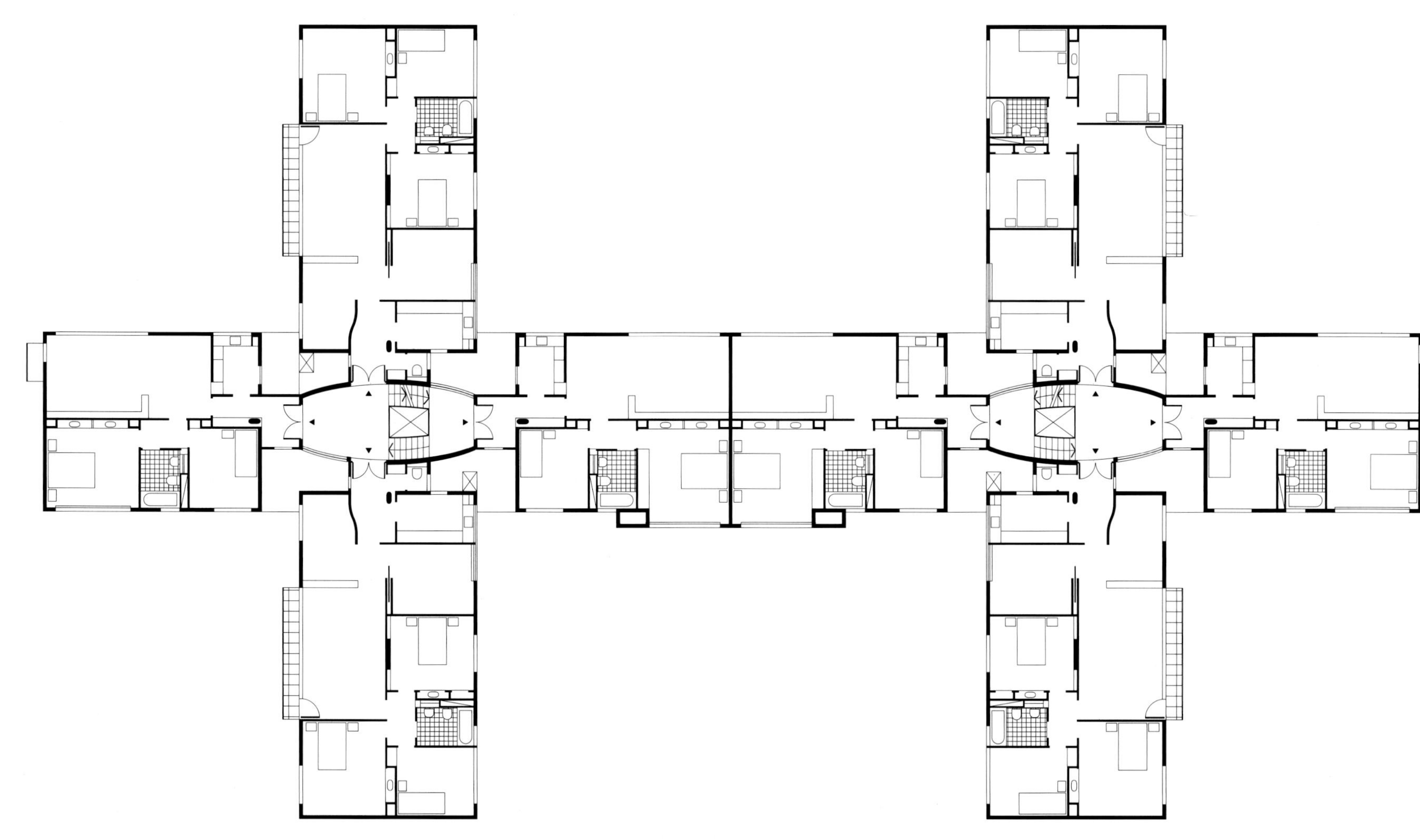

We are making this book because we believe that we shall want to escape from suburban street corridors to live in parkland with common amenities, air, and a view; and that the problems of housing cannot be solved by the provision of millions of little cottages scattered over the face of the country, whether in the garden city manner, or as speculatively built stragglers.

R.R.S. Yorke and Frederick Gibberd, Introduction to *The Modern Flat* (London: The Architectural Press, 1937, second edition 1948)

Drawing is a form of communication with oneself or with others. For the architect it is also, amongst other things a working tool, a way of learning, understanding communicating, transforming; a way of designing.

Alvaro Siza, The Importance of Drawing in *Siza: Architecture Writings*, Angelilo Antonio, ed. (Milan: Skira, 1997)

Three important books have served, to an extent, as paradigms for this one. The most significant is Roger Sherwood's *Modern Housing Prototypes*, published in 1978, not least because of his opening premise, as valid 30 years later in 2008 as it was then, that 'a re-examination of some of the great housing projects of this century (the 20th) is appropriate at a time when the design of housing commands the attention of architects the world around'. The other books are, firstly, *The Modern Flat*, published in 1937, by F. R. S. Yorke and Frederick Gibberd, and extending to their following title *Modern Flats*, published in 1958; and secondly, *Floor Plan Manual, Housing*, edited by Friedrike Schneider and published in 1994. Each of these publications has a particular perspective related to the location and time at which it was written. However, what they have in common is their acknowledgement of the role of the drawing as the primary tool of the architect, and therefore their attempt to show drawings at the centre of the work rather than as mere illustrations to a critique or historical analysis. Similarly, in this book, drawings – orthographic projections in plan, section and elevation – generally drawn to scale for comparative purposes, are the primary tool used to describe the selected buildings.

These three earlier publications all work as 'picture books', showing selected buildings through a series of drawings with an accompanying short description. Roger Sherwood's *Modern Housing Prototypes* categorizes housing as a series of types: first as Unit types, then as building types. Unit types are categorized according to their orientation to the exterior: single, double and double-orientation open-ended. Variations on these basic models result from the positioning of the entrance, bathrooms and kitchens of the dwellings. Building forms are then organized into categories based partly on characteristics such as site, orientation, density, etc. and partly on the access and circulation system: single-loaded corridors, double-loaded, split-level and skip-stop. The examples Sherwood chooses to expand on are grouped by their different building forms, arranged, according to density, as detached and semi-detached, row houses (or terraces), party wall, blocks, slabs and towers. Of the 32 examples he uses, Sherwood states that they are intended only as a representative sampling: 'well-known models of a particular housing type – Le Corbusier or Siedlung Halen by Atelier 5 for instance – or because they are particularly revealing examples of a type such as the Vienna Werkbund Exposition rowhouses of Lurçat or Brinkman's Spangen Housing.'

Writing in 1978, Sherwood speculates that, following two decades in which housing costs had risen at twice the rate of income, multiple housing projects will

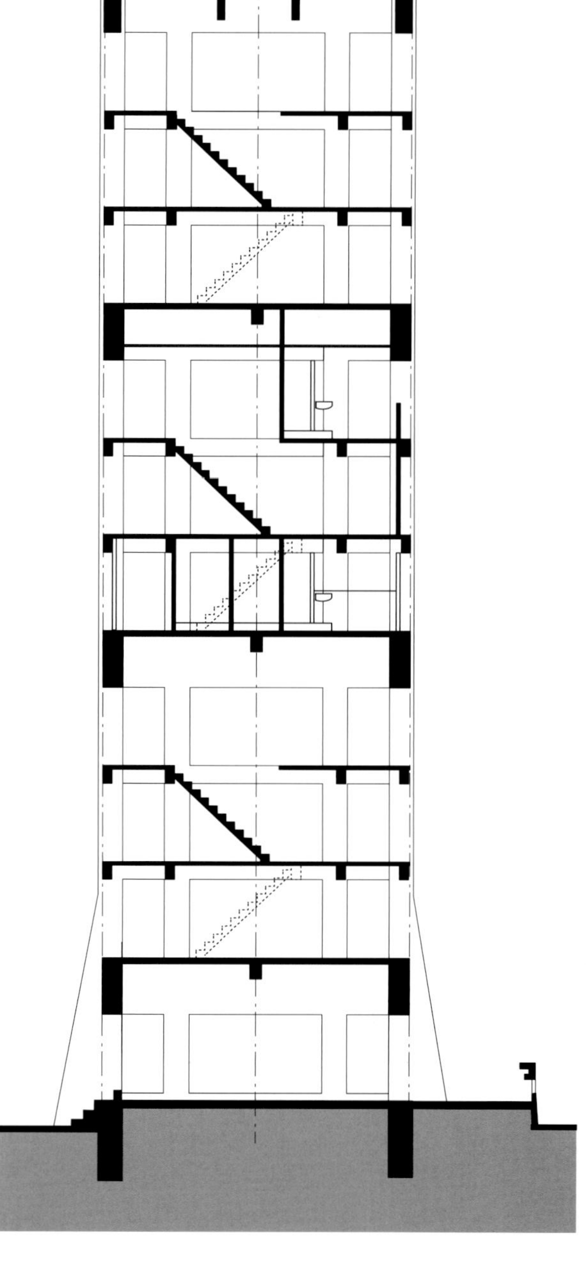

by necessity become more popular, as the norm of individual houses affordable to most middle-class families is likely to change. Additionally, although published in the United States, only a very few of the examples he chooses are American: the Pueblo Ribera Court (1923–5) by Schindler, the Peabody Terrace (1964) by Sert Jackson & Gourley, Price Tower (1956) by Frank Lloyd Wright – all of which are included here – as well as Wright's Suntop homes (1939) and the courtyard houses (1931) designed by Mies van der Rohe. The majority of his examples are well known, mainly European, ones – many of which are included here. Others that might have been included are Le Corbusier's version of the stepped section in the Durand Apartment design for Algiers (1934); the Zomerdijkstraat apartments in Amsterdam (1934), designed as ateliers with a double-height studio space; or Neave Brown's Fleet Road scheme (1967), which reworked the alternating street-and-mews pattern of traditional London thoroughfares.

The most recent of the three books, the *Floor Plan Manual*, published in 1994, similarly groups housing projects by building type, divided initially into one of two groups – either multi-storey or low-rise – and then categorized according to urban planning typology, for example 'free-standing', 'infill' or 'block-defining' structures, and, for low-rise, 'row', 'duplex' or 'detached'. An introductory essay on the 'typology of access' by Helmuth Sting examines the options possible with different plan-types and how they might be grouped into various constructional configurations.

The time period covered by *Floor Plan Manual* is rather different to that of Sherwood's book. The earliest project here is Le Corbusier's Unité d'Habitation (1947), and there are only a very few other examples from the 1950s and 1960s, most of which correspond almost exactly with the examples included here. Instances of tower blocks include Mies van der Rohe's Lake Shore Drive (1951), Denys Lasdun's cluster block (1958) and Marina City (1964) by Goldberg. Safdie's Habitat 67, the Halen scheme (1955–61) by Atelier 5 and The Ryde (1966) by PRP Architects are all included in the low-rise terraces or row housing section. The majority of the projects are those built in the 25-year period from the 1970s until the mid 1990s, with some additional, more recent, projects in the later edition. The authors claim to have 'strived for internationality but only while limiting

Opposite far left: Peabody Terrace, Cambridge, Massachusetts, 1964, Sert Jackson & Gourley. The housing for married students at Harvard University has a series of eight-storey high buildings forming quadrangles punctuated with three 22-storey high towers.

Opposite right: Harumi Apartments, Tokyo, 1958, Kunio Maekawa. Section through slab block showing access corridors at every third floor level with stairs perpendicular to the structure.

Left: 800–880 Lake Shore Drive, Chicago, Illinois, 1951, Mies van der Rohe. The two identical 26-storey high towers were early versions of apartment buildings with open plans and fully glazed façades.

Below: Halen Housing, Berne, Switzerland, 1955–1961, Atelier 5. Section of a typical terraced house stepping down to follow the contours of the sloping site.

cultural and climatic differences to a certain degree'. That is, they have focused on European countries with a similar temperate climate. *Floor Plan Manual* was published in Germany, and a very large proportion of the examples are from that country; and another sizeable selection is from the Netherlands. Once again, very few North American projects are included.

By comparison, *The Modern Flat* (1937) has a somewhat different perspective, in that it is looking at the design of flats only – a relatively new phenomenon in England at that time – rather than at all forms of multiple housing. It also groups its examples by country, following an introductory essay that explores the history of flats and analyzes the different developments in terms of type. The introduction to the first edition states that 'the flat has produced a building type peculiar to our own era: without precedent in the architecture of the past'. The book's radical approach includes describing the family thus: 'a single person, living alone or with friends, or it may consist of man and wife, with or without children, and or other dependants' – concepts that are still difficult for some developers and landlords today. Its tone is entirely optimistic, advocating higher-density urban development in place of suburban single-villa layouts, which are deemed to be taking up too much land and spoiling the potential of the countryside. For the authors, the 'modern flat' is also a key element in the new modern architecture that uses industrialized construction systems as opposed to the traditional building methods of the house builder.

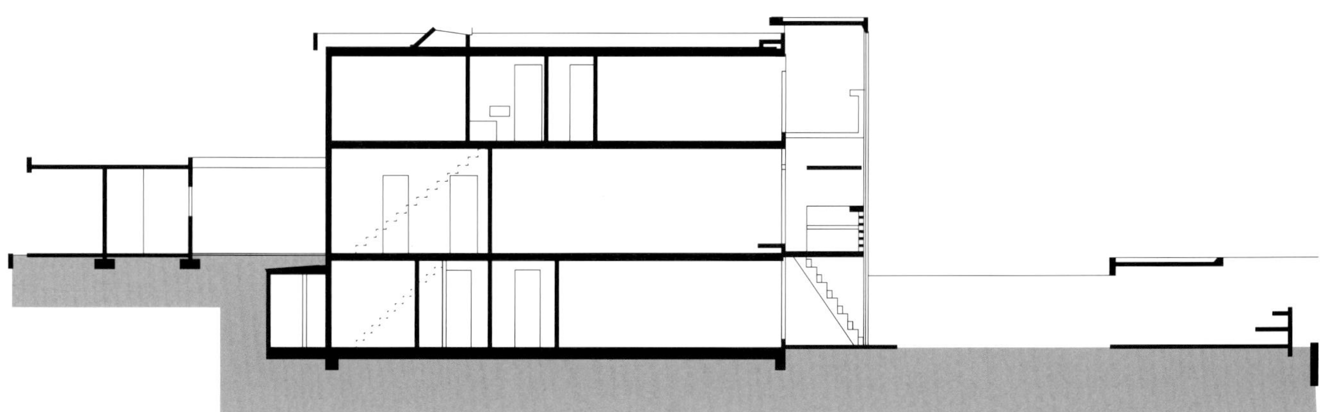

Twenty-one years later, in *Modern Flats* (1958), the same authors make no attempt to rewrite or attempt a critical appraisal of their previous work; they propose 'simply a picture book of some of the more distinguished flat buildings which have been built in recent years'. They felt any critical commentary to be superfluous to opinions expressed on the examples they chose to illustrate, which, again, included only recent contemporary examples, in this case built since 1945.

Reflecting on their earlier publication, Yorke and Gibberd recognize that there had been a 'need to make the case for flat dwelling' because conditions at that time had been very different. Then, they had criticized the poor quality of workers' housing – the dull uniform blocks in a sea of asphalt – and of luxury flats, seen only as an opportunity for developers to make more rental income. Twenty-one years on, they are observing new emerging trends: building higher, building communities rather that individual blocks, and building neighbourhoods with mixed developments of flats and houses – above all, seeing architecture as a key element in the drive to provide people with better-quality housing and a better way of living.

The intention in the current volume was to bring together housing designs that are considered to be the best examples of their kind, or those that demonstrate either a particular approach by the architect or a particular interpretation of a recognized type. All of the case studies here have been described in professional journals, and most have been included in architectural histories. The majority of projects are from Europe, reflecting the roots and development of European Modernism's focus on housing design in the middle decades of the twentieth century – and those from further afield also reflect this influence. Primarily these are what might be described as the new typology of 'modern apartment buildings', the now familiar tower blocks and slab blocks as well as the complex residential estates familiar in all cities. In parallel with these runs a second strand that records the ongoing development of the low-rise, terrace and courtyard models that continue to be a significant element in all kinds of urban housing design.

Rather than a categorization by type – either unit type or formal typology – the projects are arranged in chronological order, loosely divided into six chapters in an attempt to describe them in a more focused architectural context. The starting point, Chapter 1, *New Urban Forms*, covering the first decade of the twentieth century, looks at the emergence of the apartment block as a new building type – albeit in many forms – and at the different approaches to the relationship between housing and the structure of the urban environment. Chapter 2, *European*

Opposite left: Hansaviertel Apartments, Berlin, 1957, Alvar Aalto. The individual apartments – similar to courtyard houses with a central living space and balcony – are rotated and staggered in plan, breaking up the uniformity of the façade.

Opposite right: Britz Hufeisensiedlung, Berlin, 1927, Bruno Taut and Martin Wagner. Garden city planning with Modernist architecture, including an intense red colour on some blocks, along with geometrical layouts, gentle curves and stepped elevations.

Left: Carabanchel Housing, Madrid, 2007, Foreign Office Architects. The flexible interior space of the apartments is extended to include the additional external space of terraces, which run the full length of the building on all sides and which are enclosed with bamboo screens.

Modernism, includes the most widely published examples – buildings which are frequently included in histories of Modernism and monographs of their respective architects. Chapter 3, *Post-war Modernism*, looks at a period in which there was a pressing need for housing, especially in the bomb-damaged cities of Europe, and in which architects were able to put into practice the ideas developed by the early Modernists. By the late 1960s and early 1970s, Modernist high-rise projects continued to be built but were losing popularity, particularly as social-housing developments, and architects were experimenting with alternatives within the field of high-rise and large-scale. Some of these are discussed in Chapter 4, *Alternatives*, including projects that signalled a return to thinking about low-rise high-density housing design. By the late 1970s and early 1980s, the formalist influence of *Post-Modernism* (Chapter 5) was evident in housing design, particularly in France and Germany where large-scale suburban development and urban renewal projects required new thinking on housing design. The final chapter looks at a series of *Contemporary Interpretations*, which, among other issues, deal with current concerns of sustainability – not necessarily just with regard to the environmental impact of their energy consumption but also in terms of their social use; that is, designs that can accommodate different patterns of occupation and change over time.

New Urban Forms

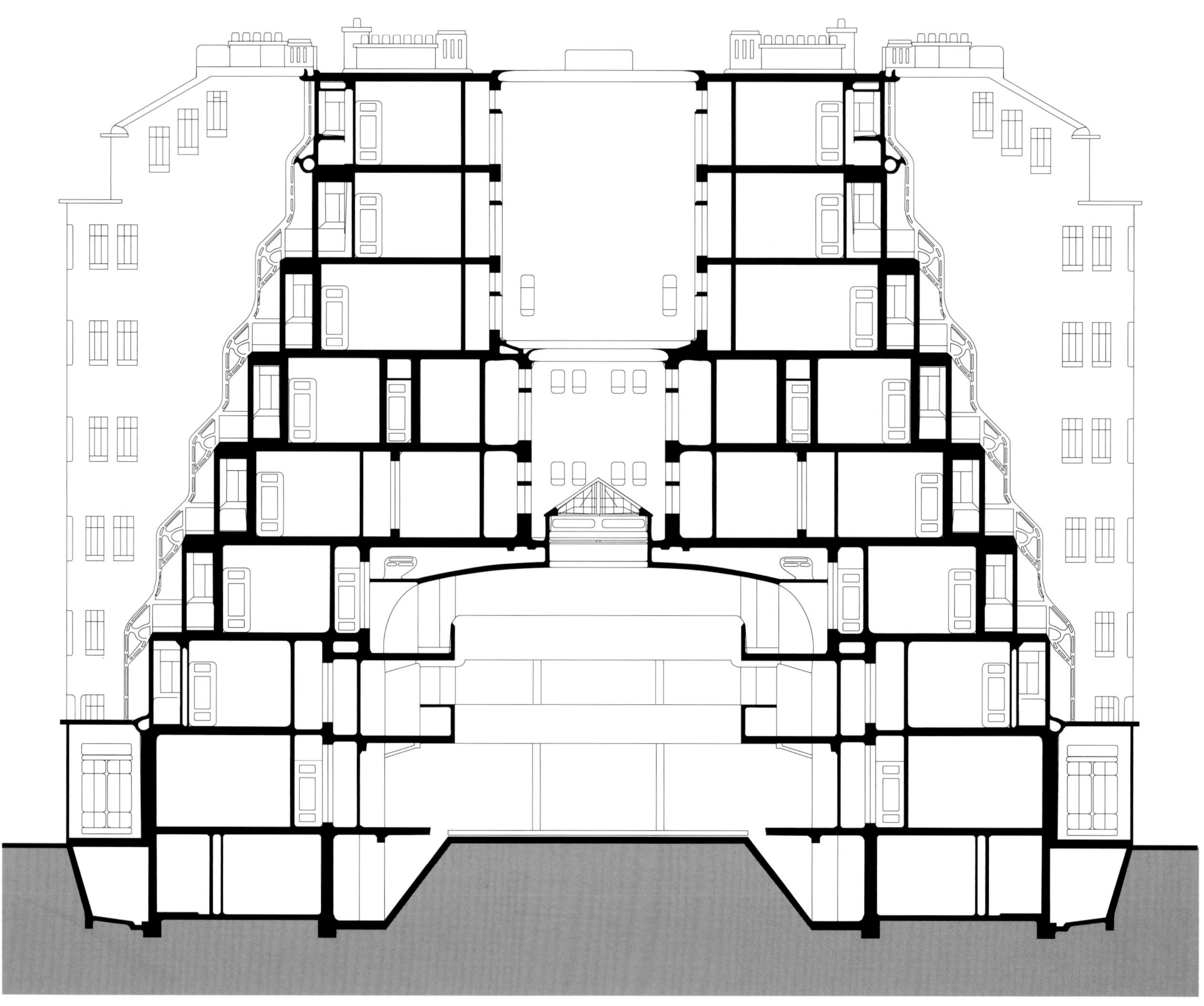

Letchworth in England (see pages 22–25), created in 1903 by Ebenezer Howard, is the first example of a garden city – a self-contained 'ideal' town, planned, according to Howard's principles set out in *Garden Cities of Tomorrow* (1902), to provide the best elements of town and country combined. In planning terms, the principles of the Garden City movement were to become enormously influential for many decades, spreading to countries across Europe and to the USA. In Germany, Richard Reimerschmid, Hermann Muthesius and Heinrich Tessenow designed the country's first garden city, **Hellerau** near Dresden, in 1909 – and, later, Bruno Taut and Martin Wagner's Berlin **Britz Hufeisensiedlung** scheme (see pages 40–41) employed the same principles but with an architecture of Modernism. In the USA, Clarence Stein and Henry Wright designed Sunnyside Gardens in Queens, New York, in 1924, the earliest example of the shared garden enclosed by a block of two-storey housing, and then **Radburn** in Fair Lawn, New Jersey in 1929, where the same ideas were extended to include planning for cars. But for those who did not support the utopian ideals of the Garden City movement – primarily its low-density, anti-urban, nostalgic approach to housing design – a commitment to the idea of the city meant finding new urban forms that would provide the much-needed better quality of housing while maintaining high densities.

In British cities, whether built by philanthropic trusts, private developers or local councils, many took the now familiar form of four- or five-storey brick 'mansion' blocks. **Navarino Mansions** (1904), built in east London by the Four Per Cent Industrial Dwellings Company, the **Sir Thomas More Estate** erected by the local council in west London, and Herne Hill mansions by the **Peabody Trust** (see pages 18–19) in south London, all share a similar approach to urban design and construction.

In the Netherlands, a close relationship between city planning and housing design and the influence of

Above left and right: **Letchworth Garden City**

Left: **Radburn**

Left: **Hellerau**

Below left: **Navarino Mansions**

Below **right: Sir Thomas More Estate**

figures like H. P. Berlage, who designed housing schemes and expansion plans for The Hague, encouraged architects to think of housing as the basic fabric of the city. Also, as in most European countries, construction legislation was now focused not only on the prevention of collapse and fire but on improving living conditions. Key aspects of the design of the individual dwelling – adequate ventilation, plumbing and sanitary arrangements; consideration of privacy; provision of external space and social space – had an impact on the overall design, that is on the urban form of the building. Michiel Brinkman's scheme at **Spangen** (see pages 34–35), for example, gives every tenant their own front door and reinvents the central space of the closed urban block as a social area, a semi-private courtyard with gardens and other amenities for the residents. Outside spaces such as balconies, gardens (both private and shared) and roof terraces were beginning to be incorporated in all types of housing; Rudolf Schindler's **Pueblo Ribera** scheme (see pages 36–37), although designed as holiday homes, has courtyards at ground-floor level and roof terraces – one of the earliest schemes to include 'outdoor rooms'.

In France, Henri Sauvage's work in Paris housing design led him to take a somewhat dogmatic approach to solving the problems associated with density in that city, and in particular its unhygienic, dank and dingy streets. Maintaining the existing street patterns, his radical proposal to build all new blocks with set-backs in order to let light and air penetrate down to street level was to replace the city's rigid Haussmannian façades. Sauvage's proposal also gave every apartment a balcony intended for growing plants that would contribute to greenery in the city (see **Gradins Vavin/ Amiraux**, pages 28–29). Although built

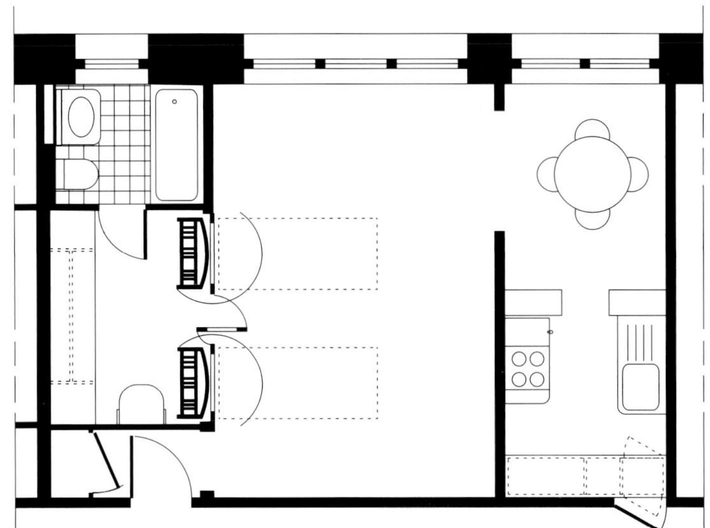

Left: **Efficiency Apartment plan**

Right: **Sherry Netherland Hotel, New York**

for wealthier tenants, Auguste Perret's **Rue Franklin Apartments** in Paris (see pages 20–21) was, according to Sigfried Giedion, significant as the forerunner of Modernism's free or open plan; however, it could also be said to have contributed to thinking about new urban forms for housing. Its concave form changes the relationship of the block to the street: from the interior, the focus is no longer directed internally to the fireside but out to the city; from the street, the lightwell or courtyard interrupts the continuity of the linear division of the façade.

Apartment living was customary in French cities, and although it had had significant influence in the USA developers there were still exploring different versions of large apartment blocks in order to shake off their association with tenements for the poor and to persuade wealthier tenants of their advantages over row houses. 'Micro-flats' of the time – apartment-hotels, such as **Schultze & Weaver's Sherry Netherland Hotel** in New York (1926–7), and **Efficiency Apartments** (see pages 38–39) that reduced an apartment to a minimal size by having one room double as living room and bedroom – were to solve problems both for developers and tenants. The much-reduced size of each apartment would lower costs and increase rents for landlords, and hotel-like services would suit the growing number of single-person households. Shared ownership schemes – like the **Hotel des Artistes** in New York (see pages 30–33) – or buildings only for single female tenants provided programmes that might distinguish one anonymous block from another. These apartment-hotels and collectives had a clear social programme that very often included public spaces such as lobbies and dining rooms, and bars such as that at the Café des Artistes, which had a direct relationship with the street and thus a direct engagement with the surrounding area, giving an identity to the building.

The 1930s were to see a shift in focus towards the design of the interior of the individual dwelling. **Karl Marx Hof** in Vienna (see pages 42–43) was one of the last of the large-scale monumental European housing estates with interior courtyards that provided schools, shops and other communal spaces along with huge numbers of very small apartments.

Peabody Buildings

Peabody Trust

London, UK; early 1900s

By 1905, the Peabody Trust (set up in 1862) had already built 226 Peabody Buildings. Their stated intention, 'to apply the fund in construction of such improved dwellings for the poor as may combine in the uttermost possible degree the essentials of healthfulness, comfort, social enjoyment and economy' resulted in buildings of the same distinctive type. The blocks are five storeys high, with an additional storey in the centre of the block for drying rooms. Although divided into separate dwellings – four per floor – these were still thought of as 'rooms' and had shared WCs and sculleries outside the flats, one for every two dwellings. Other shared facilities included laundries with coppers and washing sinks with hot water provided. Compared to much social housing built later, the rooms are spacious; living rooms are 3.45 metres (11 feet 4 inches) by 4 metres (13 feet 6 inches) and bedrooms 3 metres (9 feet 9 inches) by 4 metres (13 feet 6 inches); ceiling heights are a uniform 2.6 metres (8 feet 6 inches). The Peabody Buildings at Herne Hill in south London were included in James Cormes' *Modern Housing in Town and Country*, published in 1905, as a good example of the type and because this project was the first to include, alongside the blocks of smaller dwellings, groups of cottages with five rooms intended for larger families.

Apartments of one, two and three rooms with shared WCs, sculleries and laundries were a common type constructed by local authorities and developers all over London at a time when sanitary arrangements were a major concern. House builders even measured the success of their 'sanitary dwellings' with statistics showing evidence of a reduction in the mortality rates of their inhabitants. Fear of 'insanitary' accommodation and the dangers to health presented by WCs and sculleries that were not kept clean and properly ventilated continued to have a major influence on planning. The somewhat paternalistic view taken by the Peabody Trust was not shared by all housing providers. Self-contained flats were, of course, to become the norm, although even these often had WCs and sculleries – ventilated and accessible from open courtyards and balconies – positioned at a distance from habitable rooms. The Sir Thomas More Estate, erected in Beaufort Street by the London Borough of Chelsea, is significant as one of the earliest such buildings to provide self-contained apartments, each with its own WC and scullery, although open balconies provided the 'ventilated lobby' between the scullery and WC. Back-to-back arrangements, which remained common in much of Europe, were considered inappropriate in Britain, and all flats had high ceilings and windows on both sides to ensure through ventilation. The six-storey blocks are aligned in such a way that habitable rooms overlook either the road or a playground at least 12 metres (40 feet) wide to ensure good daylighting to even to the lowest floors. Stairs and landings are compact to maximize the amount of space available for the flats. Although all the flats had a scullery, hot water was still provided centrally, with kettles at boiling point in the mornings, so that tenants did not need to light fires for making breakfast. Communal bathrooms were provided in the basement with hot and cold water supplies.

The careful thought given to how the spaces would be occupied is clear from the attention to detail in the design of the interiors. Published drawings show coat hooks in the lobby, a food storage cupboard vented to the outside, and a fitted dresser with cup hooks as well as cupboards with shelves and hooks in each bedroom. A closed range and a cast-iron mantelpiece are fitted to the living-room fireplace and the scullery is well equipped, with a sink, copper, coal store and a gas cooker with a prepayment meter.

Opposite left and right:
Sir Thomas More Estate

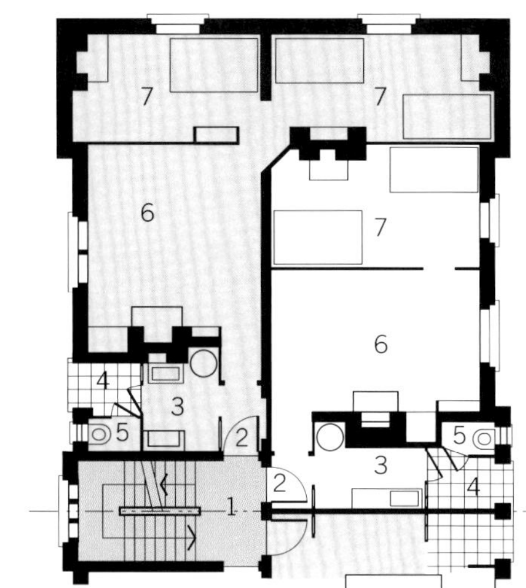

Sir Thomas More Estate, Chelsea, London

1 Part typical plan, self-contained two- and three-roomed tenements

1 Common stairs
2 Entrance lobby
3 Scullery
4 Balcony
5 WC
6 Living room
7 Bedroom

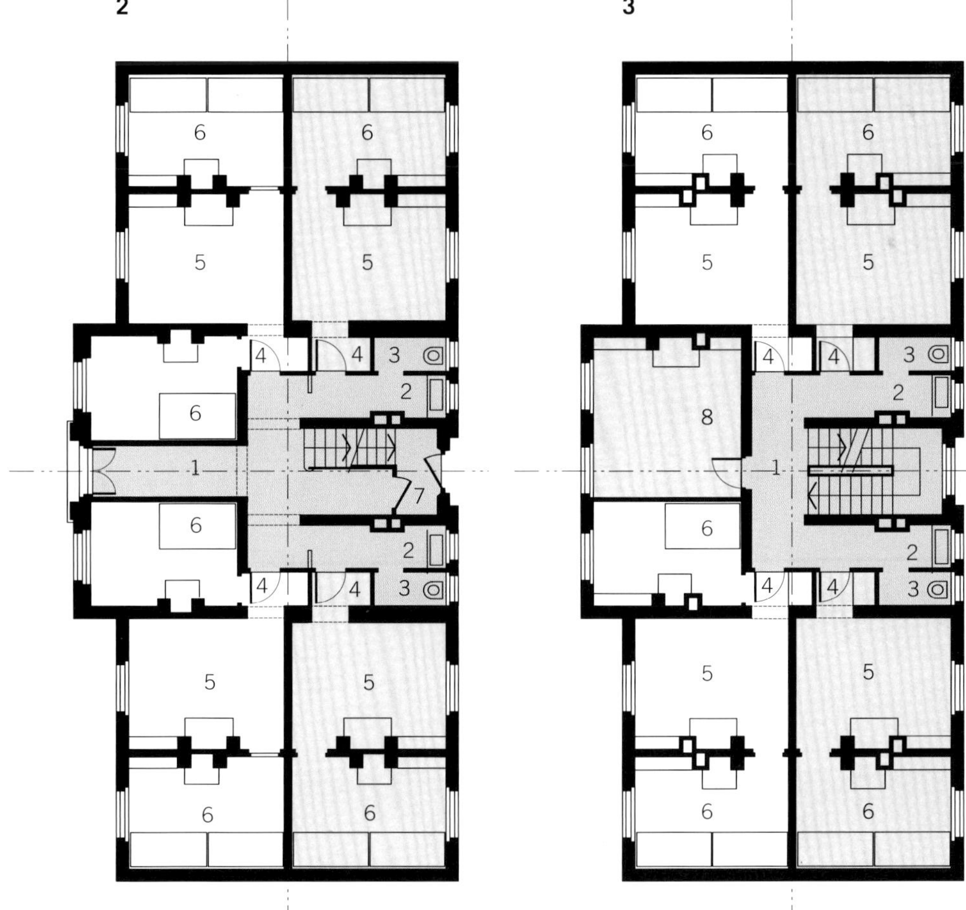

Peabody Buildings, Herne Hill, London

2 Ground-floor plan 1:200
3 Typical upper-floor plan 1:200

1 Entrance hall and common stairs
2 Shared scullery
3 Shared WC
4 Entrance lobby
5 Living room
6 Bedroom
7 Access to cellars
8 Bedsitting room

Rue Franklin Apartments

Auguste Perret, 1874–1954

Paris, France; 1903

The apartment building on rue Benjamin Franklin is included in architectural histories for its significance in constructional terms. It is the earliest of Perret's experiments with the use of reinforced concrete, which include the spectacular Theatre de Champs Elysées (1914), Nôtre Dame de Raincy (1922) and the Museum of Public Works (1937). However, it is also considered important for other reasons: stylistically it is often seen as a forerunner of Modernism, or, for Sigfried Giedion, as the first example of the flexible or 'free' plan. Significantly, it is a reinterpretation of the Parisian apartment block constructed between two party walls. The external wall, which appears to be loadbearing masonry with windows punched out of it, disappears at street level to be replaced with glazing and a terrace at roof level. The U-shape of the plan, concave towards the street, relocates the courtyard or lightwell at the front of the building and makes a visual connection possible between the different rooms in an apartment.

Above the commercial space, which occupies the two lower levels and includes a mezzanine, each of the upper floors has a single apartment. The U-shaped plan situates the stairs and lifts at the back along with the bathrooms and WCs, allowing all habitable rooms to face the street. A kitchen is located against one party wall, above the entrance and close to the service stair. The three living spaces are arranged symmetrically in the centre of the plan and interconnected in typical French manner; the central 'salon' has glazed walls all round and no fireplace, instead making the focus of the room the view outwards across Paris. A typical floor has two balconies overlooking the street, and at the upper levels the plan changes, with set-backs to accommodate roof terraces. At the seventh floor, the central salon is set back to provide a balcony across the full width. The terrace of the ninth-floor apartment (which is much smaller in surface area) has one ladder up to a terrace on the roof and another ladder down to an eighth-floor terrace inaccessible from the servants' rooms which are located there. The design of the flats – high ceilings, extensive glazing, balconies and the terraces at roof level – are all factors in a new way of thinking about apartment living, shifting the focus away from the interior towards the light and space of the exterior.

Site plan
1:500

Opposite left: Street façade

Opposite right: Detail of upper-level balconies

1

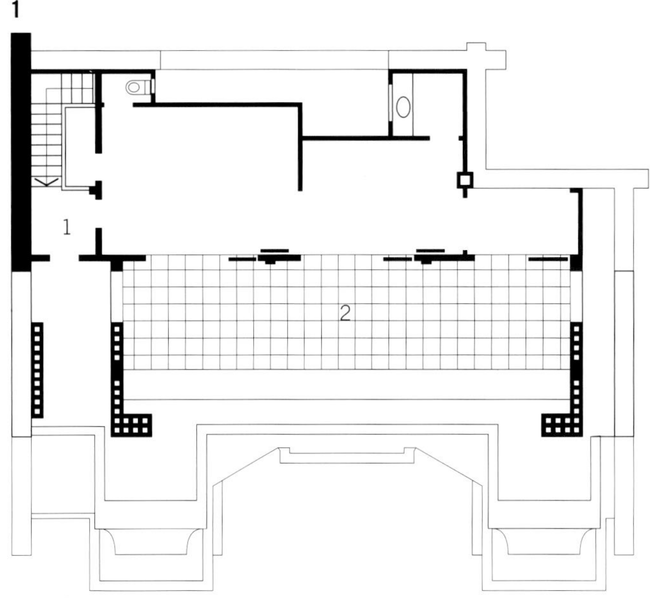

2

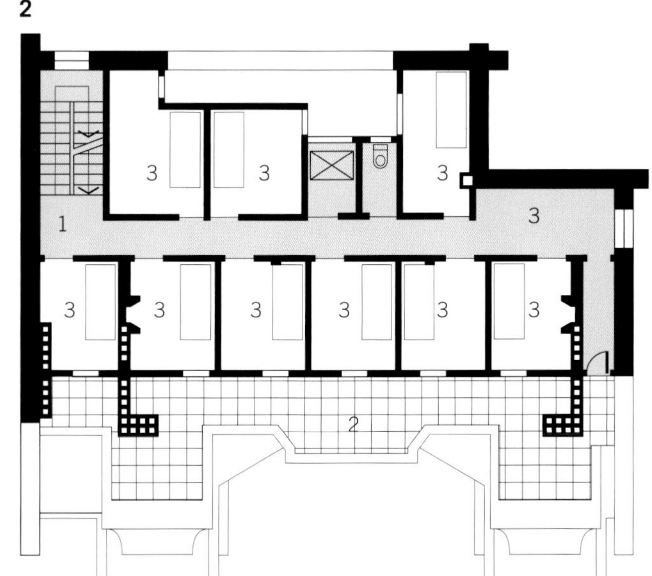

3

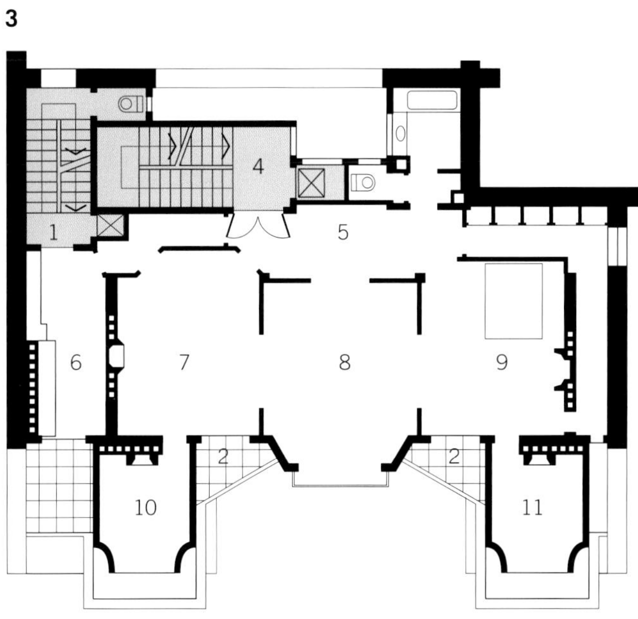

Floor plans 1:200

1 Top floor
2 Eighth floor
3 Typical floor

1 Servants' stairs and service lift
2 Terrace
3 Servants' bedrooms
4 Main stair and lift
5 Entrance/hall
6 Kitchen and scullery
7 Dining room
8 Salon/living room
9 Bedroom
10 Smoking room
11 Dressing room

4 Ground floor

1 Servants' stairs and service lift
2 Conciergerie
3 Entrance to apartments
4 Main stair and lift
5 Entrance to ground-floor shops

4

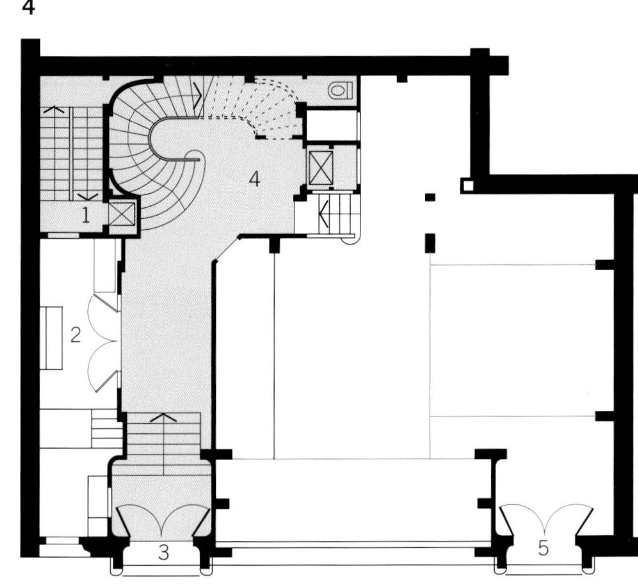

Cheap Cottages Exhibition

Fraser, Lucas, Dunkerly, Crickmer

Letchworth Garden City, UK; 1905

Rather than any stylistic innovations, probably the single most important improvement common to almost all the houses built for the Cheap Cottages Exhibition at Letchworth Garden City was the provision of plumbing services, and especially new designs for cisterns and coppers to provide hot water, baths and WCs. Most of the dwellings conform to the prevailing Arts and Crafts style, but to achieve the intended economies and build within the budgetary constraints set out by the competition many architects explored alternative types of construction and the use of different materials. Reducing the amount of fair-faced brickwork used was key to bringing down overall costs – so a whole variety of different finishes, such as roughcast and pebbledash, were applied to cheaper brickwork; and efforts were made to use timber framing at upper levels and reduce foundations by clever grouping of flues. Other cottages were built using alternative prefabricated systems. One such is the cottage built by the Concrete Machinery Company, made with their portable hand-powered concrete-block-making machine. Designed by Gilbert Fraser, its cheaper construction meant a larger cottage; a simple rectangular plan with three rooms on the ground floor along with both a kitchen and a separate scullery, and three bedrooms above.

The two blocks of four terraced cottages each, designed by Geoffrey Lucas (1872–1947) and built for the First Garden City Ltd, which won the Grouped Cottages Class in the 1905 competition, are based on the design of a handed pair of units with a simple pitched roof and the chimneys grouped at the gable ends. Locating the staircases in the centre of the plan, either side of a cranked party wall, was an economical use of space. The WC, although still outside the main house, is attached to the main building and sits under cover as part of a rear porch that can also be used to store bicycles and other household equipment. The arrangement in terraces and cranking in plan give more privacy to the gardens and create a sense of enclosure to the public green at the front.

The cottages designed by V. Dunkerly for the Letchworth Building Syndicate are larger and more elaborate. More space is given to the staircase and entrance hall, the WC is included inside the main house and the ground floor is divided between two 'living' rooms intended for different uses in summer and winter, with, between the two, a novel heating and hot-water installation. Called the 'model cottager', the combination of range, copper and bath – which might be fixed or folding – meant that the fire used in one room for heating and cooking was simultaneously used to heat water for washing clothes and bathing. A secondary grate under the copper could be used in the summer to heat only water. Access to the WC is provided in a more discreet manner, off an enclosed back porch or, in one version, off the kitchen/scullery area. Scullery activities are located in a recess, which can be closed off out of sight. Construction is of brickwork up to first-floor level, with a timber-and-machine-tile mansard above.

The group of cottages designed by Courtenay Melville Crickmer (1879–1971) includes dwellings of different sizes – a two-bed, a four-bed and two three-bed houses – arranged in two pairs around the chimneys, which are grouped on the party walls. The larger bedrooms have fireplaces and the WCs and coal stores are arranged under a covered back porch. Baths are included in the scullery, where they double up as a work surface.

***Opposite left and right*:**
Typical Letchworth cottages

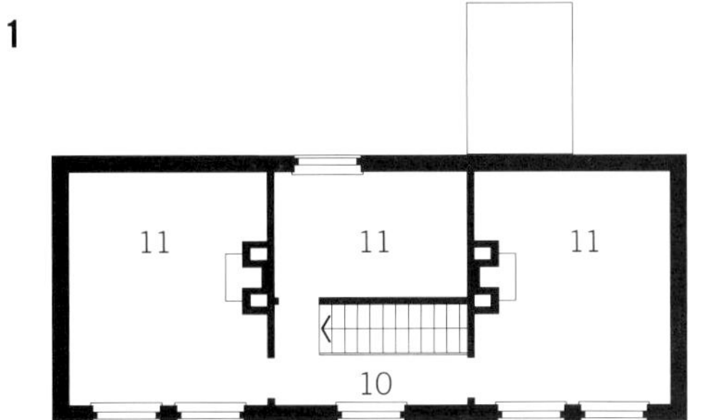

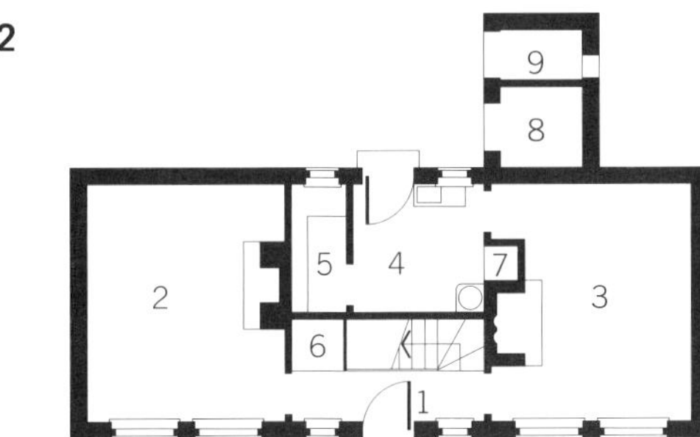

Cottage designed by Gilbert Fraser for the Concrete Machinery Company 1:200

1 First-floor plan
2 Ground-floor plan

1 Entrance
2 Living room
3 Kitchen
4 Scullery
5 Larder
6 Cupboard
7 Recess for bath
8 Coal store
9 WC
10 Landing
11 Bedroom

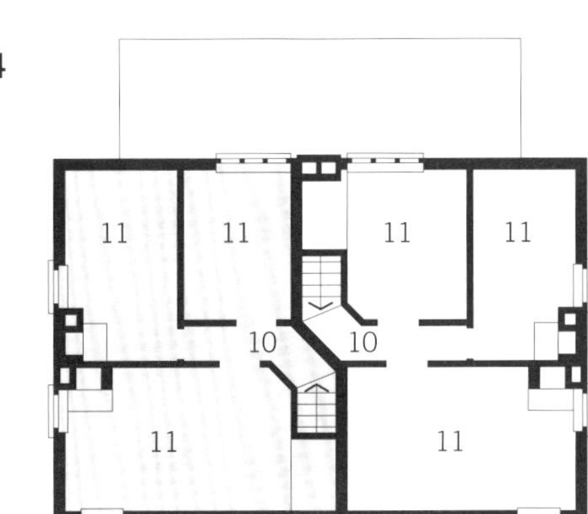

Plans of brick cottages designed by Geoffrey Lucas 1:200

3 Ground-floor plan
4 First-floor plan

1 Entrance
2 Front room
3 Living room
4 Scullery
5 Earth closet
6 Coal store
7 Larder
8 Copper and cisterns
9 Bath under stairs
10 Landing
11 Bedroom

5

5 Alternative versions of cottages designed by Geoffrey Lucas, first-floor and ground-floor plans 1:200

1 Entrance
2 Living room
3 Backroom
4 Larder
5 Coal store
6 WC
7 Back porch/bicycles/store room
8 Landing
9 Bedrooms
10 Bath
11 Combined copper and fire

Plans and sections of a pair of cottages designed by V. Dunkerly 1:200

6 Ground-floor plan
7 First-floor plan
11 Section through hall and kitchen
12 Section through hall and living room

1 Entrance
2 Living room
3 Kitchen/scullery
4 Back porch
5 Coal store
6 WC
7 Larder
8 Combination copper, stove and fireplace
9 Bath/folding bath
10 Sink and cupboards
11 Bicycles and tools
12 Landing
13 Bedroom

6

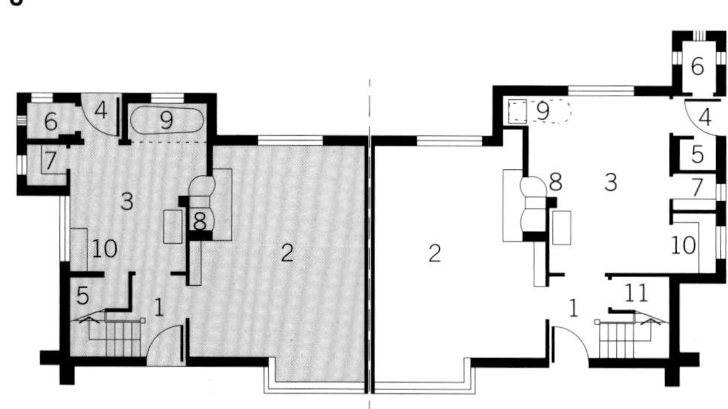

7

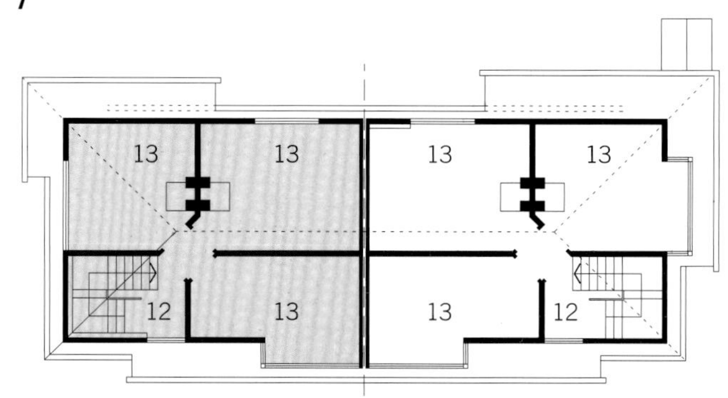

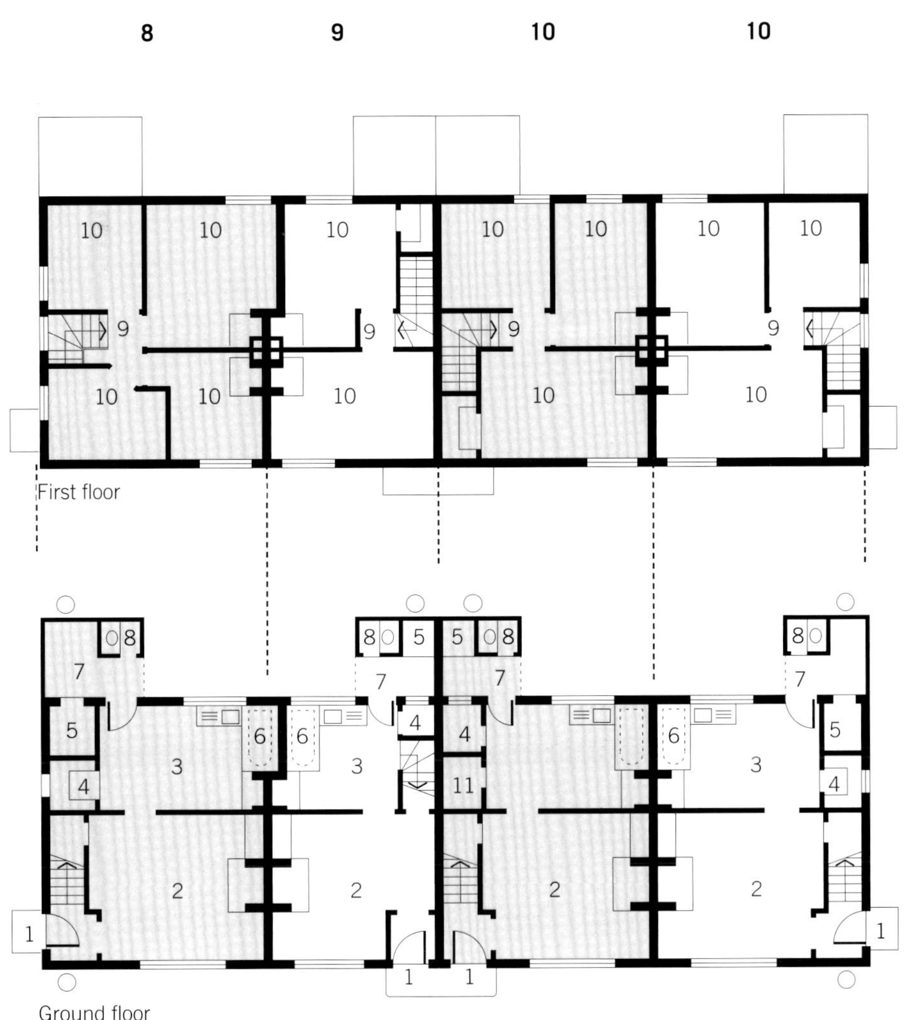

Plans of four cottages designed by C. M. Crickmer 1:200

8 Four-bedroom
9 Two-bedroom
10 Three-bedroom

1 Entrance porch with roof over
2 Living room
3 Scullery
4 Larder
5 Coal store
6 Bath/table
7 Back porch
8 Earth closet
9 Landing
10 Bedroom
11 Cupboard

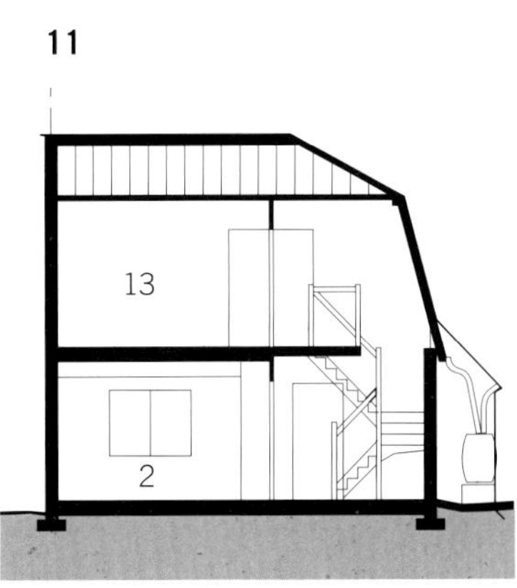

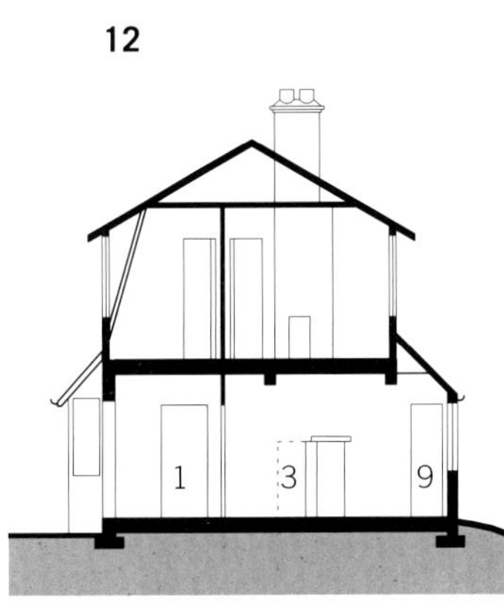

Van Beuningenstraat Housing

J. E. van der Pek, 1865–1919

Amsterdam, The Netherlands; 1909

In the Netherlands the first national Housing Act was passed in 1902. It replaced local building by-laws, which, in common with most early legislation of this kind, had aimed primarily to control the quality of construction and to prevent collapse and the spread of fire. Regulations introduced in the Netherlands as early as 1860 had attempted to deal with densification, as, in contrast to the ordered perimeter blocks that lined the streets and were controlled by building regulations, development in the open central spaces that were typical in large Dutch urban blocks had been allowed to continue unhindered. However, these regulations had had a limited impact on established developments, and by the turn of the century there was pressure to regulate further in order to reduce overcrowding and generally promote better living conditions.

Although the 1902 Act was a piece of national legislation that undoubtedly focused attention on the problems of housing – and particularly its relationship with public-health issues – it related to the design rather than the construction of the dwelling, and it required each city to draw up their own individual codes for building construction regulation. In planning terms, the Act also set out parameters, based on population-growth statistics, within which all towns and cities were expected to prepare their own expansion plans. This acknowledged relationship between city planning and housing design encouraged architects working at the time to think of housing as the basic fabric of the city. H. P. Berlage – who designed housing schemes and also expansion plans for the Hague (1905), Amsterdam (1915) and Utrecht – was a key figure in demonstrating the importance of working at all scales and in raising the profile of housing as a subject worthy of widespread attention.

The first Housing Act dwellings, designed by J. E. van der Pek and built in 1909 by the Rochdale Housing Association in Amsterdam, show considerable improvement on earlier schemes in space and layout. Ground-floor flats have their own independent entrances, there are windows on both sides to allow cross-ventilation, and each unit has a balcony. The most significant improvement was the introduction of bedrooms to replace the traditional 'cupboard' or 'alcove' beds. However, the Housing Act didn't prohibit the use of these features, and, although most housing reformers were keen to see them outlawed as unhygienic, they were the subject of much controversy, with housing associations reporting that residents missed the comfort of their 'cupboard beds'. Amsterdam was one of the first cities to ban them – in Berlage's 1915 South Extension Plan – and others eventually followed, although they were not outlawed in Rotterdam until 1937.

1

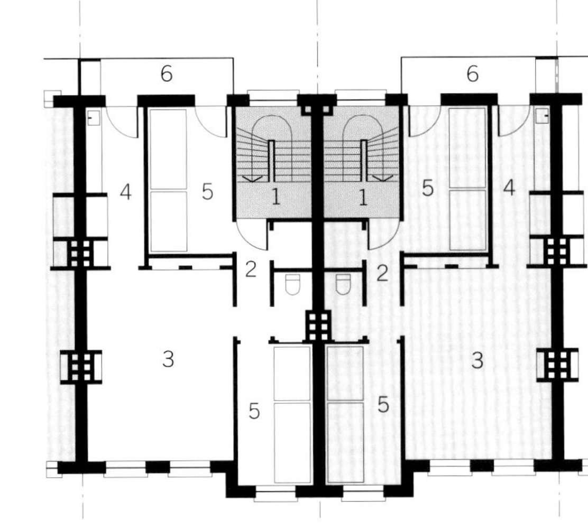

Plans of typical Housing Act dwellings 1:200

1 Second- and third-floor plans

2 First-floor plan

3 Ground-floor plan

1 Common hall/stairs
2 Entrance
3 Living room
4 Kitchen
5 Bedroom
6 Balcony
7 Sleeping alcove

2

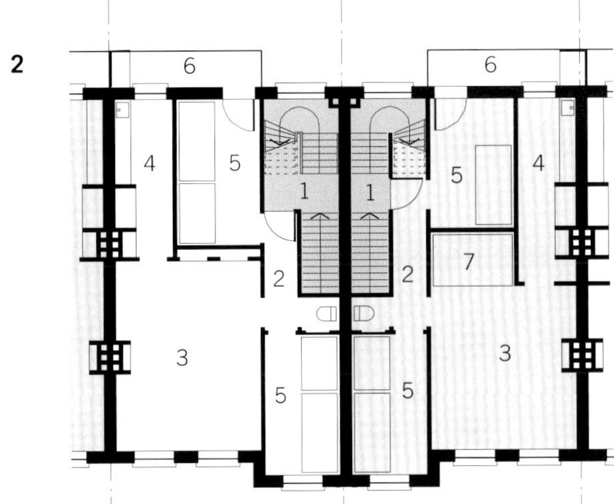

3

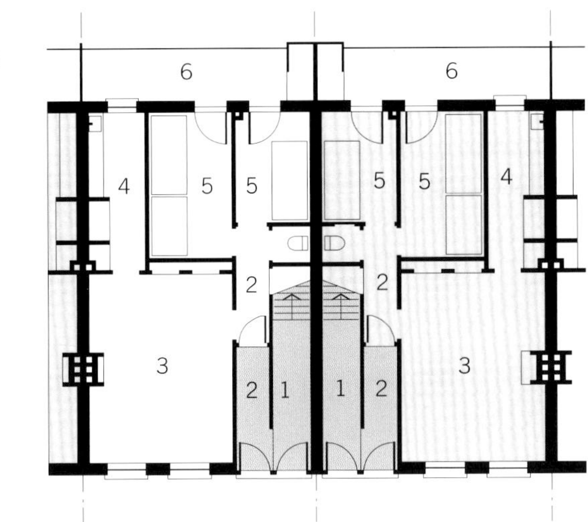

1 Plan of typical nineteenth-century dwelling 1:200

1 Common stairs
2 Entrance hall
3 Kitchen
4 WC
5 Living room
6 Sleeping alcove

4

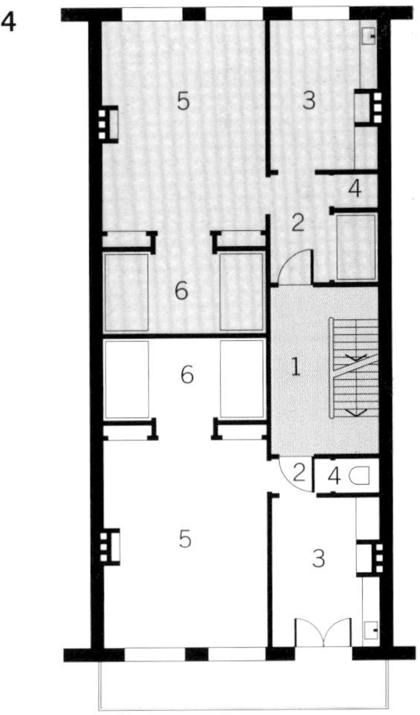

Gradins Vavin/Amiraux

Henri Sauvage, 1873–1932

Paris, France; 1912/1922

As well as working for commercial and wealthy private clients, Henri Sauvage had developed his ideas for the design of low-cost housing during the first decade of the twentieth century. He designed several apartment blocks built in Paris by the Société Anonyme des Logements Hygiéniques à Bon Marché (an organization providing low-cost, hygienic housing) that set out to improve the quality of workers' housing. The buildings were intended to provide not only for the health of inhabitants – with good lighting and ventilation, and materials and surfaces designed to promote cleanliness and prevent the harbouring of dirt and infection – but also for their mental well-being through the provision of space for activities, such as a stage for amateur theatricals, gardens and, in one development on the rue Tretaigne, a cooperative shop.

Henri Sauvage's particular interest in improving the quality of the environment led him to develop the set-back building specifically in response to the narrow and dingy streets of Paris. As well as bringing more daylight down to ground level, improving the general streetscape, a building with a stepped façade meant terraces at upper levels that could be planted, thus improving the apartments. An apartment building on the rue Vavin (1912) was the first to successfully employ the idea. In sharp contrast to the typically elaborate neoclassical façades of eighteenth- and nineteenth-century Paris, the stepped façades on the rue Vavin are covered in white glazed tiles, decorated only with occasional dark blue tiles, with natural vegetation spilling over the parapets. The nature of the section resulted in a maximum depth of around 6 metres (20 feet) and an unusable dark central space at the lower levels. The second building, completed a decade later in the rue des Amiraux (1922) and designed as workers' housing, resolved the problem of the central space with the inclusion of a swimming pool.

While many of his European contemporaries attempted to solve urban problems by creating alternatives, Henri Sauvage remained committed to the idea of the city and continued to evolve his ideas for improving the urban environment, first developing projects for the set-back building as a city block and then, at an even bigger scale, as a new urban form (although nothing of this last idea was ever realized).

1

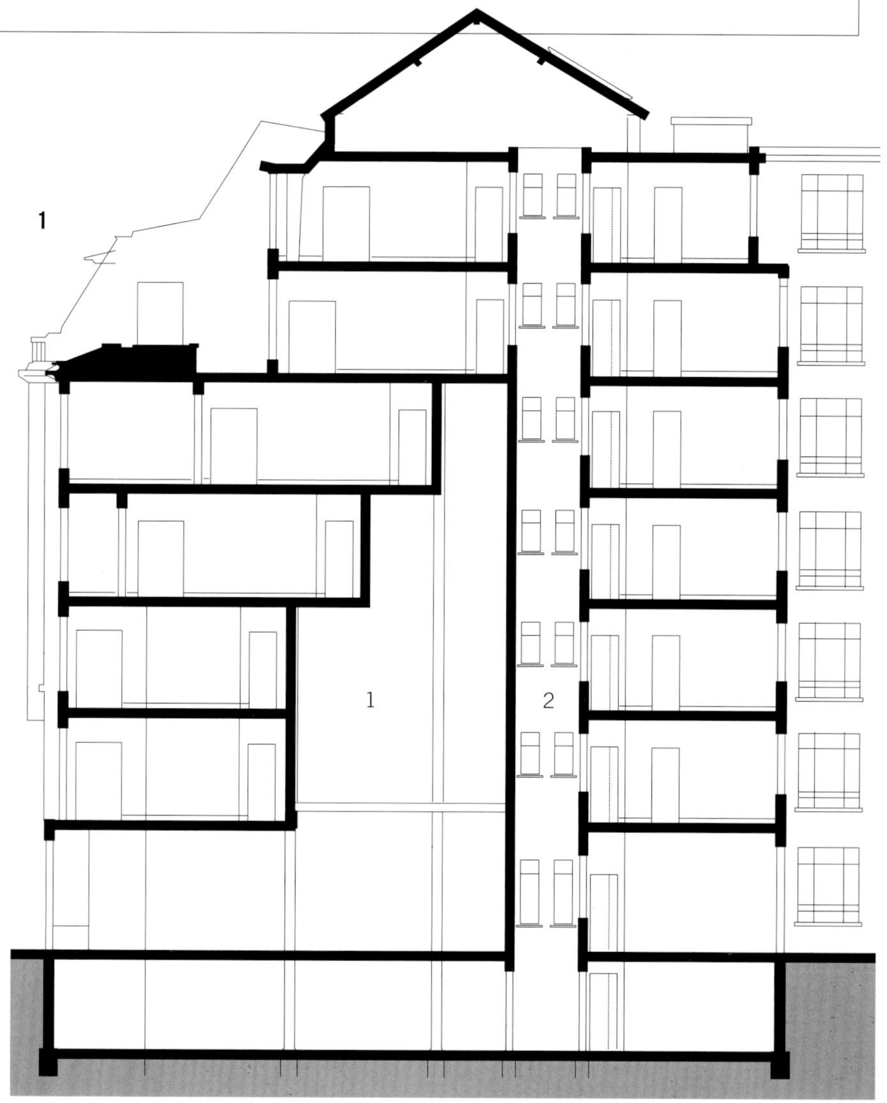

Opposite left: Rue Vavin façade

Opposite right: Rue des Amiraux façade

2

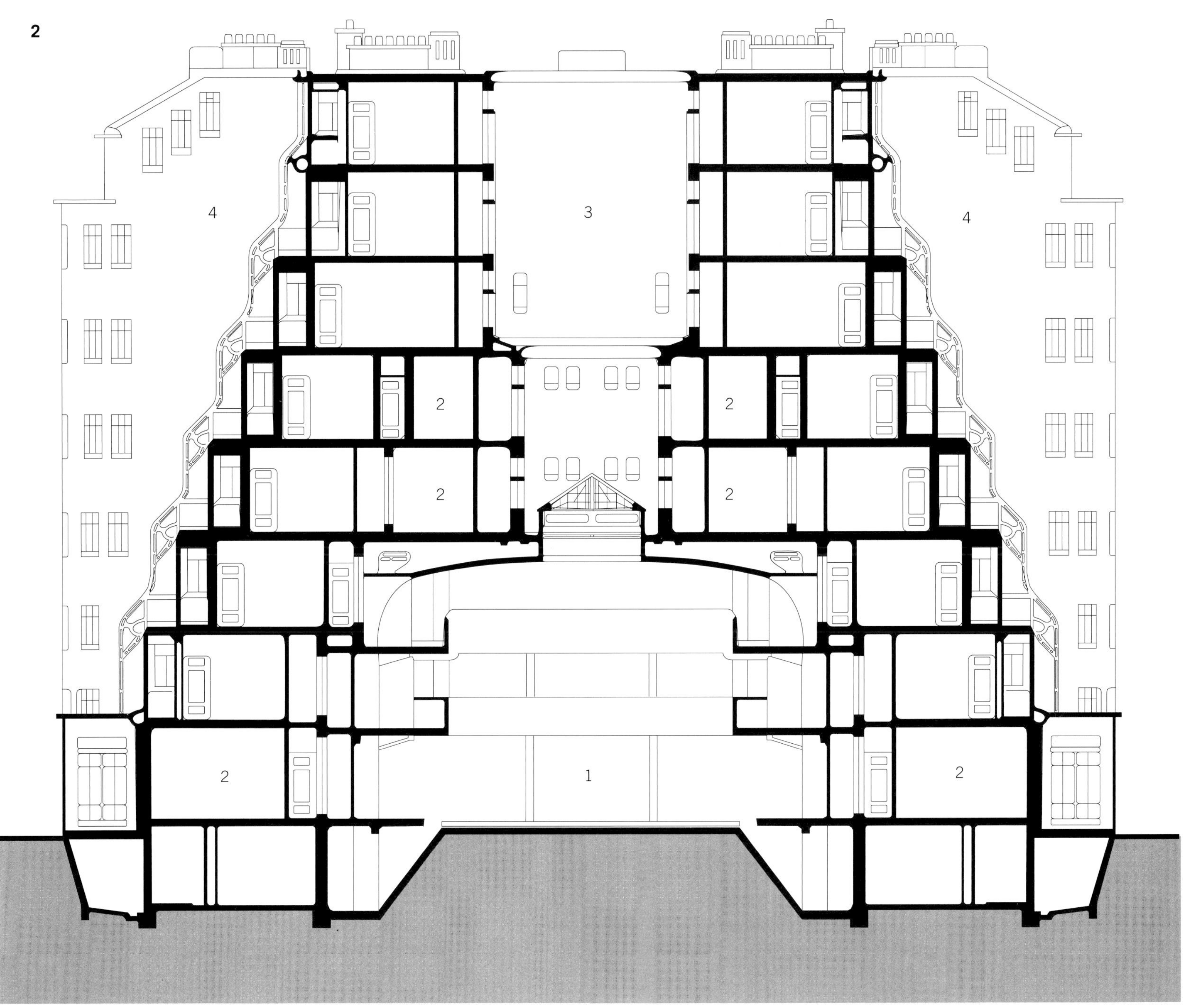

1 Section through building on rue Vavin approx 1:200

1 Interior void space
2 Lightwell

2 Section through building on rue des Amiraux approx 1:200

1 Swimming pool area
2 Storage/cellars
3 Lightwell
4 Stair towers

Far left: Detail of façade with central light well

Left: Street elevation

Hotel des Artistes

George Mort Pollard

New York, New York, USA; 1917

The Hotel des Artistes was the fifth in a series of 'artists'' apartment blocks built on West 67th Street. The first, built in 1903 at No. 27, was remarkable both for its presence on a street which until then had mainly comprised much smaller-scale buildings, such as stables and light industrial works, and for its management as a cooperative set up by a group of artists unable to find suitable affordable accommodation in New York.

Shared ownership of multiple dwellings had been in existence since the 1880s, probably the best known example being the Hubert Home Clubs built by Philip Hubert and James Prisson, but it had not become widespread. There was still considerable resistance to apartment living, and no established resale market. Sharing a building, however, seemed the perfect solution for a group of artists – like-minded people with the same particular requirements for high-ceilinged studio spaces alongside their living accommodation. Sharing purpose-built studios and apartments would be much less expensive than renting individually, and would also guarantee some income from rental units included in the building. Working together with the architects Simonson, Pollard and Steinman and builders William J. Taylor, a group of artists built No. 27 West 67th Street, comprising 14 purpose-built duplex apartments for themselves and several rental units. The success of this development meant that two more were built at Nos 15 and 33 in 1905; Pollard and Steinman designed another at No. 39–41; and Pollard designed No. 1 by himself in 1917.

The Hotel des Artistes is the most imposing of the group. With its elaborate Gothic decoration, stone fireplaces and carved stone figures, and its café on the street, it attracted wealthier and better-known tenants than the other developments. It has a centralized H-shaped plan, approximately 45 metres (150 feet) wide, with lightwells on all sides and the main lifts and stairs located in the centre. The earlier buildings had studios located at the back, facing north, and the family accommodation facing the street, or south, side; such was the demand that No. 1 also has studios that face the south side. A typical floor has eight small duplexes on the street side and four small and two double-size duplexes at the back. Servants' rooms were provided on the landings accessible from the shared corridors. The upper floors had the largest apartments, one over three floors, and included studio spaces and roof terraces. The lower floors had a swimming pool, squash court, sun room, ballroom and restaurants.

1

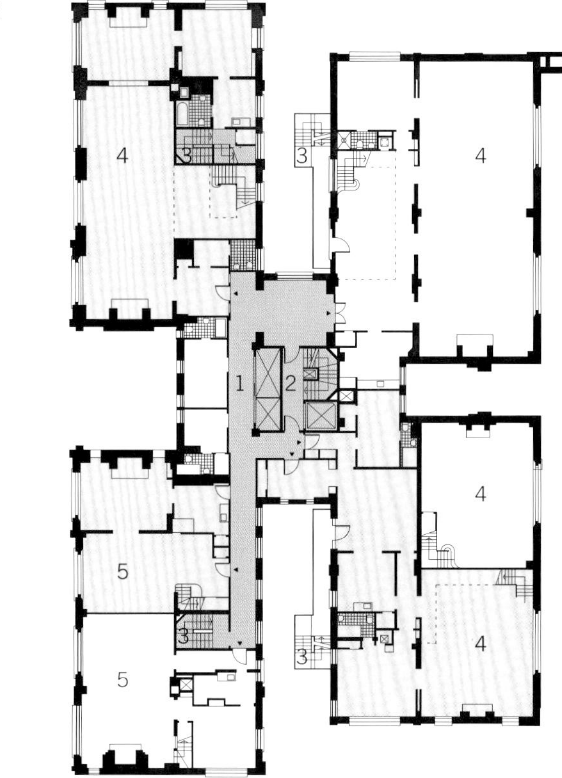

2

1 Plan of ninth floor
1:500

2 Plan of mezzanine
1:500

1 Corridor
2 Stair and lift hall
3 Fire escape stairs
4 Lower level of duplexes
5 Two-storey apartments
6 Upper level of duplexes with double-height living spaces

3

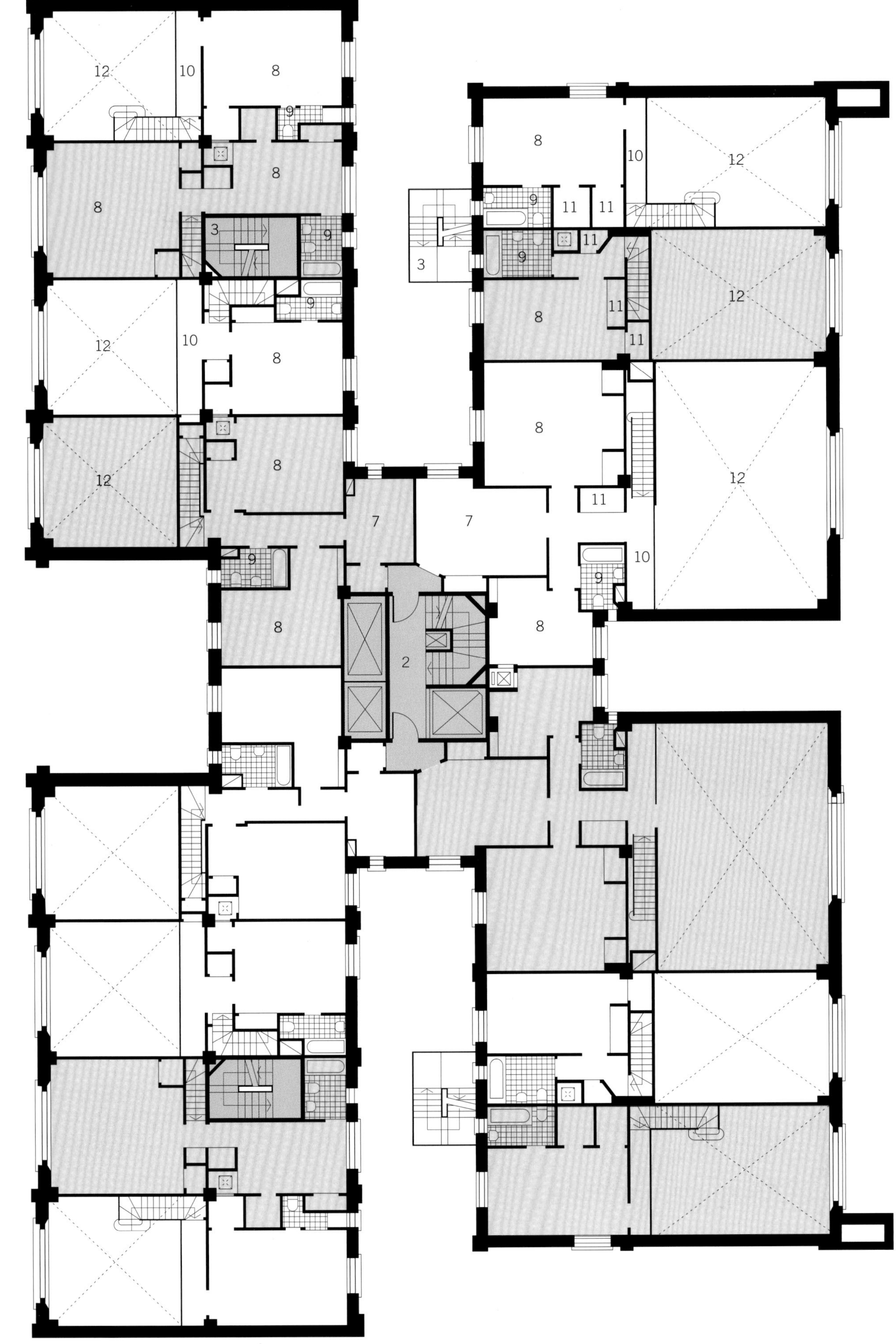
12
10
8
8
9
8
12
10
8
11
11
9
8
3
9
3
9
11
9
12
11
8
12
11
12
10
8
12
8
11
12
7
7
9
10
9
8
8
2

4

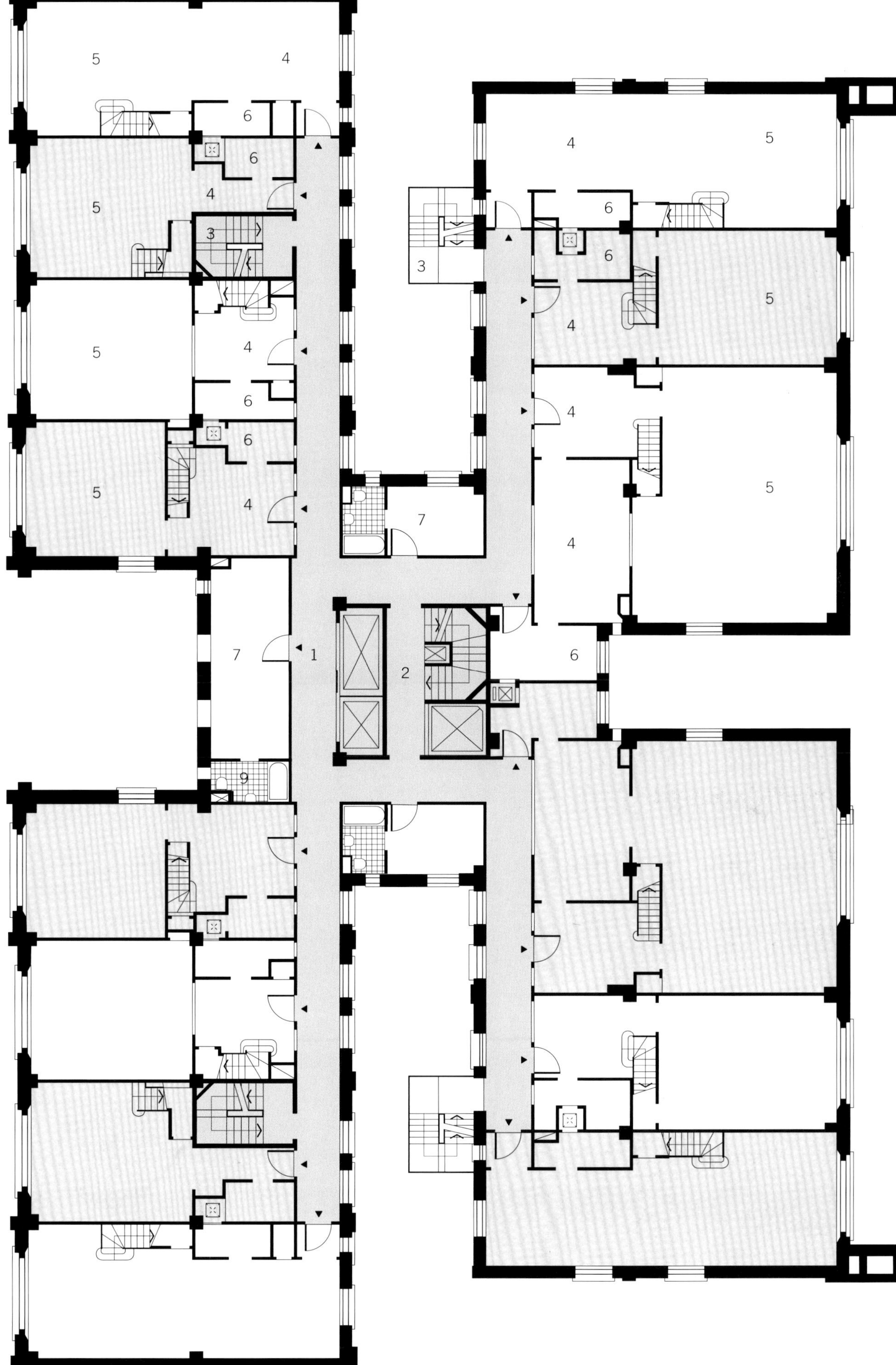

Typical floor plans 1:200

3 Mezzanine/upper-floor plan

4 Lower-floor plan

1 Corridors
2 Stair and lift hall
3 Fire escape stairs
4 Entrance/foyer
5 Living/dining/studio
6 Kitchen
7 Servants' room
8 Bedroom
9 Bathroom
10 Balcony
11 Store room
12 Void over living space

Spangen Quarter

Michiel Brinkman, 1873–1925

Rotterdam, The Netherlands, 1919–1921

The Spangen area in Rotterdam saw several housing schemes built by the municipal authorities in the first decades of the twentieth century in order to house the poor. Most follow the same plan arrangement, with anonymous façades lining the street edges and enclosing more animated courtyard spaces, sometimes with communal gardens. J. J. P. Oud, as city architect from 1918 to 1927, experimented with variations to the basic form – with, for example, much larger courtyard spaces that contain schools, and with moving the living rooms to overlook the courtyard. Brinkman's project is one of the first to disrupt the logic of the plan and question the relationships between inside and outside spaces in relation to the dwellings.

Each of the dwellings has its own private front door, either at ground level or from a wide access gallery at second-floor level. The ground-floor doors lead to flats at ground- and first-floor level, above which there are two-storey maisonettes.

Instead of the neutral space of communal gardens, the courtyard becomes an active place. Private gardens for the flats, paired at ground- or first-floor level, are crossed by a network of pedestrian paths leading to the entrances, and communal play spaces for children are included along with shared facilities such as bathhouses and laundries. The gallery, or 'street in the sky', is wide – between 2.20 and 3.30 metres (7 and 11 feet) wide. Its location on the 'private' garden side, above the private balconies to the first-floor flats, makes its use ambiguous; its size, too, means that it can accommodate use as an outdoor room, as a place to sit or gather and talk with neighbours as well as simply for access and deliveries.

Overall, the internal courtyard conveys a strong sense of identity, derived from an unusual combination of the legible, rigid and symmetrical arrangement in plan and a high level of detail – giving variety at a much smaller scale than was common in most developments of the period.

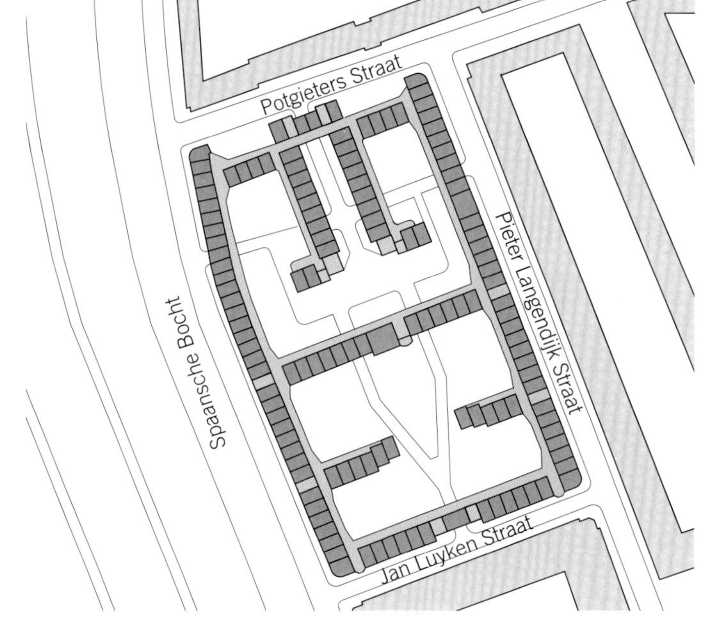

Site layout showing second-floor access galleries 1:2,500

1

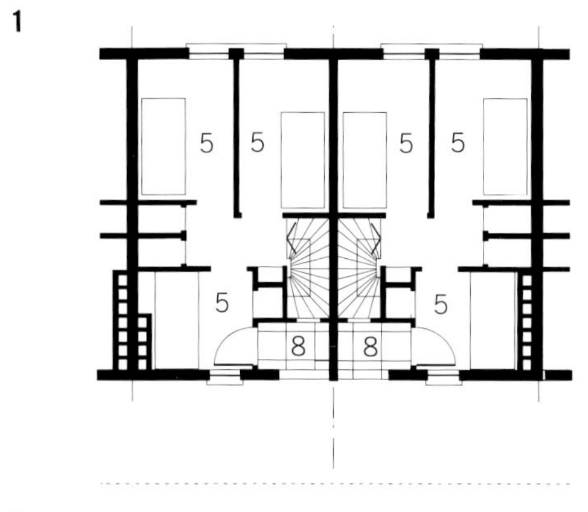

2

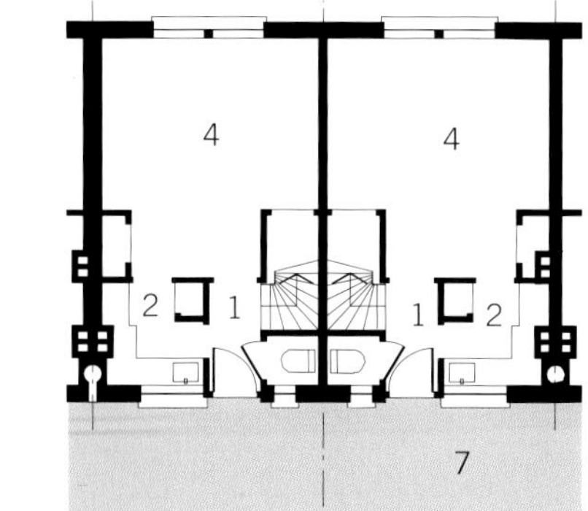

3

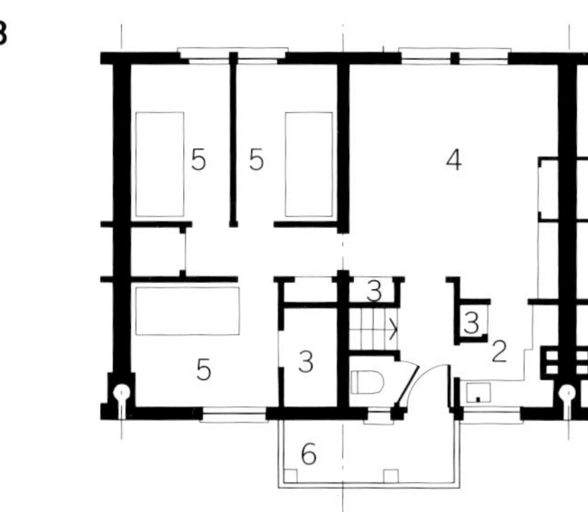

4

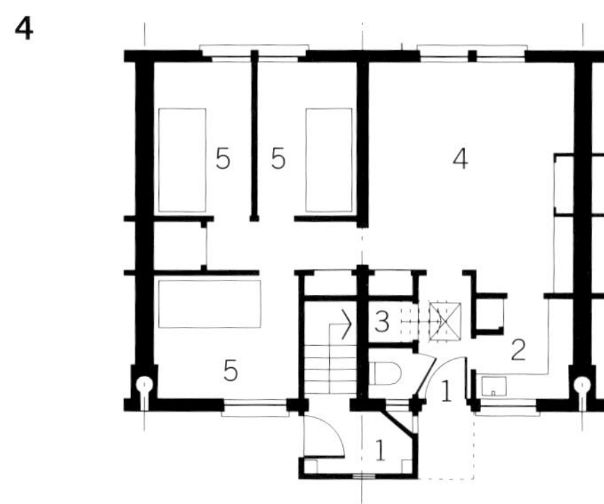

Floor plans of typical flats and maisonettes 1:200

1 Third-floor plan
2 Second-floor plan
3 First-floor plan
4 Ground-floor plan

1 Entrance/hall
2 Kitchen
3 Storage
4 Living room
5 Bedroom
6 Balcony
7 Access balcony
8 Loggia

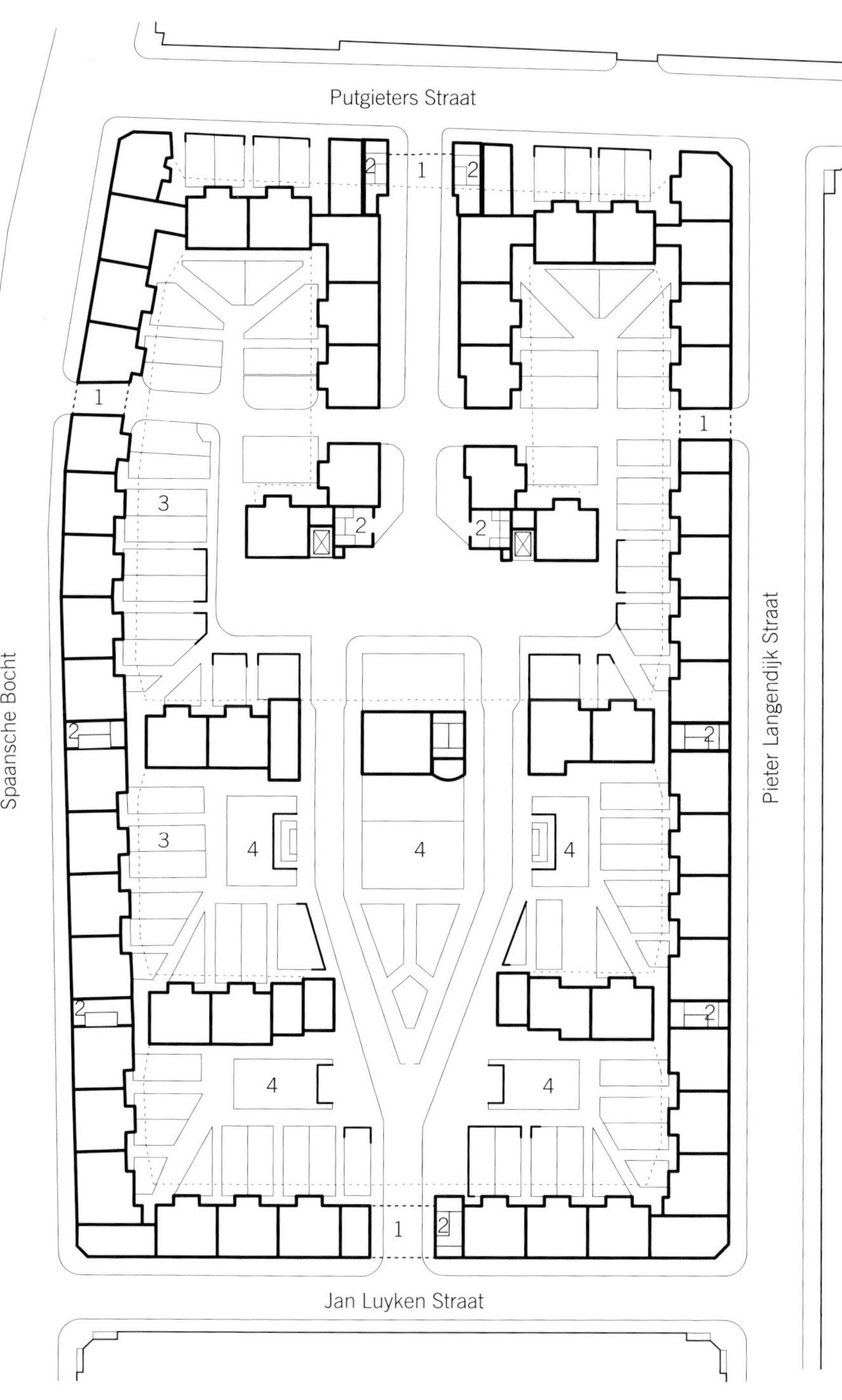

5

5 Ground-floor plan 1:1,000

1 Entrance to courtyard
2 Stairs to upper floors
3 Private gardens
4 Shared gardens and playgrounds

El Pueblo Ribera Courtyard Houses

Rudolf Schindler, 1887–1953

La Jolla, California, USA; 1925

Following the success story of his own residence, the Kings Road House built in 1922, Schindler went on to design many more houses and apartment buildings in California. The Pueblo Ribera, La Jolla (1925), was designed as holiday homes, for temporary living only, but is included here for its contribution to the development of the courtyard-house plan as a type and particularly for its incorporation of the concept of the outdoor room.

The scheme comprises 12 identical single-storey houses, U-shaped in plan, skilfully designed and laid out to maintain complete privacy. Like the Kings Road House, the dwellings are designed to facilitate outdoor living. The living room in the centre of the plan, which was also used for sleeping, has fully glazed full-height sliding panels that can be completely opened up to the courtyard, thus extending the living space outdoors. From the courtyard, an external stair leads to a roof terrace – a second outdoor living space, equipped with a fireplace, partially enclosed by parapet walls and with a timber pergola for a roof. The bedroom on one side of the plan and the 'nook' on the other both have glazed doors to the outside courtyard; the only windows are at high level, in the bathroom or above the kitchen door, purely to let light in.

Schindler used a familiar rigorous dimensioning framework – everything is based on a 100-mm (4-inch) module – and, integral to this, developed a new construction technique. The 'tilt' slab system whereby concrete was cast on site in panels and tilted up into position, and which he had used for the Kings Road House, required flat ground. Here, on a gently sloping site, he developed a 'slab-cast' system using a skeleton guide and reusable 400-mm (16-inch) planks as formwork. These were held horizontally with clamps that could be easily employed by unskilled labour – an important factor in keeping costs low in comparison with timber construction. The resulting bare concrete walls with their visible horizontal lines form the main elements of the structure, with the other elements being in timber.

1 Section 1:100

1 Living room
2 Outdoor room
3 Roof terrace
4 Fireplace
5 Pergola

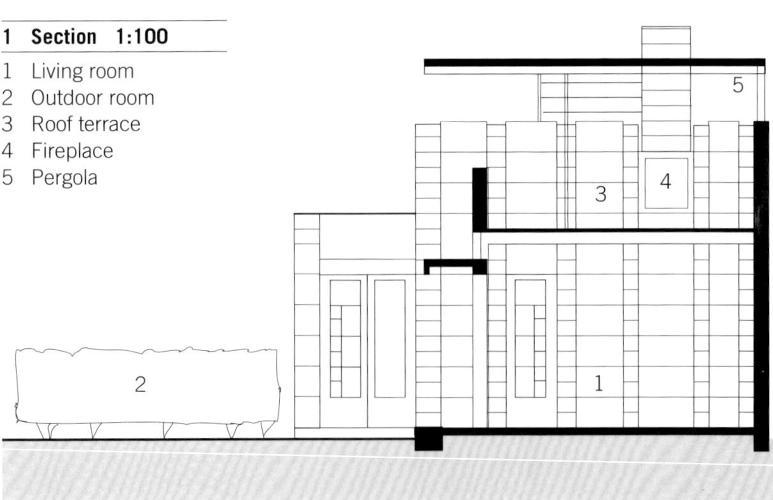

2

2 Site layout 1:500

1 Pedestrian pathway
2 Car parking
3 Outdoor room
4 Yard

3

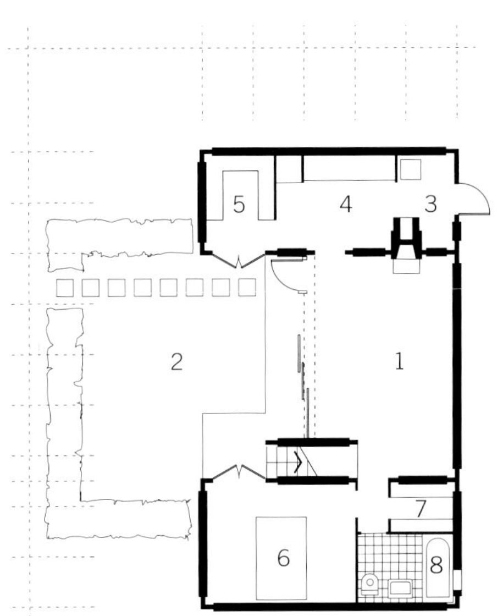

4

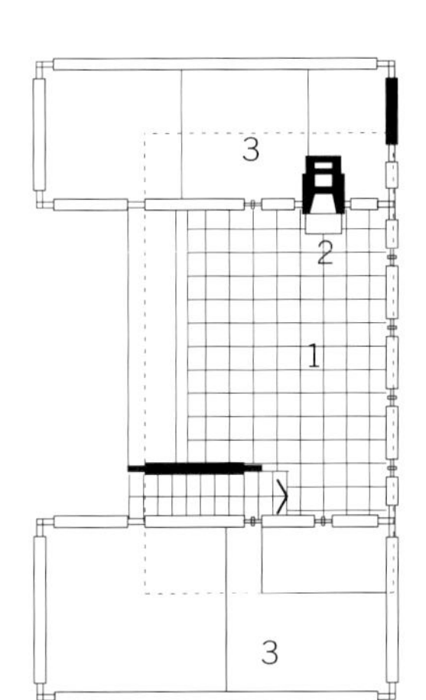

5

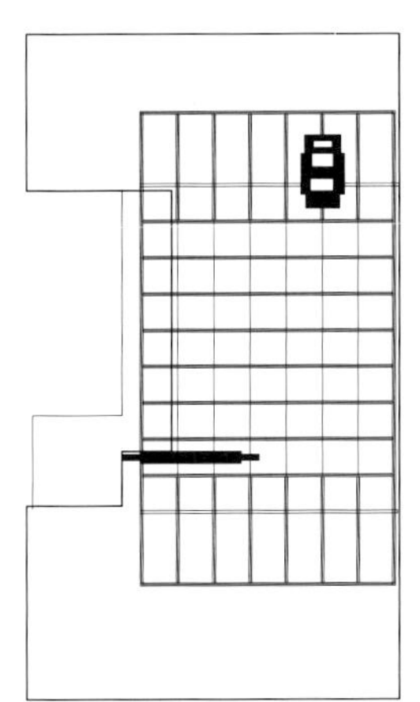

3 Ground-floor plan 1:200

1 Living room
2 Outdoor room
3 Back porch
4 Kitchen
5 Nook
6 Bedroom
7 Store room
8 Bathroom

4 First-floor plan 1:200

1 Roof terrace
2 Fireplace
3 Roof

5 Roof plan 1:200

Left: Park Lane Hotel, New York

Efficiency Apartments

Schultze & Weaver

New York, New York, USA; 1920s

The term 'efficiency' was used in the United States in the early twentieth century to describe the reduction in floor space achieved per apartment, with the aim generally of increasing the number of rental units per floor in residential blocks. There was much debate over whether the reduced space represented a benefit to those residents unable to afford larger apartments, and whether there would continue to be a market for such small one- or two-person 'living units'. According to C. Stanley Taylor, writing in *Architectural Forum* in 1924, architects should be encouraged to persuade their clients of the benefit of efficiency planning methods in terms of improved return on their investments, while such methods also encouraged development when there was a shortage of affordable housing. In the same issue of the journal, S. Fullerton Weaver – partner in Schultze & Weaver, best known for their glamorous hotels including the Waldorf Astoria and the Biltmore chain – predicted that 'it seems very likely that the next 20 or 30 years will see an almost complete abandoning of the individual city house'. One of his reasons for saying this, apart from financial ones, was the increasing problem of finding satisfactory servants. The 'apartment-hotel' offered a good solution, combining the privacy of apartments with the services of a hotel.

Efficiency is applied to the design of these apartments in two ways: firstly, by combining a kitchen and dining area in the smallest space possible; and secondly, by using one space for two different functions. New compact equipment – such as 'complete units' with hob, icebox and cupboards – was designed to fit the smaller servantless kitchens. Fittings were designed for dealing with various deliveries. Ice and groceries could be delivered directly into the back of cabinets fitted to the corridor walls; and rubbish could be removed in a similar fashion, via a container fitted into the wall to the service corridor and accessible from both sides. A similar idea was used for postal deliveries; letter boxes in doors of an increased thickness meant tenants could retrieve mail without opening their doors. Specially designed equipment was also necessary to achieve the double use of space. 'Door beds', for example, that folded and hinged, could be brought out at night and hidden away during the day in the adjacent dressing room.

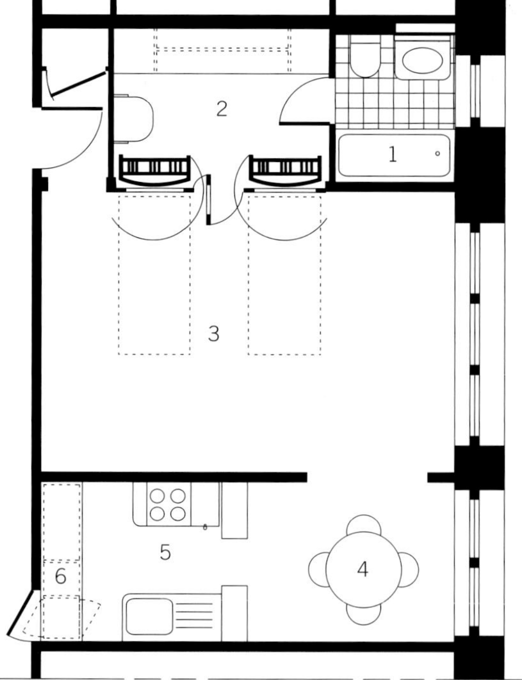

1 Plan of typical efficiency apartment 1:100

1 Bathroom
2 Dressing room
3 Living room
4 Dining space
5 Kitchenette
6 Combined cabinet and refrigerator

2

2 Typical floor plan space-saving apartment block 1:200

1 Hall, stair and lifts
2 Service hall and lift
3 Fire escape
4 Entrance/foyer
5 Kitchen
6 Living/dining
7 Bedroom
8 Bathroom
9 Cupboards
10 Lightwell

3

3 Typical floor plan efficiency planning apartment block 1:200

1 Hall stair and lifts
2 Service hall and lift
3 Fire escape
4 Entrance/foyer
5 Kitchenette
6 Dining alcove
7 Living/bedroom
8 Bathroom
9 Dressing room
10 Lightwell

Britz Hufeisensiedlung

Bruno Taut, 1880–1938, and Martin Wagner, 1885–1957

Berlin, Germany; 1925–27

The Britz Hufeisensiedlung (horseshoe housing scheme), named after the shape of the central block which is designed around a pond, was developed as part of Martin Wagner's programme for much needed housing for workers, following his appointment as planning director for Greater Berlin in 1925. Bruno Taut, best known for his conceptual writings and his Expressionist Glass Pavilion at the Cologne Werkbund Exhibition of 1914, brought a new approach to the design of housing, with a combination of garden city ideas and simple functional planning.

The layouts of the individual dwellings is conventional, and the units themselves quite small. The houses include cellars, a laundry room and additional space in the attic. The flats have a typical arrangement of main living spaces with loggias or balconies on the garden side and access landing and staircases on the opposite, street, side.

With around 1,000 dwellings in just two building types – three-storey apartment bocks and three-storey terraced houses – the Britz project uses form and layout to effectively combat potential monotony and regularity. The blocks are laid out radially from the central horseshoe, following gentle curves and stepping to correspond to level changes in the landscape. They form street edges, enclosing large internal garden spaces. Staggered plans and stairwells, either protruding or recessed, introduce vertical elements in the façades to break up the linear nature of the blocks. Recessed loggias and attic windows visible at roof level further enrich the composition and add to the possible variations in the different blocks. The small scale of the houses, the dormer windows in their steeply pitched roofs and the use of an intense red colour in some of the blocks contribute a somewhat picturesque quality to the overall composition.

Site plan
1:5,000

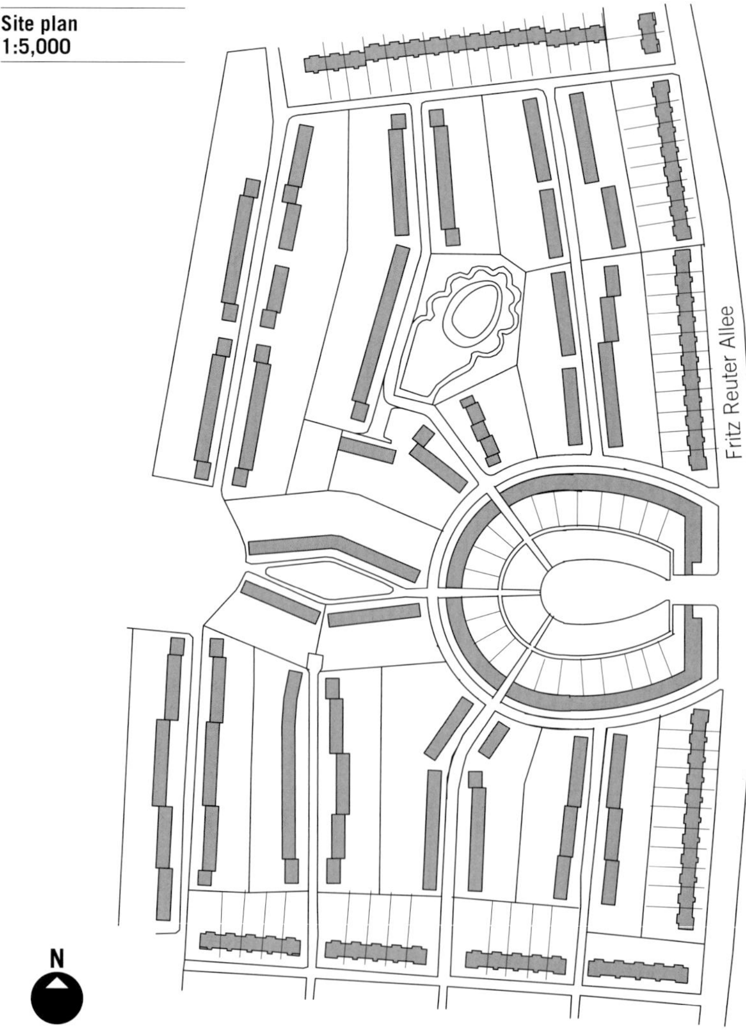

1

2

3

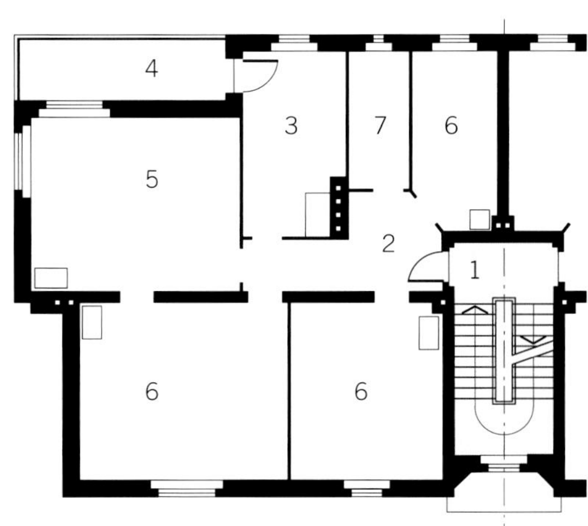

4

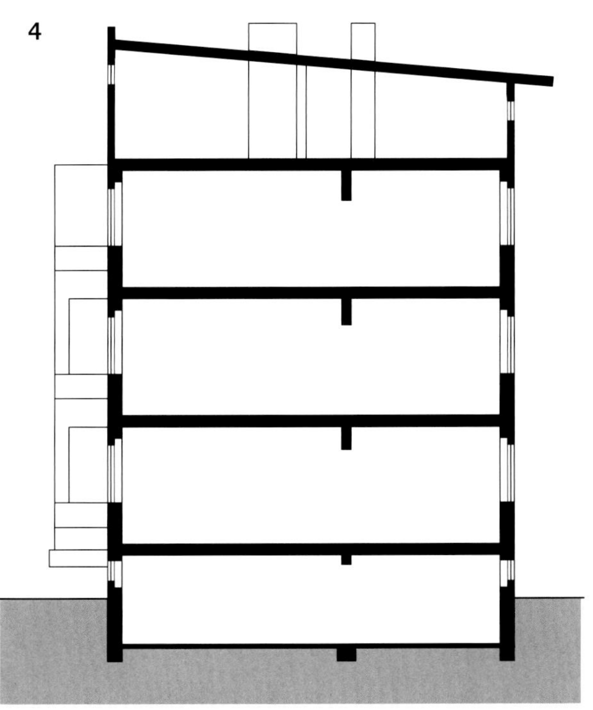

Plans of typical apartments 1:200

1 Type 1
2 Type 2
3 Type 3

1 Access stairs
2 Entrance/hall
3 Kitchen
4 Balcony
5 Living room
6 Bedroom
7 Bathroom

4 Section 1:200

Karl Marx Hof

Karl Ehn, 1884–1957

Vienna, Austria; 1926–30

During little more than a decade following the First World War, the city of Vienna's ambitious housing programme built more than 60,000 new dwellings. Rather than opting for the Modernist schemes in Germany and the Netherlands, based on garden suburb principles, the Viennese authorities chose a denser, more urban form of the closed bock surrounding interior courtyards. The 'hof', as this type of courtyard was called, became identified with the social programme and with the new modern style; developments based around it were designed by architects such as Josef Hoffmann, Peter Behrens and Josef Frank as well as those employed by the municipal authorities.

The largest example of this model is the Karl Marx Hof designed by Karl Ehn, which has come to represent the socialist housing programme of 'Red Vienna'. It was built on the site of the old market gardens, running for almost a kilometre (half a mile) alongside the Franz-Josef railway line. Its rectilinear blocks, which are generally four storeys high and approximately 11 metres (36 feet) deep, are staggered to follow the street front and enclose a courtyard accessed through huge arches cut through the perimeter wall. Towards the centre, dividing the courtyard in two, a section of the block rises to seven storeys and is crowned with a series of towers which, combined with the balconies, form a backdrop to the open space that has become the enduring monumental image of this project and the social housing of Red Vienna.

The scheme had a total of 1,382 dwellings. Generally the flats were very small: a few with one room and a few with three, but the vast majority (close to 1,000) had just two rooms. The floor area of the flats varied, along with variations in the overall depth of the blocks and the addition of balconies at some levels. Staircases – there were no lifts – generally served four apartments. All the apartments had a kitchen and a WC, sometimes with a lobby fitted with a basin, but bathrooms and shower rooms were provided collectively along with laundries. A structural wall runs down the middle of the blocks, sometimes with openings to connect both façades and provide cross-ventilation, but most flats are single aspect, overlooking either the street or the courtyard.

2

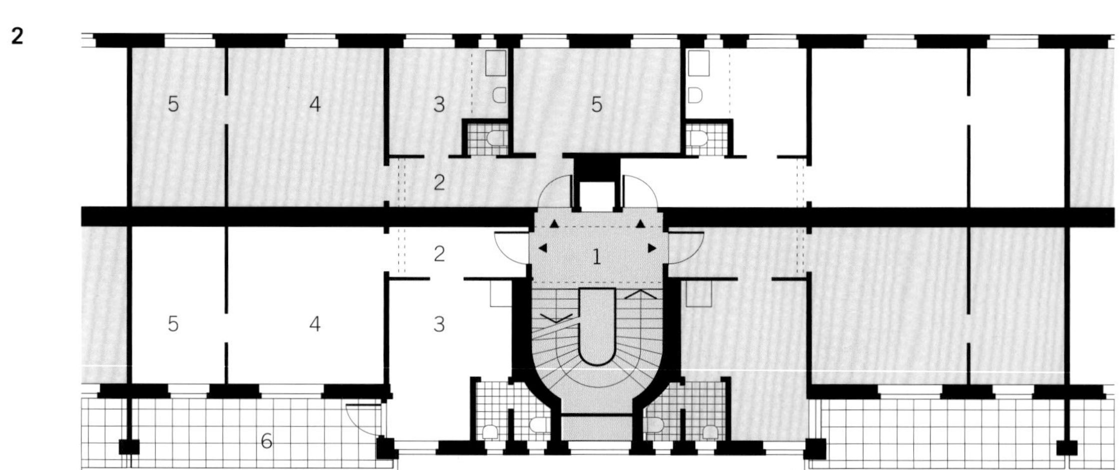

1

2

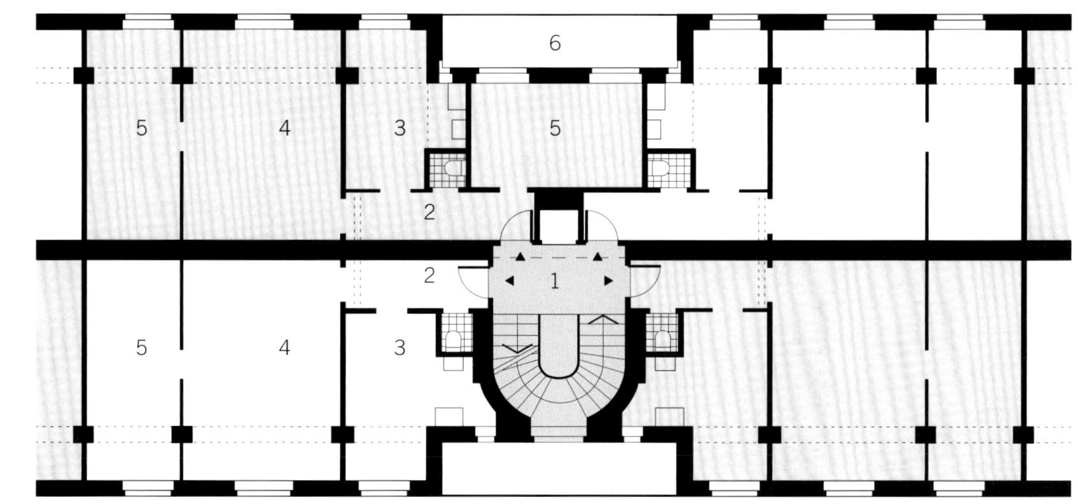

1 Part elevation 1:200

2 Typical flat plans 1:200

1 Access and circulation
2 Entrance/hall
3 Kitchen
4 Living
5 Bedroom
6 Balcony

European Modernism

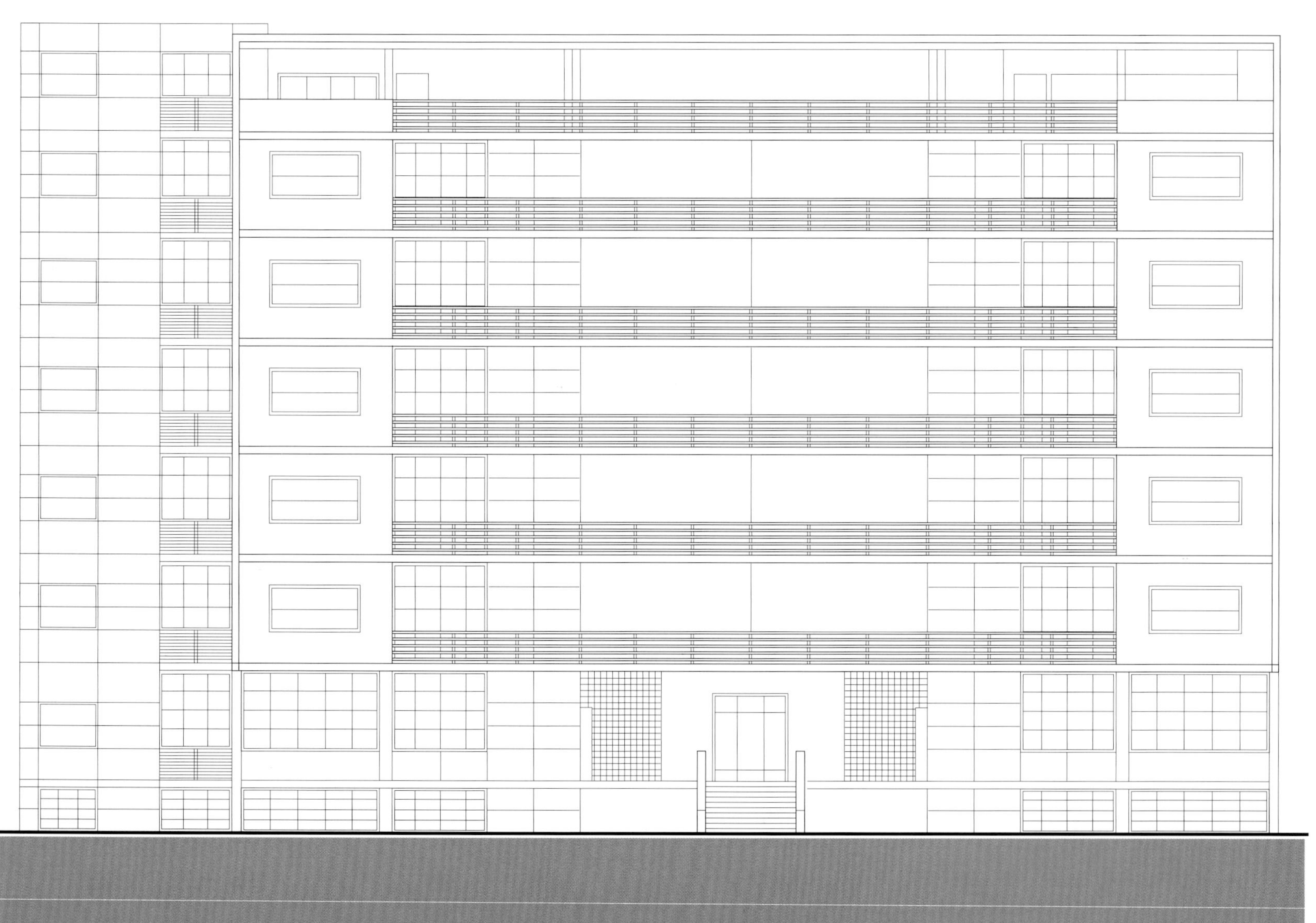

Left: **The Weissenhofsiedlung**

Right: **Elevation of Werkbund dwellings by Adolf Loos**

The foundation in 1928 of CIAM (Congrès Internationaux d'Architecture Moderne) by a group of 30 architects in Europe had crystallized the ideas and principles of modern architecture and had made clear their attitude to town planning: 'Urbanization cannot be conditioned by the claims of a pre-existent aestheticism; its essence is of a functional order … the chaotic division of land, resulting from sales, speculations, inheritances, must be abolished by a collective and methodical land policy.' The Athens Charter that was to come out of their fourth congress in 1933 was to formalize this then-radical image of the modern city, with its functional approach to planning, the separation of pedestrians from traffic and the construction of tower blocks to provide open spaces at ground level. In 1929, their second congress, held in Frankfurt, had addressed the equally pressing issue of the 'minimum dwelling', which confirmed the agenda for a rationalist and functionalist approach to planning the individual housing unit. Coupled with the use of industrialized construction methods, the employment of standardized parts and prefabrication the new architecture was expected to achieve a higher quality of housing, with the space savings and cost reductions required. Whether in larger-scale blocks or low-rise housing, the spatial planning ideas of Modernism could be applied equally. Courtyards were denounced as dirty and dingy, and existing street patterns were generally ignored in favour of the new straight blocks orientated to maximize daylight and sunlight.

The **Weissenhofsiedlung** exhibition, opened in 1927 in Stuttgart, was successful in demonstrating different versions of the new architecture as applied to housing – the only constraint imposed on the architects taking part was that they were to use flat roofs. Ludwig Mies van der Rohe's **Weissenhofsiedlung Apartment Building** (see pages 48–49), which dominates the site, turned the traditional block outside in: instead of a perimeter block around a courtyard – the familiar urban form until then – a thinner block sits alone, with flats extending through its full depth. A framed construction allows for a variety of different configurations of internal partitions. There is no hierarchical arrangement on its façades, the building is designed to be extended or repeated easily and, within the dwellings, there is no 'fixed' plan. J. J. P. Oud's **Weissenhofsiedlung Row Housing** (see pages 50–51), uses a lower-height extension, which is a familiar English device, and develops Oud's ideas from his earlier projects in the Netherlands. His two-storey buildings with balconies on the upper levels, gardens on the lower levels and direct street access had broken with the idea of the closed courtyard in the Hoek van Holland estate (1924) and again with his **Kiefhoek** workers' housing (1927), which achieved a very small (4.2 metre/14 foot) width. The constraints imposed in the Austrian Werkbund's exhibition at Vienna that followed in 1932 – only low-rise buildings were allowed – produced more new variations on terraced houses. André Lurçat's **Vienna Werkbund houses** (see pages 62–63) are very small and intricately planned over three storeys, and they demonstrate flexibility of use between day and night-time. **Adolf Loos's Vienna Werkbund houses** (see pages 60–61) have a version of his spatially sculptural *Raumplan* applied to much smaller-scale workers' houses.

Other exhibitions held by different national Werkbund organizations included Breslau (1929), Zurich (1932) and Stockholm in 1930.

The influential Berlin Siemensstadt development of 1930, under the leadership of Martin Wagner, followed the earlier Frankfurt experiment at Römerstadt by Ernst May. May had become head of the Frankfurt City Planning Department in 1925 and had

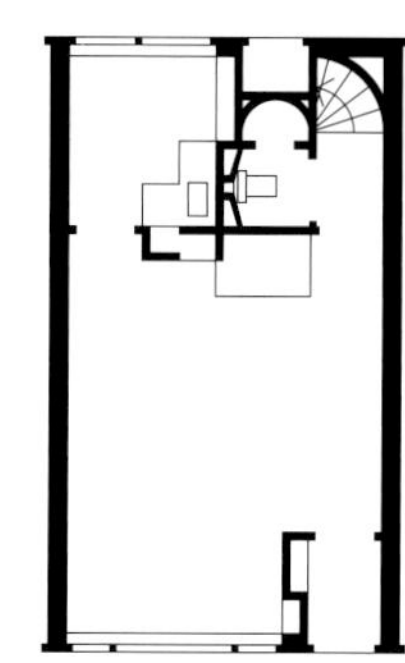

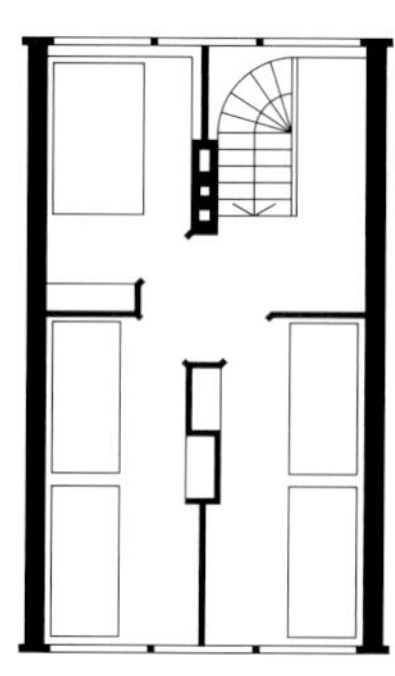

Far left: **Kiefhoek Workers' Housing**

Left: **Kiefhoek, ground and first-floor plans**

Bottom left: **Frankfurt kitchen**

Bottom right: **Siemensstadt block (Walter Gropius)**

taken ideas about English garden city planning to Germany after working with Raymond Unwin on Hampstead Garden Suburb. Römerstadt was a development on a huge scale, significant for its modern architecture, its planning (including planting schemes for the tenants' allotments) and its use of prefabrication and other standardized construction methods which were also extended to the first fitted kitchens – the '**Frankfurt kitchen**' designed by Greta Schütte-Lihotzky. Hans Scharoun had designed a prototype house for the Weissenhofsiedlung in 1927, but Scharoun's flat layouts for the **Siemensstadt development** (see pages 54–55) attracted more attention, with their centralized design focused on a living space that occupies the full (approx. 9-metre/30-foot) depth of the plan. In the Netherlands, van Tijen, Brinkman & Van der Vlugt's **Bergpolder** (see pages 64–65), with its repeated single plan-type, was much publicized, notably in Alfred Roth's *New Architecture* (**1939**), and is generally considered to be the first example of a high-rise single slab block.

During this period, facilities like heating, hot water and bathrooms were often of a higher standard in modern flats – even those designed for the working class – than in some upper-class houses, especially in cities like London. Levels of privacy and the amenities offered as part of the community of the block were also likely to be better. Maxwell Fry's **Kensal House** (see pages 72–73), built for the Gas Light and Coke Company, perfected the design of a combined kitchen

Left: **Bergpolder**

and bathroom with ducted services, ventilated larder and drying balcony, and even provided additional heating points in bedrooms as well as the living room for the comfort of the tenants. At **Highpoint** (see pages 68–71), at the other end of the social scale, Berthold Lubetkin's detailed design ensured that electric heating coils were incorporated into the ceilings of the apartments and electric radiant heaters were installed for local heating.

In Soviet Russia, the argument for higher standards for all was based on the possibilities afforded by the new mass-production methods and by proposed social changes to move away from the traditional family structure to collective living arrangements. Moisei Ginzburg and Ignati Milinis's **Narkomfin** block in Moscow (see pages 52–53), with its minimal private apartments, was one of the earliest to demonstrate these ideas. 'Bachelor apartments', like the American hotel versions for single working women or the cooperative homes of the Garden City movement such as those designed by Baillie Scott, gained little ground either in the USA or Europe. The only popular example, **Lawn Road (now Isokon) flats** in London (see pages 56–59) by Wells Coates, was built to cater for those who preferred a more secluded lifestyle.

Jean Ginsberg's **25 and 42 Avenue de Versailles** apartments in Paris (see pages 66–67), two of several similar buildings in the neighbourhood, and Giuseppe Terragni's **Casa Rustici** in Milan (see pages 74–75) maintain a continuity with the existing urban form but introduce a new relationship to the street. Ginsberg uses Modernism's horizontal bands, curves the façade to reveal the singular structural column in the centre and uses innovative sash windows that open up the interiors to the street by disappearing into the thickness of the wall. Terragni's Milanese block opens up the entire building to the street, placing the 'courtyard' in the centre and linking the two identical halves with long thin balconies on the street front.

Weissenhofsiedlung Apartment Building

Ludwig Mies van der Rohe, 1886–1969

Stuttgart, Germany; 1927

Mies's apartment block, built as part of the Weissenhofsiedlung exhibition in Stuttgart in 1927, is the largest element in the scheme, dominating the rest of the buildings from its position at the highest point of the site. As director of the project, Mies was commissioned by the Werkbund to construct an exhibition on the theme of 'the dwelling', including the master plan for the site and the selection of the participating designers. This curatorial role, which enabled him to invite the best-known Modernist architects, meant the Weissenhof demonstrated all aspects of contemporary modern design in housing. The projects included prototypes for individual villas and houses, terraced housing and blocks of apartments three and four storeys high.

Mies's scheme is a block of flats, four storeys in height, above a semi-basement level, orientated roughly north–south and standing independently in open ground. The façades are simple and regular, organized around the entrances and staircases on one side and the projecting balconies on the other; with horizontal strips of identically sized windows repeated at each floor level, they present no clues as to what goes on behind. Internally, however, the apparently rigid organization allows for a high degree of flexibility in planning. The steel-column structure, both on the façades and centrally, and the stair enclosures are arranged so that differently sized areas are created, within which lightweight partitions can be arranged in a variety of different ways. In this scheme, Mies achieved the idea of flexibility in all its various interpretations. Firstly, the structure allows different layouts which could change in the long term; secondly, apart from the kitchen and bathroom, there is no designated use for the other spaces, so the occupants can decide how to occupy the different rooms; and thirdly, the use of sliding partitions means spaces can be physically altered by the occupants. This level of flexibility means that the apartments should have a longer useful life: they can be changed either in the short term to suit the day-to-day activities of families or to accommodate a growing and changing family; or in the longer term to allow for the reconstruction of the interiors to make different units within the structural shell of the building.

Site plan 1:2,500

1 Mies van der Rohe; 2 J. J. P. Oud; 3 Victor Bourgeois; 4 Adolf G. Schneck; 5 Le Corbusier/Pierre Jeanneret; 6 Walter Gropius; 7 Ludwig Hilberseimer; 8 Bruno Taut; 9 Hans Poelzig; 10 Richard Döcker; 11 Max Taut; 12 Adolf Rading; 13 Josef Frank; 14 Mart Stam; 15 Peter Behrens; 16 Hans Scharoun

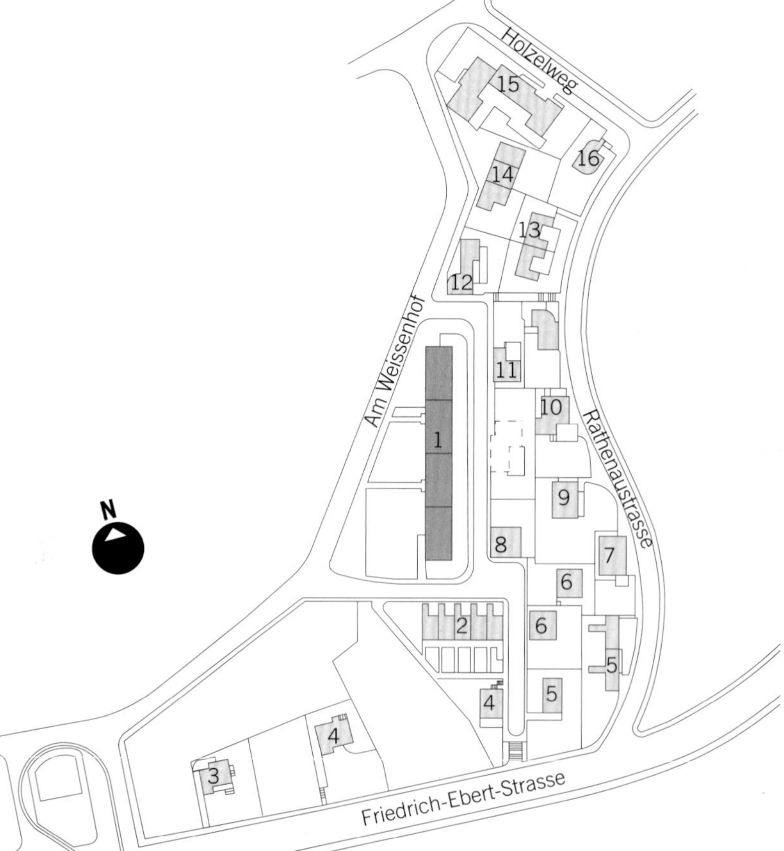

1

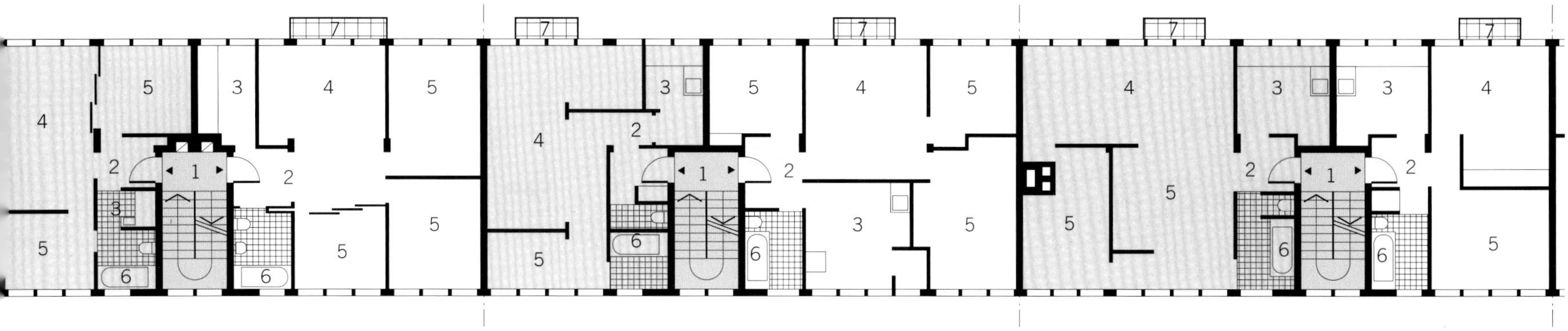

2

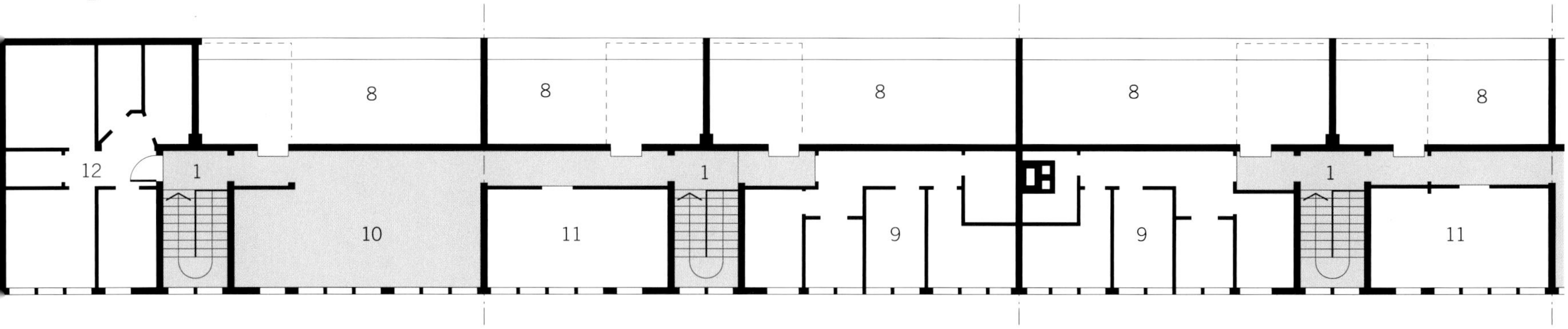

3

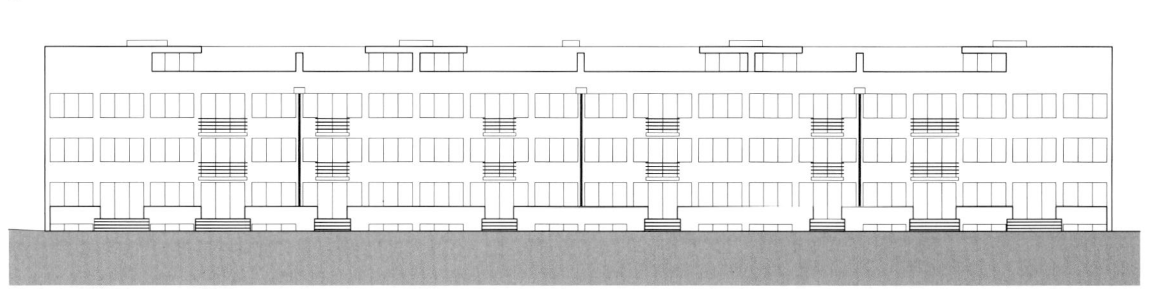

4

1 Part second-floor plan 1:200

2 Part top-floor plan 1:200

1 Access stairs
2 Entrance/hallway
3 Kitchen
4 Living
5 Bedroom
6 Bathroom
7 Balcony
8 Roof terrace
9 Store room
10 Drying room
11 Wash room
12 Attic rooms

3 Street elevation 1:500

4 Garden elevation 1:500

Weissenhofsiedlung Row Housing

J. J. P. Oud, 1890–1963

Stuttgart, Germany; 1927

The Weissenhofsiedlung exhibition was instrumental in making public much of the contemporary architectural research into the design of the 'minimum dwelling'. Oud's project at the Weissenhofsiedlung is one of a series of designs for high-density low-rise terraced or row housing that he had been working on for several years. These already included his housing estates at Kiefhoek in Rotterdam (1927), with plans only 4.2 metres (14 feet) wide, and the Hoek van Holland (1924) – both with the flat, planar, white stucco façades typical of Oud's work. These designs were the result of a pragmatic approach in response to the perceived needs of residents, rather than the more avant-garde aesthetic approach associated with the Expressionists.

This scheme is a terrace of five three -storey houses, each including a basement. Their plans are narrow – just 4.7 metres (15 feet 6 inches) wide – but relatively deep at 8 metres (26 feet) front to back. Like many English terraced houses of the nineteenth and early twentieth centuries, the main volume of the dwelling is extended with a half-width extension. This has lower ceilings so that the upper level can be reached from a half-landing on the stair. The open space formed next to the extension is enclosed and accessible from the street, forming an entrance courtyard. The houses also have a second entrance with an enclosed lobby on the south elevation, which faces gardens and a pedestrian street.

The internal arrangement of the houses follows the convention of living and kitchen spaces on the ground floor with three bedrooms on the upper level. The bathroom is located in the centre of the plan above the kitchen and has additional doors to the adjacent bedrooms which, when left open, allow daylight and ventilation into an otherwise internal room. The WC is located separately. The room on the half-landing was designed as a drying room, open to the outside at high level. A laundry room is provided on the ground floor, together with a store room which is accessible from the courtyard. Very little space is given to corridors or hallways, and the circulation space is generally included within the rooms themselves. With the street entrance via the courtyard and laundry, it is assumed the residents would use the garden entrance, particularly when receiving visitors.

Site plan
1:1,000

Elevations and plans
1:200

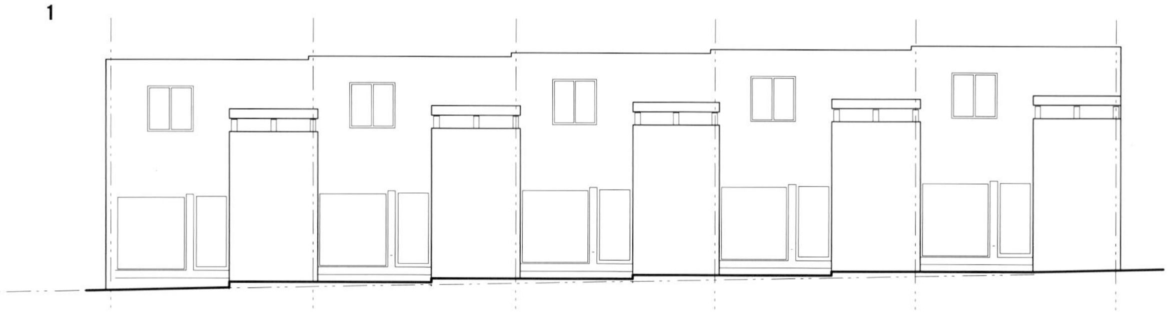

1 Street/north elevation
2 Garden/south elevation
3 First-floor plan
4 Ground-floor plan

1 Yard
2 Store room
3 Laundry
4 Stair to cellar
5 Kitchen
6 Living room
7 Porch to garden entrance
8 Drying room
9 Bedroom
10 Bathroom
11 Balcony

1

2

3

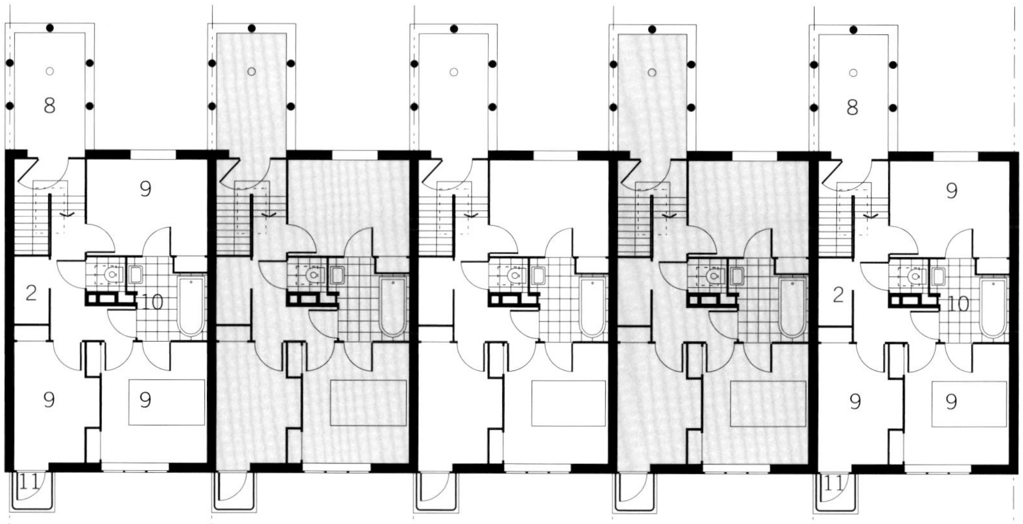

4

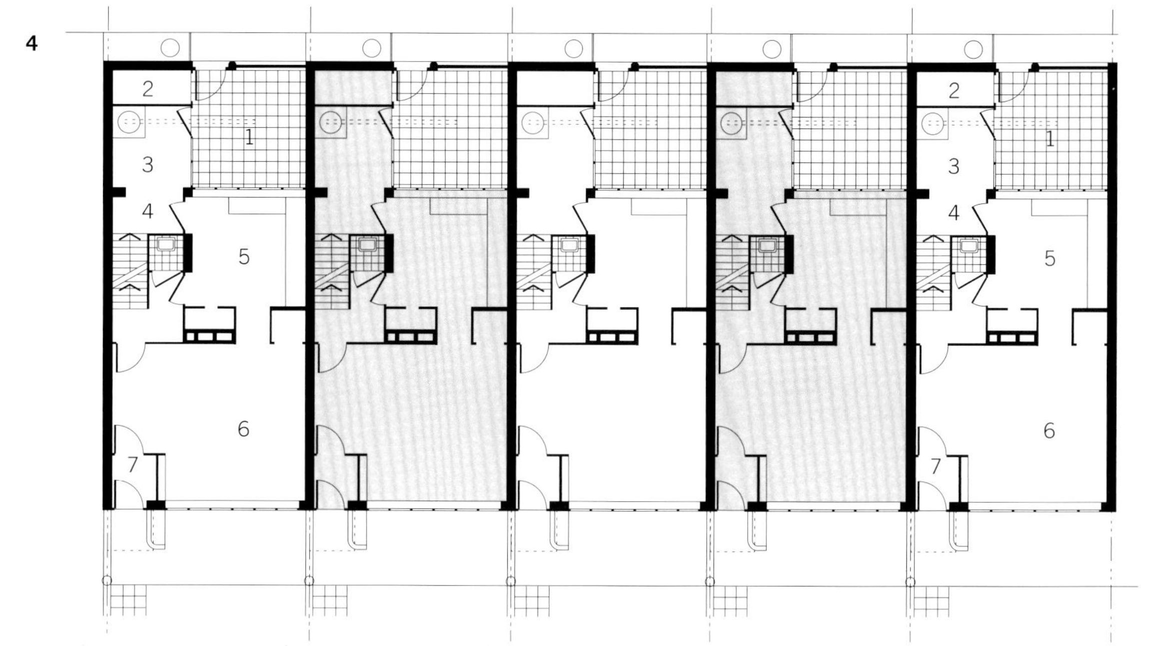

Narkomfin

Moisei Ginzburg (1892–1946) and Ignati Milinis

Moscow, Russia; 1930

Laws passed in 1918 to abolish private real estate and to nationalize land were the first steps in the government's plans to solve the housing problems in the Soviet Union. The new social order would rely on a reassessment of the family and the design and construction of new kinds of housing. Ambitious building programmes gave architects and planners accustomed to working only for the rich the opportunity to design for this new future. Changes to the family structure, the basis for so much housing design, seemed inevitable. The increasing economic independence of women as a result of political equality, together with both a desire and a need for them to join the workforce, meant that an alternative solution had to be found if they were not to be engaged in the traditional tasks of housework and childcare. The new architecture was to reflect this.

Ginzburg was a member of the OSA (Society of Contemporary Architects), a group founded in 1925 who published their project ideas and expressed their opinions in their journal *SA*. These proposals firmly established their commitment to the separation between the collective and the individual, and their enthusiasm for efficient design in living spaces that would allow for the provision of social spaces – gyms, kindergartens and canteens. Following his appointment in 1928 as head of the standardization section in the construction committee, Ginzburg worked on the development of a whole series of standard plan-types for use in all new housing developments. These were 'transitional' types, that is, with minimal provision of kitchens and bathrooms so that they could be occupied during the transitional phase that was necessary before fully communal housing could be provided. The Narkomfin building, built by Ginzburg in 1930, uses a version of a split-level apartment known as the 'F' type, which was the most popular, in combination with a larger two-storey type. The apartments are grouped in one block with a second, adjacent, block at right angles containing all the communal facilities. As well as a similarity in the overall approach to provision for the community, the individual 'F' type apartments share many features with those found in Le Corbusier's Unité (see pages 82–85); this is a dwelling type that continues to reappear in contemporary housing design.

1 Part outline section 1:200

1 Access gallery
2 Entrance
3 Kitchen/living
4 Bedroom

1

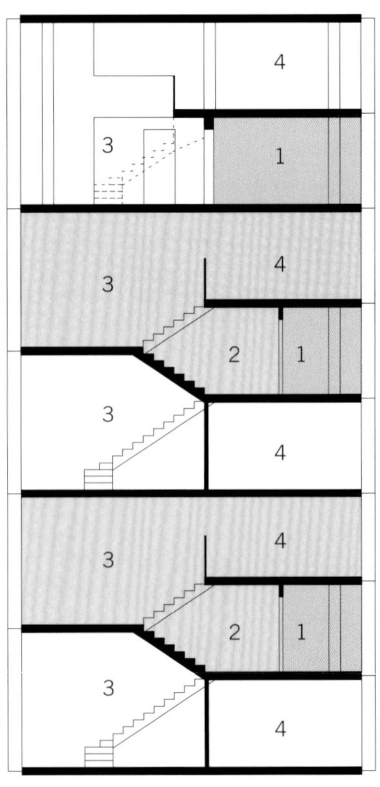

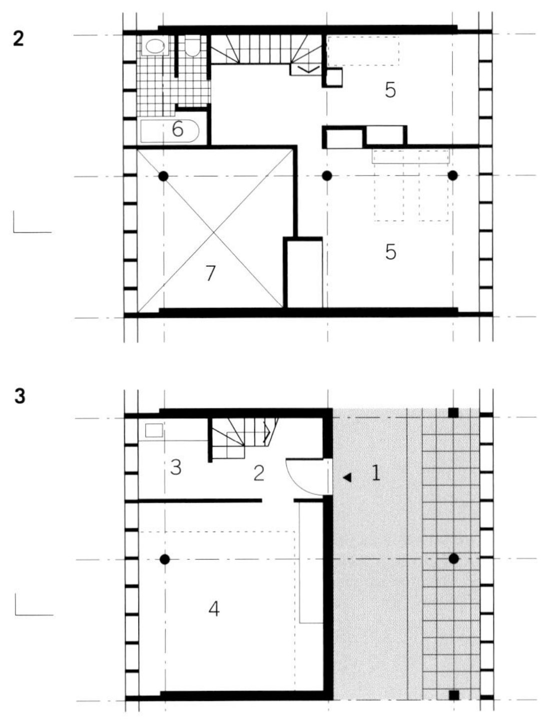

Plans of duplex apartment 1:200

2 Upper-level plan
3 Lower-level plan

1 Access gallery
2 Entrance/hallway
3 Kitchen
4 Living room
5 Bedroom
6 Bathroom
7 Void over living room

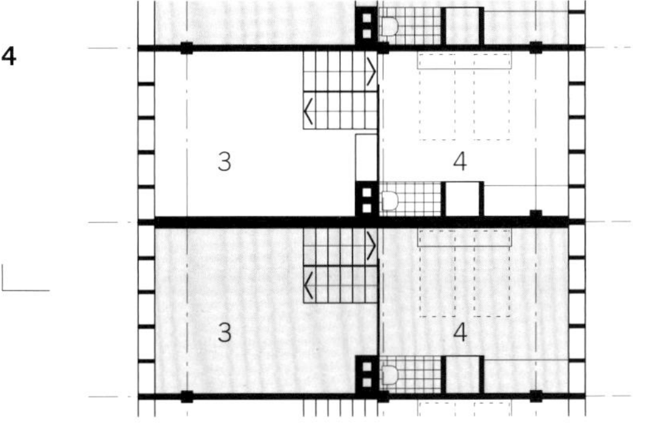

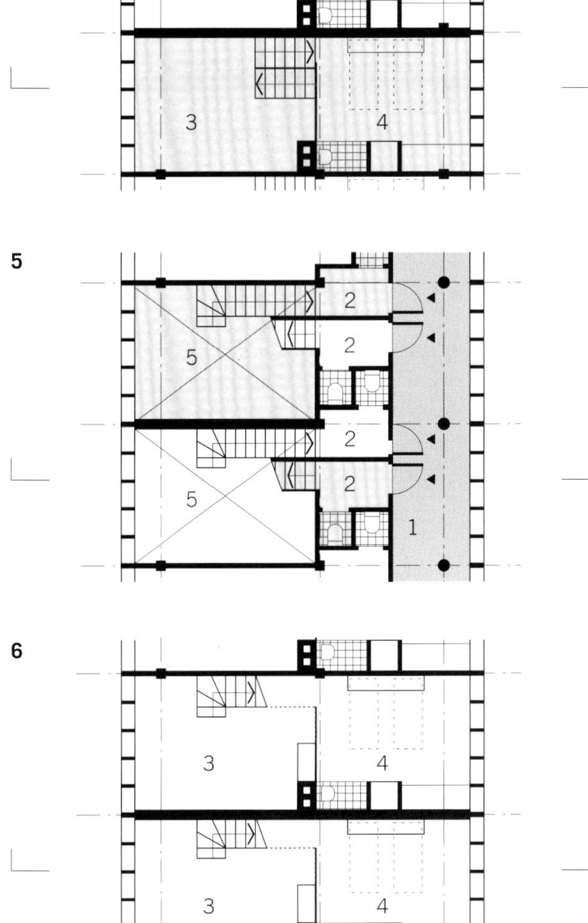

Plans of split-level one bedroom flats 1:200

4 Upper-level plan
5 Middle-level plan
6 Lower-level plan

1 Access gallery
2 Entrance
3 Living/kitchen
4 Bedroom
5 Void over living room

Siemensstadt Housing

Hans Scharoun, 1893–1972

Berlin, Germany; 1930

The Seimensstadt project, for low-income groups and electrical workers, was built on a large site on the outskirts of Berlin. Planning director Martin Wagner gave Scharoun responsibility for the master-planning of the site, which included projects by Walter Gropius, Hugo Häring and Alfred Forbat. For his own project, Scharoun chose a corner of the site, cut off by the curve of the railway. He designed three different dwelling types in blocks laid out in response to the specifics of the site, neither following the roads nor lined up in north–south-orientated parallel *Zeilenbau* blocks. The form of the blocks is also a response to the design and layout of the apartments, rather than the more usual Modernist approach of fitting the apartments into an external volume or organizing structure. Referring to the scheme in his 1978 monograph as looking 'wilfully untidy', Peter Blundell Jones suggested that in reality perfect geometry in plan drawings does not necessarily result in good spatial relationships, and maintained that Scharoun's planning gives a better 'sense of place', which was lacking in the rest of the site – and, indeed, in many other Modernist housing schemes.

The three blocks by Scharoun explore different aspects of planning. All have similar stair access with two apartments per landing, in blocks which are a similar depth of approximately 9 metres (30 feet). Type A uses the staircase, which protrudes from the façade, to position balconies and as the angle in its faceted plan. Circulation space is reduced to two small lobbies, one at the entrance and one to the bathroom and bedroom, which means a maximum amount of space can be devoted to the living room, which extends the full width of the apartment. In type B, the living room is in the middle of the plan, extending the full depth of the building with windows on both sides. These have a deep window box on one side and a loggia recessed into the block on the other, thus extending the interior space to the outside. The other rooms are accessed from the living space. The third variant, type C, rotates the plan in order to have living rooms and staircases alternately on different sides of the building, and both curved and rectangular cantilevered balconies.

Scharoun had designed a prototype house for the Weissenhofsiedlung in 1927 and he continued working in Germany throughout the 1940s and 1950s, designing both one-off houses and social housing schemes. The 'Romeo and Juliet' project in Stuttgart is one of his best known designed, in response to the site, with two very different blocks – a tower with vertical access and a slab block with horizontal access, both overlaid with a curving, radial planning approach to afford the maximum number of different views out.

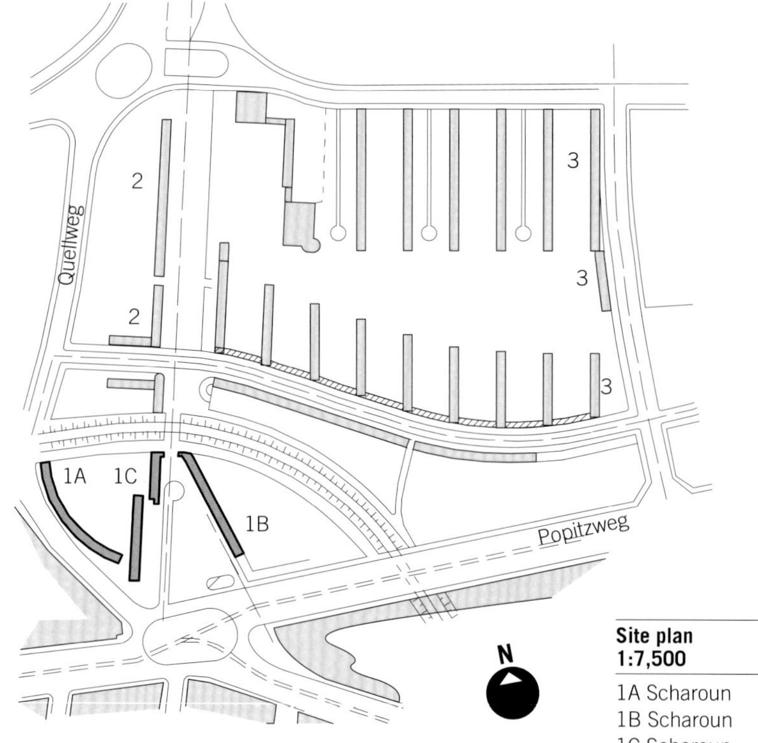

Site plan
1:7,500

1A Scharoun
1B Scharoun
1C Scharoun
2 Gropius
3 Forbat

Opposite left: Type A block

Opposite right: Type C block

1

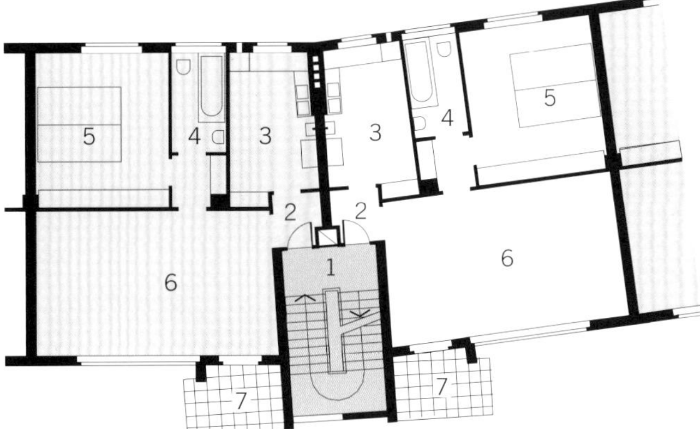

1 Typical one-bedroom flat, Block A 1:200

1 Access stairs
2 Entrance
3 Kitchen
4 Bathroom
5 Bedroom
6 Living room
7 Balcony

2

2 Typical two-bedroom flats, Block B 1:200

1 Access stairs
2 Entrance
3 Kitchen
4 Dining alcove
5 Living room
6 Bedroom
7 Bathroom
8 Loggia

3

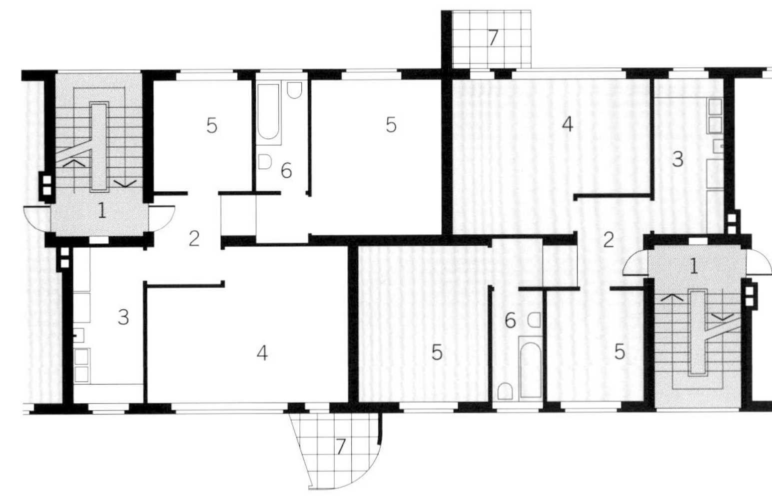

3 Typical two-bedroom flats, Block C 1:200

1 Access stairs
2 Entrance
3 Kitchen
4 Living room
5 Bedroom
6 Bathroom
7 Balcony

Lawn Road (now Isokon) Flats

Wells Coates, 1895–1958

London, UK; 1934

Wells Coates is a key figure in the development of modern design in Britain in the 1930s. He was a member of the Twentieth Century Group formed in 1930, which was devoted to the promotion of the principles of modern design, and subsequently of the Modern Architecture Research group (MARS) formed in 1933. He had trained as an engineer and had established his reputation as a designer before taking on architectural work. As an industrial designer his modern practical approach won him the competition for the EKCO radio with a design that was circular in form, based on the speaker, and which exploited the fluid properties of its Bakelite material so that it could be easily and cheaply mass-produced. Wells Coates designed production furniture for the PEL and Isokon companies as well as one-off pieces for individual clients. His interior design work focused on fitted furniture – he is the acknowledged inventor of the D handle – and he believed that furniture should be the defining element of a modern domestic interior, an integral part of the architecture of housing.

The block of flats at Lawn Road in London, for Isokon directors the Pritchards, was Wells Coates' first major building project and it demonstrates his commitment to the principles of modern design. In a single four-storey block, 5.5 metres (18 feet 6 inches) wide with external access balconies, there were originally 31 apartments (there are now 36 following restoration), 22 of them minimum single-person apartments, with, at the ends, larger studio and two-roomed flats. The project, with detailed drawings of its furniture and fittings, was included in Yorke and Gibberd's *The Modern Flat* published in 1937, and was referred to as 'flats for bachelors'. The spaces are very small, perhaps the result of a preoccupation with ideas of 'efficiency' and cleverly designed gadgets, rather than a focus on ideas about better accommodating the residents. The roof level had just one large flat with a private roof terrace, and the ground floor had a garage and accommodation for resident staff who provided cleaning services and meals served in the tenants' flats.

A complete restoration of this Grade I Modernist landmark was completed in 2004 by Avanti Architects.

Site plan 1:2,500

Opposite left: Rear façade

Opposite right: Lawn Road façade

Elevations 1:200

1 Lawn Road elevation
2 North elevation

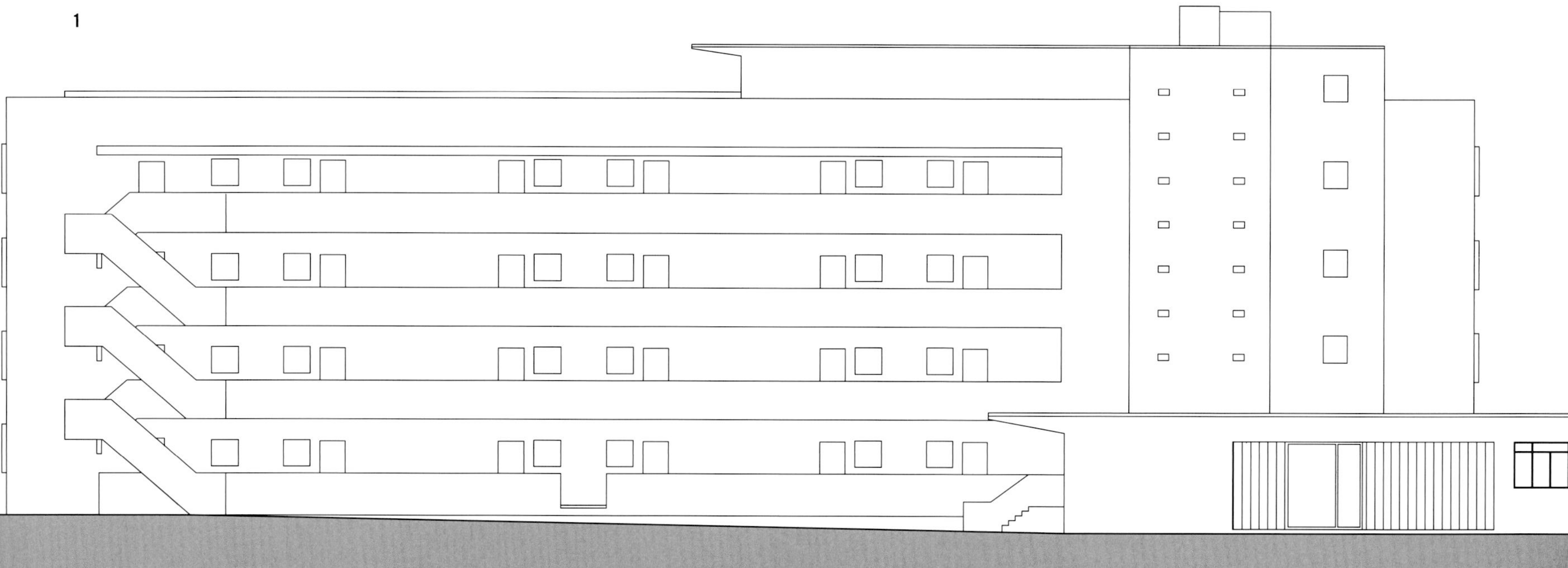

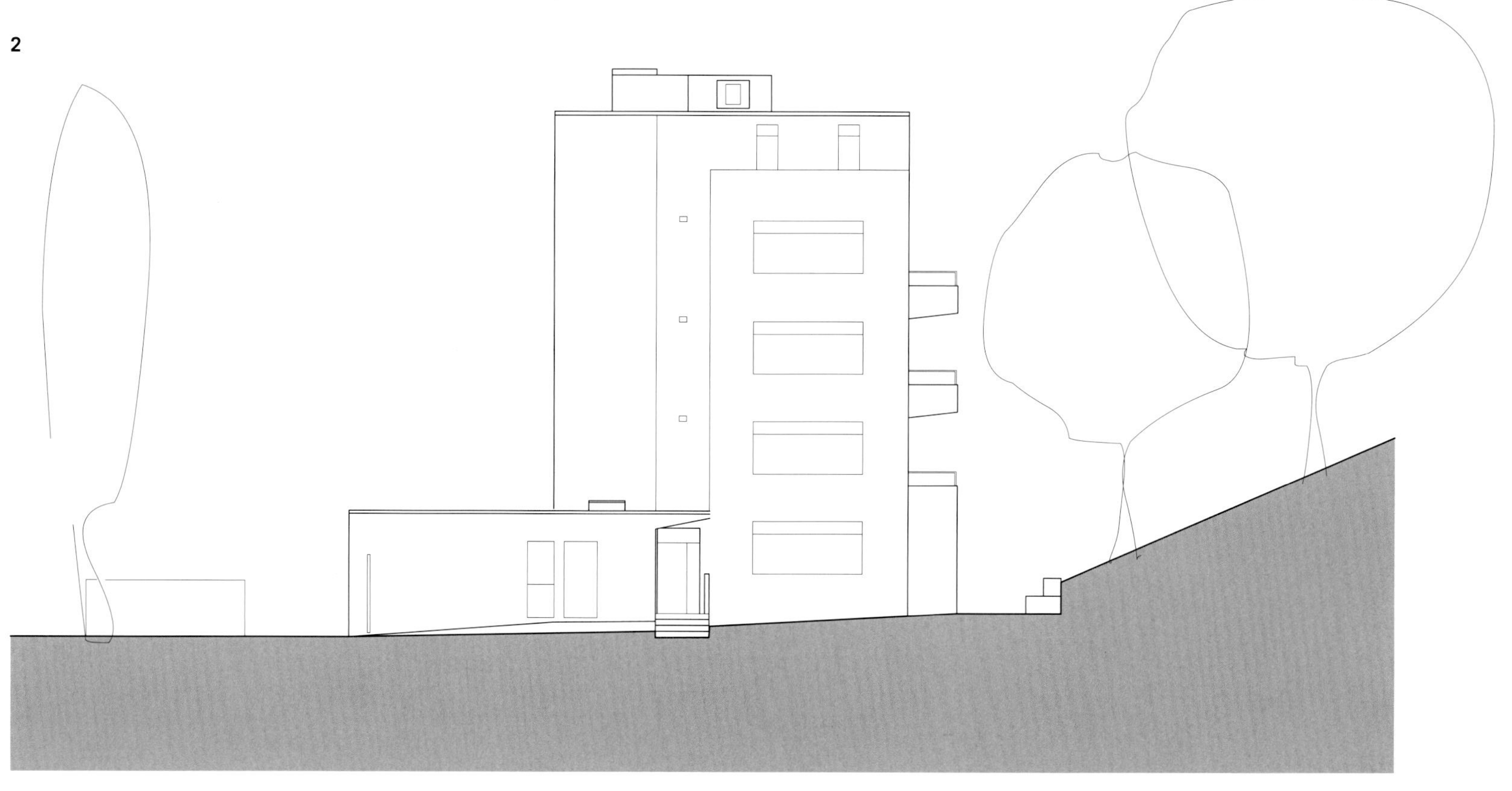

3

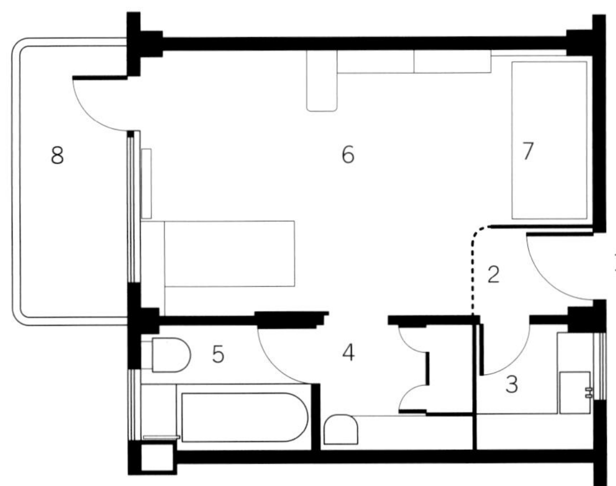

3 Plan of single person apartment 1:100

1 Open gallery access
2 Entrance
3 Kitchenette
4 Dressing room
5 Bathroom
6 Bedsitting room
7 Bed
8 Balcony

4

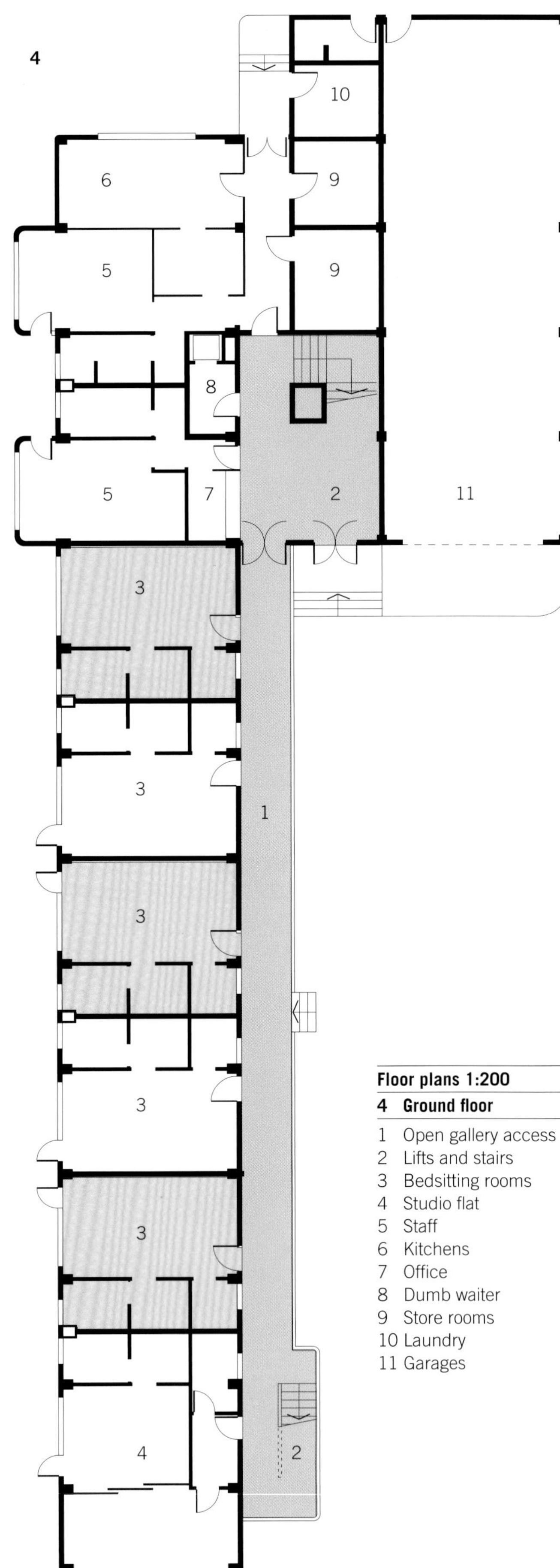

Floor plans 1:200

4 Ground floor

1 Open gallery access
2 Lifts and stairs
3 Bedsitting rooms
4 Studio flat
5 Staff
6 Kitchens
7 Office
8 Dumb waiter
9 Store rooms
10 Laundry
11 Garages

5

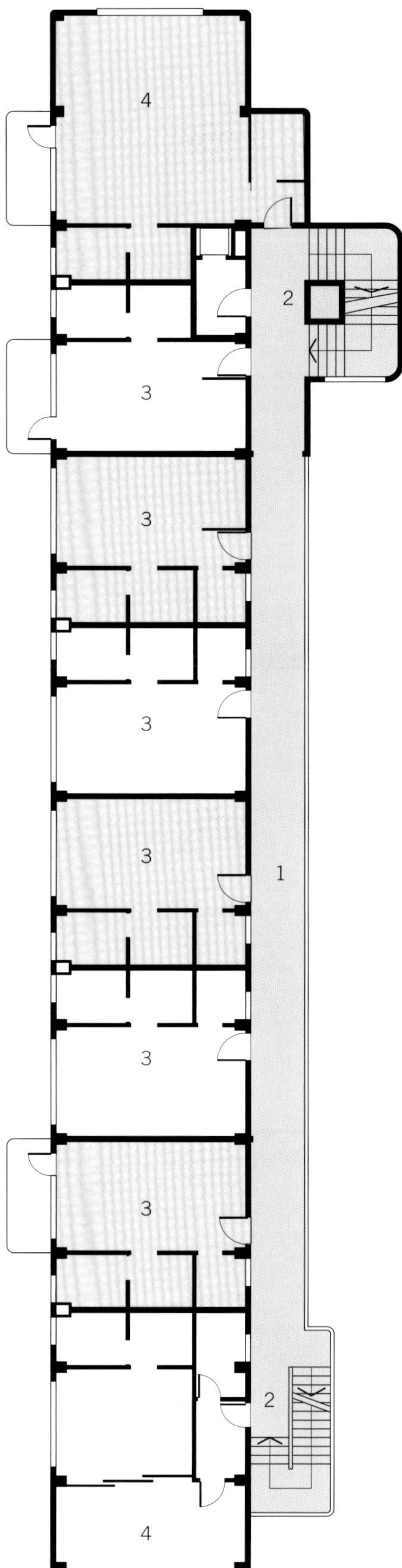

6

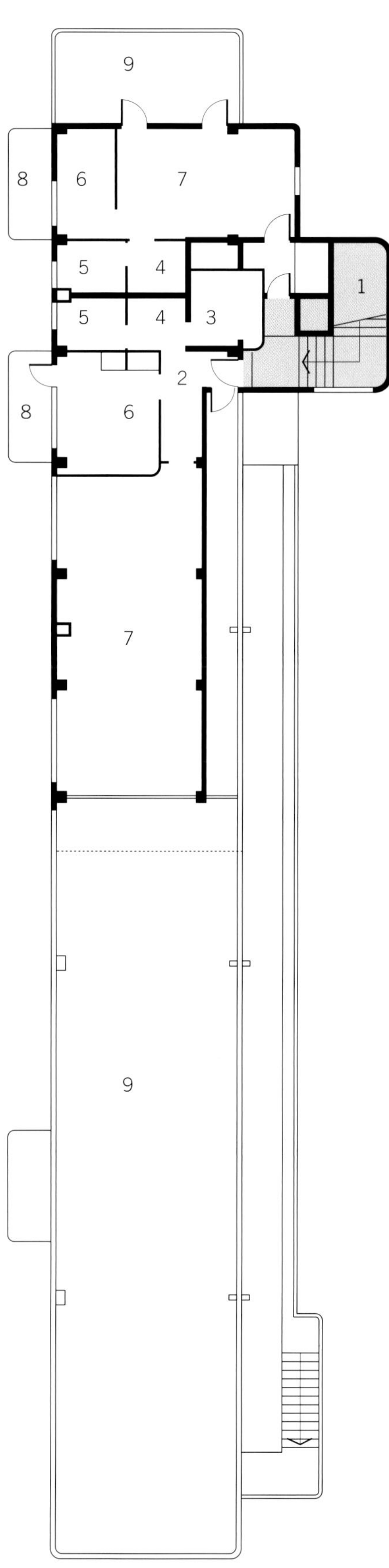

Floor plans 1:200

5 Typical upper floor

1 Open gallery access
2 Lifts and stairs
3 Bedsitting room
4 Studio flat

6 Top floor

1 Lifts and stairs
2 Entrance/hall
3 Kitchen
4 Dressing room
5 Bathroom
6 Bedroom
7 Living room
8 Balcony
9 Roof terrace

Vienna Werkbund Houses

Adolf Loos, 1870–1933

Vienna, Austria; 1931

The Austrian Werkbund was set up in 1910 following the German Werkbund, which had been founded in 1907 by Hermann Muthesius. Its intention was to demonstrate the value of embracing the potential for collaboration between art and machine technology. Adolf Loos was, however, critical of its work under the direction of its first president, Josef Hoffmann. Loos referred to the Werkbund members as 'the superfluous ones' in an article published in 1918, because of their adherence to work that he considered to be merely fashionable and wasteful. Once Josef Frank took over, however, Loos changed his view of the organization and accepted its invitation to design a row of dwellings for a 1932 exhibition of working-class housing. The exhibition was intended to show 'the maximum exploitation of space' and 'the greatest comfort possible in accordance with a strict observance of the principle of minimum wastage of space.'

Loos had been appointed as chief architect of the housing department of the city of Vienna in 1921, but had resigned in 1924 when he found it too difficult to realize his designs. His entire approach – based on a belief in the social impact of housing and the important role that architecture played in society – was at odds with those in power. He considered projects like Ehn's Karl Marx Hof of 1926–30 (see pages 42 –43) oversized and inadequately equipped. In 1922 Loos had delivered a lecture at the RIBA conference on the garden city, persuaded that his ideas would be better accepted in England than in Austria. Many of the elements of the designs for earlier projects which he put forward, and which were refused, were based on the Scheu House of 1912. This dwelling was conceived as a series of interconnected volumes or spaces: its main stair was located within a large high-ceilinged hallway, and roof terraces outside the bedrooms on the upper floors extended the space outside, resulting in a stepped section. These ideas were developed further in housing projects, such as the group of 20 villas with roof terraces for the Côte d'Azur and the Inzersdorfstrasse housing scheme for Vienna, both in 1923. The Werkbund houses, two pairs of semi-detached dwellings, although small display Loos's best known characteristic – a double-height living and dining space overlooked by a gallery, in this instance with a study desk incorporated. There are bedrooms on the top floor with a large balcony, and a cellar at the basement level. The utilitarian appearance, with flat unadorned surfaces, large windows facing south and cubic volume appears to be very much part of the overall aesthetic of the other buildings in the exhibition.

1 Oswald Haerti; 2 J. Wenzel; 3 E. Plischke; 4 J. Jirasek; 5 O. Wlach; 6 André Lurçat; 7 Josef Hoffmann; 8 R. Bauer; 9 H. Häring; 10 M. Fellerer; 11 G. Schütte-Lihotzky; 12 Hugo Gorge; 13 J. Groag; 14 Richard Neutra; 15 H. Vetter; 16 Adolf Loos; 17 Walter Loos, K.A. Bieber, O. Niedermoser, Josef Frank, E. Wachberger; 18 G. Guevrekian; 19 G. Rietveld; 20 A. Grunberger; 21 Josef S. Dex; 22 Otto Breuer; 23 H. Wagner

Site plan
1:2,500

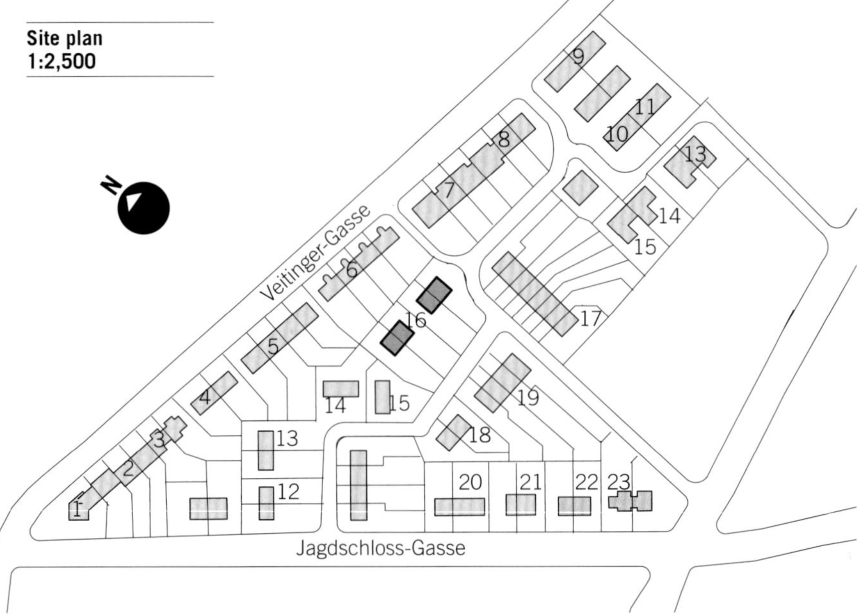

Plans, elevations and sections 1:200

1 Front elevation, north façade
2 Rear elevation
3 Section
4 Second-floor plan
5 First-floor plan
6 Ground-floor plan
7 Basement plan

1 Storage
2 Laundry
3 Cellar/heating
4 Entrance
5 Hall
6 Living/dining
7 Kitchen
8 Pantry
9 Terrace
10 Void over living
11 Gallery
12 Small room
13 Bedroom
14 Bathroom
15 Balcony

1

2

3

15
13
13
11
9
6
1
3

4

15
13
14
13
13

5

10
12
11

6

9
6
8
4
5
7

7

1
2
3

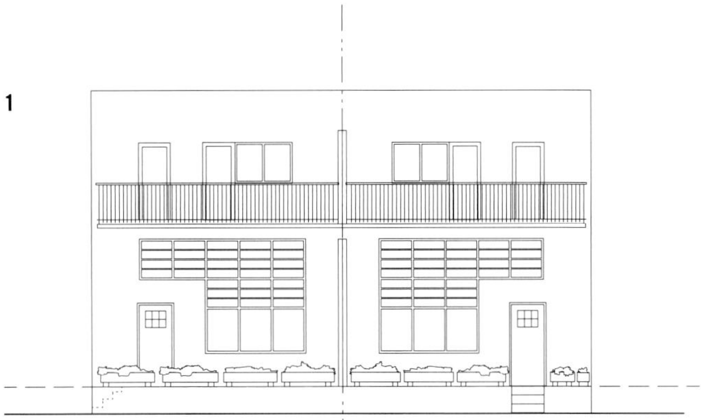

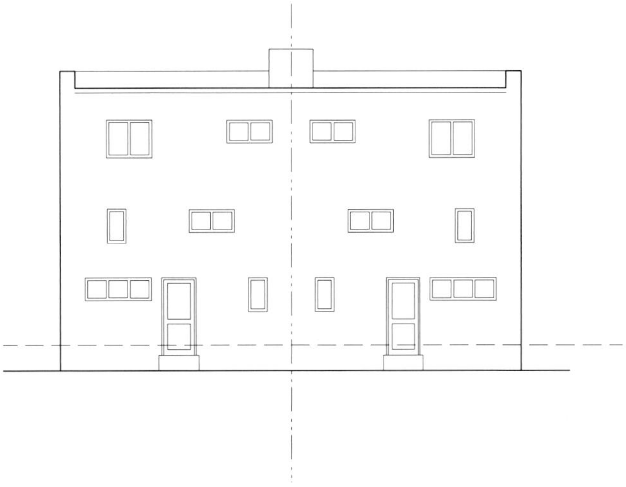

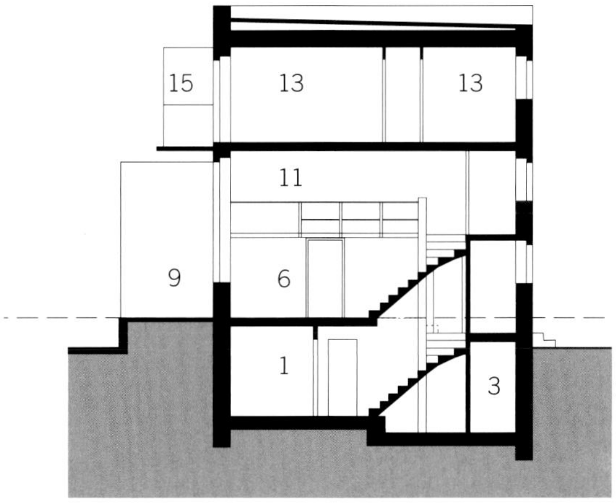

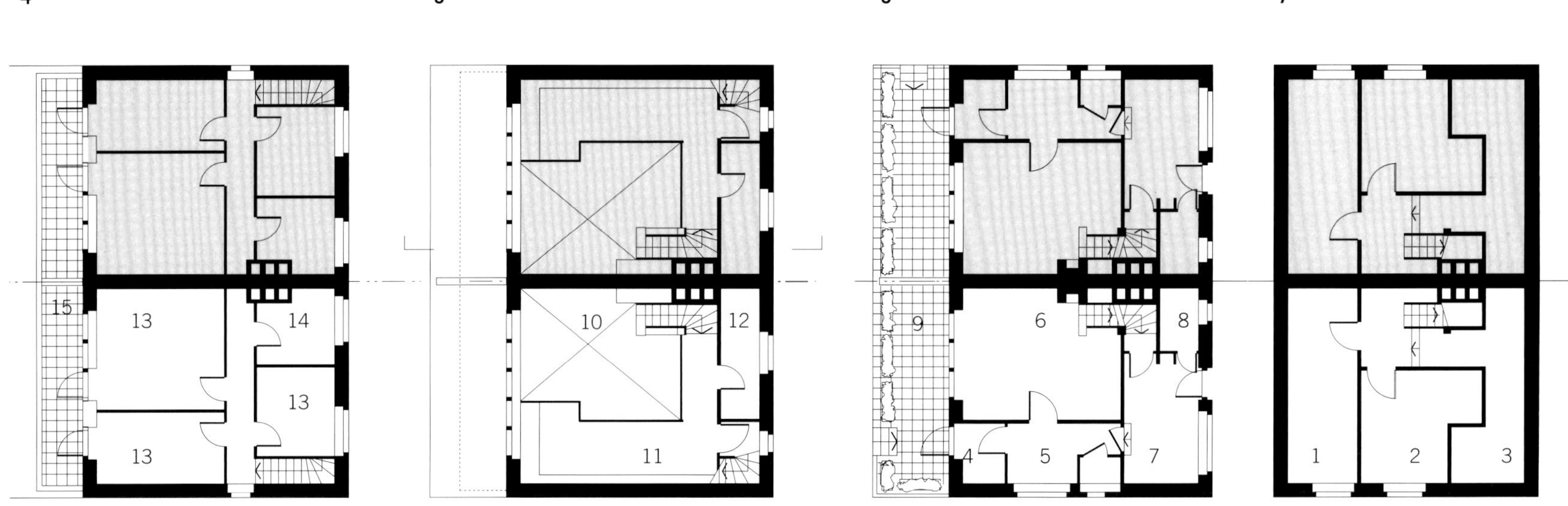

Vienna Werkbund Houses

André Lurçat, 1894–1970

Vienna, Austria; 1932

André Lurçat originally proposed a small block of apartments for the Vienna Werkbund exhibition, but changed the design to this row of terraced houses when it was decided by the city authorities that the dwellings would be sold rather than rented. The exhibition boasted buildings by well-known Viennese architects such as Adolf Loos (see pages 60–61) and Hoffmann alongside buildings by the less well-known Häring and Neutra. However, Lurçat's reinterpretation of the row house was one of its most interesting projects, in the context both of the exhibition itself and the design of the row-house type in general.

The overall layout of the individual houses is novel. Rather than the usual deep plan with central staircase, the plan is very shallow – 4.16 metres (13 feet 6 inches) internally – and, in consequence, relatively wide, at 8-metre (26-foot) centres. This configuration avoids the common problem of achieving good daylighting, and most rooms have windows at both front and back. The staircase is taken outside the envelope and enclosed by a curved wall, adding articulation to the otherwise flat façade and partially defining an open yard at the front of the house. Detailed attention is paid to the design of the internal layout of the dwelling in terms of the spaces themselves and how they might be occupied in different ways, including being flexible over time. In addition, the idea of a house as 'equipment for living' led to the inclusion of fitted furniture, such as shelving and cupboards that line the walls and, in most rooms, folding tables and pull-down beds. Drawings were made of each floor, showing daytime and night-time arrangements for the furniture in order to demonstrate the flexibility of the plans. At ground floor, the level of detail includes storage for wood and coal, an outside yard for hanging washing as well as an inside laundry, and a 'breezeway' – a covered open space connecting the front yard with the back garden and acting as a buffer between the residential spaces and the street. The houses could also be easily extended, either at roof level – one was built with a terrace – or the breezeway could be filled in and the servant's room converted to other uses.

Site plan
1:2,500

1 Oswald Haerti; 2 J. Wenzel; 3 E. Plischke; 4 J. Jirasek; 5 O. Wlach; 6 André Lurçat; 7 Josef Hoffman, 8 R. Bauer, 9 H. Häring; 10 M. Fellerer; 11 G. Schütte-Lihotzky; 12 Hugo Gorge; 13 J. Groag; 14 Richard Neutra; 15 H. Vetter; 16 Adolf Loos; 17 Walter Loos, K.A. Bieber, O. Niedermoser, Josef Frank, E. Wachberger; 18 G. Guevrekian; 19 G. Rietveld; 20 A. Grunberger; 21 Josef S. Dex; 22 Otto Breuer; 23 H. Wagner

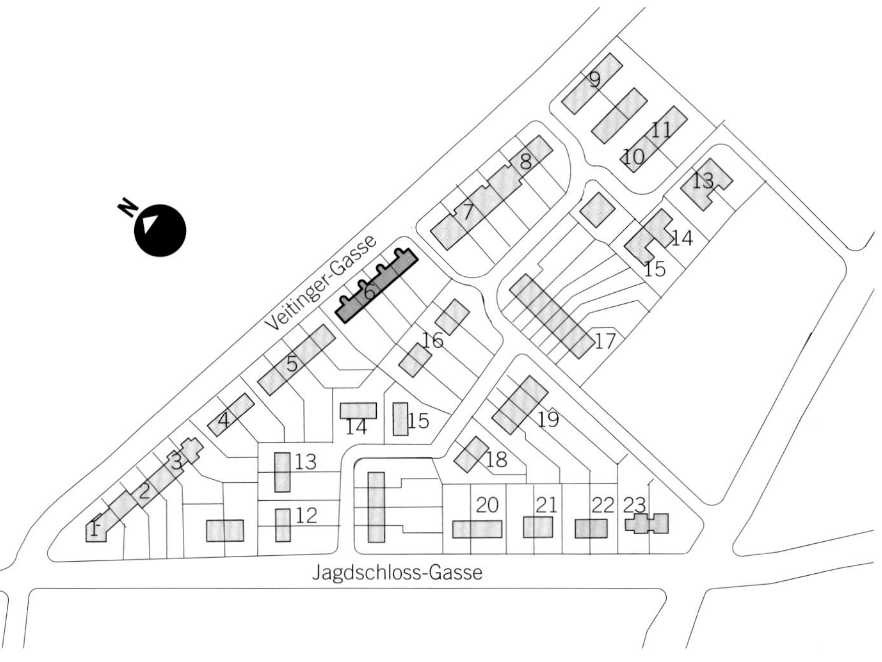

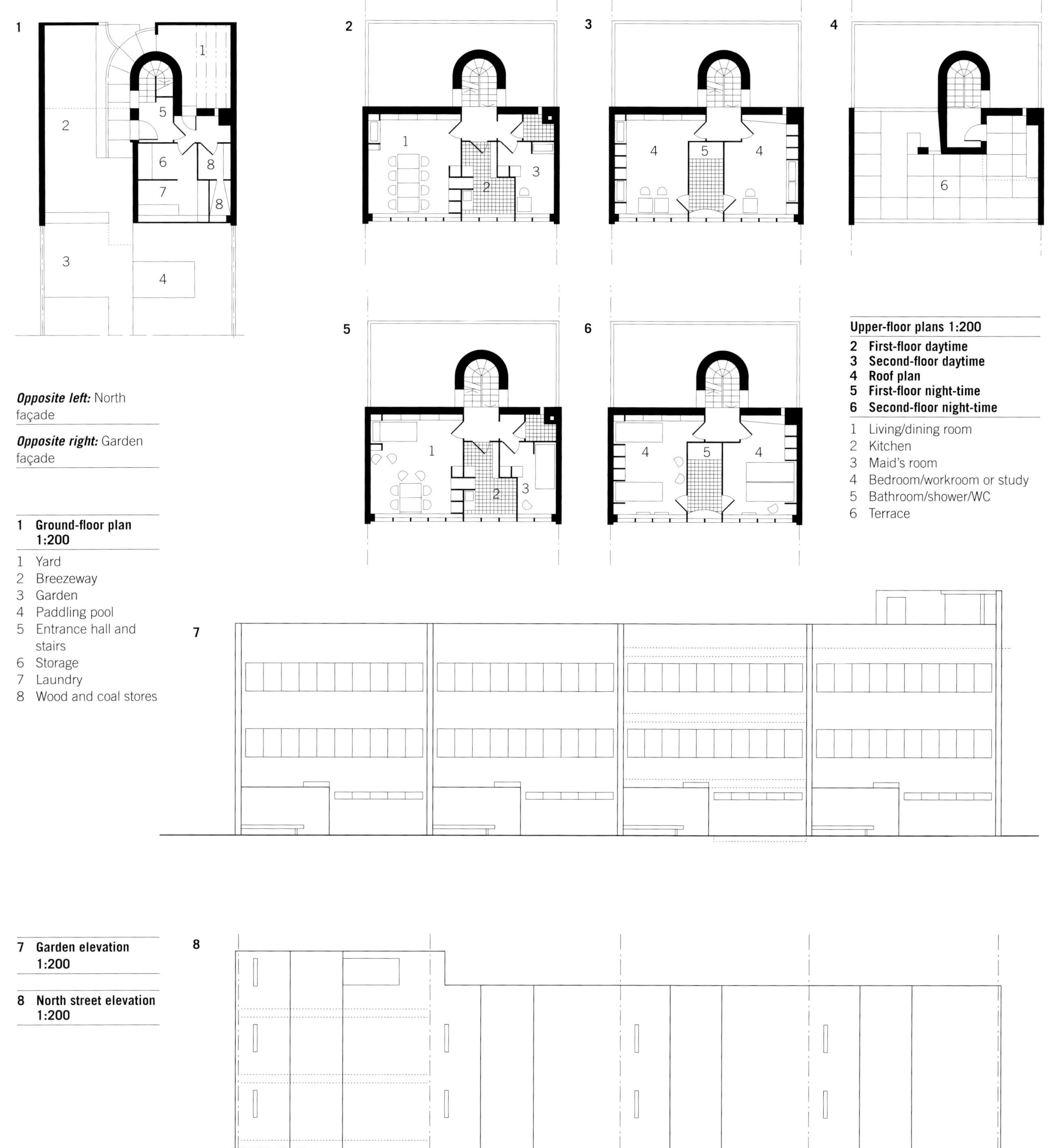

Opposite left: North façade

Opposite right: Garden façade

1 Ground-floor plan 1:200

1 Yard
2 Breezeway
3 Garden
4 Paddling pool
5 Entrance hall and stairs
6 Storage
7 Laundry
8 Wood and coal stores

Upper-floor plans 1:200

2 First-floor daytime
3 Second-floor daytime
4 Roof plan
5 First-floor night-time
6 Second-floor night-time

1 Living/dining room
2 Kitchen
3 Maid's room
4 Bedroom/workroom or study
5 Bathroom/shower/WC
6 Terrace

7 Garden elevation 1:200

8 North street elevation 1:200

Bergpolder Building

Willem van Tijen (1894–1974), Brinkman & Van der Vlugt

Rotterdam, The Netherlands; 1934

The Bergpolder building is one of the earliest experiments in modern high-rise construction for residential buildings in the Netherlands, where developments in the design of modern social housing had tended to focus on terraced houses and low-rise blocks. In contrast to the apparent solidity of low-rise buildings in familiar brickwork, the Bergpolder – at nine storeys high, set back in open space and raised half a level from the ground – had a light and transparent appearance. It is constructed of steel frames at 6.2-metre (20-foot 4-inch) centres – the width of a flat, with cross-bracing concealed within the dividing walls. It has timber floors and its external walls are of an insulated framed construction, faced with zinc-coated steel panels. The simple linear form, aligned north–south to maximize sun penetration, has continuous balconies on both elevations. On the east side is an open access gallery with stairs at both ends and a solid balustrade; on the west side are the private balconies, which are accessible from the flats. These private balconies have a transparent balustrade and are equipped with canvas blinds, stretched on adjustable metal frames. The visibly thin open structure supporting the balconies forms a continuous open framework around the entire block, contributing to the apparent transparency and insubstantial quality of the building.

The 72 flats, eight per floor, are all identical units. Generally, there is minimal circulation and service space in order to maximize storage space and the area of the living spaces. Wide sliding doors from the living room allowed tenants some flexibility to use the adjacent room as a dining room or study – or even as a bedroom. Functionally the private balcony, the same size as the access balcony on the other side, is too narrow to work well. Technical innovations at the time included a central-heating plant and the provision of one radiator in the living room of each flat, although only cold running water was provided. A lift was, of course, necessary, but it stopped only on alternate floors to improve speed and minimize potential safety problems in operation; it was also of concern that it should be an adequate size to accommodate stretchers and coffins, and collapsible doors were avoided so that it would be for safely used by children.

At the time of its construction, the collective facilities on the ground floor of the Bergpolder were as important as the individual apartments. A single-storey block had shops and the caretaker's office, where a hot-water point for the tenants' use was located. The semi-basement level had laundry and drying rooms, store rooms and cellars. Bicycles were stored under the lowest access gallery.

1

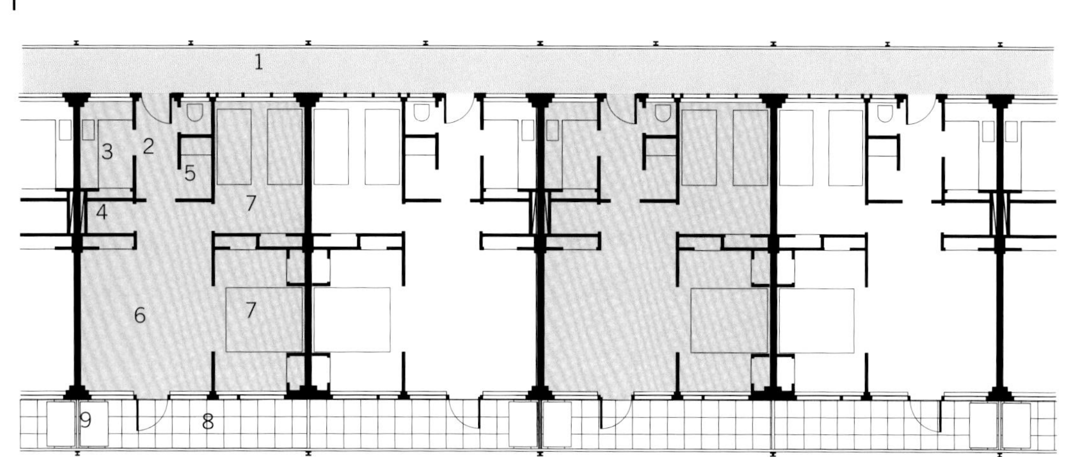

2

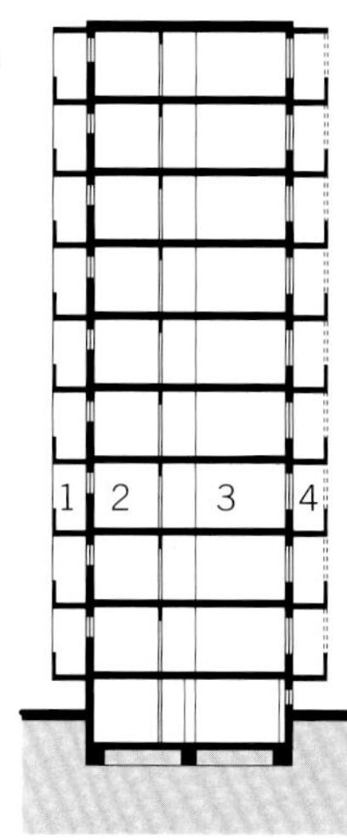

1 Typical flat plans 1:200

1 External access gallery
2 Entrance/hall
3 Kitchen
4 Store room
5 Shower
6 Living room
7 Bedroom
8 Private balcony
9 Broom cupdoard

2 Section 1:500

1 External access gallery
2 Entrance/hall
3 Living room
4 Private balcony

3

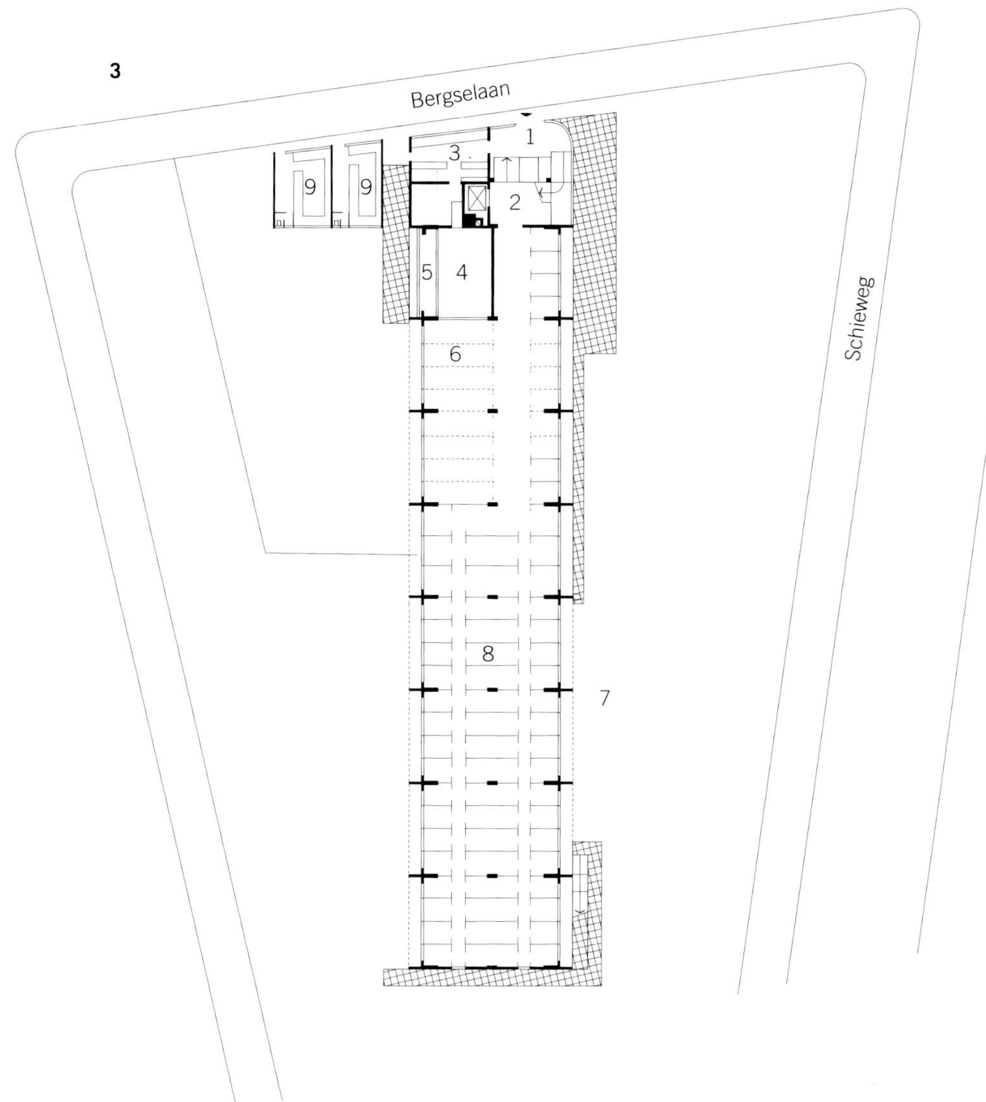

4

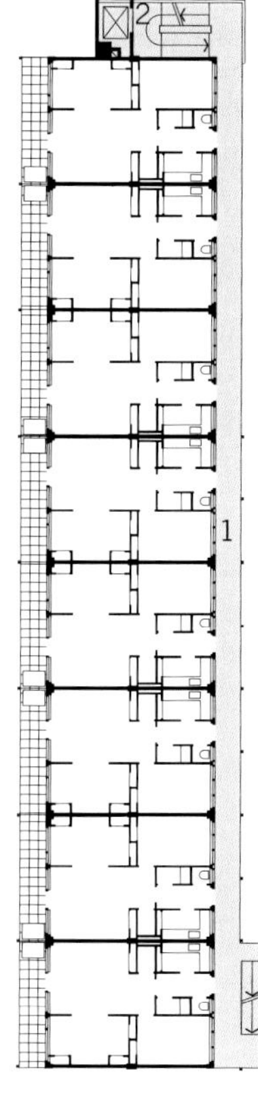

3 Ground-floor plan 1:500

1 Entrance lobby
2 Lift and circulation
3 Caretaker
4 Pump and heating plant room
5 Coal store
6 Laundry and drying space
7 Rubbish chute
8 Cellars and store rooms
9 Shop units

4 Typical upper-level plan 1:500

1 Open access gallery
2 Lift and stair access

25 and 42 Avenue de Versailles

Jean Ginsberg, 1905–83

Paris, France; 1932 and 1933

The apartment building at No. 25, designed in collaboration with Berthold Lubetkin, was the first of Ginsberg's projects. It is a small building, L-shaped in plan, with two flats per floor sharing a central circulation space. An article in the *Architectural Review* in 1932 suggested that the façade of this building had been designed with cars in mind; that is, that a level of detail like the intricate and elaborate decorations of the surrounding neoclassical façades typical of Paris's 16th arrondissement would be wasted on it, as the building was intended to be appreciated at speed. Whether or not the concept of speed did consciously influence its designers, the façade of this building is clearly important. Windows in horizontal bands appear continuous from one side to the other, curving behind the central column to form a recess or small loggia. The horizontality is emphasized at the roofline with parapet balustrades of tubular steel with sweeping curves at the corners. In response to the then fashionable ideas about the health benefits of the open air, the roof has space for the inhabitants to exercise and take a shower outdoors. Furthermore, the windows, especially imported from Germany, have vertical sashes that 'disappear' into a cavity in the concrete wall below, visually opening up the interior spaces to the outside.

Completed a year later, this time in collaboration with François Heep and Maurice Breton, No. 45 demonstrates a similar, modern approach. Horizontal strip windows are continuous across its street façades and around the dramatic curve forming the corner of the block. To provide light and maximize space within the apartments, a shelving unit is used as a room divider to separate living and dining space but to maintain views through in order to make the space seem bigger. The balconies, which have one of the earliest examples of glass balustrading, physically extend the space and give unobstructed views to the outside. The floor plans include a service lift and access at the rear. Careful internal detailing includes bathrooms and kitchens back-to-back, ducted services – the vertical ducts ingeniously disguised as cupboards – and low-level radiators underneath tiled sills.

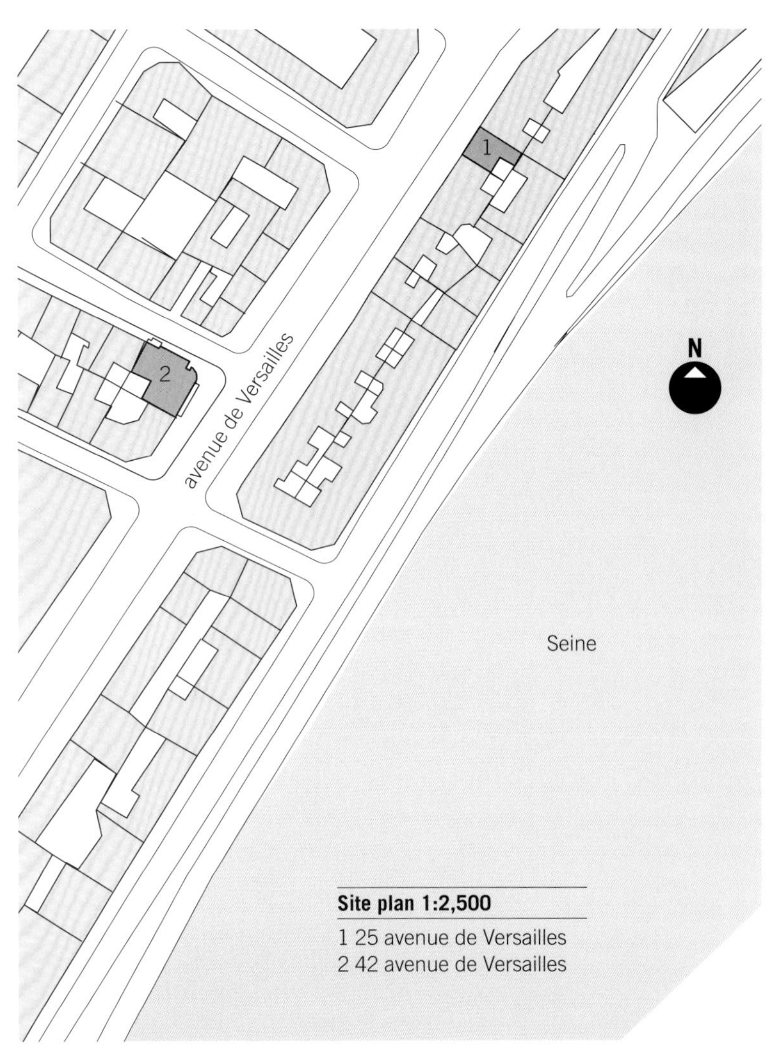

Site plan 1:2,500

1 25 avenue de Versailles
2 42 avenue de Versailles

1

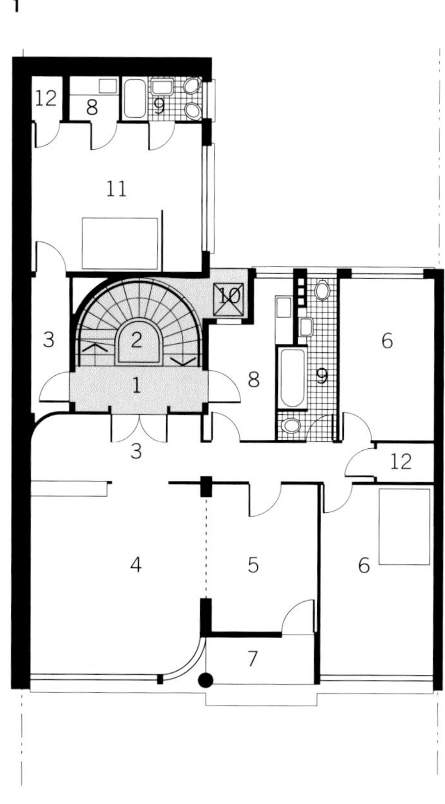

1 Plan of typical floor 25 avenue de Versailles

1 Access stair
2 Lift
3 Entrance/hallway
4 Living room
5 Dining room
6 Bedroom
7 Balcony
8 Kitchen
9 Bathroom
10 Service lift
11 Studio/bedsitting room
12 Store

2

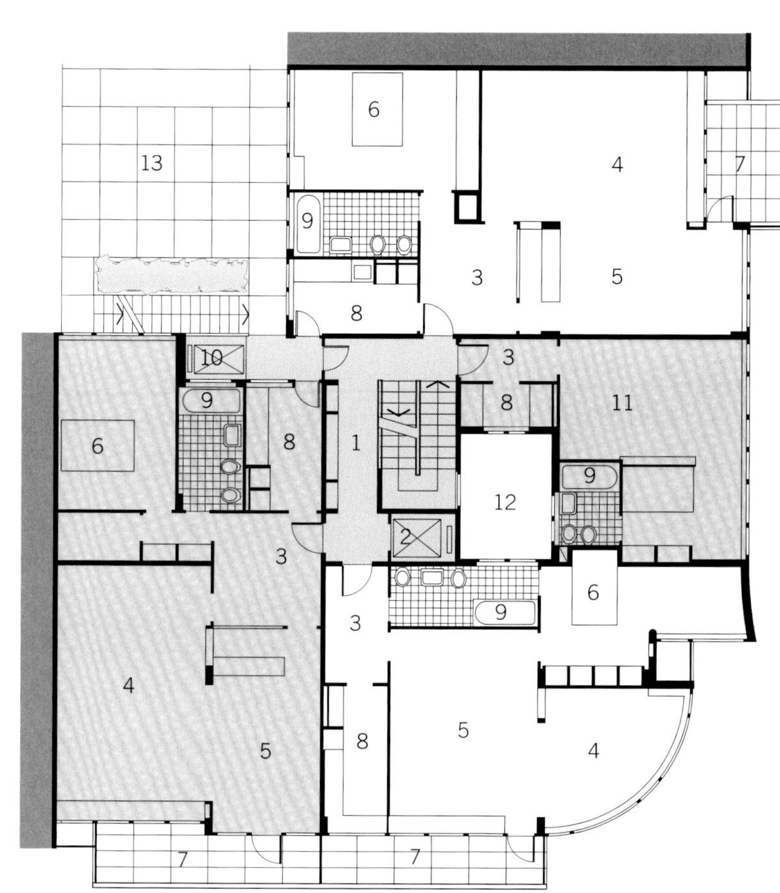

2 Plan of typical floor 42 avenue de Versailles

1 Access stair
2 Lift
3 Entrance/hallway
4 Living
5 Dining
6 Bedroom
7 Balcony
8 Kitchen
9 Bathroom
10 Service lift
11 Studio/bedsitting room
12 Lightwell
13 Area

Highpoint Flats

Berthold Lubetkin, 1901–90

London, UK; 1935

Since its publication in Frederick Gibberd's *The Modern Flat* in 1937, very soon after it was built, Highpoint I has become one of the best-known Modernist residential projects and is extensively referred to as the first example of Le Corbusier's 'Five Points of a New Architecture' in the UK. As Miles Glendenning and Stefan Muthesius point out in the much later *Tower Block* (1994), while it doesn't follow the single north–south *Zeilenbau* format, it does have pilotis, a free plan, long horizontal windows and roof terraces. The cruciform plan used in place of the linear configuration, the result of Lubetkin's rational approach to planning, was arrived at in order to improve isolation from neighbouring flats. There are eight apartments per floor, four to each circulation core, with the central part of the cruciform at half-storey level to reduce overlooking from adjacent windows. Most flats have external walls on three sides, giving cross-ventilation as well as exposure to the sun on two sides and uninterrupted views across London. Junctions of the cruciform are articulated with open balconies and vertical service shafts for WCs and dumb waiters.

Compared to London's draughty and unheated terraced houses, day-to-day living in a modern flat such as those at Highpoint would have presented distinct advantages for those able to afford them. The inclusion of new technology, much of it aimed at women, and improvements in household management – for example, amenities and facilities for laundry within the building and a design that was easier to clean and maintain – would reduce the numbers of servants needed. The kitchens had central refrigeration, and stainless-steel sinks and worktops; central heating was provided by heating coils in the ceilings and an electric fire in all the living rooms for local heating. Attention to detail extended to 50-mm (2-inch) thick doors on the fitted cupboards and wardrobes to prevent warping, and lights fitted inside that were operated by opening the doors. There is an additional basin and vanity unit recessed behind curtains in the second bedroom in the larger flats.

There are two flat types, one with two bedrooms and one with three. In both, the bedroom and bathroom areas are separated by a lobby from the open-plan arrangement of the living and dining rooms. The apartments are large – at either 70 square metres (750 square feet) for a two-bed unit, or approximately 110 square metres (1,200 square feet) for a three-bed. Maids' rooms are included on the ground floor and gardens shared with Highpoint II, which followed in 1938, have tennis courts and tea rooms.

Highpoint II follows the alignment of its predecessor, but is a more conventional single-slab block with much larger four-bed apartments. Between the ground floor with maids' rooms, garages and the porter's room and the roof level, with a penthouse flat, there are six floors of maisonettes – four per floor. The plan is rational and rigorously symmetrical. All the apartments have balconies, spacious entrance hallways and stair lobbies, and two bathrooms; the larger flats in the centre of the plan have curved staircases giving onto double-height living rooms. Access is by lifts which open directly into the apartments, with a separate service elevator giving onto the staircase, and separate entrance lobbies for servants.

Opposite left: Exterior of Highpoint I

Opposite right: Living room, Highpoint I

1

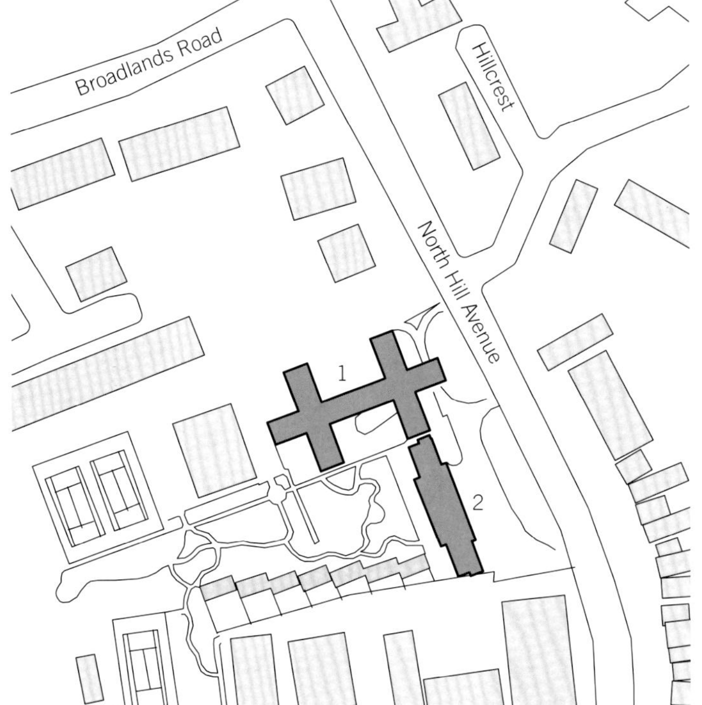

1 Site Plan 1:2500

1 Highpoint I
2 Highpoint II

2

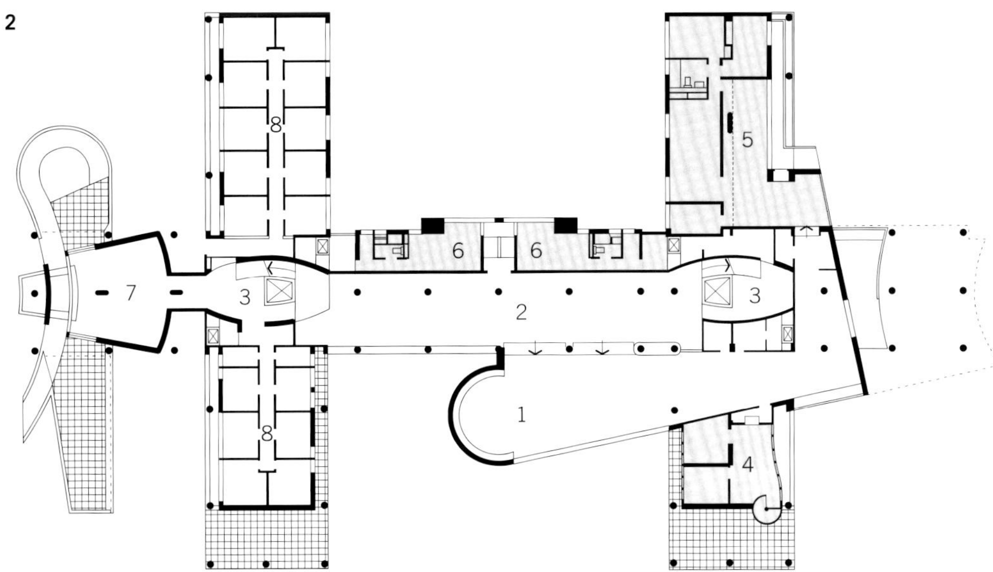

3

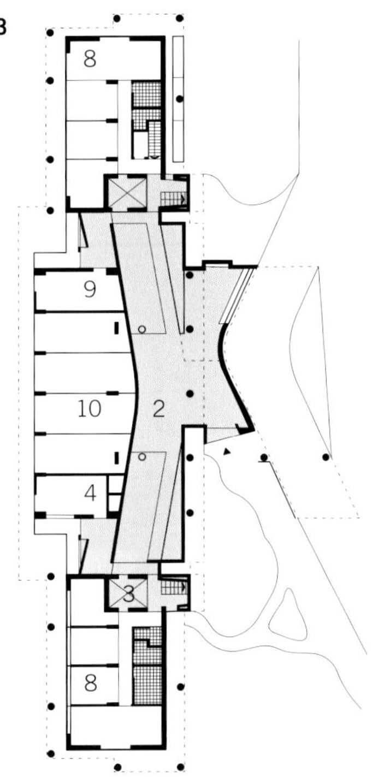

2 Highpoint I Plan of ground floor 1:500

3 Highpoint II Plan of ground floor 1:500

1 Hall and winter garden
2 Entrance hall
3 Lifts and stairs
4 Porters
5 Large flat
6 Studio flats
7 Tea room
8 Maids' rooms
9 Pram store
10 Garages

4

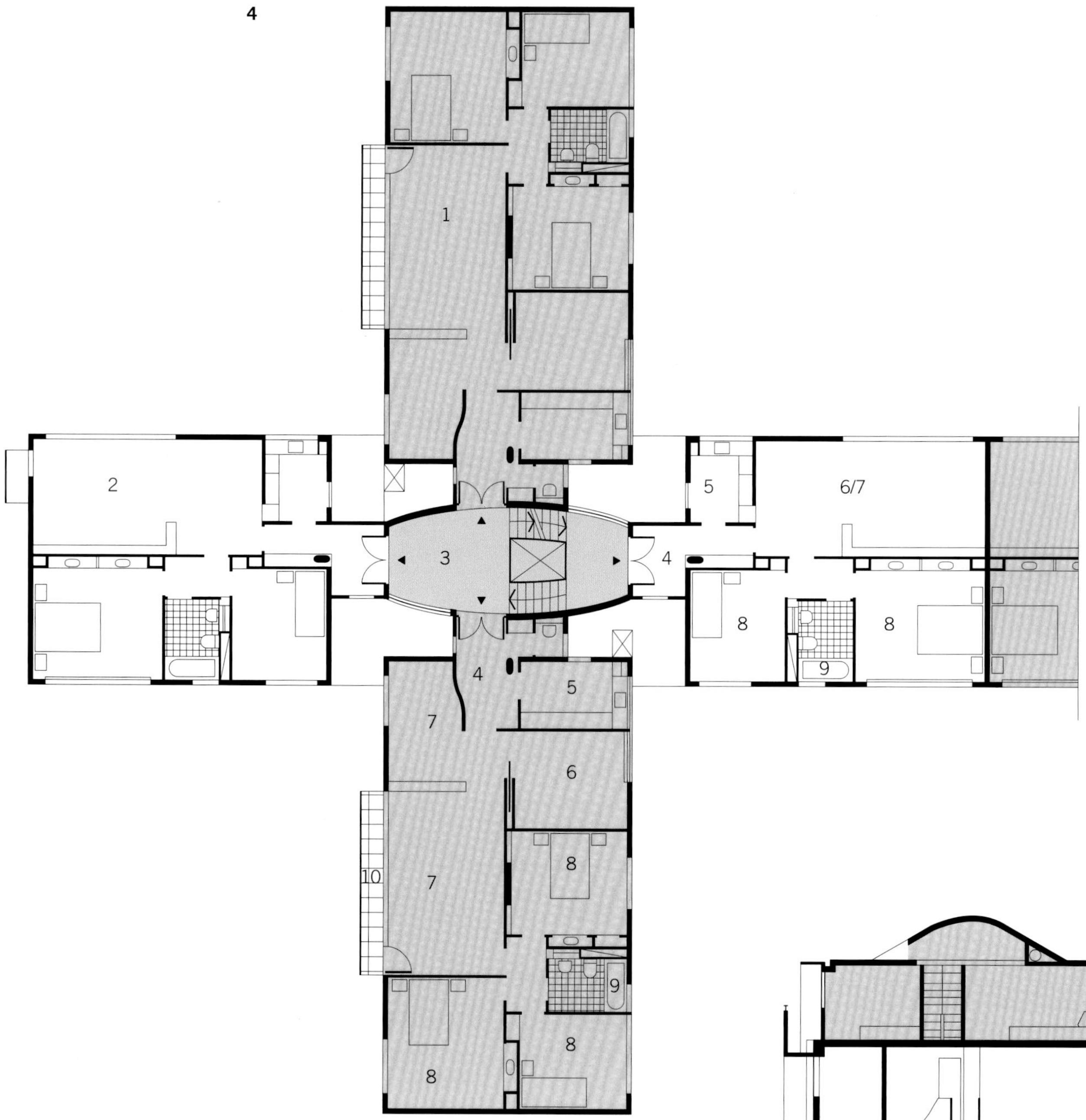

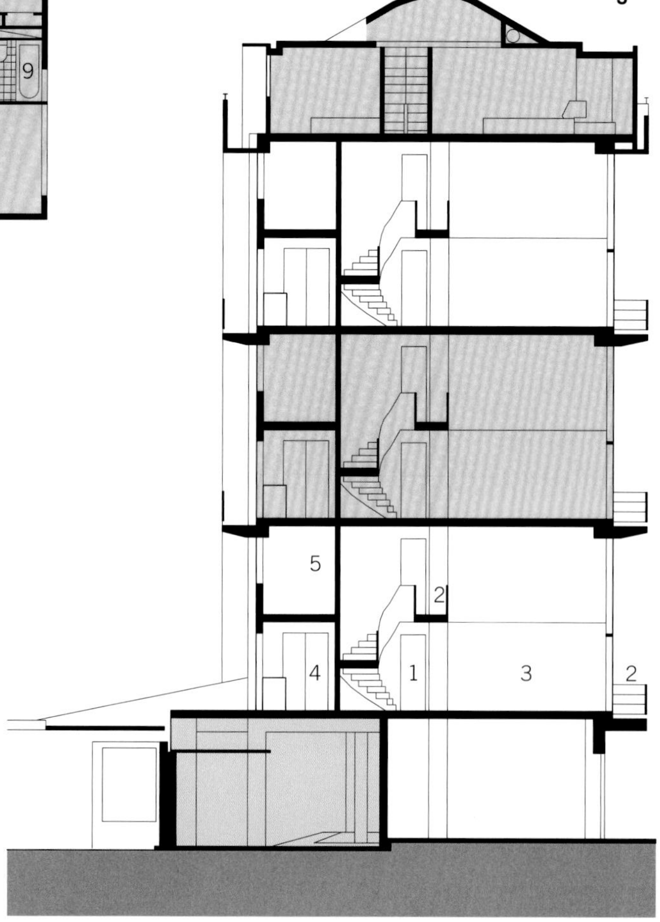

4 Highpoint I
Part plan typical floor 1:200

1 Three-bedroom flat type A
2 Two-bedroom flat type B
3 Stairs and lift
4 Entrance/hallway
5 Kitchen
6 Dining room
7 Living room
8 Bedroom
9 Bathroom
10 Balcony

5

5 Highpoint II
Section 1:200

1 Hall/stairway
2 Balcony
3 Double-height living room
4 Kitchen
5 Bathroom

6 Highpoint II Lower level of maisonettes, 1st, 3rd and 5th floors 1:200

7 Highpoint II Upper level of maisonettes, 2nd, 4th and 6th floors 1:200

1 Access lift
2 Entrance/hall
3 Stairs
4 Servants' entrance
5 Kitchen
6 Dining
7 Living
8 Study
9 Balcony
10 Bedroom
11 Void over double-height living room
12 Bathroom

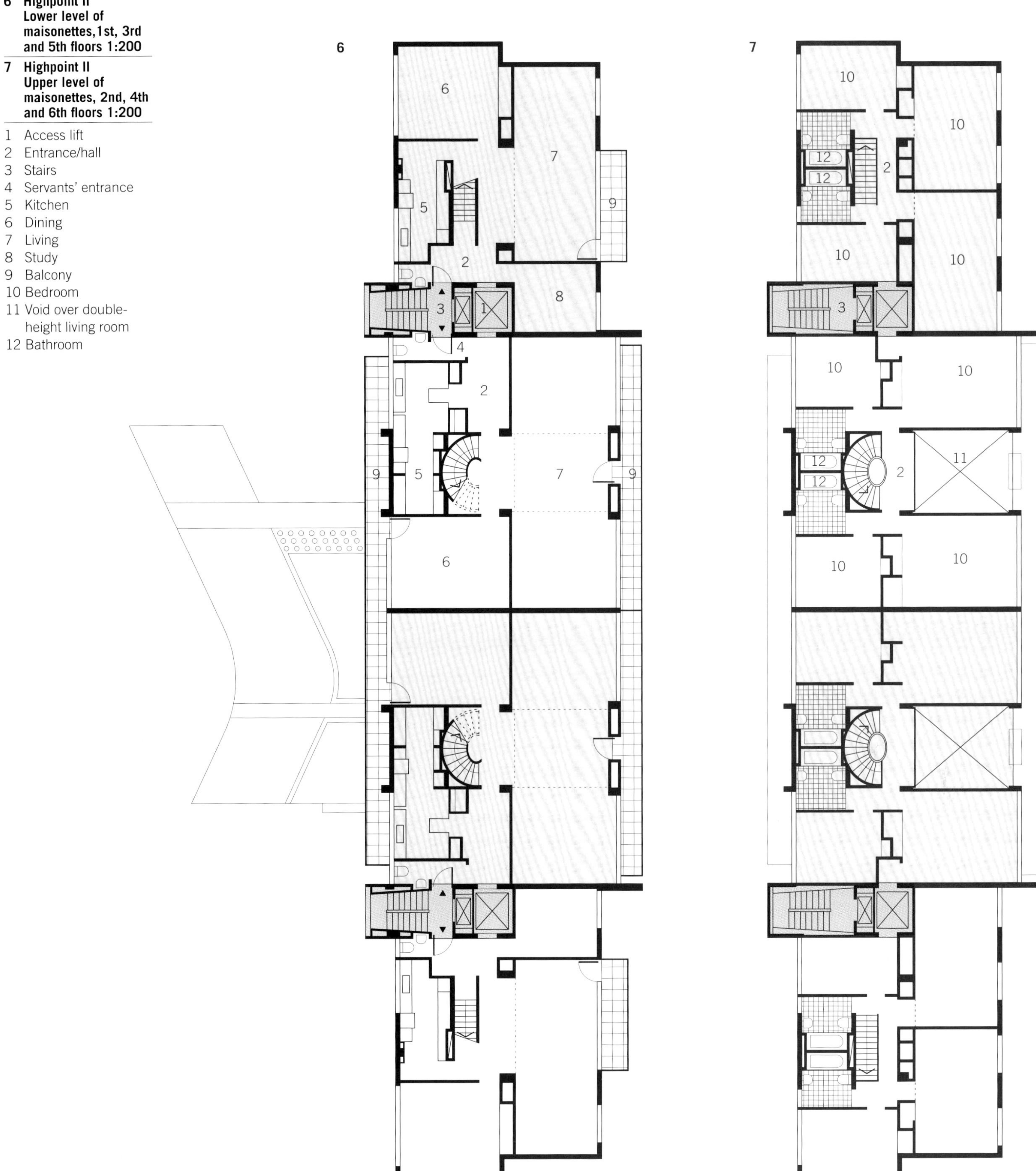

Kensal House

Atkinson, Fry, James and Wornum

London, UK; 1936

The building of Kensal House, by the public utility company the Gas Light and Coke Company, was used as an opportunity to test and evaluate the most appropriate equipment for working-class homes, in actual use based on advice from a committee comprising four architects – Robert Atkinson, Maxwell Fry, C. H. James and Grey Wornum – and Elizabeth Denby, a housing consultant. The estate was developed in accordance with the then current Slum Clearance and Re-housing Act (1930), in collaboration with the local borough authority. The estate housed 68 families and included club rooms for adults and children, allotments, a nursery and a playground. Published alongside technical information as one of a series of examples of urban flats in England, it was referred to as an 'urban village': a development that boasted a community element alongside its technical innovations. This social element extended to the management of the estate, and included the participation of tenant representatives from each of the 'staircases' in the management committee – an experiment in self-government.

The industrial mass-production techniques that could provide the new building components at economical costs could also provide the model for developing a plan-type for the flats themselves: 'rather than plan a building around this funny unequal site' the design starts with a standard flat plan. The flats are arranged in two blocks, aligned north–south to maximize sunlight, and are accessed from internal staircases, two per landing. Internally, each unit has a living room and three bedrooms plus a carefully designed 'working unit' comprising the kitchen and bathroom with a double wall between to accommodate gas and water pipes, and a balcony for drying clothes which also provides ventilation to the larder. The whole was designed around the instantaneous hot-water heater, which provided hot water direct to the sink, bath and a copper for clothes washing. The grouping of the kitchen and bathroom and the introduction of the second, drying, balcony were also intended to make a clear separation between the activities of housework and the leisure pursuits of the rest of the family, which could continue uninterrupted in the living room. Gas lighting was installed, the large bedroom had a gas fire, and a gas poker was provided for the open fire in the living room.

Opposite left: Façade looking onto nursery school

Opposite right: Façade looking onto courtyard

1

1 Part typical upper-floor plan 1:200

1 Access stairs
2 Entrance/hall
3 Kitchen
4 Drying balcony
5 Bathroom
6 Living room
7 Bedroom
8 Balcony

2

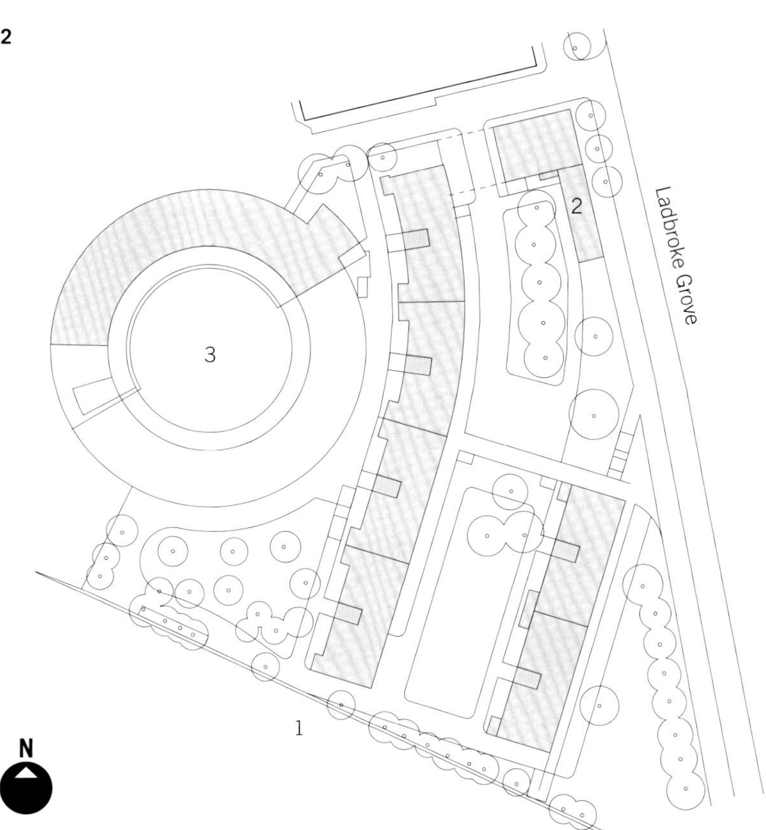

2 Site plan 1:1,000

1 Railway line
2 Shops
3 Nursery school

Left: Street façade

Right: Detail of open balconies connecting the two blocks

Casa Rustici

Giuseppe Terragni (1904–43) with Pietro Lingeri (1894–1968)

Milan, Italy; 1936

According to Thomas Schumacher in his 1991 work on Terragni, the principles of Modernism were not introduced in Italy as quickly as they were in other rapidly expanding European cities. Instead of the isolated blocks and open parkland of the new style, Italian urban designers clung longer to the street as the principal organizational device, with its hierarchies of scale and individual building plots. In this context, each of the five apartment buildings in Milan designed by Terragni and Lingeri, although rationalist in their approach to planning, are not free-standing structures resulting from the design of a typical dwelling but have been designed to fit a particular site and location.

The Casa Rustici, built in 1936, is the best known of these Milanese apartment buildings and is the most innovative in plan. On a relatively deep site, the designers eschewed the nineteenth-century urban form, which followed the street edge with a dense block enclosing a lightwell behind. Instead, two rectangular blocks face each other across an open courtyard and are connected at each floor level by open balconies, replacing the dense street façade while maintaining a continuity along the edge and bringing light deep into the plan. The building thus has an independent or distinct 'object-like' quality, even while fitting its site and location.

The blocks on either side of the central open space are roughly symmetrical, with two or three apartments per floor. Access is up broad steps from the Corso Sempione, via the courtyard space to lifts and stairs on each side. There are offices on the ground floor, and storage space and garages beneath the raised courtyard in the basement. The penthouse is particularly elaborate, occupying both sides of the building with a bridge connecting them and having a circular hallway and a huge roof terrace. The apartments are large, intended for professional people, and include servants' rooms. They have spacious halls and lobbies, and a layout of adjacent interconnecting living rooms more usual in French planning.

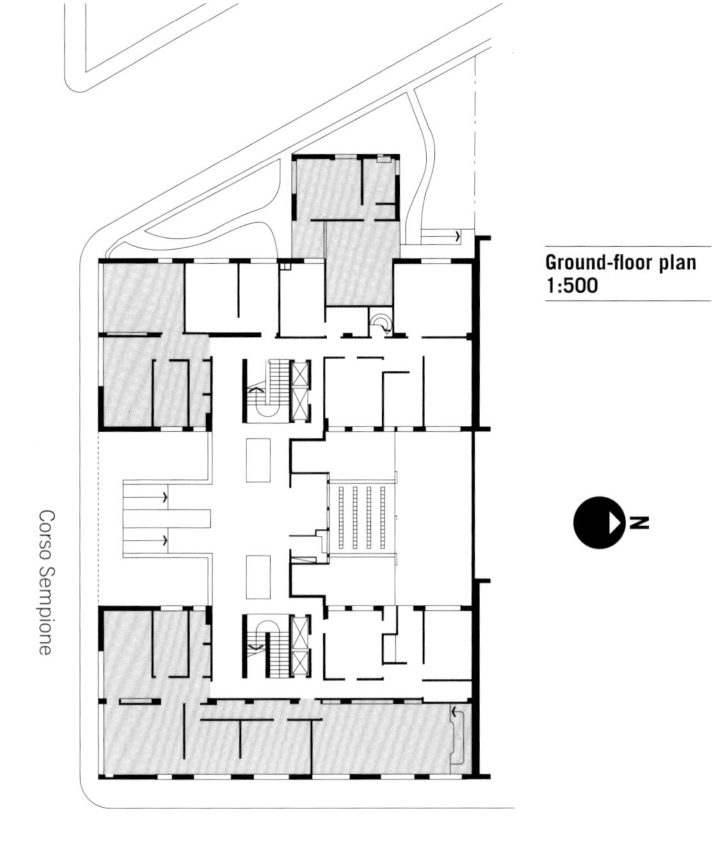

Ground-floor plan 1:500

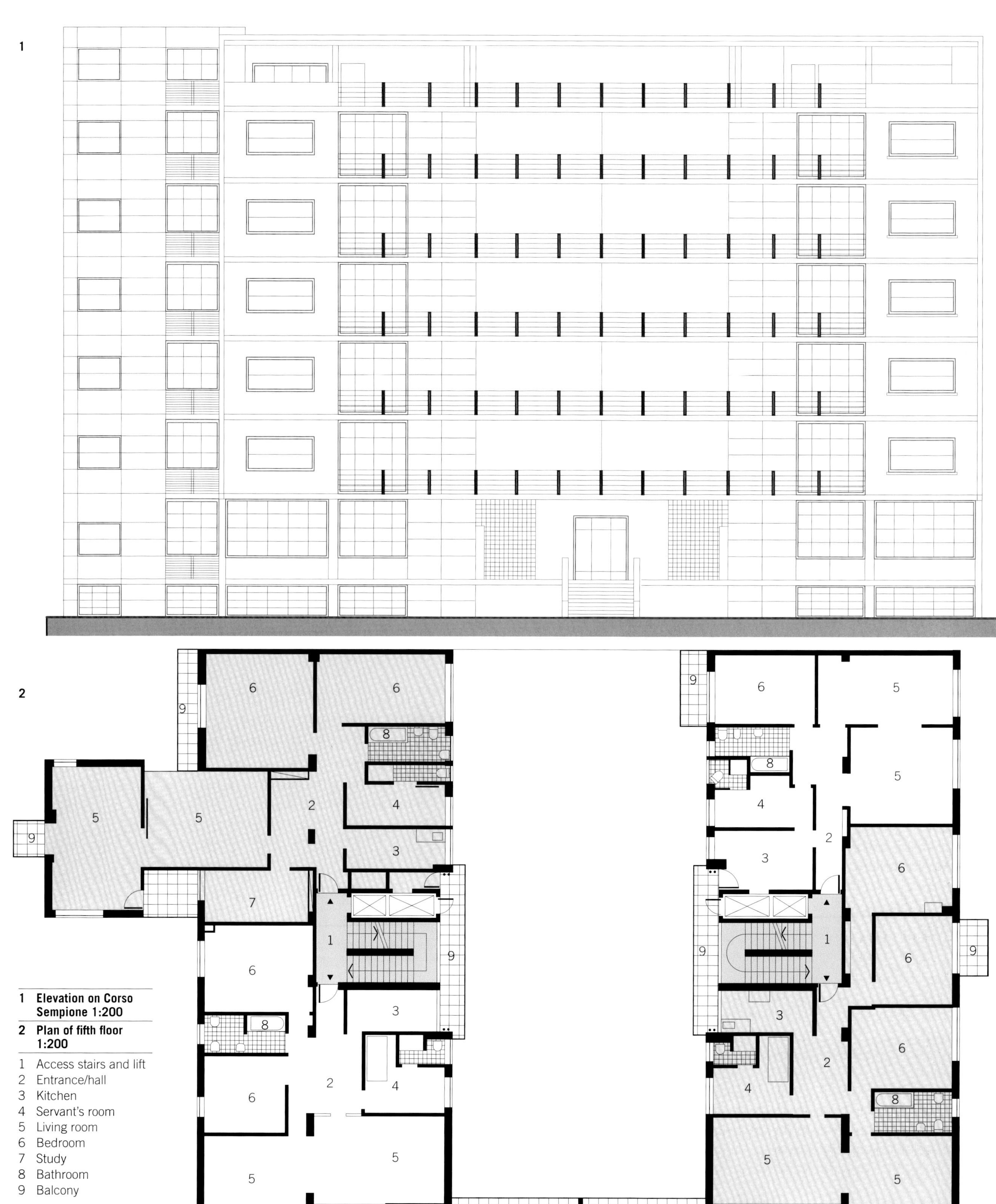

1 Elevation on Corso Sempione 1:200

2 Plan of fifth floor 1:200

1 Access stairs and lift
2 Entrance/hall
3 Kitchen
4 Servant's room
5 Living room
6 Bedroom
7 Study
8 Bathroom
9 Balcony

Bubeshko Apartments

Rudolf Schindler, 1887–1953

Los Angeles, California, USA; 1938–41

The Bubeshko has six apartments on three levels above ground-floor garages. The building is divided into two blocks, with four flats on one side and two on the other separated by a central passageway. The entrances to the apartments are on either side, where external staircases lead to each individual dwelling, while the central entrance is reserved for service access, with back doors to each apartment, storage spaces and a backyard for those on the top floor. This scheme uses a familiar form with a stepped section following the steeply sloping site. Overhanging eaves and external terraces on the roofs of the lower apartments extend the horizontal planes in contrast to the verticality of the site.

Each of the apartments is different; two studios and one duplex are included in the scheme, but they have common design characteristics, with the other flats. Entrance doors generally open direct into the living rooms, but are positioned in one corner. This gives the longest possible external view diagonally across the space, through windows situated in the opposite corners and across terraces or balconies. The double-height apartment has its living room on the upper level and has several outdoor rooms, as well as terraces at both levels on the street side and a patio beyond a covered porch at the rear on the upper level. The other apartments all have terraces on the street side, apart from one studio which has only a small garden area at the entrance.

Following his early experiments with concrete construction, Schindler employed a more economical construction method – that of timber framing and stucco – for this and other apartment blocks he designed during the Depression years in the 1930s. Schindler went on to develop his own version of timber-frame construction which he used for the design of several more apartment buildings in Los Angeles in the following decade. These included the Falk Apartments (1943) and Laurelwood (1946–49), which continued the same spatial devices of angular shifts, diagonal views and stepped terraces.

1

1 Street-level plan 1:200

1 Access stairs
2 Service access
3 Garages/parking

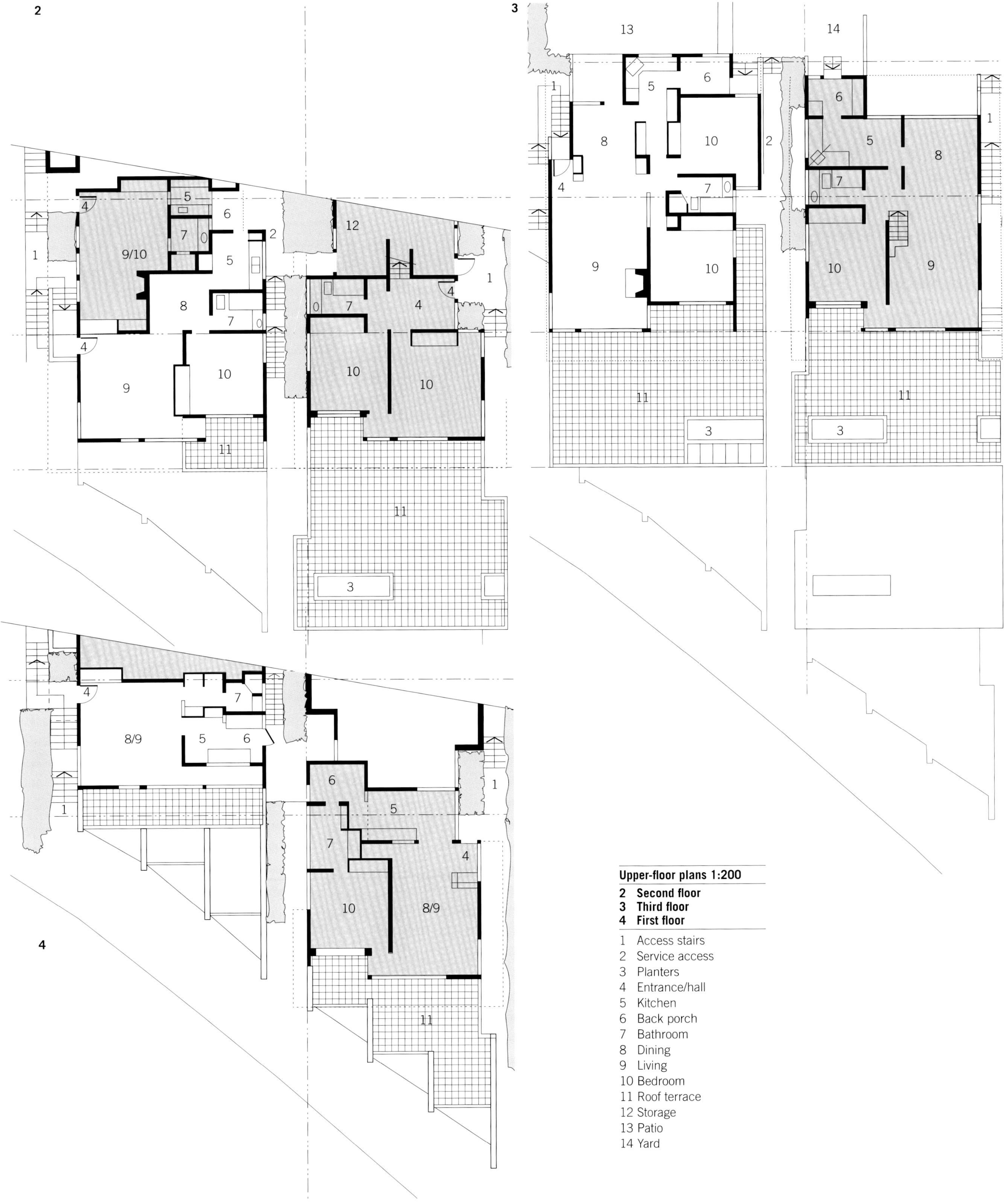

Upper-floor plans 1:200

2 Second floor
3 Third floor
4 First floor

1 Access stairs
2 Service access
3 Planters
4 Entrance/hall
5 Kitchen
6 Back porch
7 Bathroom
8 Dining
9 Living
10 Bedroom
11 Roof terrace
12 Storage
13 Patio
14 Yard

Post-war Modernism

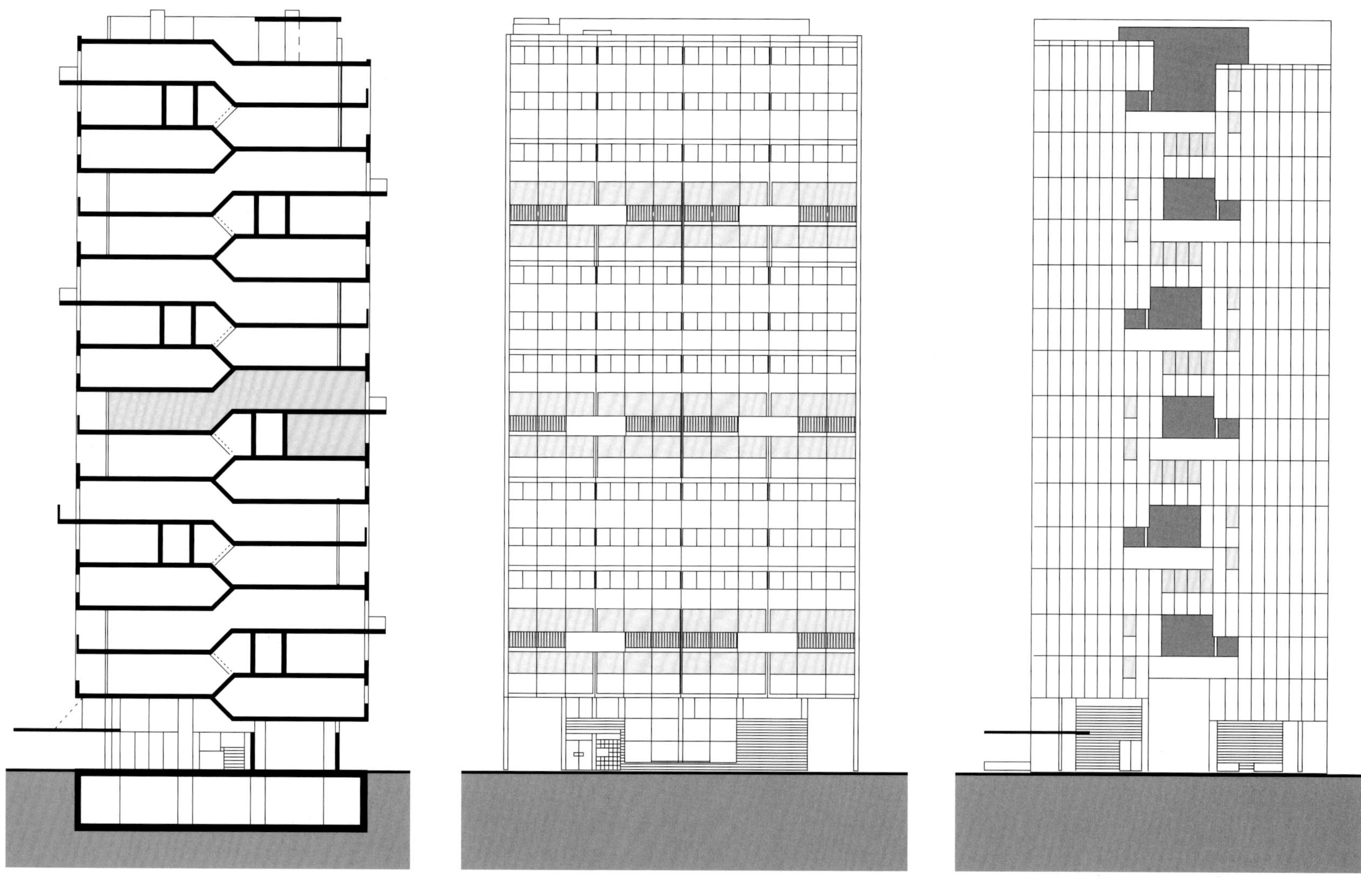

Left: **Unité d'Habitation, roof terrace**

Right: **Churchill Gardens estate**

In the post-war years, the urgent need for reconstruction in Europe and pressure to build more homes meant that many public housing authorities and government bodies adopted the current ideas, those of pre-war Modernism, and embarked on large housing schemes closely linked to areas of urban renewal. Good public housing schemes were increasingly concerned with the provision of amenities and facilities for residents, including the local infrastructure beyond the dwellings themselves: nursery schools, playgrounds and community centres. In addition, the absence of servants, coupled with advances in technology, was to have a significant impact on the design of interior layouts. Central heating seemed more economical and appropriate in apartment buildings, and open fires, flues and fuel stores remained a feature of individual houses only. Shared electric washing machines started to appear in apartment buildings in Europe as well as the USA, as well as the all-important drying space for dwellings with no gardens and only small balconies. Great attention was paid to the location and design of kitchens and bathrooms in the name of efficiency, both in relation to the routing of pipework and drainage and in the carrying out of household tasks such as cooking and cleaning.

The best-known housing project of this period – probably of all time – is, of course, the first of Le Corbusier's **Unités d'Habitation**, which was built in Marseilles (see pages 82–85). Inspired, perhaps, by some aspects of the earlier **Narkomfin** building by Moisei Ginzburg and Ignati Milinis (see pages 52–53), with which it shares some similarities in section, the Marseilles Unité was original in almost every respect: its extraordinary overall depth of apartments, at 24 metres (80 feet) each; the interlocking section, which reduced circulation to every third floor; the massive structural form; the use of exposed concrete; the landscaped roof; and its claim to provide a new version of urban space – the 'vertical garden city'. In Brazil, Affonso Reidy's **Pedregulho** (see pages 86–87) similarly demonstrated new forms for housing. In contrast to the great depth of the Unité, in Reidy's block very small flats and maisonettes are strung out in a wall-like sinuous curving form following the contours of the terrain and looking out over a landscape dotted with buildings housing the other facilities including a gym, kindergarten and medical centre. And in England, Powell and Moya's **Churchill Gardens Estate** (see pages 88–89) successfully overlaid modern slab blocks on London's existing street plan.

The drive to reduce costs in public housing projects that led to compromises such as balcony access and lower ceiling heights in the later blocks at Churchill Gardens also favoured duplexes or maisonettes for their potential to reduce circulation space, which was seen as unnecessary and costly. In England particularly, the maisonette was popular – often referred to as having the appearance of a house. At **Golden Lane Estate** (see pages 90–91) adjacent to the **Barbican** in central London, Chamberlin Powell and Bon's intricately designed maisonettes also reduced circulation space within the dwelling by locating the staircases within the living rooms. Kunio Maekawa's **Harumi Apartments** (see pages 102–3) building in Japan used a rigorous development phase to achieve a reduction in its circulation space. It employs an access gallery on every third floor, but maintains access to the flats above and below by staircases, unusually running perpendicular to the access corridor.

Ludwig Mies van der Rohe had become head of the architecture department at the Illinois Institute of Technology in 1938, and together with other European immigrants such as Walter Gropius and Marcel Breuer he is credited with the introduction of the new style of architecture to the USA. By the late 1940s and early 1950s, a second phase in skyscraper

Left: **Tower block, Barbican development**

Right: **Price Tower, section**

Below left: **Keeling House, plan**

Below right: **Bellevue Bay atrium houses**

Opposite left: **Hansaviertel Apartments, Alvar Aalto, detail of terrace**

Opposite **right: Alexandra Road**

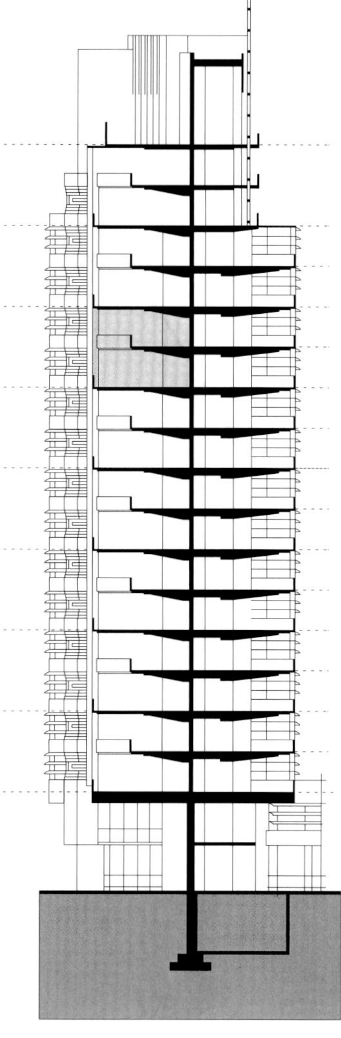

developments was under way – this time with even taller structures than those of the earlier turn-of-the century phase. Mies's **860–880 Lake Shore Drive** (see pages 96–97), with its two towers of identical form but with very different floor plans, brought a style of construction to residential building that had previously been associated purely with office developments. Frank Lloyd Wright's **Price Tower** at Bartlesville, Oklahoma (see pages 98–99) claimed to be the first to incorporate dwellings and offices in the same building, with residential duplex units forming one quarter of each 'pinwheel' floor plan. Wright was convinced, however, that the tower block as a residential building type was better suited to the open spaces of suburbs or small towns, where it could offer privacy to inhabitants, rather than to the proximity of other towers in the congested spaces of cities. Denys Lasdun's **Keeling House** in London (see pages 100–101) explored important issues of privacy and proximity. This project, and other 'cluster blocks', are tower blocks at a smaller scale, and were popular partly because their small footprint was seen as less disruptive

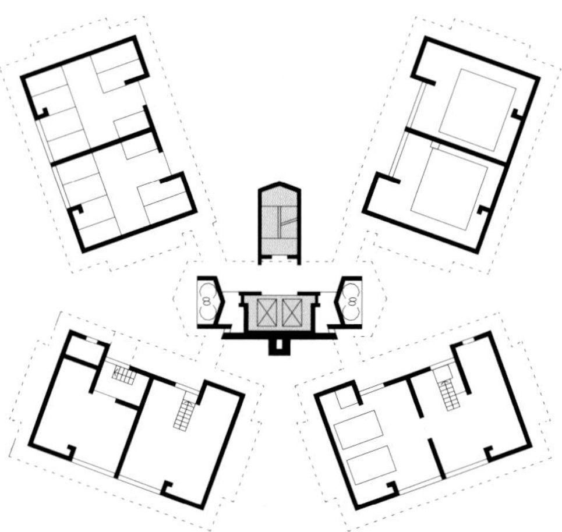

in areas where they were to replace existing terraced houses. At Keeling House, groups of four maisonettes are clustered around the central circulation core, physically separated but accessible by bridges, thus minimizing corridor lengths and improving privacy by reducing noise disturbance.

At the same time that mainstream architectural practice and theory explored the possibilities for very large-scale housing projects, other architects developed existing models using ingenuity and inventiveness to rework the traditional forms of terraces and courtyard houses. Giancarlo De Carlo's **workers' housing** in Italy (see pages 94–95) is the result of a modular approach, the development of a plan-type designed in such a way that it could be rotated, mirrored and grouped in several different ways to arrive at different building forms. The unusual form of **Casa de la Marina** in Barcelona by José Antonio Coderch (see pages 92–93) is in part related to its site – it forms the end of an urban block – and in part to its unusual circulation system, with linked lobbies within the flats and the use of several loggias as an integral part of the individual dwelling plans. In Arne Jacobsen's **Bellevue Bay flats and houses** scheme at Klampenborg, Denmark (see pages 110–11), the apartments have a sunken sitting room in the darkest, central part of the plan, which is intended for use in the winter and equipped with an open fire. In the courtyard houses opposite, this feature is replaced by an outdoor room: a courtyard, or 'summer living room'.

The 1957 housing exhibition at the Hansaviertel (Hansa quarter) in Berlin, with projects by many of the same architects who had participated in the Weissenhofsiedlung 30 years earlier, displayed a range of building types including towers, slab blocks and low-rise terraced schemes. Alvar Aalto's **Hansaviertel Apartments** (see pages 106–7) employs a reworking of a courtyard house plan with multi-purpose living and circulation space in the centre, while Van den Broek en Bakema's **Hansaviertel Tower** (see pages 108–9) reworks Le Corbusier's Unité duplex in a more compact, 20-metre (65-foot) deep version. **Halen** in Berne, Switzerland (see pages 112–15), by Atelier 5, is still regarded as one of the most inventive designs for low-rise, high-density terraced housing – the inspiration for many later schemes, particularly those built by London's Borough of Camden Architecture Department under the direction of Neave Brown, with schemes such as Branch Hill (1978), **Alexandra Road** (1979) and Maiden Lane (1981).

Unité d'Habitation

Le Corbusier, 1887–1965

Marseilles, France; 1952

The realization of the Unité d'Habitation in Marseilles represents the culmination of more than 20 years of research by Le Corbusier into the design of dwellings. This work had included individual prototypes, such as the Domino and Citrohan houses (1915 and 1921 respectively), as well as examining the relationship of the dwelling to the urban environment in ambitious urban planning proposals such as the Ville Contemporaine (1922) and the Ville Radieuse (1935). The Marseilles Unité (first of a series) is an 18-storey block with 337 apartments of 23 different types. Its ingenious access system utilizes corridors on levels 2, 5, 7, 8, 10, 13 and 16 only. Although the Unité is often compared to the work of Moisei Ginzburg, whose Narkomfin building in Moscow (see pages 52–53) radically reduced personal space and replaced it with communal living areas, it is not certain that Le Corbusier subscribed to the same principles in his design. Ginzburg's proposal reflected a belief in the need for a reassessment of the traditional family as a part of the transition to a more egalitarian society, whereas the Unité provides a high level of facilities and communal spaces to support and strengthen the idea of the family unit.

The standard Unité apartment – interlocked in pairs around a central access corridor – is designed for families with two children. Bedrooms – the most private spaces – are kept to the absolute minimum in order to give more space to the open-plan kitchen/living room, intended to be the focus of servant-less post-war family life. The kitchen is located in the central part of the plan, close to the entrance, and connects directly with the double-height living space that extends either above or below. Although small (98 square metres/1,055 square feet), and a narrow 3.66 metres (12 feet) wide, the apartments extend the full depth of the block and have balconies on both sides. The provision of central heating, partial air-conditioning and refuse chutes and iceboxes in every kitchen raised the standard of services – in addition to the inventive planning that gives the majority of apartments sunlight, controlled by brise-soleils, both morning and afternoon. Variations on the unit types include the side addition of a second pair of bedrooms for larger families, single-aspect two-person apartments (generally west- or south-facing) and studios – the only type without a double-height living space.

Communal facilities included laundries with electric washing machines, a crèche, a kindergarten and a restaurant, and instead of guest rooms in the flats the block had a hotel with 18 rooms. The landscaped roof terrace provided playgrounds and a paddling pool for children, a running track and an open-air gym as well as spectacular views. There were also shops, a sick bay and dispensary, and a bar included within the block. Despite numerous attempts to imitate many of the design ideas in the Unité (the streets in the sky, 'skip-stop' access arrangements and the north–south orientation) most have not achieved the same quality – a criticism also levelled at the Unités that followed in Nantes-Rezé, Briey-en-Forêt, Berlin and Firminy, where budgetary constraints reduced the programme.

Opposite left: Exterior view from south-west

Opposite right: Interior of apartment type E1 showing kitchen

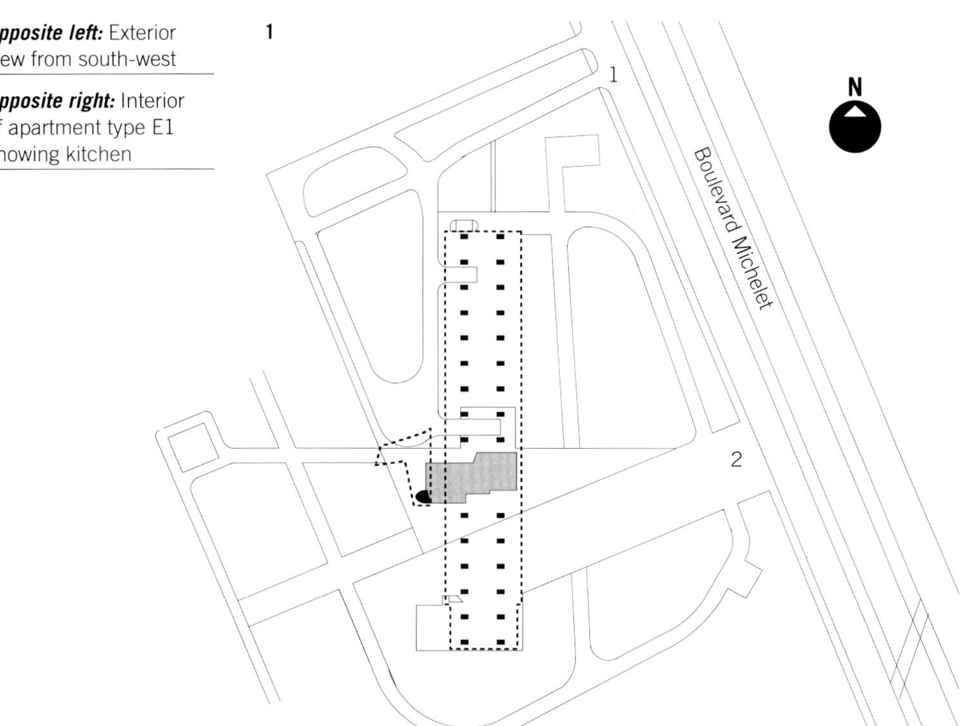

1 Site plan 1:2,500

1 Entrance for cars
2 Entrance for pedestrians

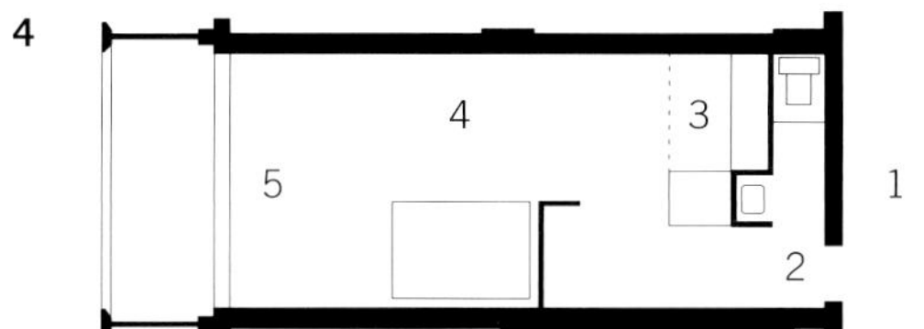

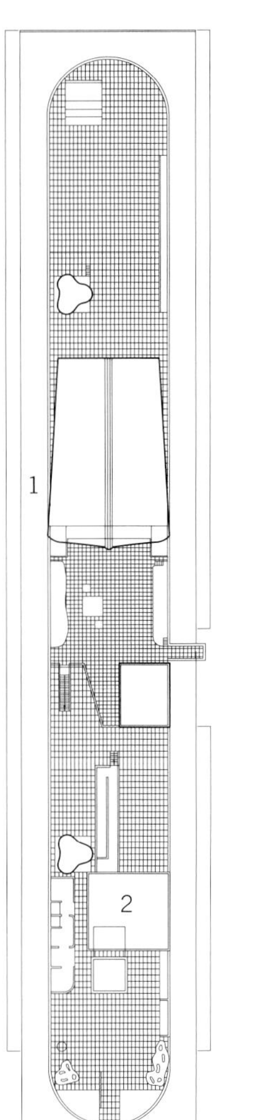

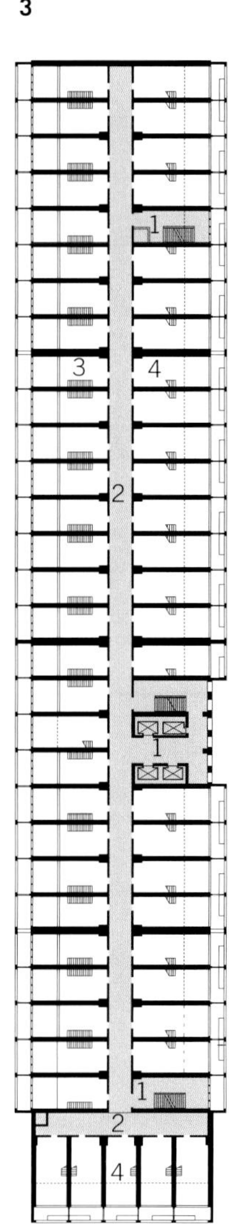

2 Roof plan 1:1,000

1 Running track
2 Paddling pool

3 Plan of typical access floor 1:1,000 Levels 2, 5, 10, 13 and 16

1 Lifts and stairs
2 Access corridor
3 Upper level of lower maisonette
4 Lower level of upper maisonette

4 Type E1 single-person studio flat plan 1:200

1 Access corridor
2 Hall
3 Kitchen
4 Dining/living
5 Double-height living

Maisonette for family with 2–4 children Plans 1:200

5 Upper level
6 Lower level

1 Access corridor
2 Hall
3 Kitchen
4 Dining/living
5 Double-height living
6 Balcony
7 Sleeping

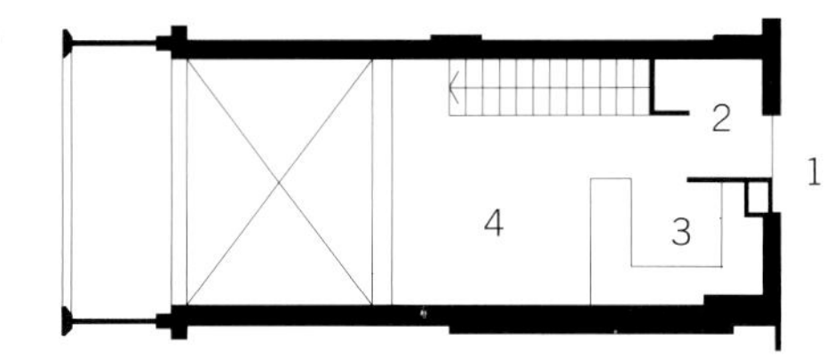

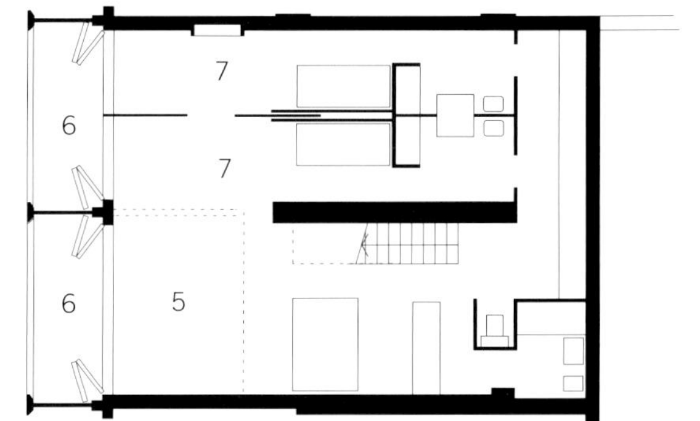

7

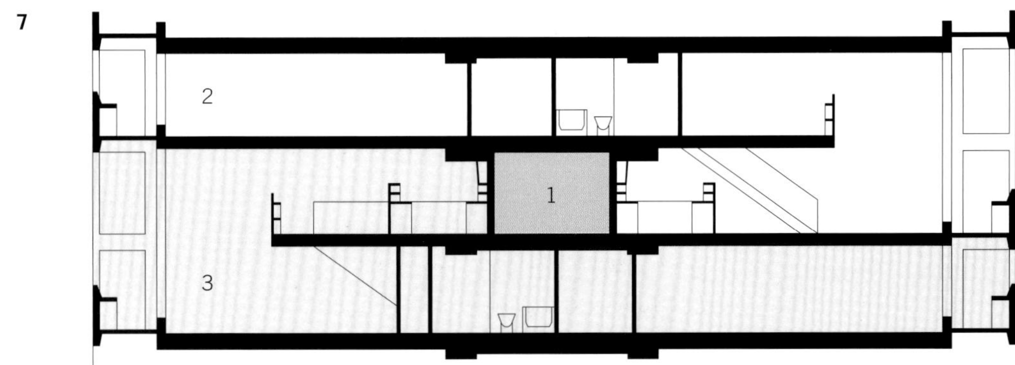

7 Pair of maisonettes for family with 2–4 children Section 1:200

1 Access corridor
2 Upper maisonette
3 Lower maisonette

8

9

10

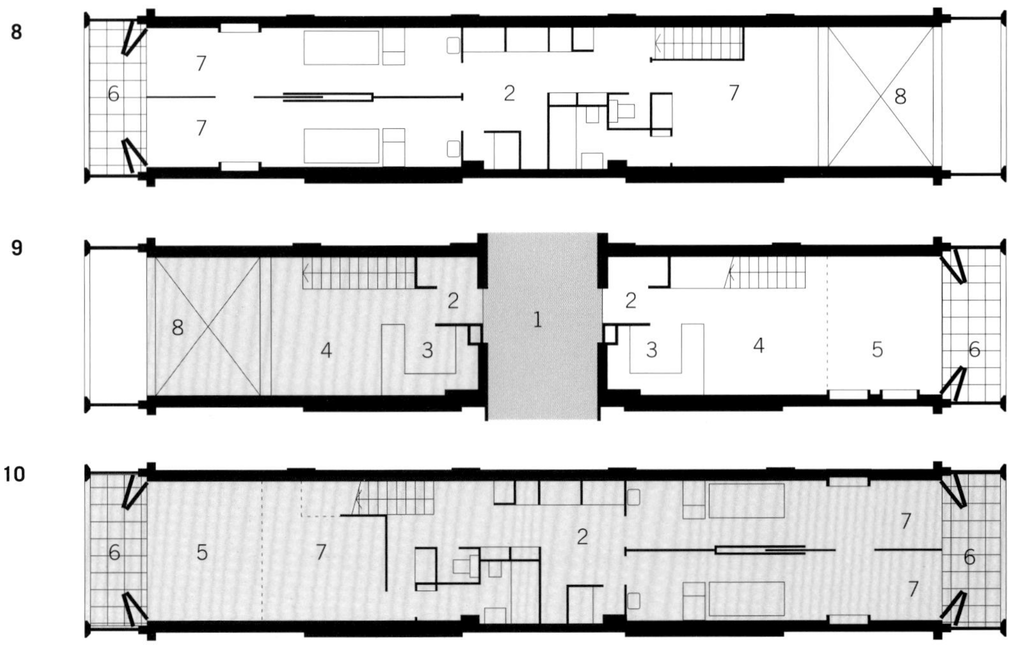

Pair of maisonettes for family with 2–4 children Plans 1:200

8 Upper level

9 Middle level with access corridor

10 Lower level

1 Access corridor
2 Hall
3 Kitchen
4 Dining/living
5 Double-height living
6 Balcony
7 Sleeping
8 Void over double-height living

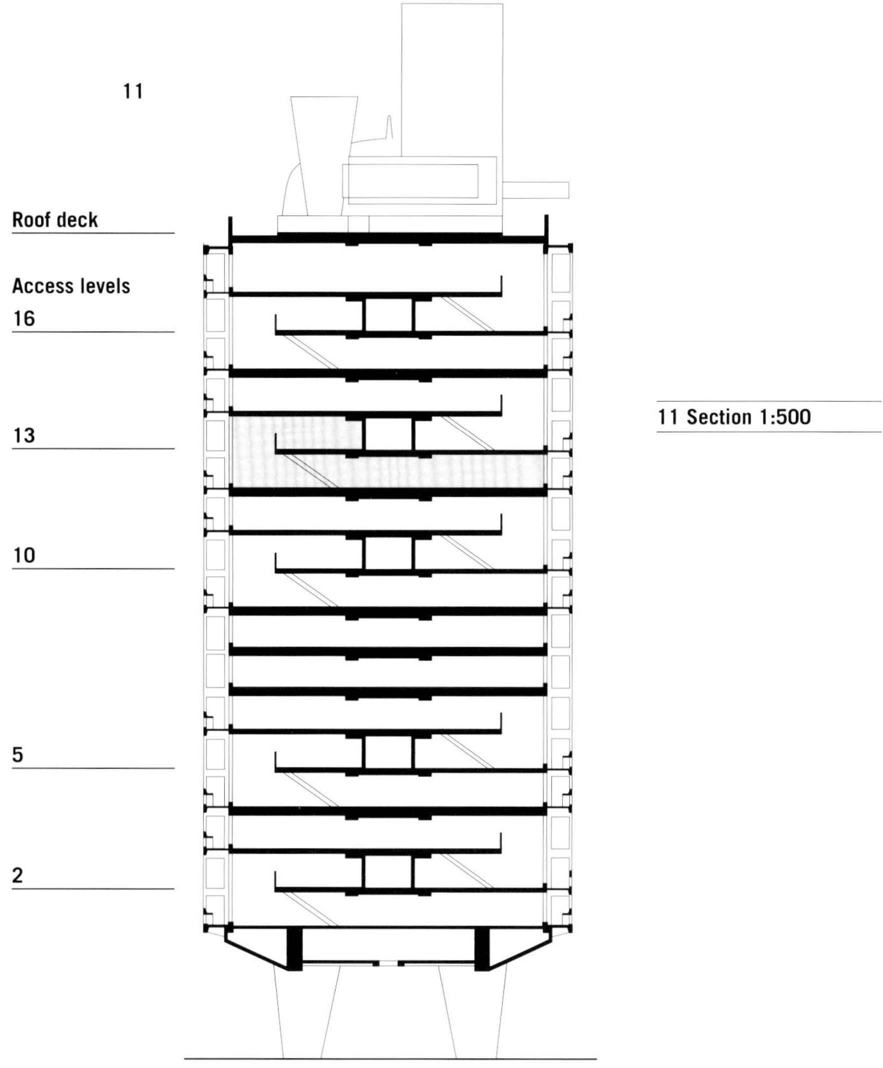

11 Section 1:500

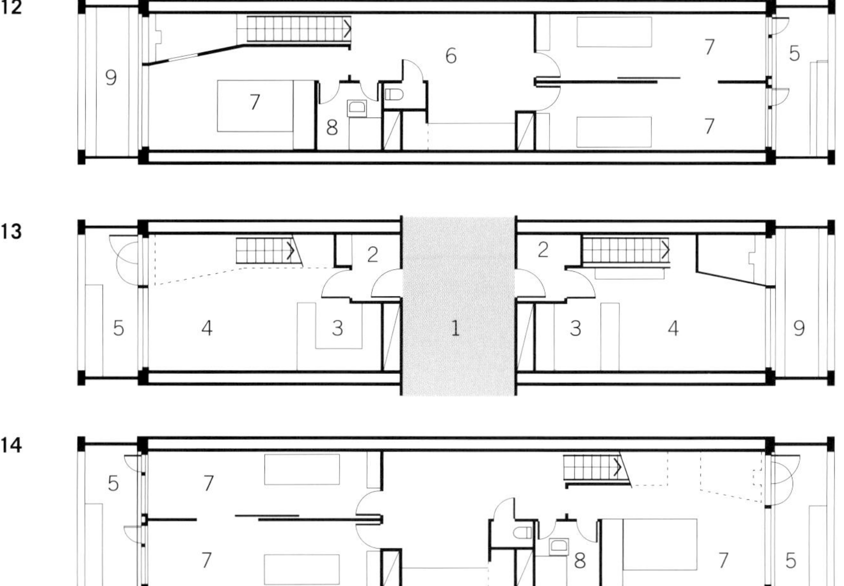

Plans of a pair of Unité apartments at Nantes-Rézé 1:200

12 Upper level

13 Middle/access level

14 Lower level

1 Interior street/access corridor
2 Entrance/hall
3 Kitchen
4 Living
5 Balcony
6 Landing
7 Bedroom
8 Bathroom
9 Brise-soleil

Pedregulho Housing

Affonso Eduardo Reidy, 1909–64

Rio de Janeiro, Brazil; 1950–52

The Pedregulho project was awarded the first prize in the International Biennale in São Paulo in 1953 by a jury presided over by the influential historian and critic Sigfried Giedion who claimed it was 'a simple example of how every city should be built'. Its critics were less concerned about the architectural qualities, which remain highly regarded, than they were about the paternalistic stance and rigid regulations enforced by the municipal housing office. Prospective tenants were given medical examinations to avoid introducing diseases, and had to agree to inspections of themselves and their flats from time to time to check up primarily on cleanliness. The design was intended as a model, and the overall scheme included four housing blocks, a school, playground, health centre, shops and a fully equipped laundry – all set in a landscape designed by Roberto Burle Marx. The most significant element in the composition is the largest housing block, which sits at the top of the steeply sloping site.

It stands seven storeys high, raised on pilotis, and with a very long sinuous shape (260 metres/853 feet in length), curving to follow the contours of the site. The building has no lifts; all access is by stairs, with the entrances into the building either at ground level or at the third floor where two bridges connect to the higher ground level further up the hill. This third-floor level is partly open space, and contains a playground, municipal administrative offices and a kindergarten with staff rooms for the teachers.

On the lower levels, there are small one-bedroomed flats, and on the four floors above are maisonettes with, generally, two bedrooms. The space below the building and the open area at third-floor level provide shaded open space and air circulation, important given the local climate. The access corridors are wide enough to be occupied, and are partly enclosed with perforated terracotta screens to provide shading and maintain ventilation. Inside the flats, all the rooms have windows and are arranged to allow cross-ventilation. The flats are arranged in handed pairs, divided by a perpendicular wall alternating with structural columns. The latter follow the curve in plan, and are enclosed by oblique partitions or fitted cupboards.

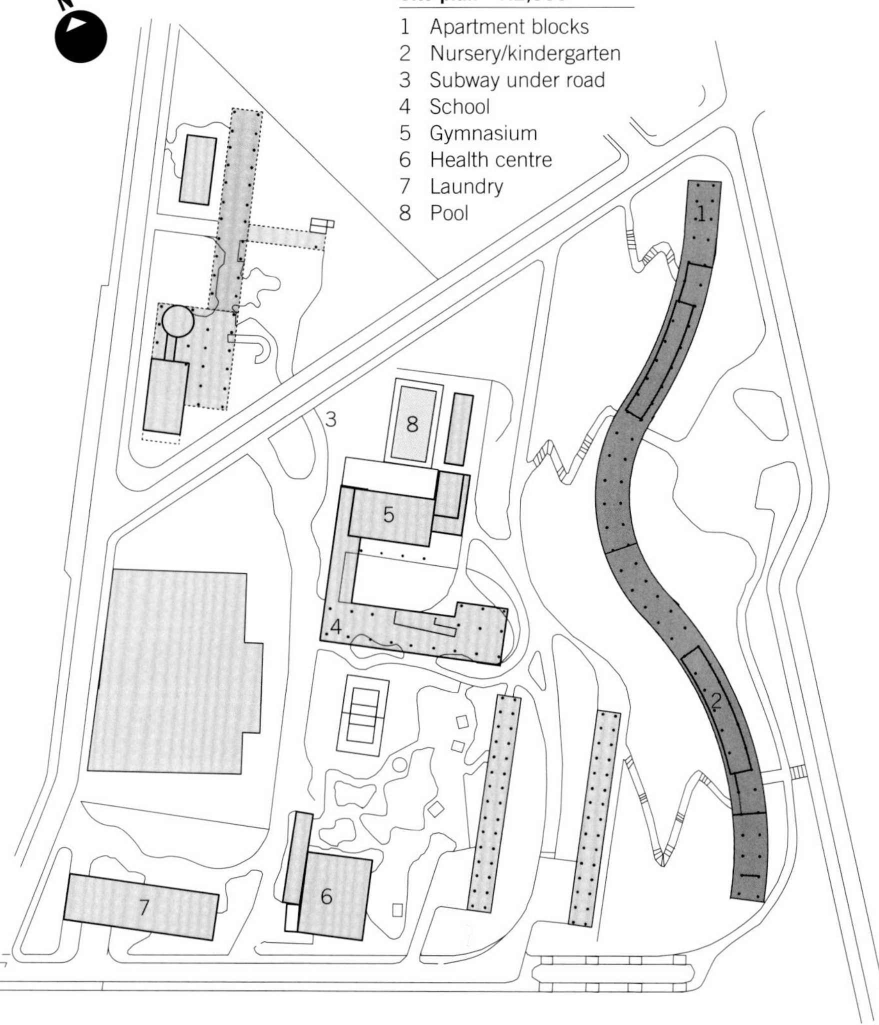

Site plan 1:2,500

1 Apartment blocks
2 Nursery/kindergarten
3 Subway under road
4 School
5 Gymnasium
6 Health centre
7 Laundry
8 Pool

1 Plan of intermediate floor, level 3 1:1000

1 Bridge
2 Administrative offices
3 Nursery school
4 Children's theatre
5 Kindergarten

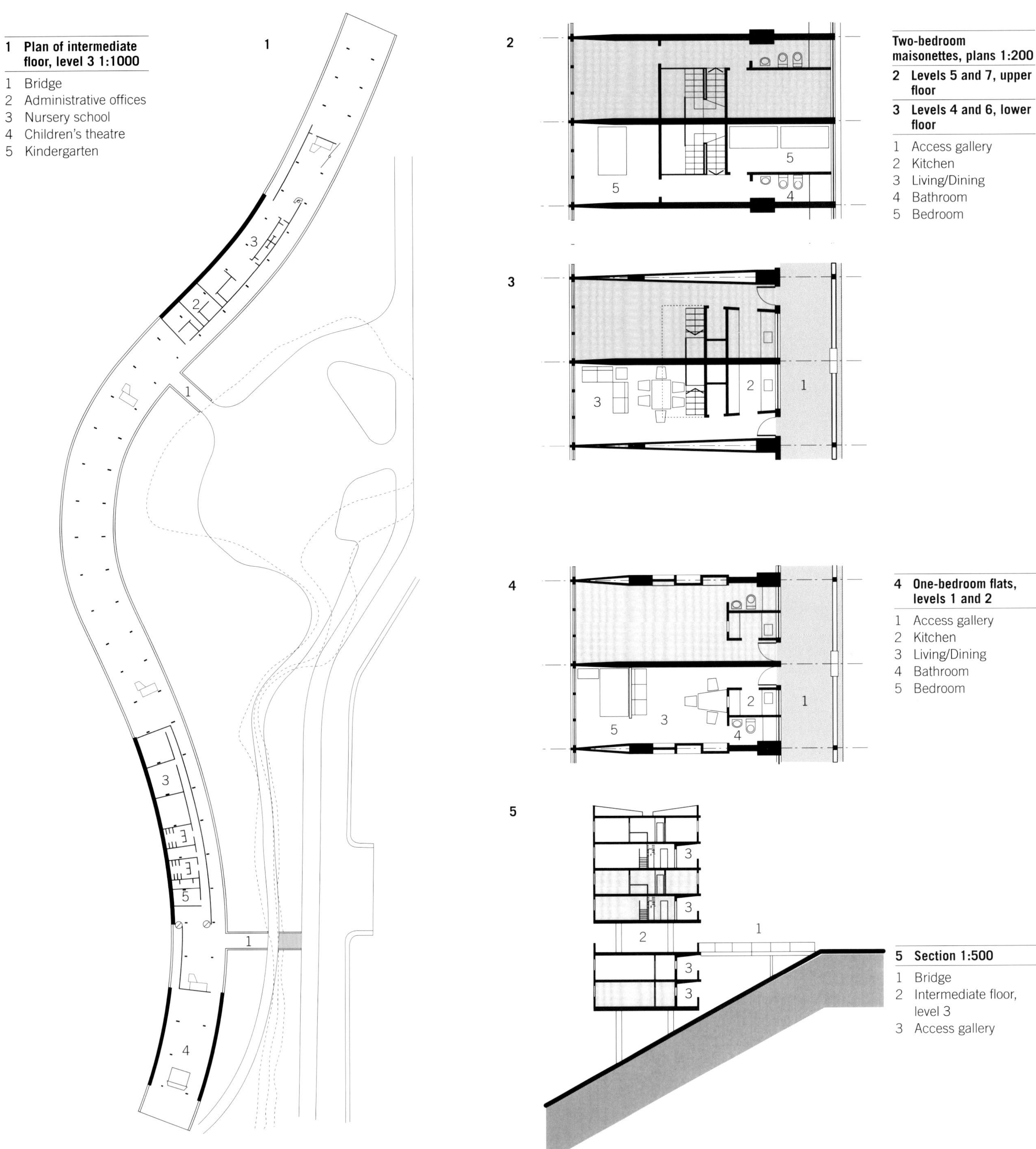

Two-bedroom maisonettes, plans 1:200

2 Levels 5 and 7, upper floor

3 Levels 4 and 6, lower floor

1 Access gallery
2 Kitchen
3 Living/Dining
4 Bathroom
5 Bedroom

4 One-bedroom flats, levels 1 and 2

1 Access gallery
2 Kitchen
3 Living/Dining
4 Bathroom
5 Bedroom

5 Section 1:500

1 Bridge
2 Intermediate floor, level 3
3 Access gallery

Churchill Gardens Estate

Powell and Moya

London, UK; 1949

Powell and Moya's housing project in London's Pimlico district was considered of such significance at the time of its building that it was the subject of a major article by the Modernist critic Henry Russell Hitchcock, published in the *Architectural Review* in September 1953. Two significant aspects were discussed: firstly, that housing programmes should be of interest to young architects, largely as a result of interruptions to career opportunities caused by the war years; and secondly, that housing could be considered to have a monumental quality. Hitchcock compares the initial blocks (only the first two sections were built by this time), for their quality as landmarks, to Mies van der Rohe's Lake Shore Drive in Chicago (1951; see pages 96–97) and Lever House by SOM (1952) in New York. This was probably one of the first times that housing was discussed in terms of urban design; the project's commitment to the ideas of European Modernism or the International style was clearly visible in its concrete-frame structures, use of colour and the importance of the site layout.

Churchill Gardens is undoubtedly one of the most successful large-scale housing schemes in London, and is of particular interest because of its combination of the familiar urban arrangements of a coherent network of streets and squares with Modernism's ideas of orientation and the structural form of buildings. Hitchcock makes scant reference to the layout of the flats themselves or the ingenuity of their design (especially marked in terms of developments in services). The project had an innovative collective heating and hot-water system based on reusing the waste heat from one of London's major power stations at Battersea on the opposite side of the Thames.

Central heating, significantly, freed the plan from the constraints of flues, and enabled the architects to approach the design of the apartments from a different perspective. Privacy was considered of great importance, as was efficient planning to maximize living space. A commitment to efficiency is also demonstrated by Powell and Moya's taking part in the BRE (Building Research Establishment) project to survey housewives' work in order to improve on the design of their kitchens. The flats are paired, with the bathrooms and kitchens grouped together with shared ducts on the adjoining wall. Each has a private balcony on one side and the entrance on the other. The stair towers are separated from the main volume of the block, enclosed in glass, and give access to just two flats per landing, designed to accommodate a separate 'porch' space for each flat.

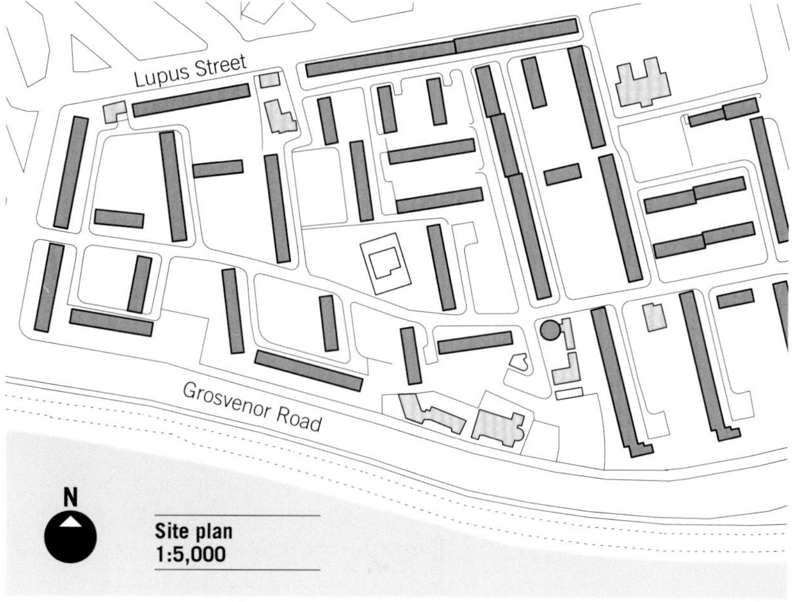

Site plan
1:5,000

Plans of typical apartments 1:200

1 Top-floor plan, one and two-bedroom flats

2 Typical floor plan, three-bedroom flat

1 Stairs and lift
2 Porch
3 Entrance/hall
4 Bathroom/WC
5 Kitchen
6 Living room
7 Bedroom
8 Private balcony
9 Escape stairs

3 Section 1:200

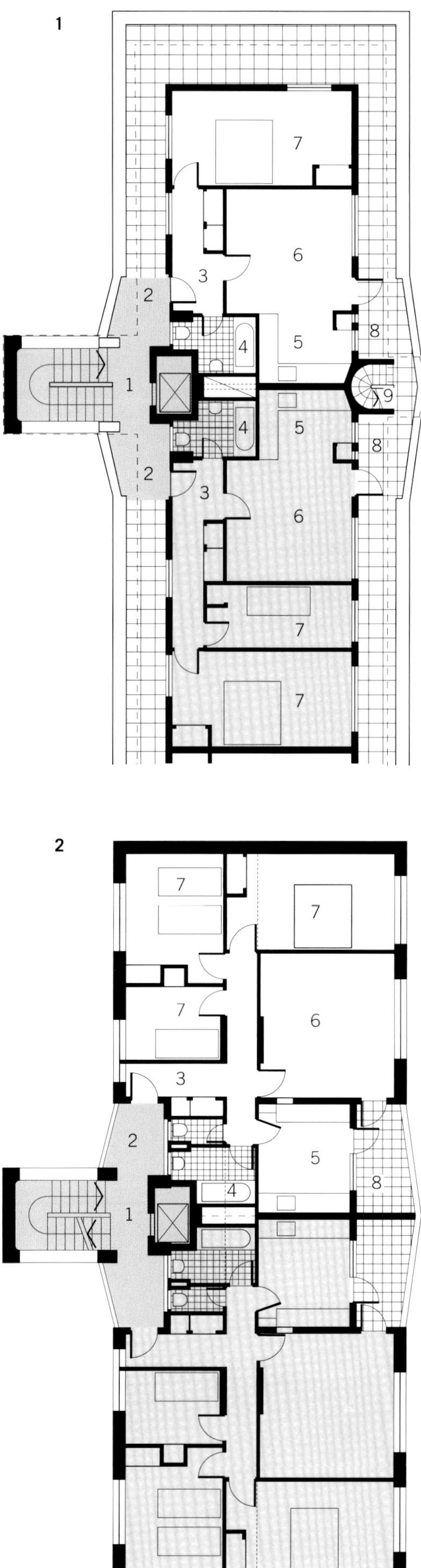

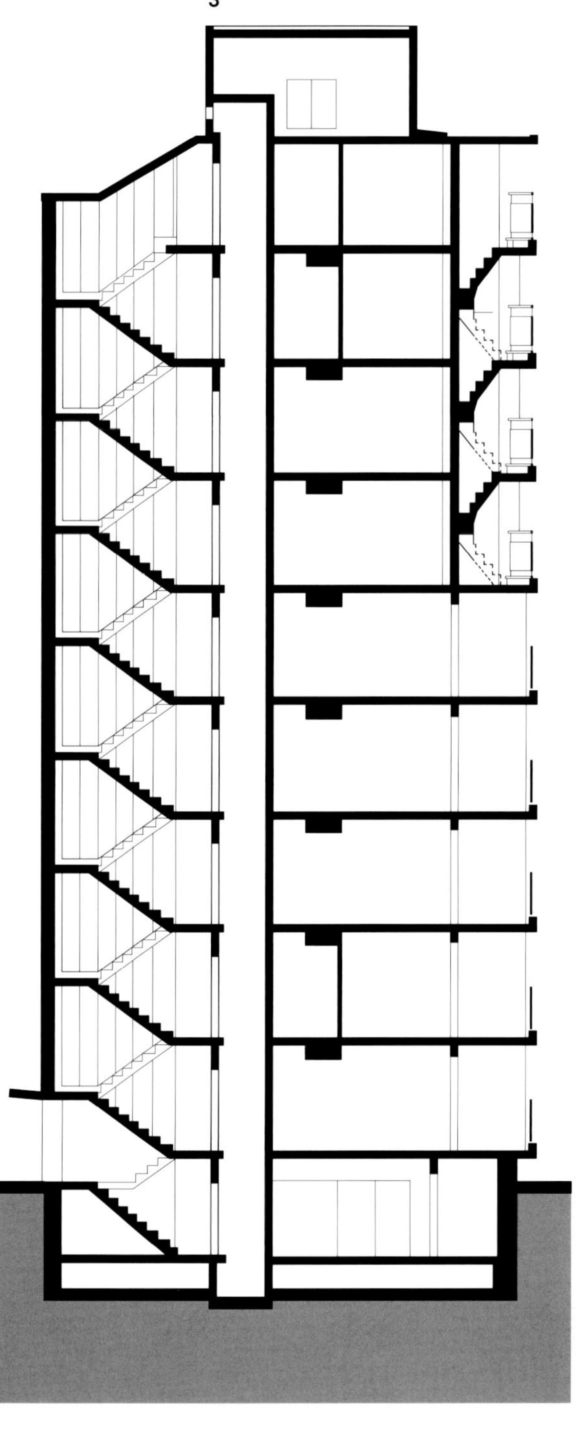

Golden Lane Estate

Chamberlin, Powell and Bon

London, UK, 1952–62

There are three different building types that make up the Golden Lane Estate, built over a period of ten years between 1952 and 1962. The first to be built were four- and six-storey blocks of flats and maisonettes intended mainly for families, located closer to the open spaces and playgrounds for children. These used a loadbearing brick construction, with concrete floors between the dwellings and timber within. The second building type was the 16-storey high tower – an early example of curtain walling, using bright yellow glass panels – which has eight two-room flats per floor, intended for single people or couples without children. The last block to be completed was Crescent House, bordering the site along Goswell Road and including commercial units at street level.

The low blocks have either two or three levels of maisonettes accessible directly at ground-floor level or by external balconies at the upper levels. The paired entrances are positioned behind brick piers rising up on the external face of the building, and recessed to improve privacy. Daylighting to the access balconies and the kitchens overlooking them is enhanced by the use of open grilles for the escape balconies from the bedrooms a level above. Also, despite rather small overall dimensions – a width of just over 4 metres (13 feet 4½ inches) between dividing walls – double-height glazing to the stairwell within the living space and the screen between the kitchen and living space contribute to a greater sense of spaciousness. Externally the dividing walls are extended beyond the façade, clearly defining the separate units. The Golden Lane Estate is significant as one of the first in England to employ urban planning ideas promoted by Le Corbusier. On a key central London bomb site, it demonstrated the potential for urban redevelopment as an alternative to the growing suburbanization and New Town ideals. The use of different housing types provided for a mixed community: facilities such as a swimming pool, community centre and playgrounds provided amenity for the residents, and the layout – tower highly visible at the centre, with the lower buildings forming a series of squares – gave a strong sense of identity to the estate and to the neighbourhood.

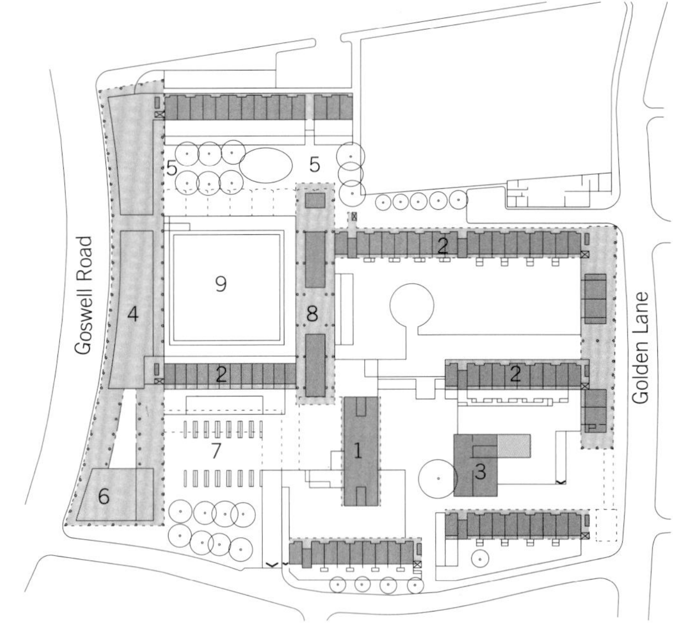

Site layout 1: 2,500

1 16-storey tower block
2 Slab blocks with flats or maisonettes
3 Community centre
4 Shops
5 Playground
6 Pub
7 Pedestrian courtyard with garages underneath
8 Sports courts and gym
9 Sunken court

Opposite left: 16-storey tower block with slab block in foreground

Opposite right: Lower-level interior of a maisonette

1

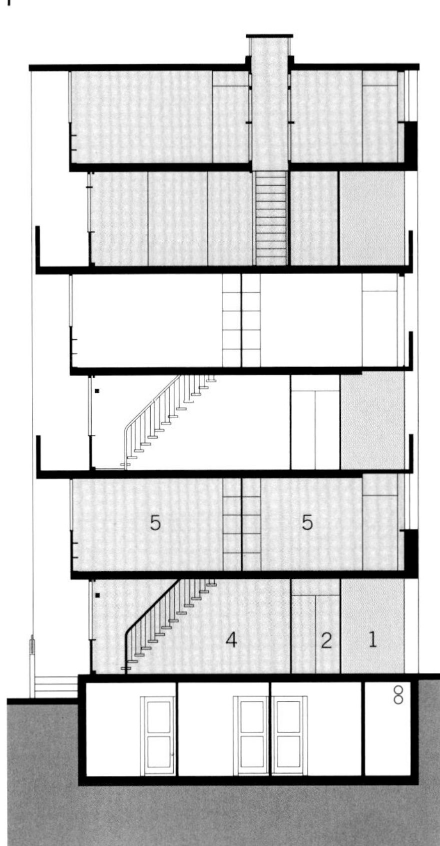

2

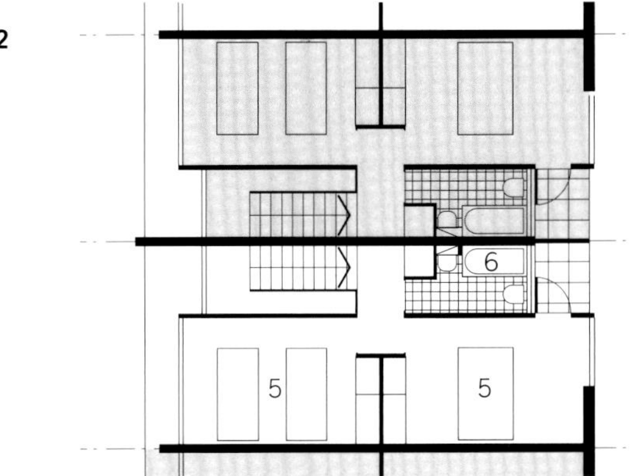

3

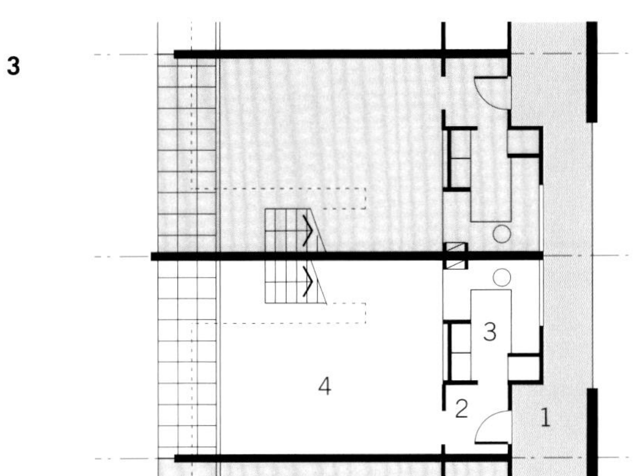

1 Section through typical slab block 1:200

Plans of typical maisonette 1:200

2 Upper-floor plan
3 Lower-floor plan

1 Access gallery
2 Entrance
3 Kitchen
4 Living
5 Bedroom
6 Bathroom

Casa de la Marina

José Antonio Coderch, 1913–84

Barcelona, Spain; 1951–54

Casa de la Marina, built by the ISM (Instituto Social de la Marina) for local fishermen and their families, is located on the water's edge in the Barceloneta dock area of Barcelona. The building forms the end of a block with exposed façades on three sides. Behind full-height glazing set back from the main building, it has a raised ground floor and semi-basement, which contains commercial space, a caretaker's flat and storage spaces. At roof level, the top floor is set back beneath an oversailing roofline and contains two studio apartments and a terrace. The six intermediate floors each contain a pair of identical, handed apartments separated by a central stair.

The geometry of oblique and angled planes that creates the 'undulating' façades is also used in the plan – a kind of labyrinthine approach to make the small spaces appear larger. A series of partitions parallel to the adjoining building divide the space in each unit between the living room and the bedrooms. The partitions between them are arranged at seemingly random angles, producing an intricate arrangement of interconnected spaces. A corridor leads diagonally from the entrance to the living room at the farthest corner of the plan, and the view is from the door at the corner looking across to the full-height glazing in the corner and beyond. A sharp angle in the corridor leads to the kitchen and a terrace, and a second corridor separates access to the bedrooms and bathroom. The bedrooms are also connected via doors leading to loggias. The faceted elevation consists of either solid panels, containing the enclosed spaces of flues and cupboards, or adjustable timber louvred panels to windows in the living rooms and the loggias.

Coderch maintained that there were functional reasons for the oblique plan arrangements. The ideas developed in this scheme – particularly the use of louvres, a variation of the traditional Mediterranean shutter, and an emphasis on aspect as a key idea in developing the plan, were used in other larger housing projects by Coderch such as Compositor Bach, Barcelona (1958); Girasol, Madrid (1966) and Las Cocheras, Barcelona (1969–75).

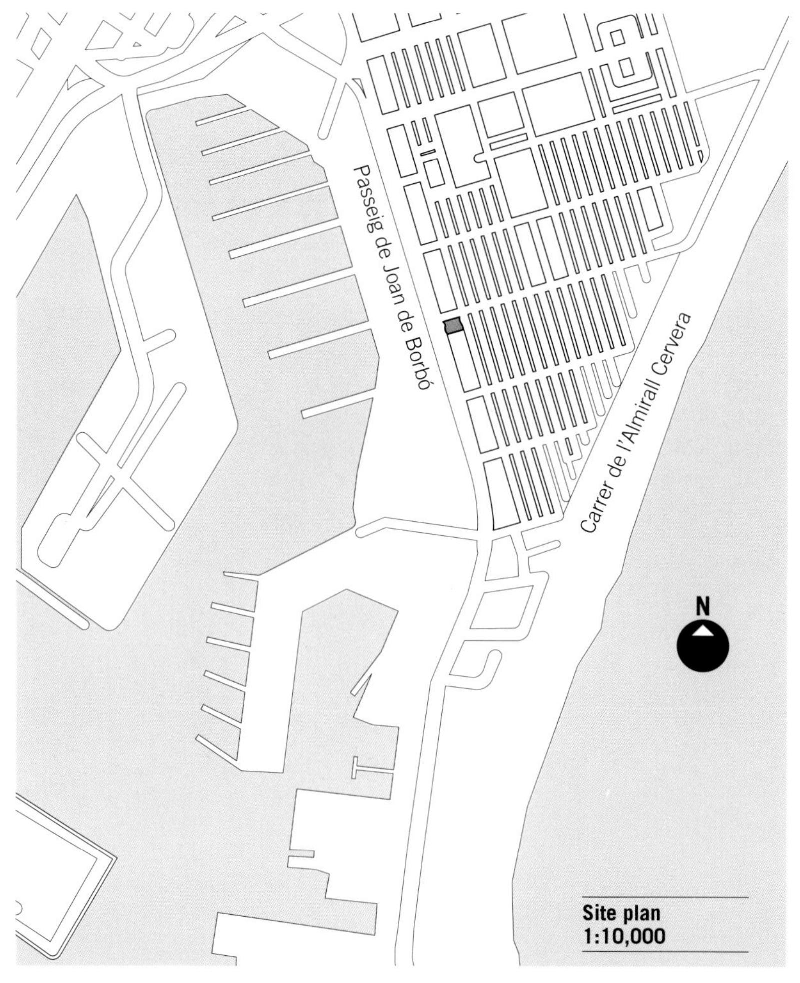

Site plan
1:10,000

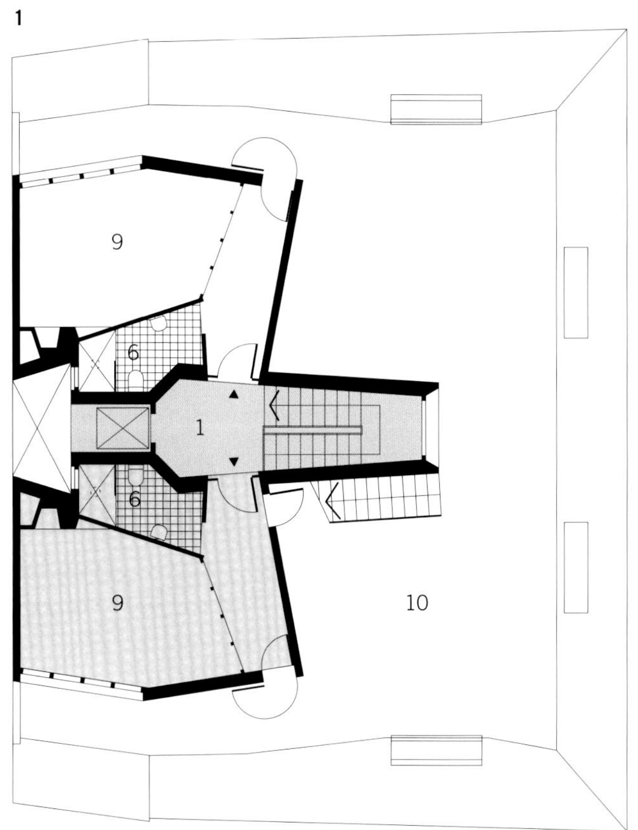

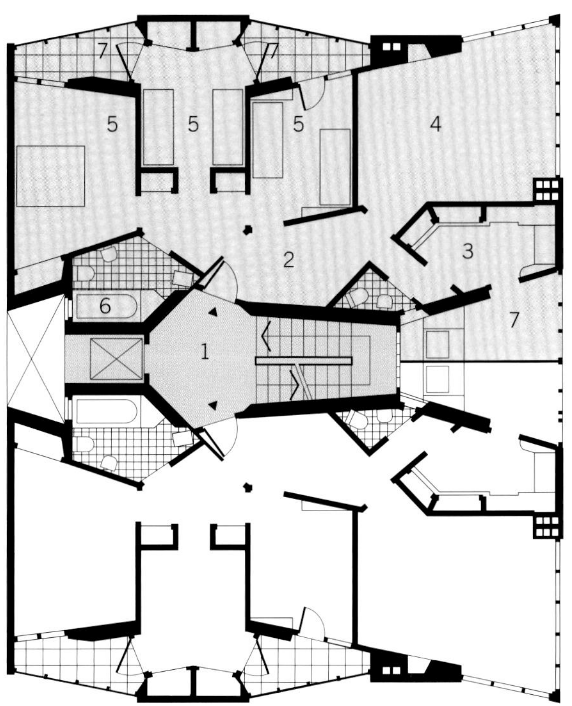

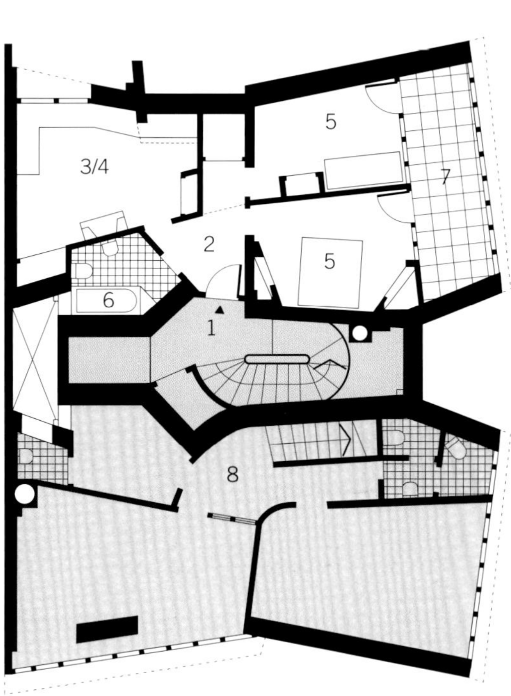

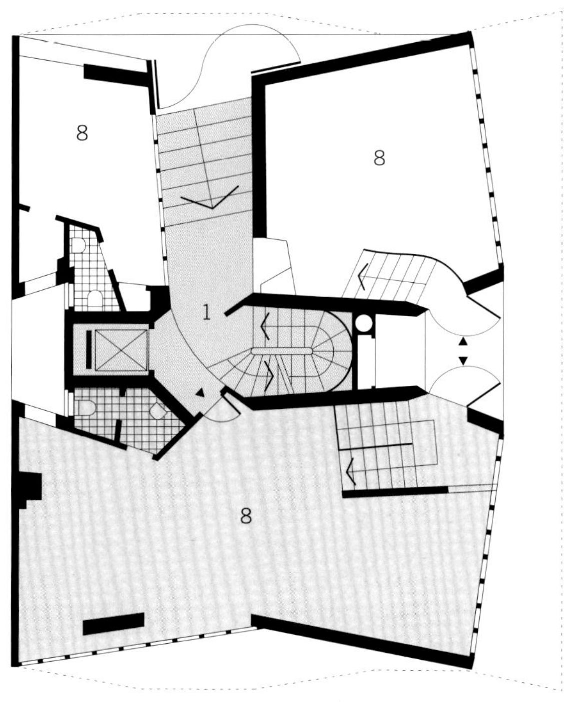

1 Attic floor plan 1:200

2 Typical upper-floor plan 1:200

3 Upper-ground-floor plan 1:200

4 Lower-ground-floor plan 1:200

1 Stairs and lift
2 Entrance/hall
3 Kitchen
4 Living
5 Bedroom
6 Bathroom
7 Loggia/terrace
8 Commercial/retail spaces
9 Studio/bedsitting room
10 Roof terrace

Workers' Housing

Giancarlo De Carlo, 1919–2005

Baveno, Italy; 1950–53

De Carlo's first independent project, which he won in competition in 1950, was a block of 50 workers' apartments at Sesto San Giovanni, on the outskirts of Milan. The design showed a familiar, logical, rational approach to planning. Between slightly larger apartments at either end, identical dwellings were organized in a linear block with access balconies on the north side, separated from the main block to reduce disturbance and noise. Private balconies were located on the south side, with views out to the surrounding landscape. De Carlo's aim had been to provide the families with the best possible spaces and the maximum possible degree of privacy. Having completed this project, however, and witnessed how the residents occupied the flats, De Carlo changed his entire approach to housing design. Writing in *Casabella* in 1954 he observed that the views from the private balconies were obscured by laundry, and that people were sitting on the north-facing side where they could see their neighbours and watch passers-by. He concluded that social communication is as important as – if not more important than – orientation, greenery, light and privacy.

This questioning of a rational or logical approach – which had, to some extent, resulted in Modernism's typologies or systems developed out of form and structure – led De Carlo to focus on the idea of the city, or systems of organization.

This approach was first demonstrated in his project at Baveno, which grew out of a series of design studies done for a competition held by the FIE (Building Promotion Fund). The competition brief stipulated that residents were to be consulted before construction, which would imply fixed plans, and that the site location was to be determined by the developer, which would imply a flexible or typological approach. To deal with these contradictions, De Carlo developed a series of studies for a new typology, to be based on a series of design stages. The first stage was to identify the basic building type; the second, to develop that type as housing; the third stage was to be an investigation of the chosen site; and the fourth and final stage, the grouping of the new buildings on the site. The different types demonstrated how the basic unit could be modified and grouped in different ways. The resolution of the project at Baveno has two-storey masonry and timber buildings with pitched roofs. There are six clearly defined sections, with two flats per floor and a shared open staircase enclosed within the building volume. Each of the apartments has a living/dining room, two bedrooms, a kitchen and a bathroom.

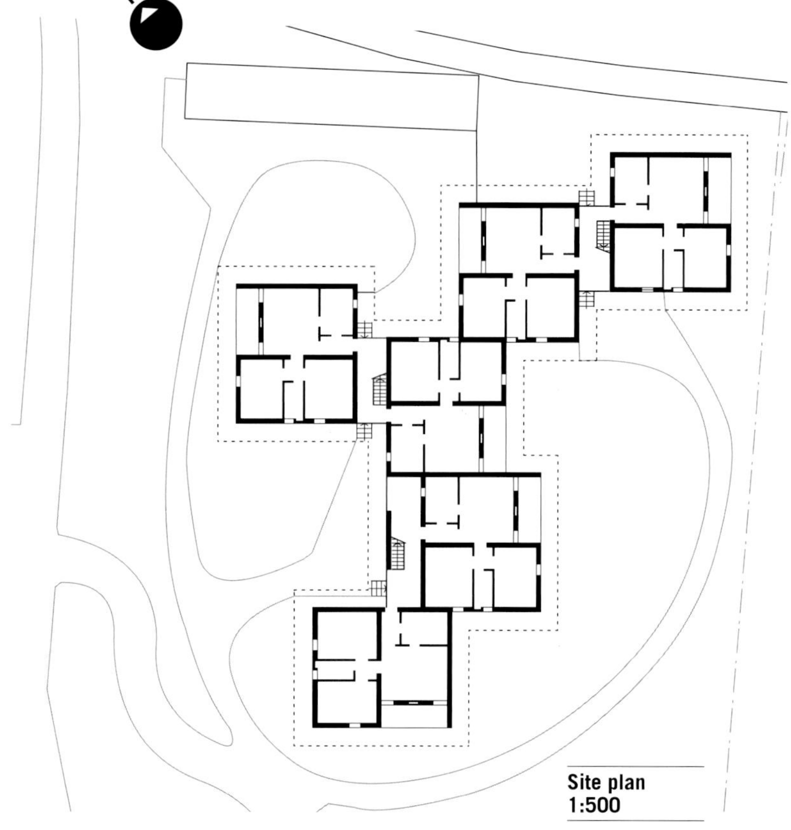

Site plan
1:500

1 Upper-floor plan 1:200

1 Shared circulation
2 Entrance hall
3 Kitchen
4 Living room
5 Balcony
6 Bedroom
7 Bathroom

2 West elevation 1:200

1

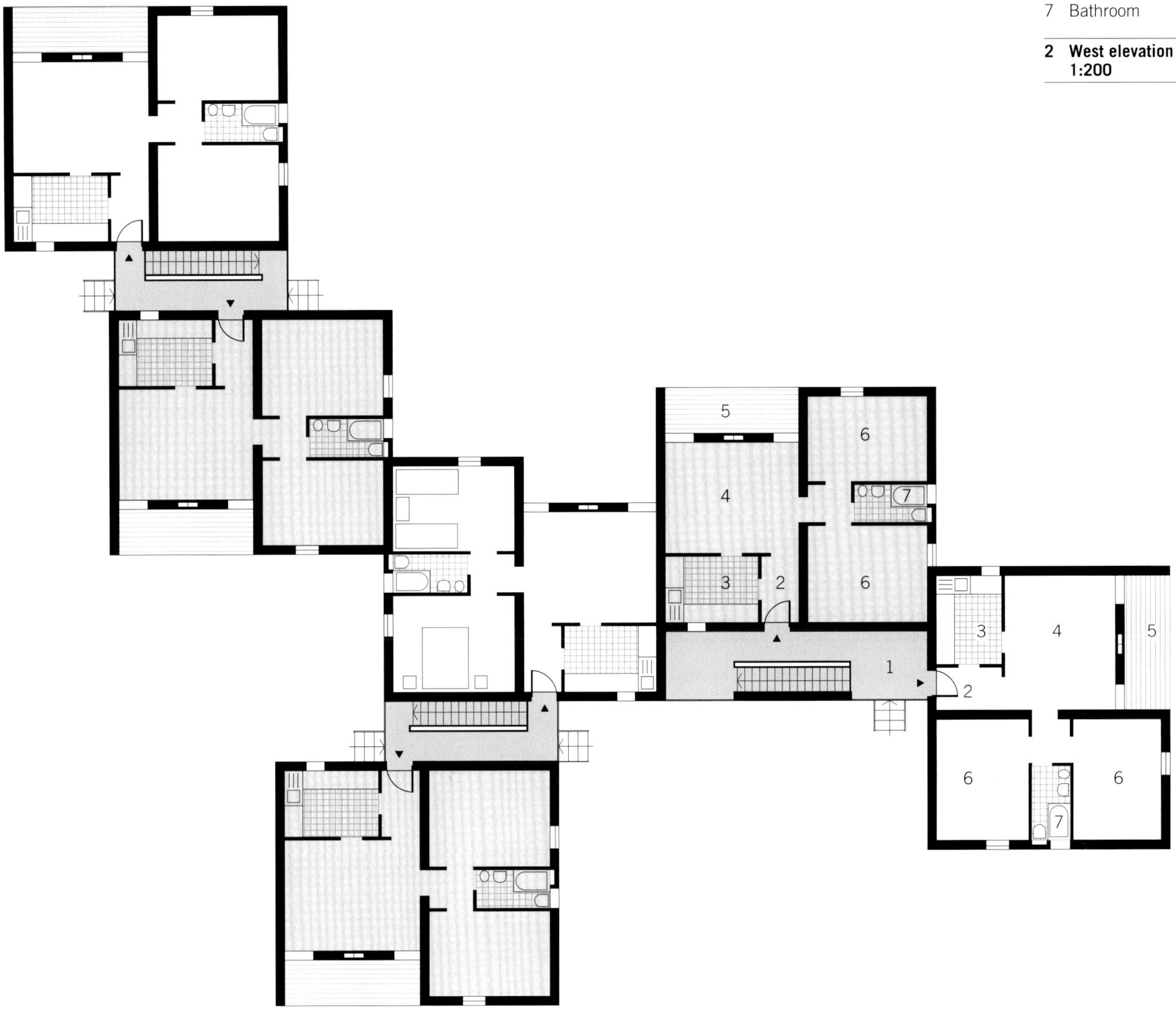

2

860–880 Lake Shore Drive

Ludwig Mies van der Rohe, 1886–1969

Chicago, Illinois, USA; 1951

'The effect of windows going right down to the floor level in a flat at this great height is magnificent and startling.' This caption, to an interior photograph in Frederick Gibberd's *Modern Flats*, published in 1958, makes clear the impact that these two 26-storey steel-and-glass towers at 860–880 Lake Shore Drive must have had in the 1950s. The towers are famous for their construction, a seemingly effortless expression of a precisely dimensioned and detailed steel-frame and glazing system – an architectural language of a new generation of skyscrapers that was to be developed during the next two decades, primarily for office buildings. Independent of the topology of the site, the triangular plot and the shoreline of Lake Michigan, the two identical rectangular towers stand 26 storeys high at right angles to each other, an uncompromising demonstration of the best of International Modernism.

Although identical from the outside in dimension, form and construction the plans inside the two towers are not the same. Both are based on the same starting point, with a pair of centrally placed stair and lift shafts and a single central access corridor. Then the kitchens, bathrooms and cupboards are arranged in the centre with the entrance halls, leaving the perimeter for the living spaces with the benefit of better daylighting levels and views out. Each floor of the north tower contains eight two-roomed flats (approximately 66 square metres/700 square feet), and the south tower has just four five-roomed flats (approximately 133 square metres/1,400 square feet) per floor. The lower storeys, including two basement levels, provide individual storage spaces, car parking and the shared spaces of a sitting room, laundries and deep freeze. Originally the flats were designed to be more 'open plan': the spaces similarly arranged, but with only minimal partitioning to the kitchen and to enclose the bathroom. The plans, however, were redesigned to suit the developer's preference for a more conventional approach to the layout.

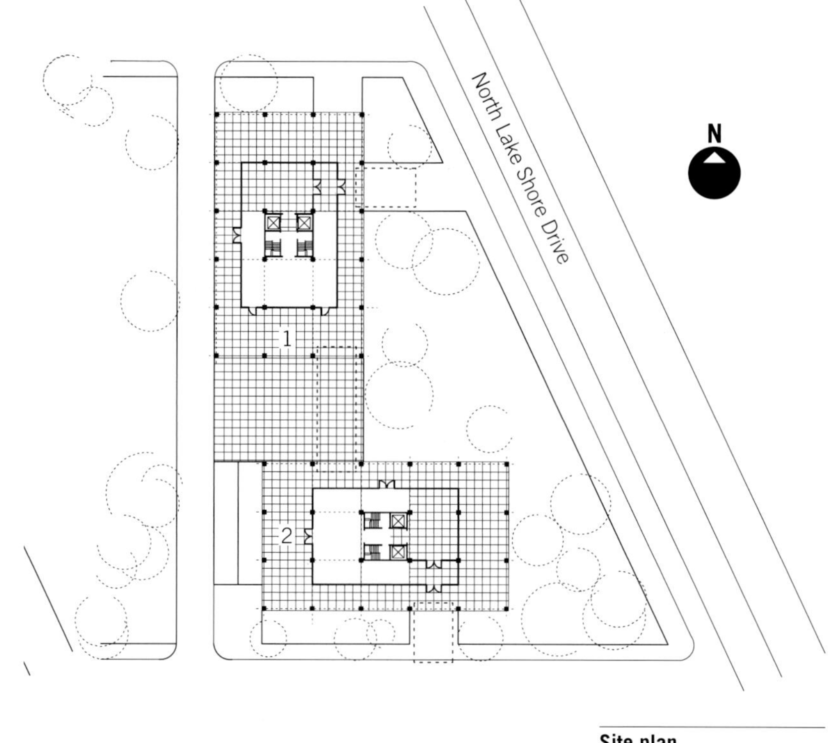

Site plan
1:1,000

1 North building
2 South building

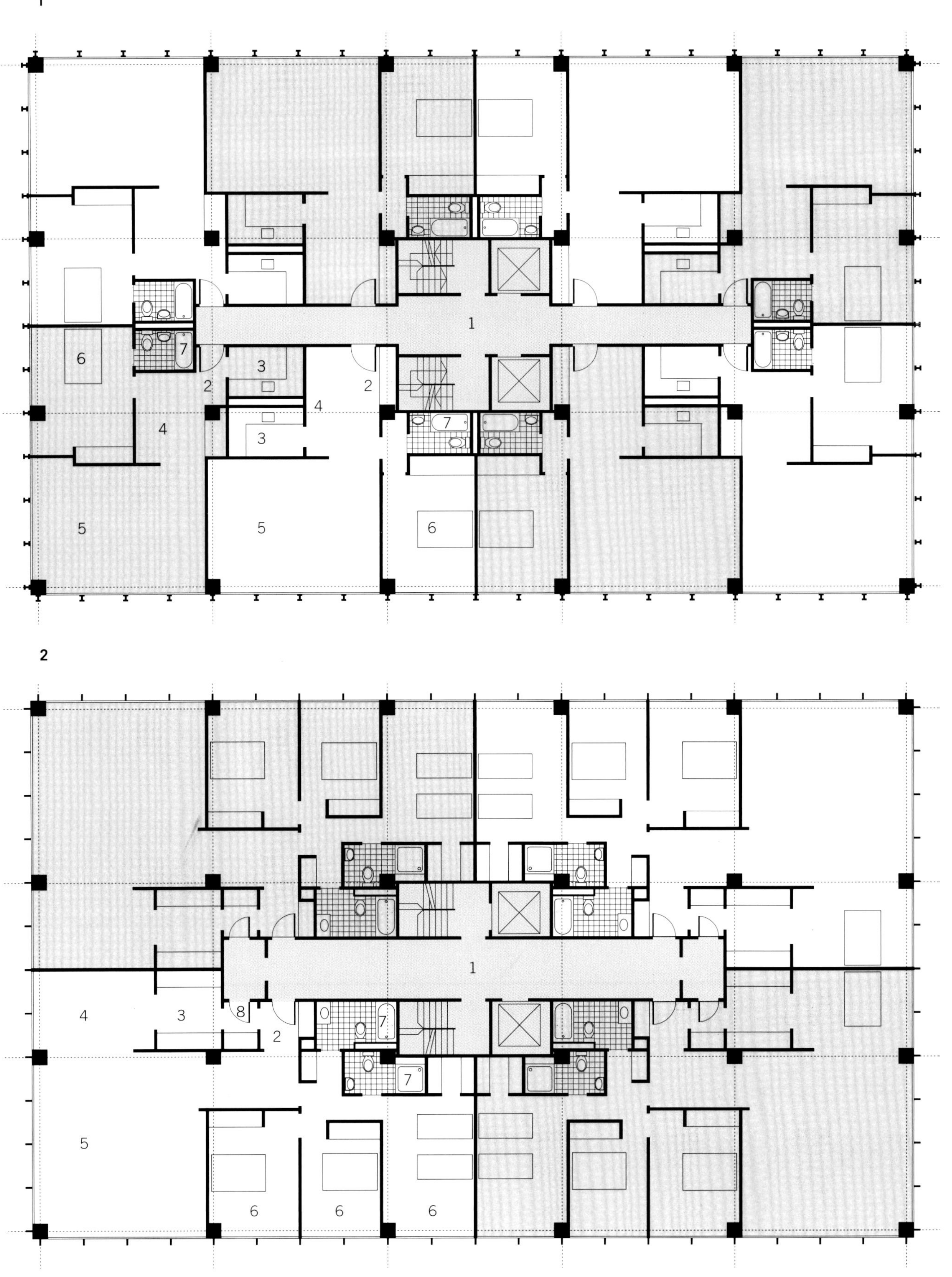

1 North building typical floor plan 1:200

2 South building typical floor plan 1:200

1 Access corridor, stairs and lifts
2 Entrance/hall
3 Kitchen
4 Dining space
5 Living room
6 Bedroom
7 Bathroom
8 Service hall

Price Tower

Frank Lloyd Wright, 1867–1959

Bartlesville, Oklahoma, USA; 1956

At the time of Price Tower's construction, discussion in the architectural press focused on Wright's theories of tall buildings and their relationship to the urban landscape. Wright's earlier projects for tall buildings – the unbuilt St Mark's Tower in New York (1929), the Chicago Towers (1930) and Broadacre City (1934) – were all based on a central structural core supporting cantilevered floor slabs. In a book published to commemorate the construction of Price Tower, Wright used the metaphor of a tree: in order to survive and blossom, unlike the densely packed towers of other American cities the tower of the future needed to stand free from the 'forest', away from other tall buildings. Accordingly the Bartlesville tower stands isolated, overlooking the low-lying city and the Oklahoma prairie beyond.

Price Tower claimed to be one of the first projects to include both residential accommodation and office space. Within a roughly square 'pinwheel' plan, each floor has a duplex apartment in one quadrant and offices in the other three. The apartments have living and kitchen spaces on their lower floors and bedrooms and bathroom on their upper, mezzanine, levels where there are timber shutters to close off the sleeping area or to open it out onto the living space below. The planning is based on a diamond shape, with 120- and 60-degree internal angles which Wright claimed were more easily suited to the arrangement of spaces. As a consequence, the fitted furniture and partitioning all had to be specially designed and made. Services and environmental controls were highly developed. The concrete fins that house the 'self-operated' elevators also contained pipework and ducts that fed air-conditioning plenums. Glazed external walls on two sides have tinted glass and external vertical louvres that provide shading from the sun and protection from heavy rain and high winds. As well as its contribution to the engineering and design development of tall buildings generally – and especially the lightness of its structure, which made it economical to build – Wright made further claims for Price Tower's contribution to modern thinking: 'the tower affords privacy, safety and beauty.'

At street level, the tower sits on a 140 x 150-metre (460 x 490-foot) corner lot with separate access and covered parking for the offices and the dwellings. Double-height entrance spaces extend beyond the tower to encompass a caretaker's flat and public service company offices, which are all linked by planted roofs. The penthouse has a suite for the owner, Harold C. Price, and a canteen and external terraces for Price employees.

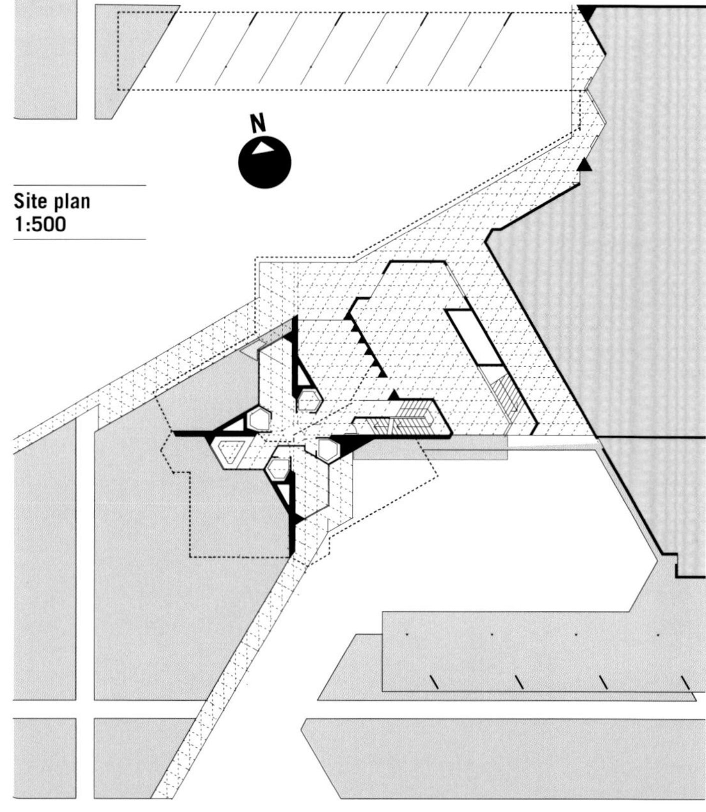

Site plan
1:500

Opposite left: Exterior

Opposite right: Interior of an apartment

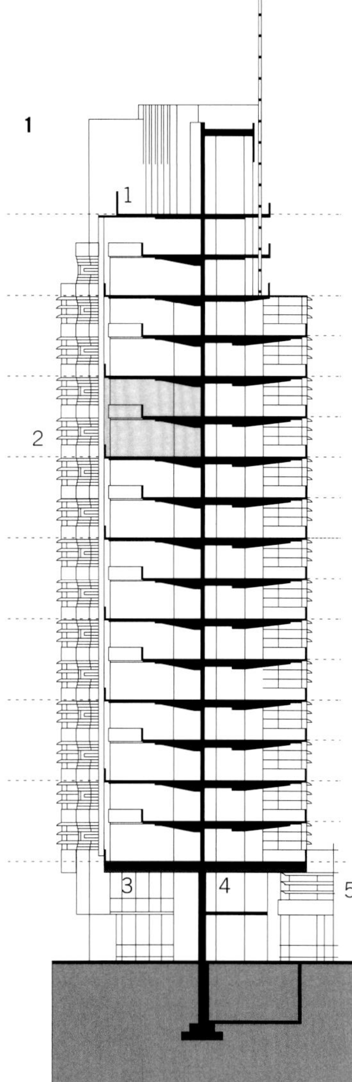

1 Section 1:500

1 Roof terrace
2 Duplex apartment
3 Double-height entrance to office
4 Entrance to apartments with mezzanine gallery
5 Two-storey building beyond with planted roofs

2 Penthouse floor plan 1:200

1 Lift
2 Roof terrace
3 Entrance lobby
4 Planting

3 Typical floor plan 1:200

4 Mezzanine floor plan 1:200

1 Kitchen
2 Entrance
3 Dining
4 Living
5 Lift
6 Offices
7 Void over living space
8 Bathroom
9 Bedroom

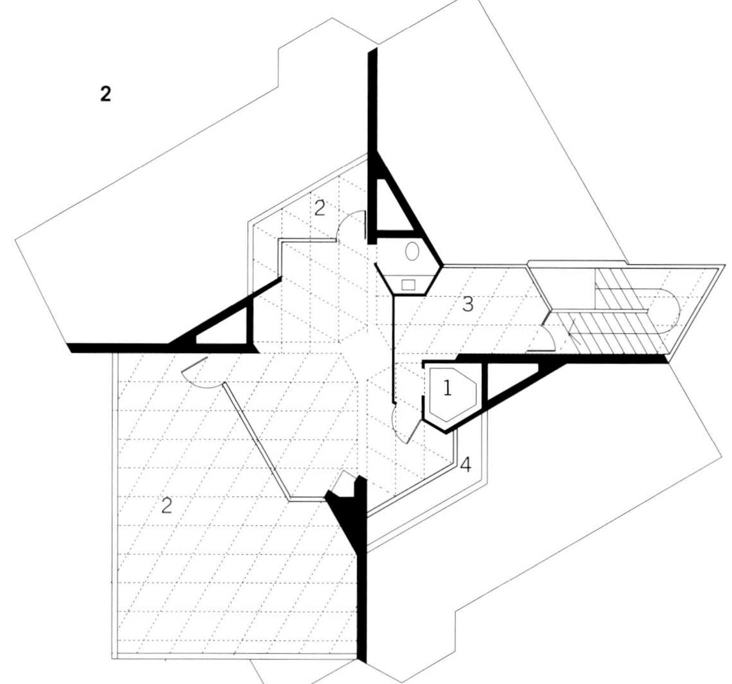

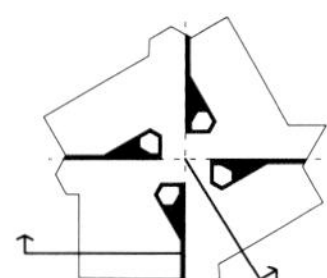

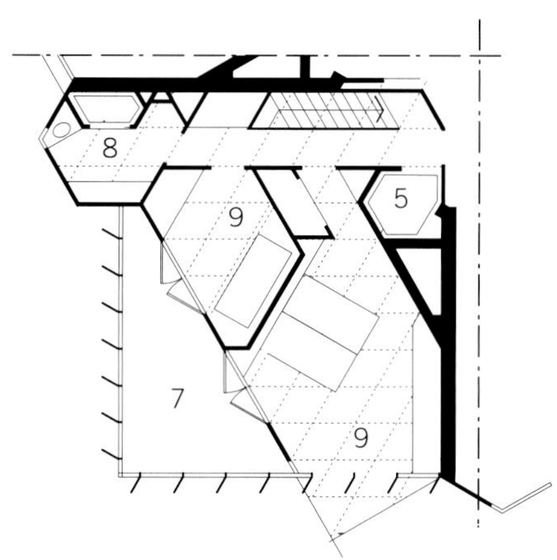

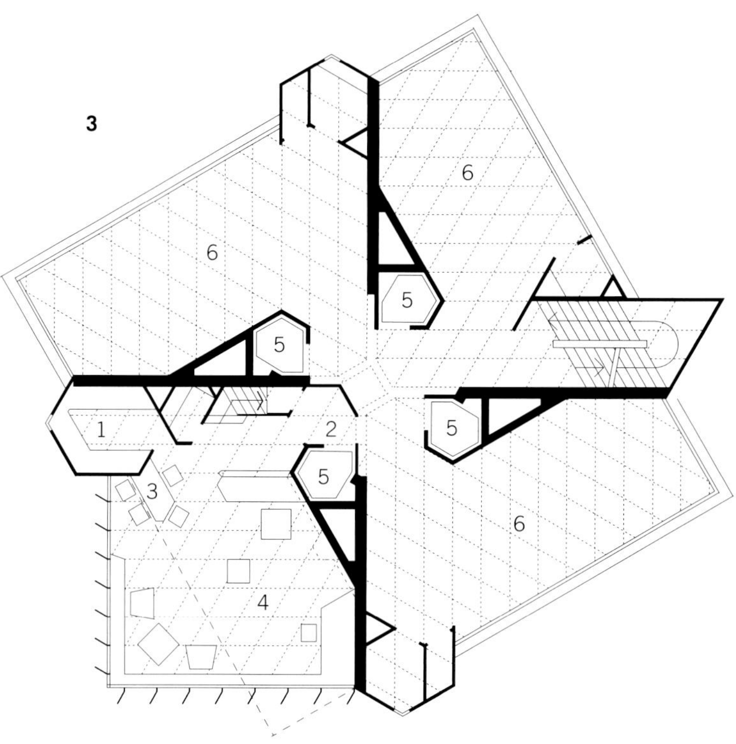

Keeling House

Denys Lasdun, 1914–2001

London, UK; 1958

The highly experimental nature of this project was justified during a period of slum clearance and rebuilding following wartime bomb damage. The small footprint of the 'cluster blocks' meant that families could be more efficiently and easily decanted than usual, as far more of the houses scheduled for demolition could be retained for longer. According to the *Architectural Review* in May 1960, the term 'cluster' also had roots in theoretical discourses referred to by geographer Kevin Lynch and the architects Alison and Peter Smithson.

Architects were already questioning the application of Modernism's universal principles and looking for ways to work more closely with existing urban forms. The 'grain' of the city was an important concept in architecture and town planning; at a broad scale it referred to the analysis of the mix and density of different elements that made up the urban fabric. In relation to grain, the idea of the 'cluster' referred to a particular focus – either individual buildings or a recognizable place in a particular part of a district. The Smithsons had referred to the cluster as the built form of a 'social unit' (*Architectural Review*, November 1957) – the identifiable neighbourhood, such as the working-class street.

The cluster blocks built in London's East End, Trevelyan House in Usk Street (1952) and Keeling House in Claredale Street, were seen as the solution to many contemporary housing problems. Firstly, they would reduce the overall mass of building: the apartments appeared as recognizable smaller units within the whole. Secondly, their open structure allowed views through, preserving a more open relationship with the surroundings. Thirdly, and perhaps most importantly, they were to provide much-improved privacy for the residents. The services in Keeling House are all arranged in the central vertical core, and bridges lead to the private living units. The units themselves, apart from eight studio apartments (bedsitting rooms) on one floor, are all maisonettes, paired in each of the four towers that cluster around the central core. Bridges, connecting with short access balconies on alternate floors, are each shared by two apartments and are only directly overlooked by windows to hallways, stairs and bathrooms. The overall arrangement of the plan allows maximum sunlight into each apartment during at least some part of the day. The ground floor contains the various plant rooms for heating and electric supply, as well as bicycle stores; 'platforms', located in the central core on the same level as the bedrooms, were provided for drying laundry.

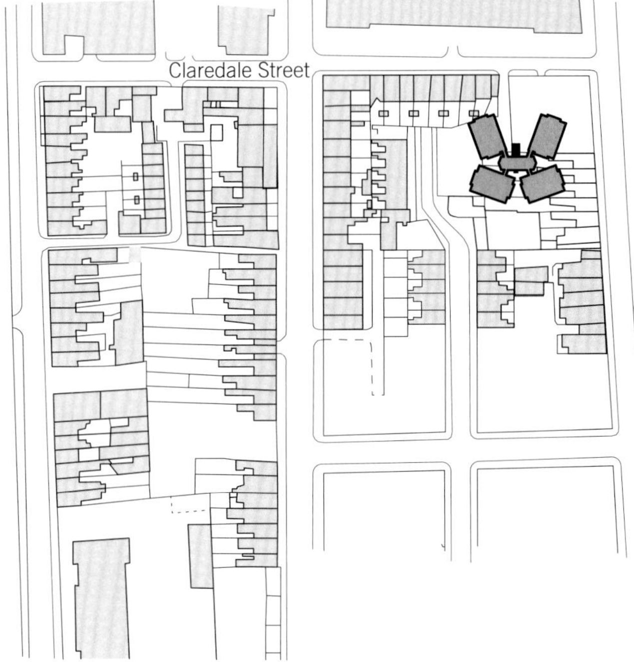

Site plan
1:2,500

1

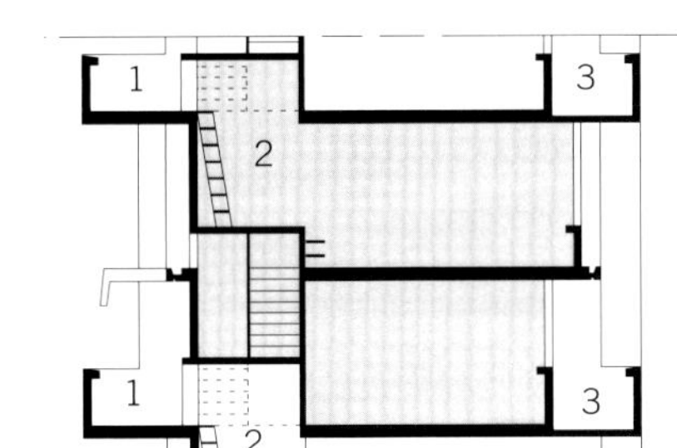

1 Part section 1:200

1 Public balcony
2 Fire escape
3 Private balcony

Plans of maisonettes 1:200

2 Upper level
3 Lower level

1 Access balcony
2 Entrance/hall
3 WC
4 Kitchen/dining
5 Living
6 Private balcony
7 Bathroom
8 Bedroom
9 Fire escape

2

Plans 1:500

4 Upper level of maisonettes, levels 2, 4, 7, 9, 11, 13, 15

5 Lower level of maisonettes, levels 1, 3, 6, 8, 10, 12, 14

6 Ground-floor level

1 Fuel stores
2 Boilers
3 Electricity substation
4 Tenants' store rooms
5 Main stair
6 Bin stores
7 Rubbish chutes
8 Bridge
9 Access gallery
10 Drying platform

3

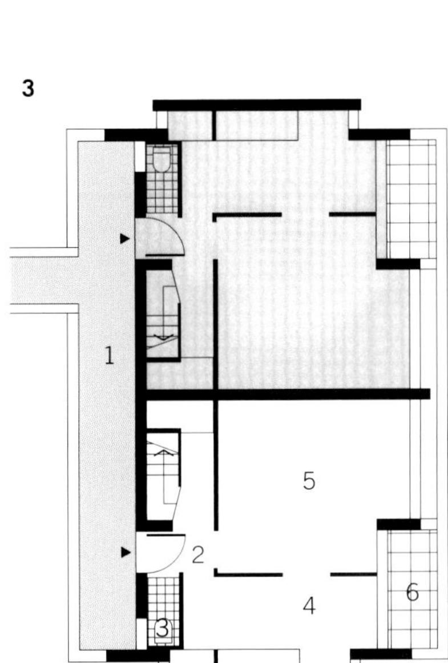

4

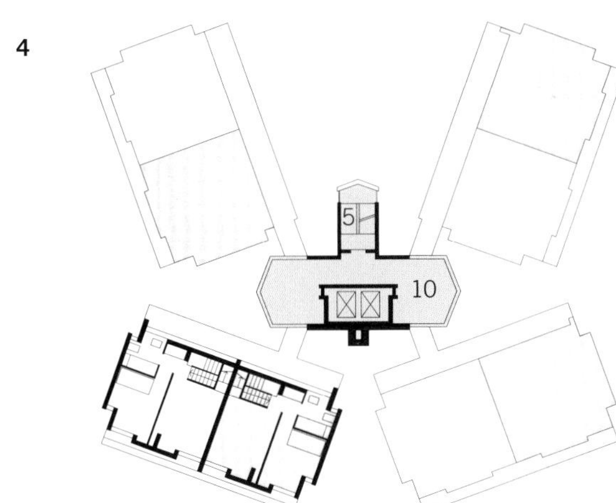

5

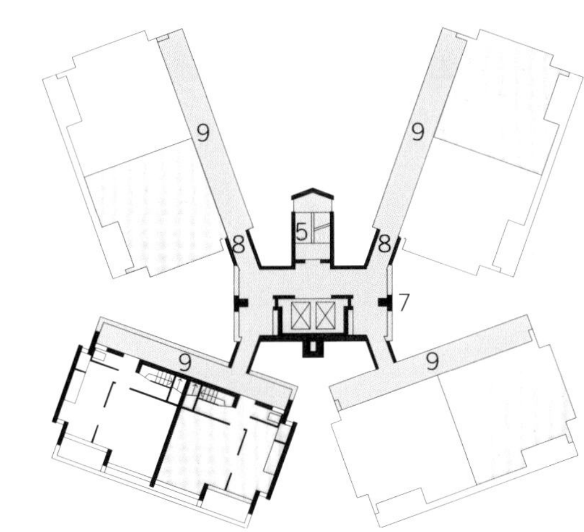

6

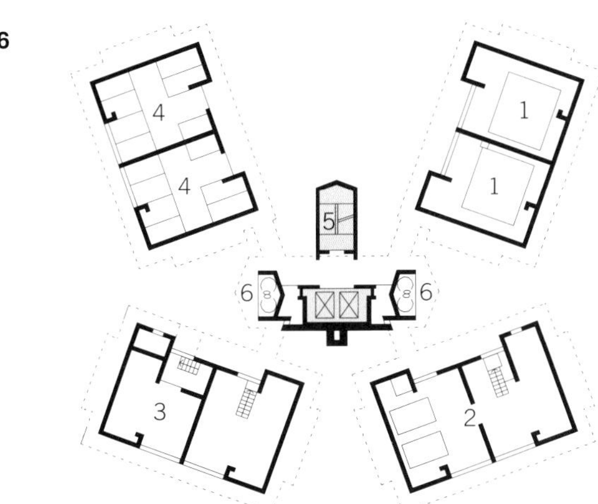

Harumi Apartments

Kunio Maekawa, 1905–86

Tokyo, Japan; 1958

Writing in 1958, Noboru Kawazoe claims that one of the most significant aspects of this building is the use of concrete. He likens it – because of its appearance of permanence – to a naturally occurring rock, thought of as part of the landscape and distinct from buildings, considered as objects placed within it. It is, of course, also much discussed in the context of the 'New Brutalists', a term adopted by young architects in Britain and described by the Smithsons as an 'ethic rather than an aesthetic' – that is, a way to re-think architectural design through abandoning stylistic and metaphorical constructs. More simply, it is associated with rough-cast concrete buildings, deriving its name from the French term '*béton brut*' used by Le Corbusier in reference to his Unité d'Habitation in Marseilles (see pages 82–85), built ten years earlier and clearly influential in this case. The Harumi building also distinguishes between its structure and infill elements – the former including, in this case, earthquake protection and particular attention to erosion from sea air and high winds. Maekawa defines this separately as the solid, permanent 'infrastructure', within which the more fragile partitioning systems that form the apartments are organized. The architect here conceives the building as a 'backdrop' – unlike fellow Japanese architect Kenzo Tange, who reportedly complained about the way hanging laundry spoils the façade of apartment buildings. Such things are here seen as signs of life and action, without which the building is nondescript.

The Harumi slab block is also notable as the first building of its type, a high-rise apartment house, to be funded by the Japan Housing Corporation. The design was approached as a typological exercise based on six or seven variations in possible basic plan-types, which were published alongside the final designs. Much of the initial decision-making was pragmatic and related to earthquake-proofing, weatherproofing (the site is close to the sea), height restrictions and keeping the number of lifts down to two. The decision to keep the circulation to a minimum by providing access corridors only on every third floor level led to the unusual arrangement of stairs perpendicular to the access gallery, organized with the vertical service ducts adjacent to the main structural walls. The effect is to leave the rest of the space open for more flexible planning. Each landing, either above or below the access gallery, is shared by two apartments, handed in pairs, with their separating wall made up of storage units. The final layout has two tatami rooms, one each side, with the WC, shower and storeroom along the stair wall separated by a long narrow corridor-like living and kitchen space. The apartments on the gallery level have both tatami rooms on the south side and the kitchen and a corridor-like living space on the north, access-gallery side. The access corridor is wide, intended by the architect to be used as a street with children playing and neighbours in conversation.

Opposite left: Exterior

Opposite right: Tatami room (right) and living space (left)

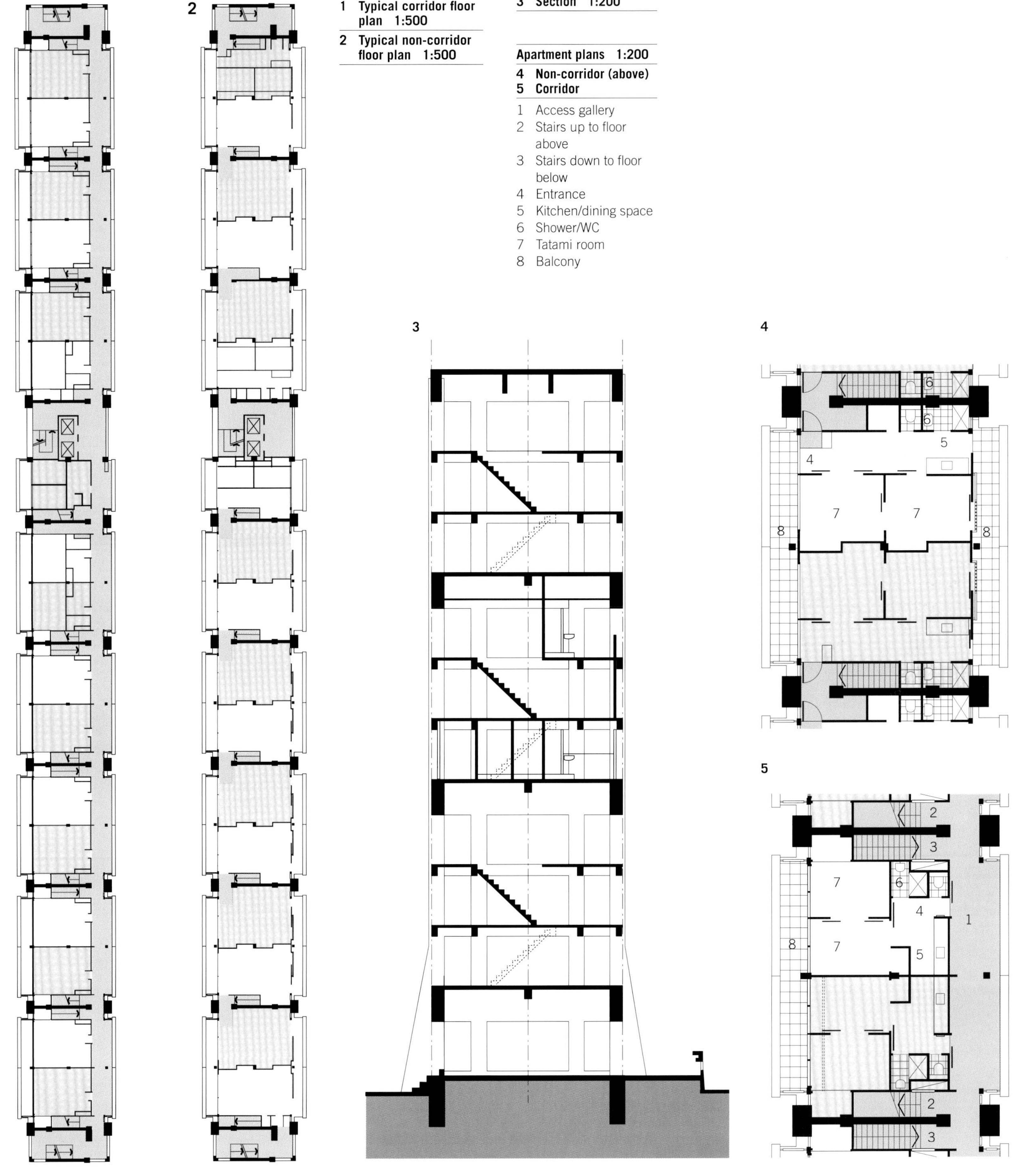

1 Typical corridor floor plan 1:500

2 Typical non-corridor floor plan 1:500

3 Section 1:200

Apartment plans 1:200

4 Non-corridor (above)
5 Corridor

1 Access gallery
2 Stairs up to floor above
3 Stairs down to floor below
4 Entrance
5 Kitchen/dining space
6 Shower/WC
7 Tatami room
8 Balcony

Beacon Street Apartments

The Stubbins Associates

Boston, Massachusetts, USA; 1959

This 17-storey block of 78 apartments on Beacon Street in Boston, built in 1959, belongs to the realm of op art, its façade a composition of faceted bays evoking an illusion of movement rather than the expected solidity of an apartment building. The projecting bays closely relate in form and dimension to the bay windows on the adjacent brownstone tenements. Built in Beacon Hill, one of the most long-established expensive residential districts in Boston, the apartment building provides high quality and very large living units. The architect, Hugh Stubbins Jr of The Stubbins Associates, is less well known for his residential work than for commercial projects such as the always recognizable Citicorp Center in New York with its 45-degree angled top, built in 1978, or the 1993 Yokohama Landmark Tower.

There are three vertical circulation cores in the Beacon Street building, thus reducing the need for shared corridors. These are located only on every third floor, which means that most landings serve just two apartments. The plans of three typical floors are then repeated. A regular column grid divides the plan into nine equal sections, with bedrooms – evenly spaced between the columns – on the street side facing south-east and the living spaces on the north-west façade with full-height glazing and balconies overlooking the Charles River. Sound reduction between bedrooms in adjacent flats is assured with double-wall construction and cork insulation. The kitchens and bathrooms are all located in the central part of the plan. On the floors without corridors, all the apartments occupy the full depth of the plan. Sizes of apartments vary by the number of bedrooms – one, two or three – and the number of structural bays – either one and a half or two – they occupy on the opposite side. On every third floor the access corridor runs in the centre, linking the three lift and stair cores and giving access to storage spaces and to two single-aspect flats and one duplex apartment. Some of the larger units have a second entrance door for servants and tradespeople, and one car space is provided for each flat in three levels of basement parking.

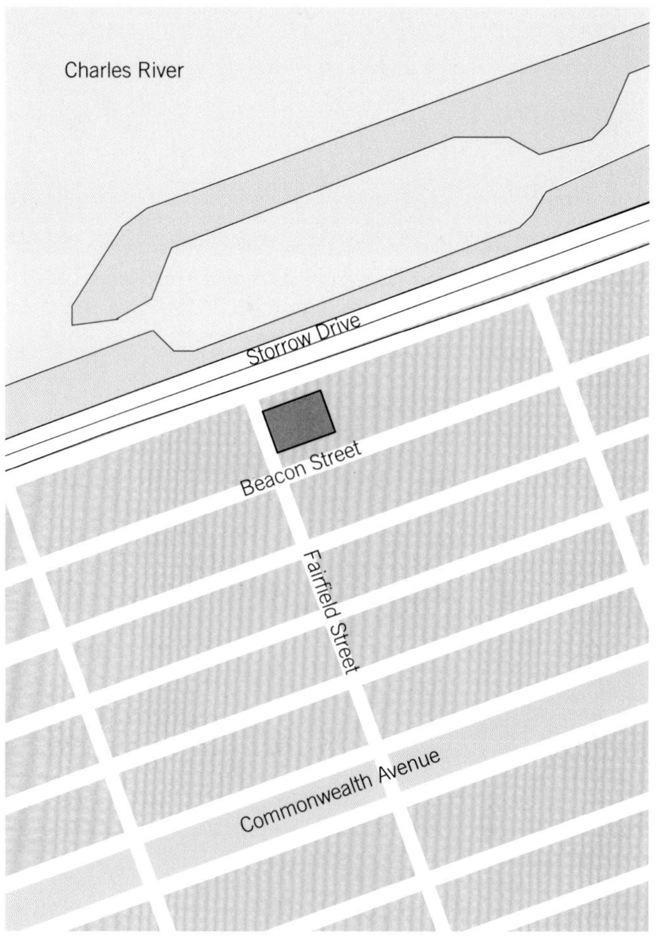

Site plan
1:5,000

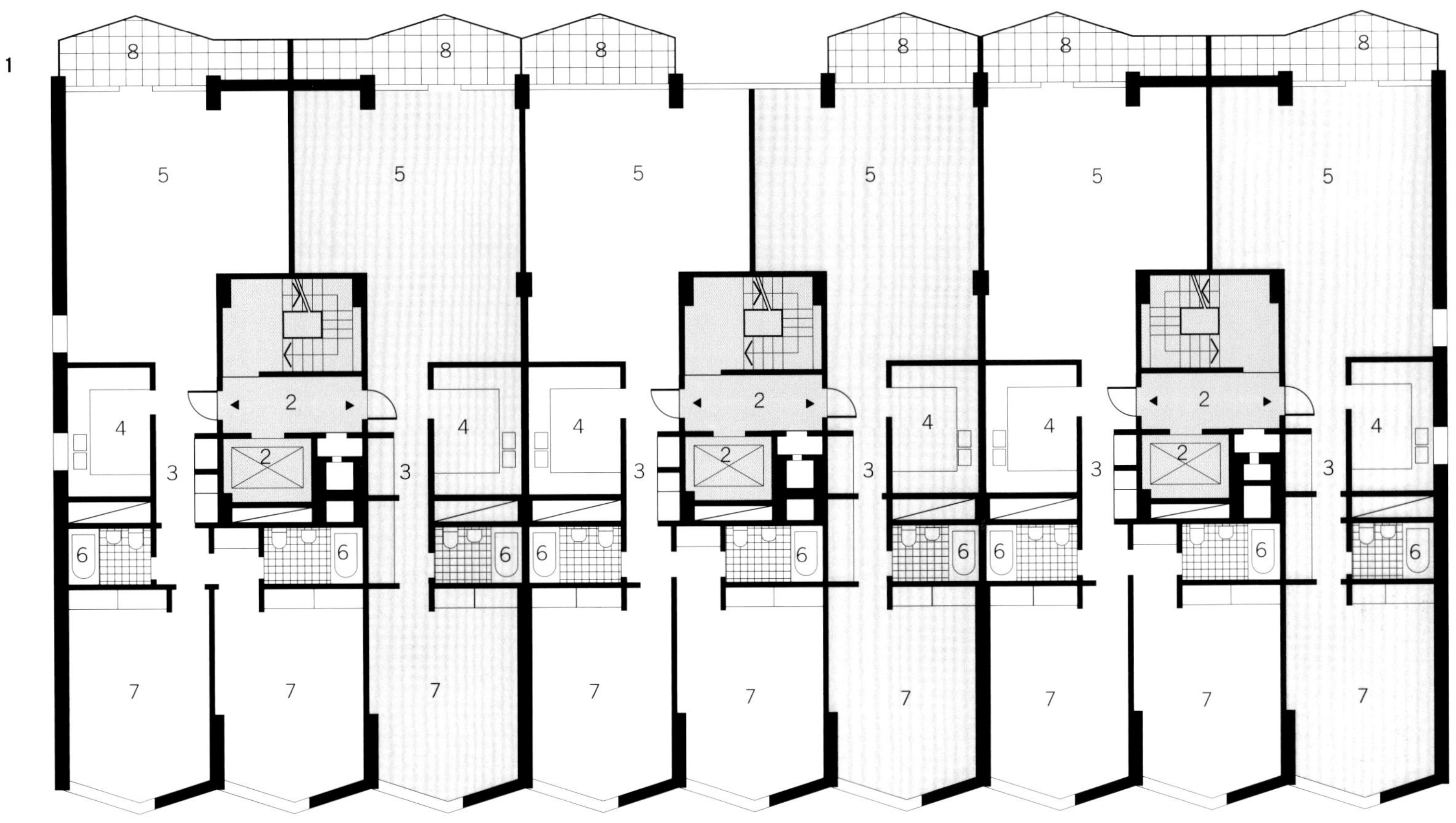

1 Typical above corridor floor plan 1:200

2 Typical corridor floor plan 1:200

1 Access corridor
2 Stairs and lifts
3 Entrance/hall
4 Kitchen
5 Living/dining
6 Bathroom
7 Bedroom
8 Balcony

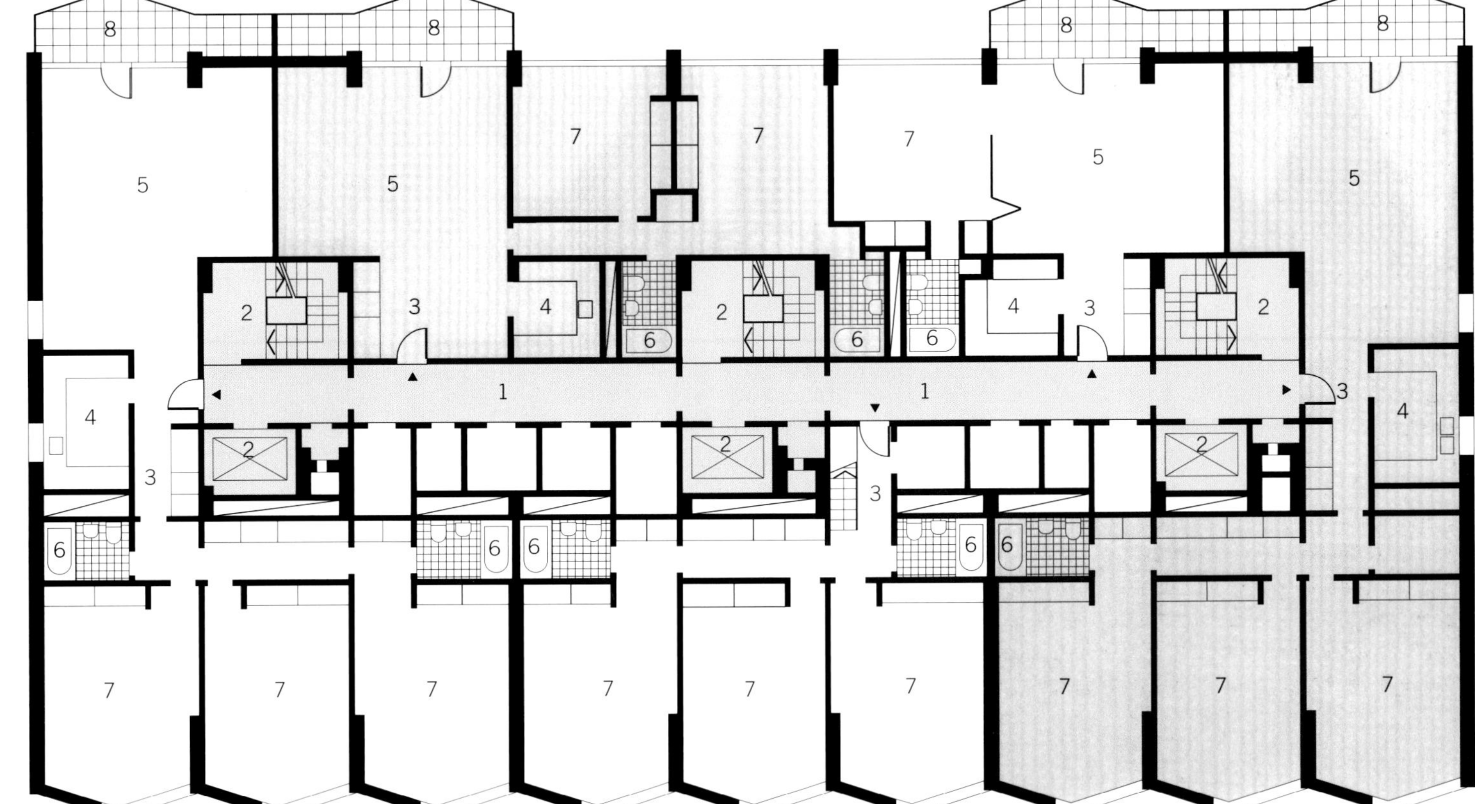

Hansaviertel Apartments

Alvar Aalto, 1898–1976

Berlin, Germany, 1957

Aalto's first 'high-rise' housing project was built as part of the Berlin International Building Exhibition of 1957 on a bomb-damaged site. The intention of the exhibition was to demonstrate the potential of a new kind of architecture that was modern rather than traditional, and was clearly different to the stripped classicism associated with Soviet style and the Nazi era. The buildings are laid out in a park-like setting with a range of different types, from single-storey houses to tower blocks. Established modern architects were commissioned: Le Corbusier, Gropius, Mies, Van den Broek en Bakema – most of them contributors to the Weissenhof project of 1927.

Aalto's project has an inventive plan that rotates the ten dwellings per floor in two linked blocks around a central stair and lift. A shift in plan between the two blocks and a slight shift at each balcony line breaks up the horizontality and the overall mass of the block. At ground level, the building is raised up on pilotis with ramps leading up to and through a breezeway between the two blocks. Laundry and drying rooms, along with store rooms, are included in the basement, and garbage chutes are located at every floor level next to the lifts.

The plan of the individual flats is based on the plan of a courtyard house with a multi-purpose living and circulation space in the centre. Very deep balconies, or loggias, extend the living space to the outside and are accessible from the adjacent main bedroom and dining room. Referred to as 'patios', the balconies were intended to create an 'intimate, private, atmosphere'. The Hansaviertel block is considered the most successful of Aalto's housing projects, particularly in terms of its internal planning and in bringing the quality of the individual dwelling to apartment design. Later projects were considered more successful in terms of pure form – particularly the Neue Vahr tower in Bremen, completed a year later, which further developed the shift in plan in a series of single-aspect, much smaller apartments with corridor access laid out in a fan-like arrangement.

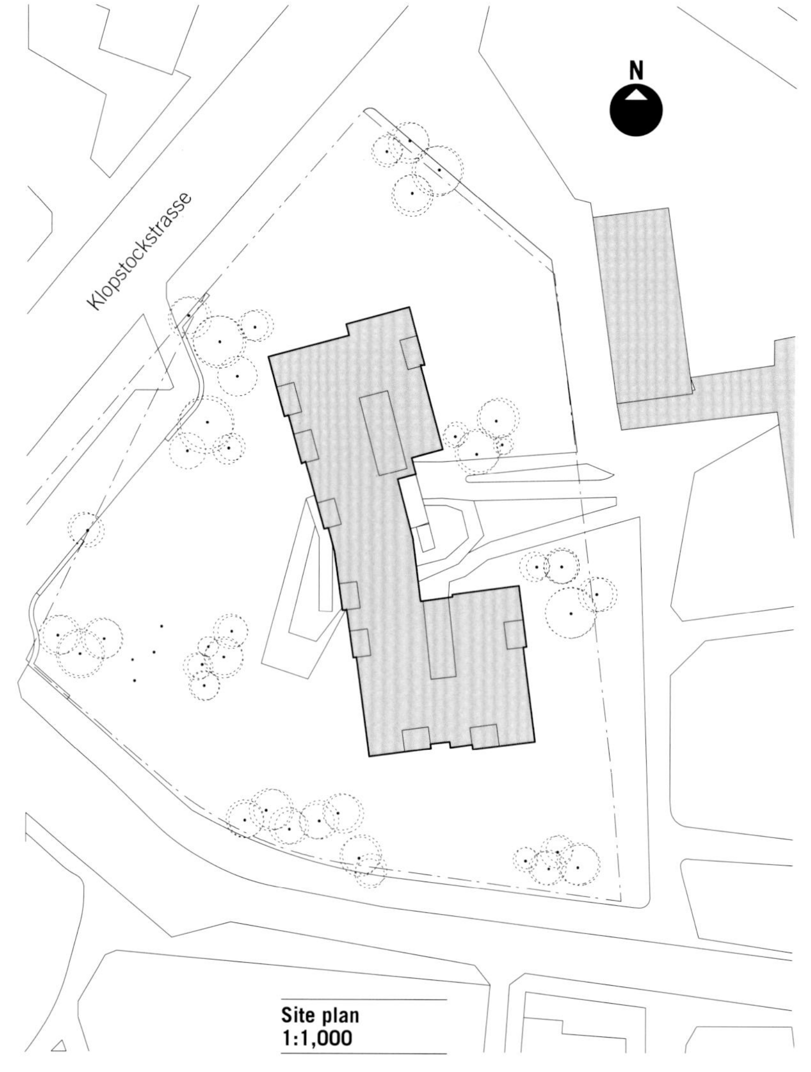

Site plan
1:1,000

1

2

1 Typical floor plan 1:500

1 Access stairs and lift
2 Three-bedroom flat
3 One-bedroom flat
4 Studio flat

2 Part typical floor plan 1:200

1 Access stairs and lift
2 Entrance/hall
3 Kitchen
4 Dining
5 Living room
6 Loggia
7 Bedroom
8 Bathroom

Far left: View from the south-west

Left: Interior of studio apartment

Hansaviertel Tower

Van den Broek en Bakema

Berlin, Germany; 1960

The bombed Hansa quarter of Berlin was rebuilt as part of the International Building Exhibition of 1957, which included the work of more than 50 architects including names such as Aalto (see pages 106–107), Gropius, Le Corbusier and Niemeyer. The overall project provided around 3,000 dwellings in a range of building types – tower blocks and slab blocks as well as low-rise terraced housing. The 15-storey high Van den Broek en Bakema tower, one of six on the site, is approximately square in plan – 20 x 24 metres (66 x 80 feet) – but, rather than a more usual symmetry, its markedly different elevations reflect a complexity in the plan and section.

The tower is largely made up of identical two-bedroom apartments, 6 metres (20 feet) wide, which extend the full depth of the block (20 metres/ 66 feet) from west to east. They comprise 48 of the 73 units in the block, and have a floor area of approximately 85 square metres (915 square feet) each. A stepped section – an effective, more compact, development of Corbusier's typical Unité section – connects living spaces on one side with bedrooms on the other. The apartments are identical, but the orientation alternates for each pair. The west and east elevations show the living spaces, one above the other with full-width loggias, with bedroom floors either directly above or directly below. Between the pairs of apartments, the half-depth of the plan adjacent to the access corridor is occupied by studio apartments – 24 in all, with a floor area of 33 square metres (360 square feet). These are single-aspect flats with kitchen alcoves off the living space. The lifts and stairs, which are located in the centre of the block, have six landings and an access corridor running north–south. At the northern end, a second stair provides additional means of escape and on the south end a double-height open sun terrace for shared use brings sunlight into the corridor and animates the elevation. At the lower levels there is a flat for a caretaker, as well as pram and bike stores; and, at roof level, a children's playground.

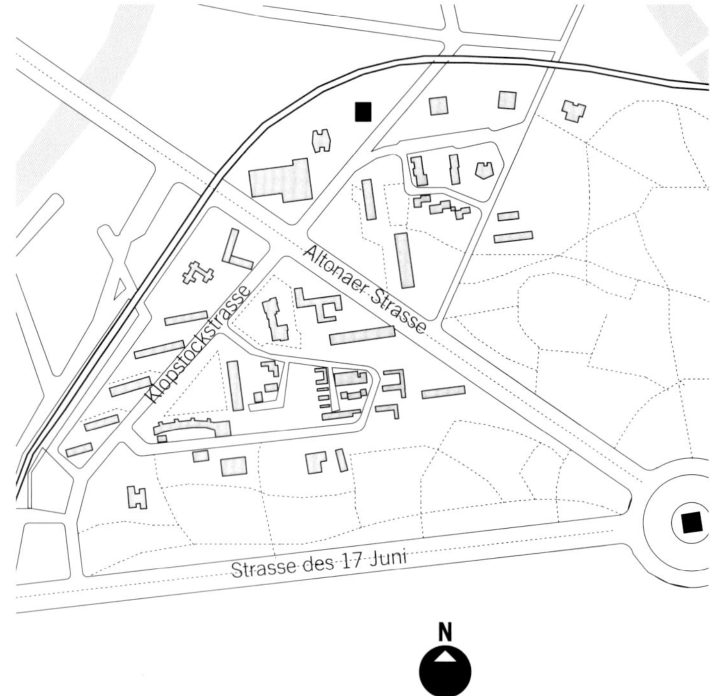

Site plan
1:10,000

1

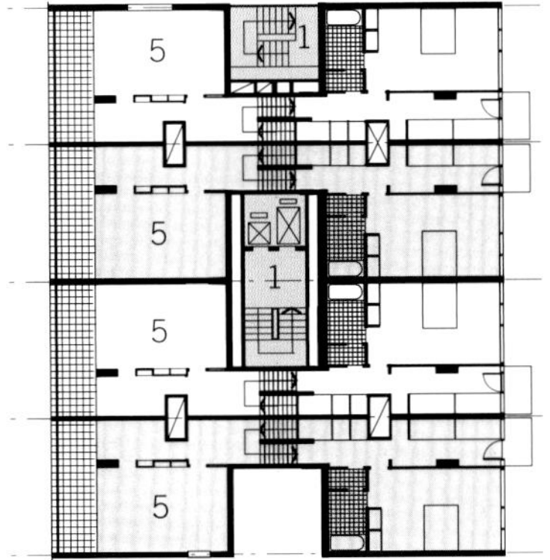

2

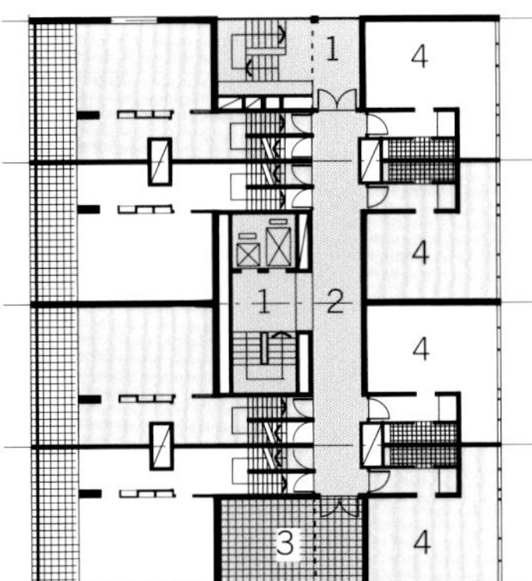

3

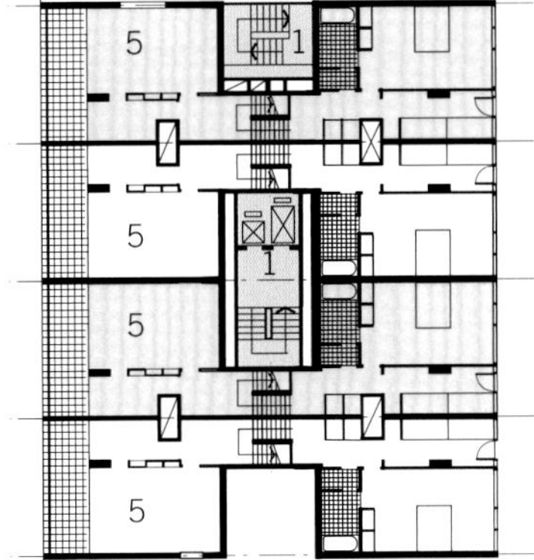

Plans at 1:500

1 Upper-level two-bedroom split-level flat

2 Middle/access-level studio flats

3 Lower-level two-bedroom split-level flat

1 Circulation/lifts/stairs
2 Access corridor
3 Double-height shared terrace
4 Studio flats
5 Two-bedroom split-level flats (upper level)

Part Plans 1:200

4 Split-level two-bedroom flat

5 Access level with studio flat (on right)

1 Access corridor
2 Shared terrace
3 Entrance/hall
4 Living/dining
5 Kitchen
6 Bathroom/WC
7 Store room
8 Bedroom
9 Balcony/loggia
10 Bedsitting room

4

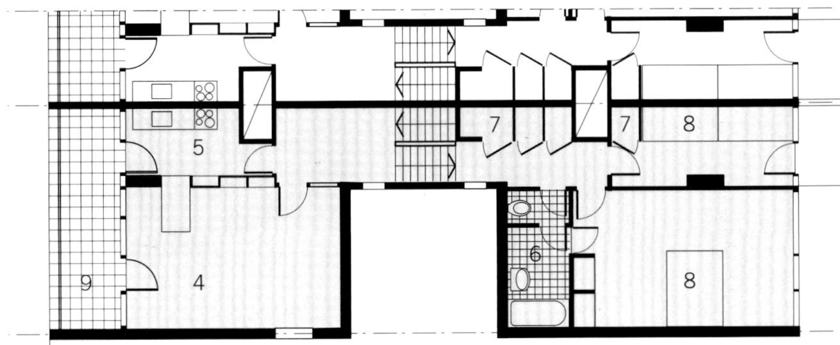

5

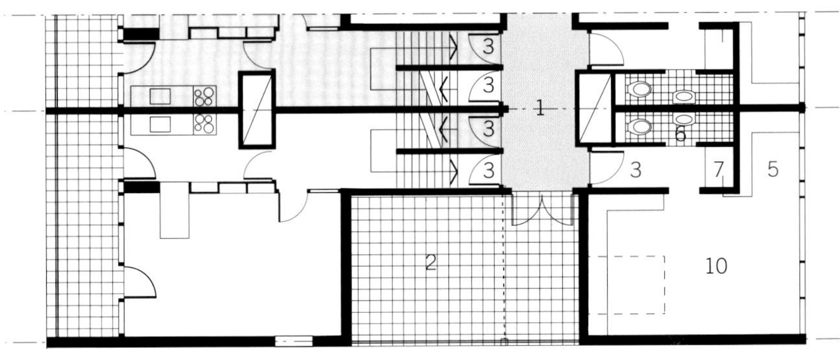

6 7 8

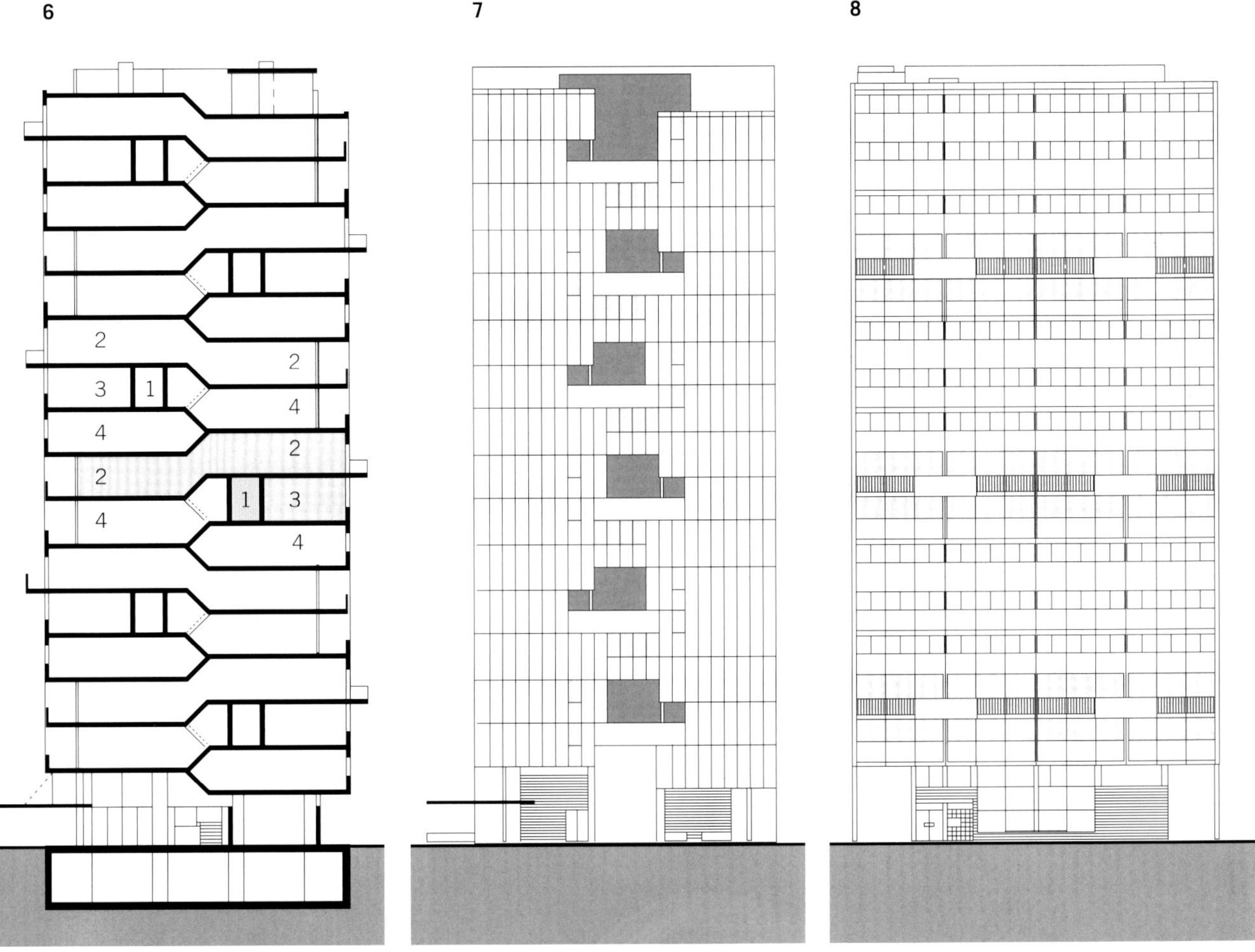

6 Section 1:500

1 Access corridor
2 Upper two-bedroom flat
3 Studio flat
4 Lower two-bedroom flat

7 South elevation 1:500

8 West elevation 1:500

Bellevue Bay Flats and Houses

Arne Jacobsen, 1902–71

Klampenborg, Denmark; 1961

The Bellevue Bay project juxtaposes two very different models for housing – one a slab block, the other single-storey atrium houses. Both have particularly deep plans and there are similarities in their approach to the organization of living spaces.

In the apartment building the flats extend the full depth of the block, with access stairs and lifts, located in the centre of the plan, serving two flats per landing. Within the flats, bathrooms, WCs and cupboards are located in the central, darkest parts of the plans and the living spaces are closer to the façades, with balconies on both sides to benefit from daylight and views. Other than an entrance hallway and a small lobby to the bedrooms, circulation space is a part of the living room. In the central part of the plan, where the living space is extended, it forms a 'fireside lounge'. This space, which is treated differently with unplastered white-painted brickwork walls, one of which incorporates a built-in open fireplace and log store, sits a step below the surrounding area. A fixed seating unit on one edge frames the space and acts as a balustrade to the change in level. Variations in the plans include the location of the kitchen either at the front or back of the plan, and the number of bedrooms. From the outside, the dark finish of the frames to the glazing and balcony dividing walls adds to the impression that they recede, emphasizing the horizontal elements of the scheme.

The courtyard houses have a similarly very deep plan. The entrance is set back beyond the garages and a courtyard garden. A wide hallway separates the bedrooms and bathroom, which are grouped around a separate corridor at the front of the house, from the kitchen and living rooms at the rear. Instead of the central 'fireside lounge' – the winter living space in the flats – the houses have a central courtyard that could be thought of as an outside, or summer, living room. A shared garden extends the full width of the plan beyond the living rooms.

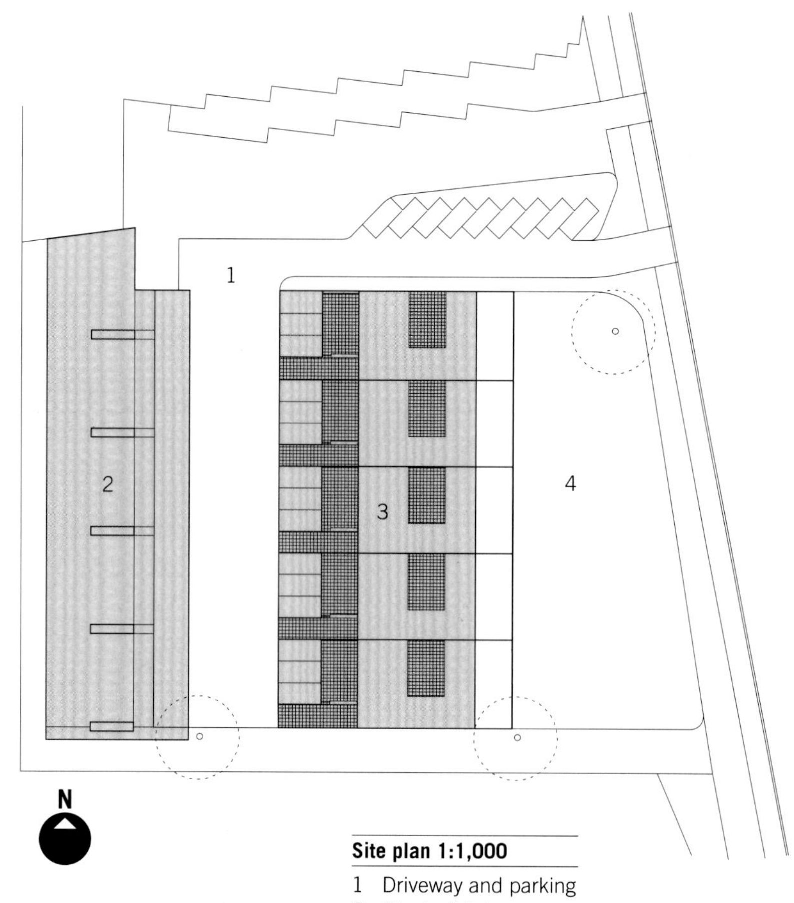

Site plan 1:1,000

1 Driveway and parking
2 Block of flats
3 Single storey courtyard houses
4 Shared garden

1

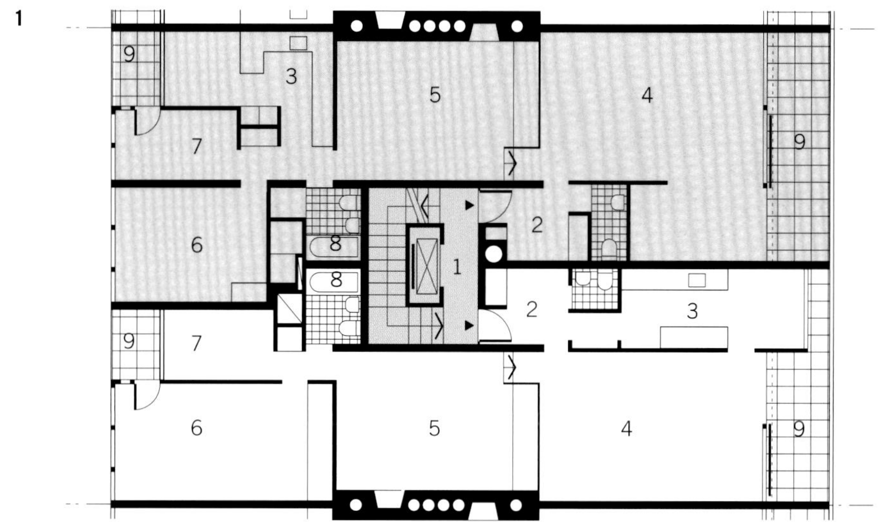

1 Plan of typical flats 1:200

1 Access stair and lift
2 Entrance/hall
3 Kitchen/dining
4 Living room
5 'Fireside' living room
6 Bedroom
7 Study/bedroom
8 Bathroom/WC
9 Balcony

2

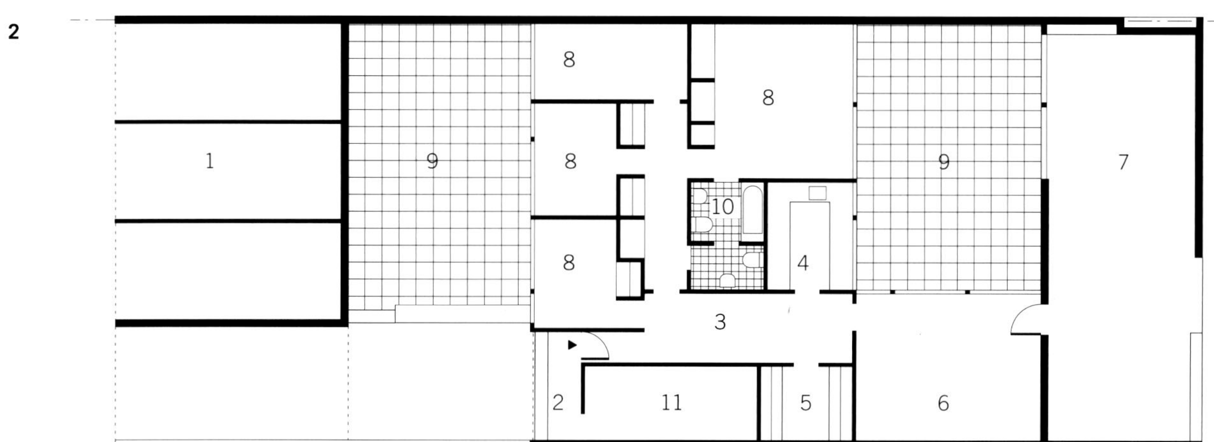

2 Plan of courtyard house 1:200

1 Parking
2 Entrance
3 Hallway
4 Kitchen
5 Cupboard
6 Dining
7 Living
8 Bedroom
9 Courtyard
10 Bathroom/WC
11 Store room

Halen Housing

Atelier 5

Berne, Switzerland; 1955–61

The terraced housing scheme at Halen by Erwin Fritz, Samuel Gerber, Rolf Hesterberg and Alfredo Pini, the founders of group practice Atelier 5, is one of the few residential projects to make a significant impact outside the field of housing design. Two things make it an important contribution to histories of architecture: one is the form of the estate; the other, the skilful development of the terraced house as a type. The form of the estate, intended to enhance the idea of place and therefore a sense of belonging and identity in the residents, uses traditional urban elements such as streets, squares and courtyards – recognizable features of a settlement. There are two basic terraced-house types: one 3.8 metres (12 feet 6 inches) wide with the stair perpendicular to the party walls and one 4.7 metres (15 feet 6 inches) wide with the stair parallel to the party walls; both are three storeys high. There are then several variations possible within each type, including, for example, additional bedrooms, a roof terrace, an atelier and a second bathroom.

On the sloping south-facing site the houses, 79 in total, are all orientated in the same way, perpendicular to the slope with gardens on the south side and their entrances facing north. Cars are parked on the boundary, and only pedestrian pathways pass between the terraces. At the centre, the space opens up to form a square with one side comprising commercial spaces for small shops, and a small group of studios and two-bedroom apartments. This scheme's success is directly attributable to the skilful handling of that perennial problem in housing design: the conflicting demands of privacy and community. The architects were particularly concerned, on such a high-density estate, to provide for both. To ensure adequate privacy for the occupants proximity is reduced to a minimum with the deep plan of the houses and the high walls that shelter the gardens, and with good acoustic separation ensured by the use of dense concrete and cavity party-wall construction. The buildings use a central-heating plant, and ownership is based on a cooperative model whereby each resident is a shareholder in the whole estate, including its roads, pathways and open spaces, and the swimming pool, laundry, caretaker's house and garages.

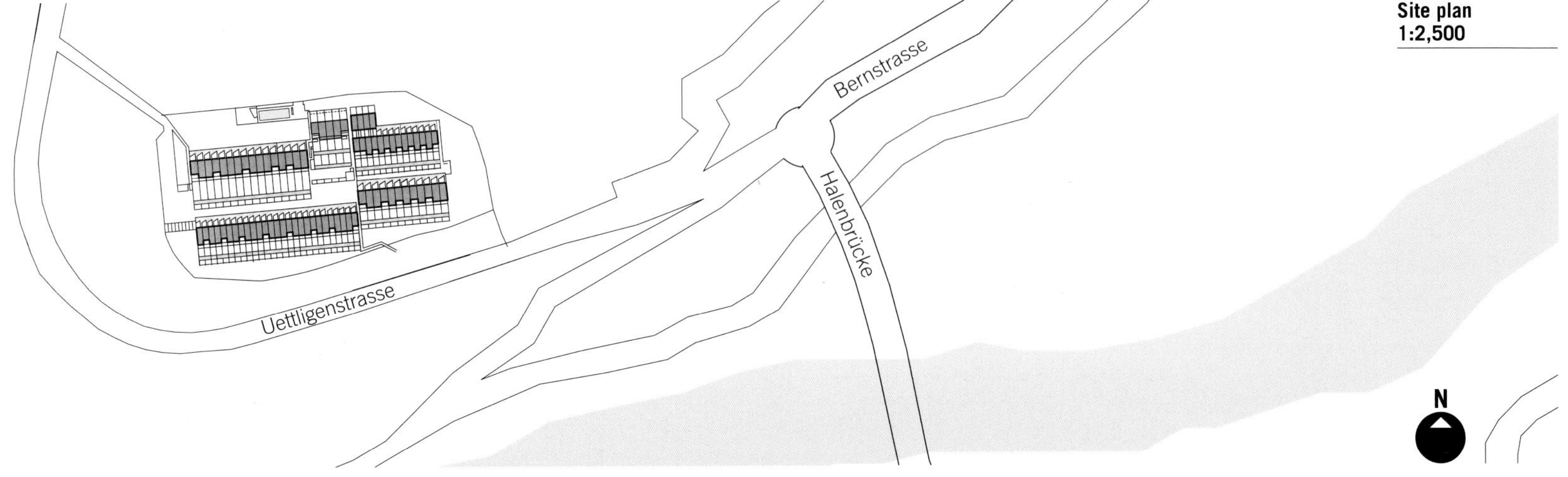

Site plan
1:2,500

House type 380 plans 1:200

1 Upper level

2 Entrance level

3 Lower/garden level

4 Alternative garden level

5 Section

1 Covered walkway
2 Pathway
3 Store room
4 Patio
5 Entrance/hall
6 Bathroom/WC
7 Kitchen
8 Living/dining
9 Loggia
10 Cupboards
11 Study
12 Bedroom
13 Balcony
14 Sun terrace
15 Cellar
16 Service route
17 Garden terrace

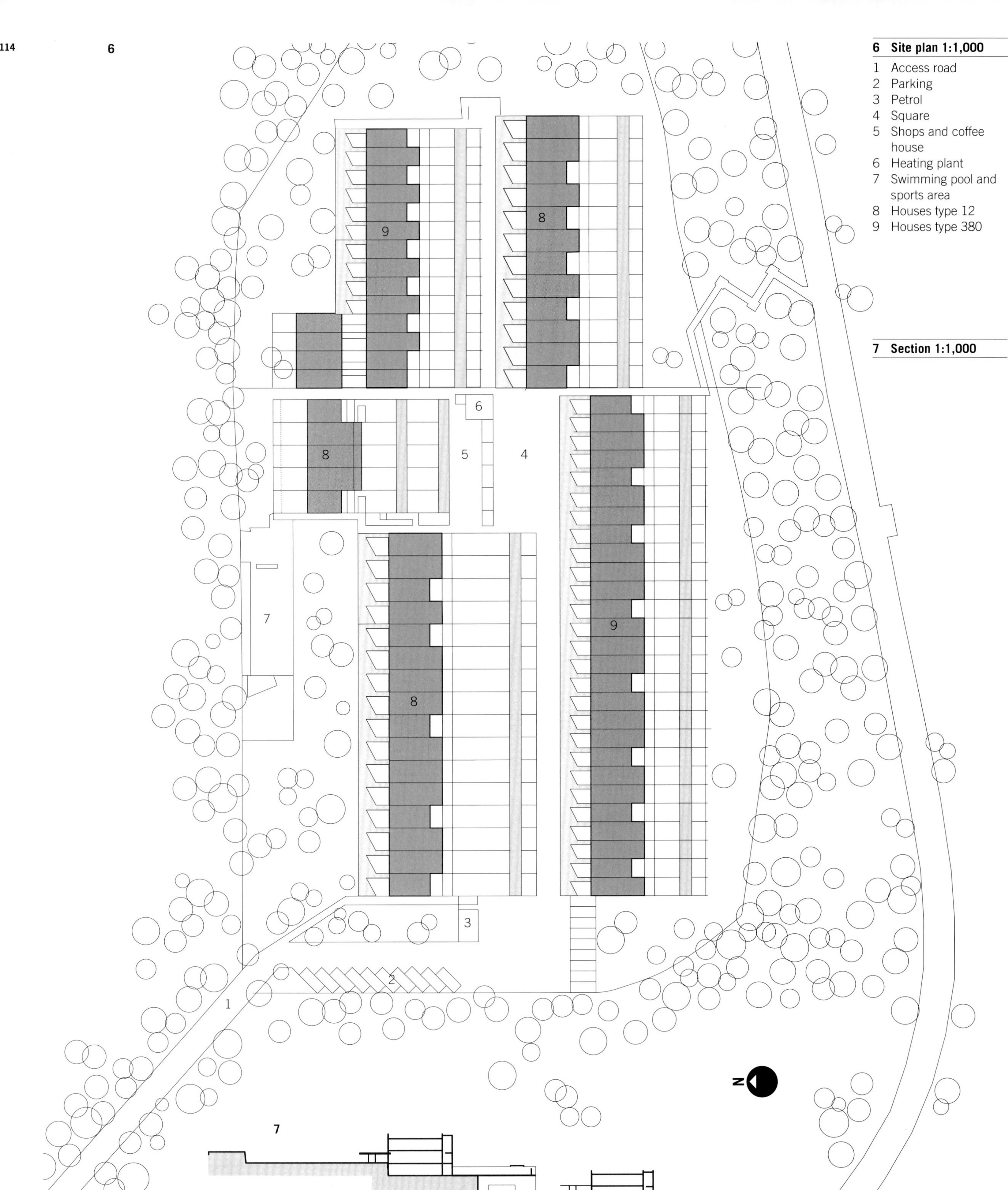

6 Site plan 1:1,000

1 Access road
2 Parking
3 Petrol
4 Square
5 Shops and coffee house
6 Heating plant
7 Swimming pool and sports area
8 Houses type 12
9 Houses type 380

7 Section 1:1,000

House type 12 plans and section 1:200

8 Alternative upper level

9 Upper level

10 Entrance level

11 Lower/garden level

1 Covered walkway
2 Pathway
3 Store room
4 Patio
5 Entrance/hall
6 Bathroom/WC
7 Kitchen
8 Living/dining
9 Loggia
10 Cupboards
11 Study
12 Bedroom
13 Balcony
14 Sun terrace
15 Cellar
16 Service route
17 Garden terrace

12 Section 1:200

8

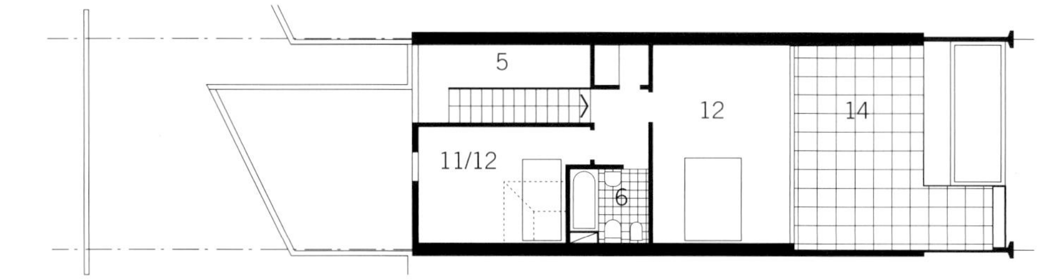

9

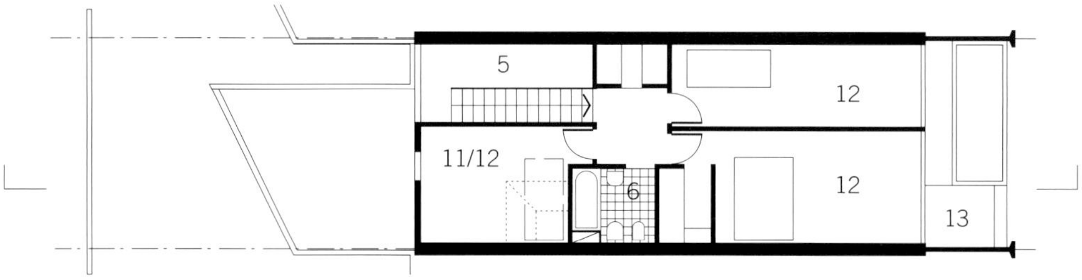

10

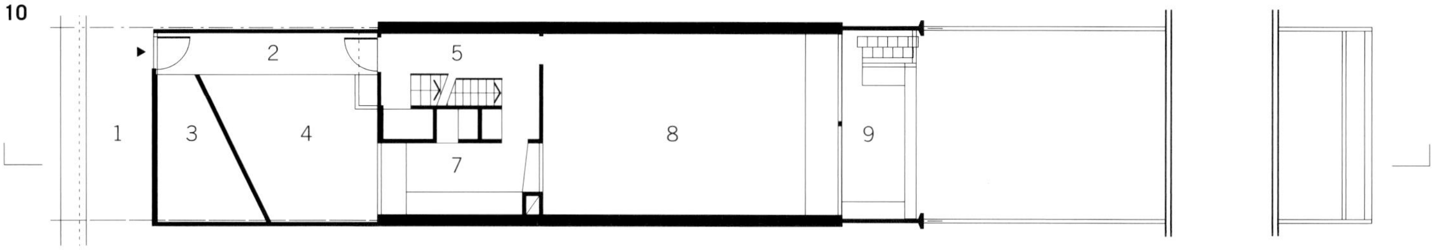

11

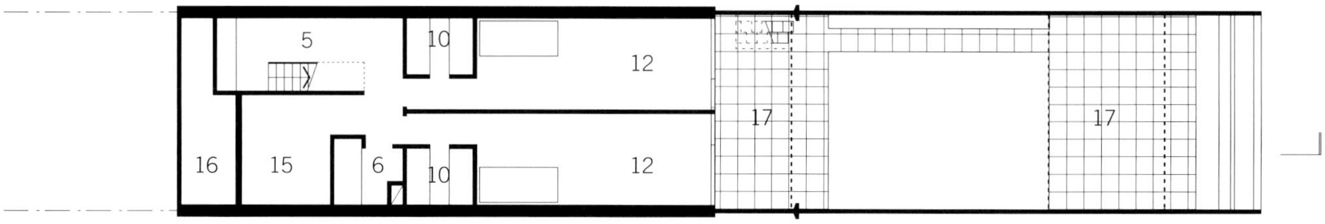

12

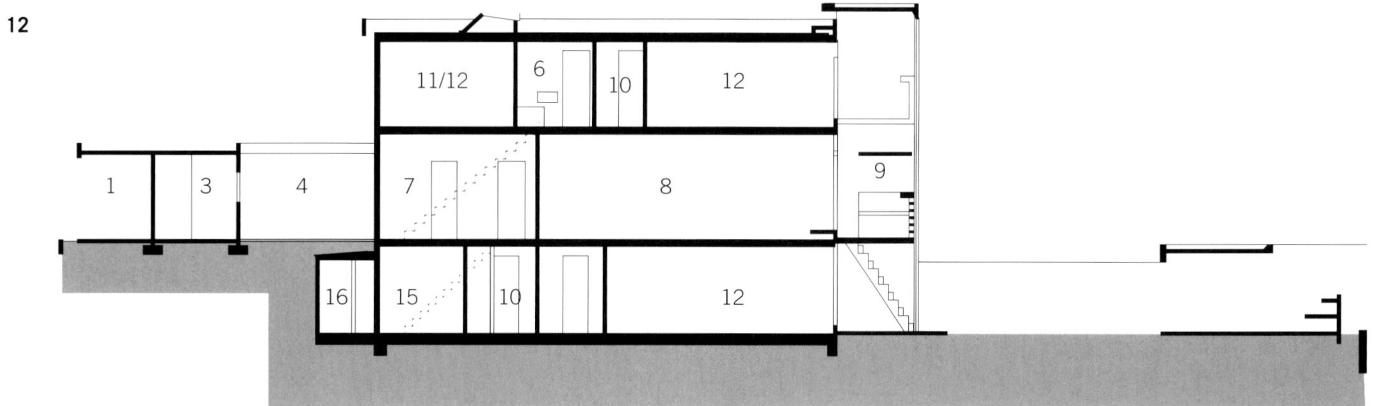

Tapiola Housing

Aulis Blomstedt, 1906–79

Espoo, Finland; 1954

Aulis Blomstedt was a successful practitioner throughout the 1950s and 1960s and a leading Finnish academic. He was Professor of Architecture at Helsinki University of Technology from 1958 to 1966, and spent some time as a visiting professor at Washington University in St Louis, Missouri, USA. He also set up the Standardization Institute at the invitation of the Finnish Association of Architects in 1941. More importantly he was a prolific essayist, writing on many different themes in modern architecture. From 1941 to 1945 he was editor of the Finnish architectural review *Arkkitehti* and was the editor of the *feuille internationale d'architecture*, founded in 1958 by the Helsinki CIAM group, which was to become the magazine *Le Carré Bleu*. Its emphasis was on three aspects of the relationship between theory and material expression: architectural form, function (in social terms) and structure. Excerpts from Blomstedt's writings and unpublished diaries and manuscripts are included in Scott Poole's *New Finnish Architecture* (1991), which was dedicated to Alvar Aalto and Aulis Blomstedt.

Blomstedt, however, approached architecture in a more objective manner than Aalto, and he developed a theory based on the application of modular systems in aesthetic and social terms. He designed a prefabricated construction system, Kenno, and his own version of a modular system, based on the human body and musical harmonics, called the Cannon 60, which was first published in *Le Carré Bleu* in 1961. He applied his rationalist principles to the design of housing projects, notably in Tapiola, part of the multi-centred Espoo garden suburb of Helsinki. In contrast to Aalto's work, Blomstedt's buildings follow rigid dimensioning systems, regular layouts and standardized elements with a cool precision, reflecting his commitment to Modernism's ideal of an industrially produced architecture. This simplicity and clarity is demonstrated in the Tapiola blocks, many of which were variations of the same principles. Structural walls laid out at regular intervals, 3.6 or 5.6 metres (12 or 18 feet) apart, form linear blocks with bathrooms and storage located in a central strip and habitable rooms on either side. Different-sized apartments are formed by combinations of the subdivided spaces. At four or five storeys high, there are no lifts; the staircases protrude from the façades, accommodating windows on either side of half-landings. Deep loggias and balconies mean that each apartment has some outside space.

Opposite left:
Karhunpojat block

Opposite right:
Riistapolku block

1

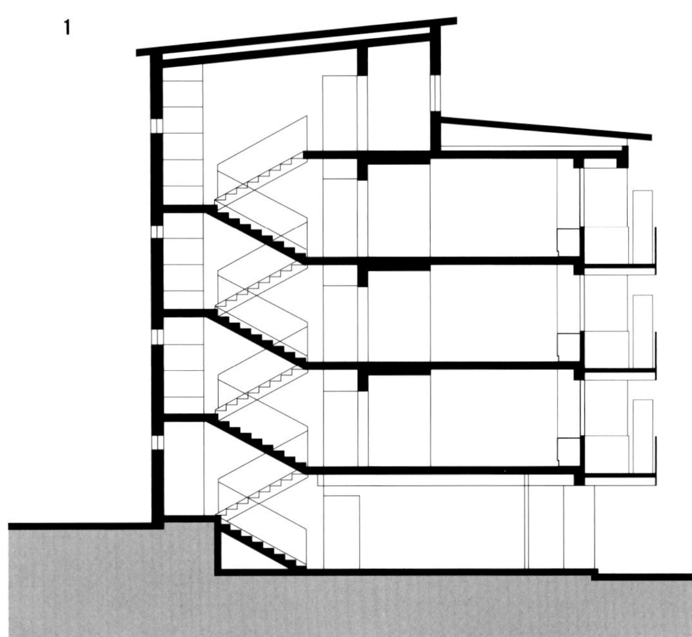

2

3

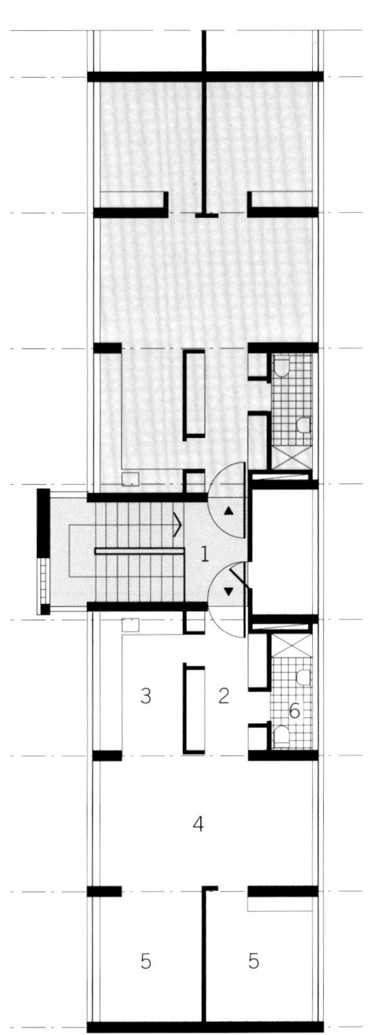

1 Section 1:200

2 Part typical floor plan 1:200

1 Stairs and circulation
2 Entrance/hall
3 Kitchen
4 Dining
5 Living
6 Bedroom
7 Bathroom
8 Balcony

3 Part top-floor plan 1:200

1 Stairs and circulation
2 Entrance/hall
3 Kitchen
4 Living/dining
5 Bedroom
6 Bathroom

Alternatives

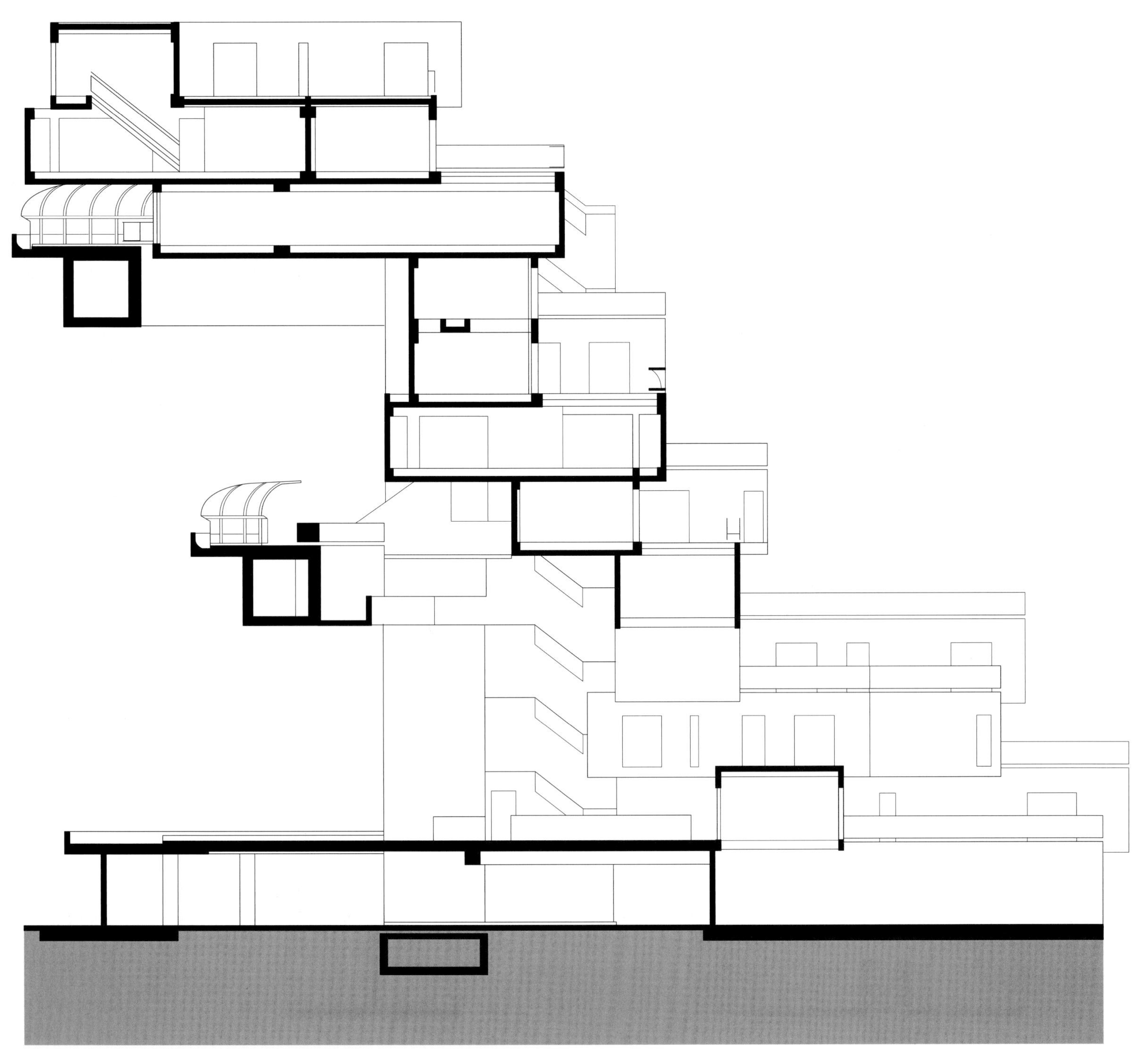

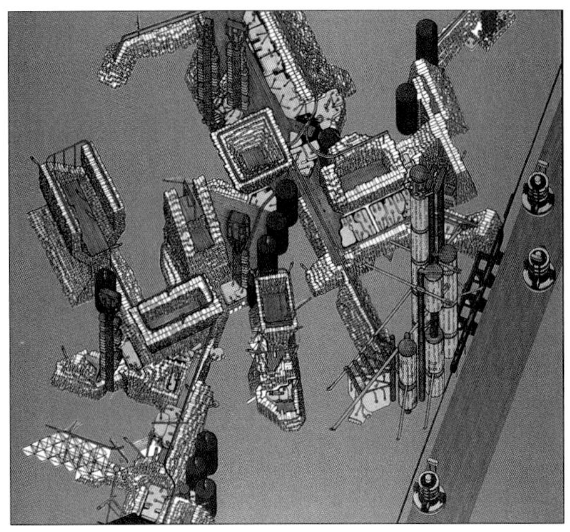

Above: **Plug-in City**

Right: **Aircraft Carrier City**

The 1960s and 1970s constituted a period of intense architectural speculation, linked to a growing dissatisfaction with the prevailing reworking of the ideas of Modernism that had, perhaps, lost their raison d'être in a different social and economic context. In Europe particularly, unlike during the preceding decades immediately following the Second World War when reconstruction was a necessity, building was no longer a guaranteed outcome for project work. However, younger architects continued to develop their own theories, and, although much was never built, many projects became significant for their questioning of the dictum of Modernism, their critical approach to earlier planning notions and an intellectual conservatism. Common to much of this work was the acceptance that the city could not be considered a fixed or static environment. Instead, plans needed to take on board the idea not only of change but of a tapestry of constantly shifting elements woven together, which gave any urban environment its identity. In a period in which historical reference was to become increasingly important, these young architects questioned the idea that new cities could not be conceived as old ones – as static, fixed places – but had to be thought of as dynamic.

In the UK, Archigram's **Plug-in City** project of 1964, in which pods could be 'plugged in' wherever the residents decided and the whole city strode around on mechanical legs until it found a place to stop, personified this idea of the lack of a fixed state for the city. In Italy, No Stop City (1969) by Archizoom, a group inspired by Archigram, took an anti-design stance, describing the city through commercial models of the 'factory' and the 'supermarket', and Superstudio's *Il monumento continuo* foresaw creeping globalization in a proposal that envisaged an utterly uniform continuous grid enveloping the whole planet. In Austria, Hans Hollein's drawings showed visual parodies of Le Corbusier's concept of architecture as an object in the landscape. **Aircraft Carrier City** in Landscape Project led Hollein on to a group of site photographs he took in 1964, dispensing with buildings altogether and declaring the forms of the land themselves to be architectural statements – further proof of the contention that 'everything is architecture'.

Many of the built projects of this period that have remained influential were at the time considered equally extreme; different ways to generate design briefs and design ideas were found and the projects often made clear a divergence from the pervading polite Modernism. A growing interest in the use of geometry to generate form and to avoid the uniformity of façades associated with Modernism was particularly suited to the scale and repetitive nature of apartment buildings. Bertrand Goldberg's **Marina City** in Chicago (see pages 122–23) uses a bold circular form in plan, extended with petal-like curved balconies, and Harry Seidler's **Blues Point Tower** in Sydney (see pages 128–29) modulates its façade by rotating an identical plan through 90 degrees around a fixed core at alternate floor levels. In Japan, Kisho

Left: **Nagakin Capsule Tower**

Bottom left: **Habitat 67**

Bottom right: **Walden 7, atrium**

Kurokawa's **Nagakin Capsule Tower** (see pages 142–43) is the embodiment of the idea of the fixed enduring infrastructure and the movable living pods, and Ricardo Bofill's **Walden 7** project in Barcelona (see pages 148–49), described as a 'vertical labyrinth', defines its dwellings as multi-functional space grouped around a public arena. At the Montreal International Exposition, Moshe Safdie's **Habitat 67** (see pages 134–35) formally put into practice ideas about modular construction and prefabrication.

Looking for ways to develop further the established ideas of Modernism, Aldo Rossi's and Carlo Aymonino's **Gallaratese housing** project in Milan (see pages 154–55) grouped together slab blocks to define space, and, in London, Ernö Goldfinger refined planning and circulation layouts in two similar blocks, **Balfron and Trellick Towers** (see pages 138–39). In the USA, where the skyscraper had been adopted as the 'American building type' in response to the problems of diurnal depopulation caused by too many office blocks, zoning laws in several states were relaxed to make way for mixed-use developments, such as Skidmore Owings & Merrill's **Olympic Tower** in Manhattan (see pages 146–47), in order to encourage activity round the clock. Using similar conventional planning principles, Prentice & Chan, Ohlhausen's **Twin Parks Northwest** tower in the Bronx district (see pages 136–37) developed a honeycomb-like cellular plan to produce a much higher than usual density of occupation in a range of flats and duplexes of varying size.

In addition to the preoccupation with alternatives to the formal constraints of Modernism, the 1970s saw a return, in the field of social housing, to a focus on internal layouts. Questions were explored about how people occupied space in a period of increasing leisure time and changing family structures. The Smithsons' sympathy with the

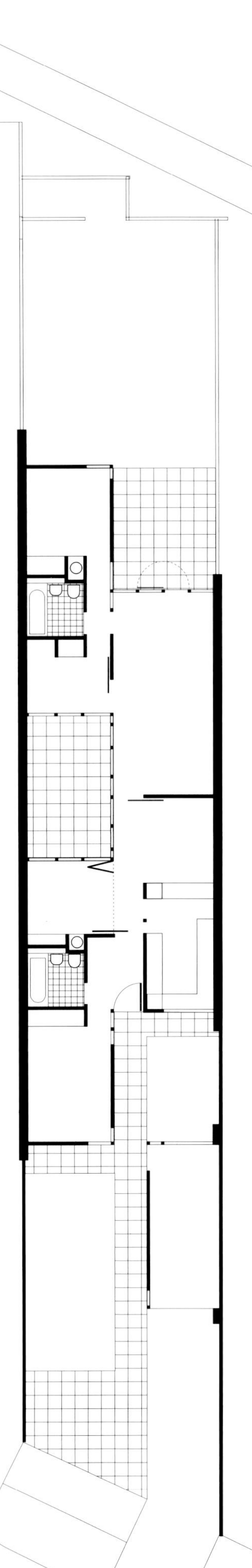

***Left:* The Ryde, plan**

***Right:* The Ryde, interior looking out to private garden**

Modern Movement did not prevent them seeing it as puritanical and fraught with compromises based on decisions taken for the good of the many. They proposed what they described as a 'legible form language', demonstrated in their scheme at **Robin Hood Gardens** in London's East End (see pages 140–41) and published in *Changing the Art of Inhabitation*.

At the same time, in the UK high-rise and mixed-use schemes were becoming increasingly unpopular both with residents and landlords, and it became necessary to investigate other types. Studies at Cambridge University carried out in the 1960s by Leslie Martin and Lionel March had demonstrated how low-rise schemes could achieve the same high densities as high-rise tower blocks. *Urban Spaces and Structures*, published in 1972, used hypothetical models to show that courtyard houses could provide far higher densities than either terraces or tower blocks. **The Ryde** in Hatfield (see pages 132–33), by Phippen Randall and Parkes, is an exemplary model that reinvents the terraced house as a single-storey courtyard house, and furthermore successfully introduces the idea of the estate as a coherent social group with residents being members of a shared ownership club. In common with Jørn Utzon's **Bakkedraget** courtyard dwellings at Fredensborg in Denmark (see pages 130–31) and Alvaro Siza's **Quinta da Malagueira** patio-houses in Portugal (see pages 156–57), these last-mentioned projects develop a series of variations on a basic flexible plan-type that can be inhabited in different ways, and can accommodate adaptations over time in order to reflect the changing needs of a growing family.

Far left: Exterior of the two towers

Left: Detail of curved balcony segments

Marina City

Bertrand Goldberg, 1913–97

Chicago, Illinois, USA; 1964

In 1964 when they were completed, the twin 60-storey towers of Marina City were the tallest concrete structures in the world. With apartments between the 21st and 60th floors they were also the tallest residential buildings, and were a bold experiment at a time when architects and city planners were seeking to find new high-density forms for the future of the city. At the base of the towers, at the first- and second-floor levels, a more conventional structure that fills two city blocks incorporates commercial spaces and a 700-boat marina with, above it, a skating rink, auditoria and a 16-storey office block. Parking for 900 cars is located in the lower 18 storeys of both towers, where the floors are a continuous spiralling ramp. Goldberg described his 'city within a city' as a remedy for the problems created by zoning, which separates out residential areas from commercial districts, and as a way to plan for two 'shifts' – by stacking daytime and night-time uses on one site.

Within the towers, the approach to the distribution and internal layout of the apartments is straightforward. The circular plan means consistent detailing and planning, with no special conditions and no alteration to layouts to take account of orientation. At the centre of each tower, a 10.7-metre (35-foot) diameter structural core contains lifts and stairs and carries all the services. Radiating beams span from the centre to concentrically placed columns on the façade, dividing the space into 16 segments, and semicircular balconies project externally beyond the faceted glazed façade. The entrances to the apartments are from access corridors encircling the lifts at every level. Inside the units, kitchens and bathrooms are located beyond the entrance lobbies, with the living spaces arranged closest to the façades. The smallest apartment occupies one segment; larger ones are created by adding another complete or half segment. Although some were intended for the rental market, all have independent heating and hot water.

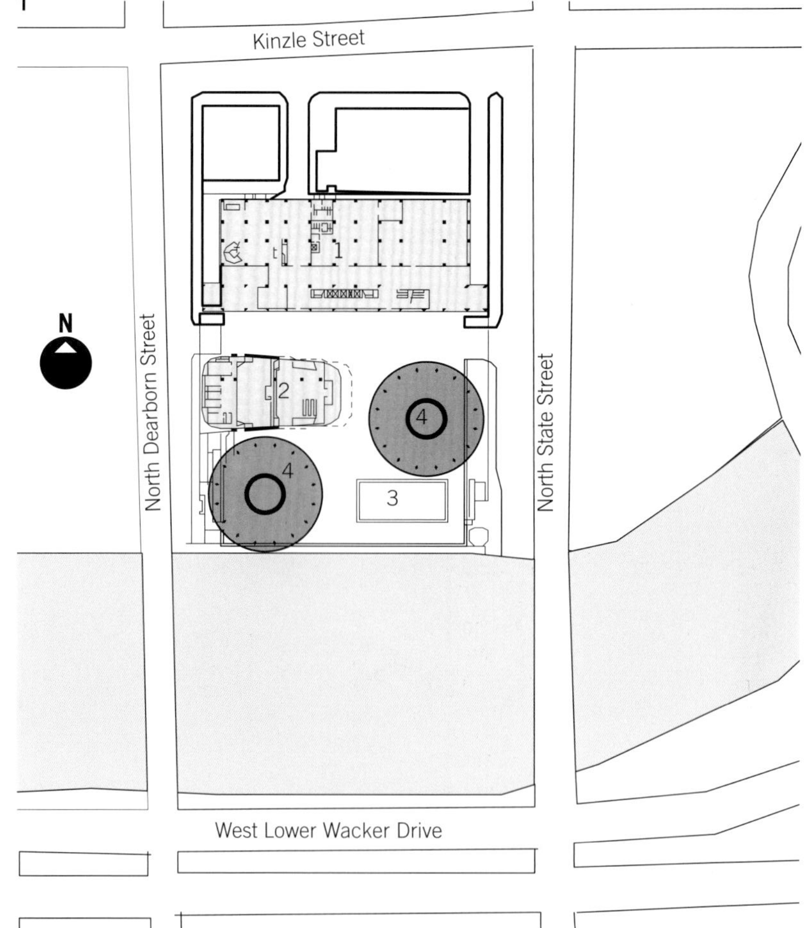

2

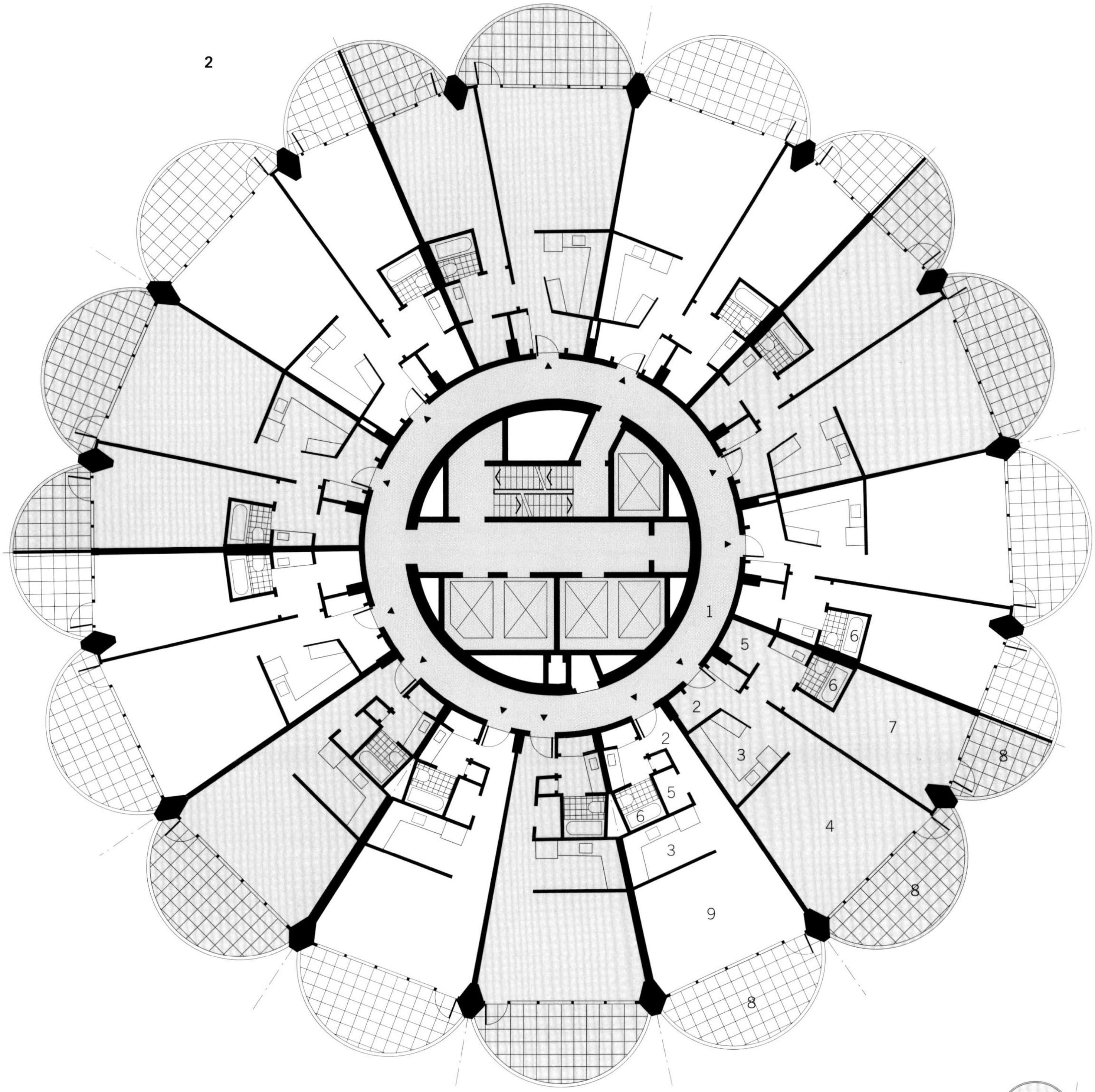

1 Site plan 1:2,500

1 Retail and commercial space
2 Theatre
3 Ice rink
4 Apartment tower

2 Typical floor plan 1:200

1 Access corridor
2 Entrance/hall
3 Kitchen
4 Living/dining
5 Store room
6 Bathroom
7 Bedroom
8 Balcony
9 Living/bedroom

3 Typical floor plan 1:500

1 Lifts/circulation core
2 One-bedroom flat
3 Studio flat

3

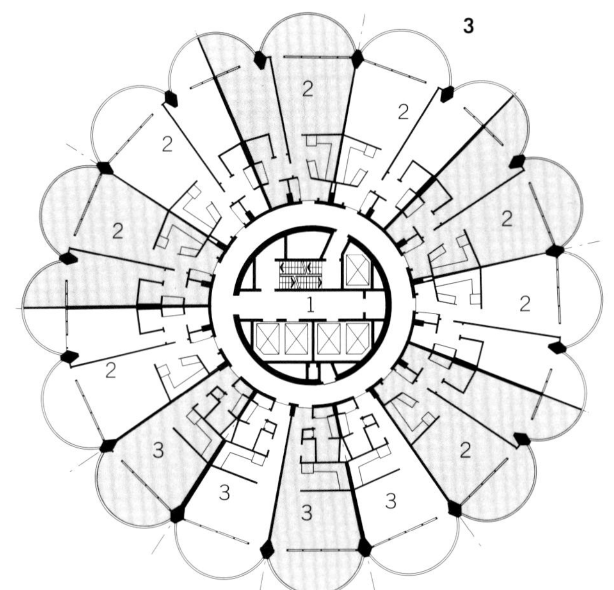

Lafayette Park Apartments

Ludwig Mies van der Rohe, 1886–1969

Detroit, Michigan, USA; 1963

The urban renewal project at Lafayette Park, which recently celebrated its fiftieth year, is considered to be one of America's most successful regeneration projects and an outstanding example of Modernist architecture. It combines apartments in 21-storey high tower blocks with one- and two-storey terraced houses around a 6.5-hectare (16-acre) landscaped park. Situated close to the centre of Detroit, it replaced a run-down slum area, and was intended to rejuvenate the locality by attracting people back to the city centre. The site was bought and developed by Herbert Greenwald, who invited the architect and planner Ludwig Hilbersheimer and the landscape architect Alfred Caldwell to work alongside Mies van der Rohe. The site has three main interconnected sections: on the east side, two apartment towers sit either side of a shopping centre; running north–south on the west side are the town houses, arranged around planted culs-de-sac; while the central strip is occupied by open parkland with a school and recreation facilities. Crucially, the dwellings and parkland are raised above the partially sunken roadways and parking spaces.

The key ideas of Modernism are continued in the construction and detailing of the apartments and town houses. Both have the same Modernist concrete structure and tinted glass framed in aluminium or steel. The town houses are a less familiar part of Mies's work: both types are 'open plan', with the kitchens and bathrooms located in the centre and with, in the two-storey houses, the staircase rising up from the living room. The more conventional upper levels have three bedrooms and a bathroom with, in each pair, the third bedroom straddling the party wall. All the houses have basements intended for 'recreation rooms' and the single-storey dwellings have the addition of a private walled courtyard garden at the rear. Parking is grouped away from the houses, which are reached by pedestrian alleys and pathways leading to paired front doors. The only difference in construction materials is the brickwork end walls.

Site plan 1:2,500

1 Two-storey terraced houses
2 Single-storey terraced houses
3 Parking

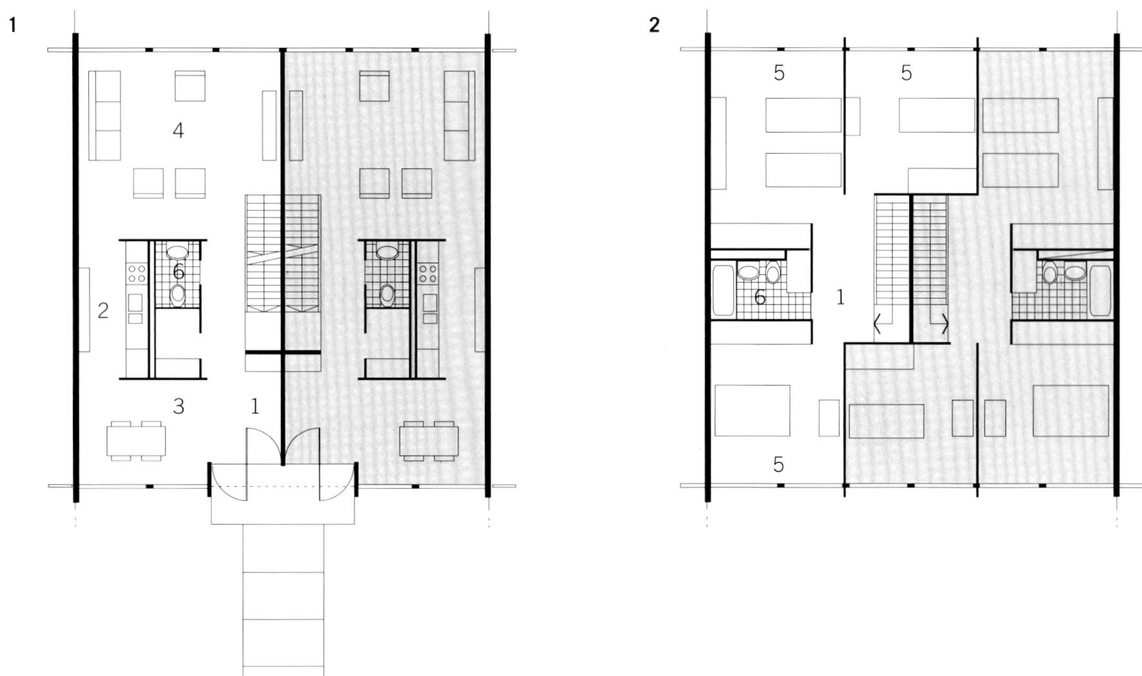

Two-storey houses
1:200

1 Lower-floor plan
2 Upper-floor plan

1 Entrance/hall
2 Kitchen
3 Dining
4 Living
5 Bedroom
6 Bathroom/WC

3 Single-storey houses
1:200

1 Entrance/hall
2 Kitchen
3 Dining
4 Living
5 Bedroom
6 Bathroom/WC

3

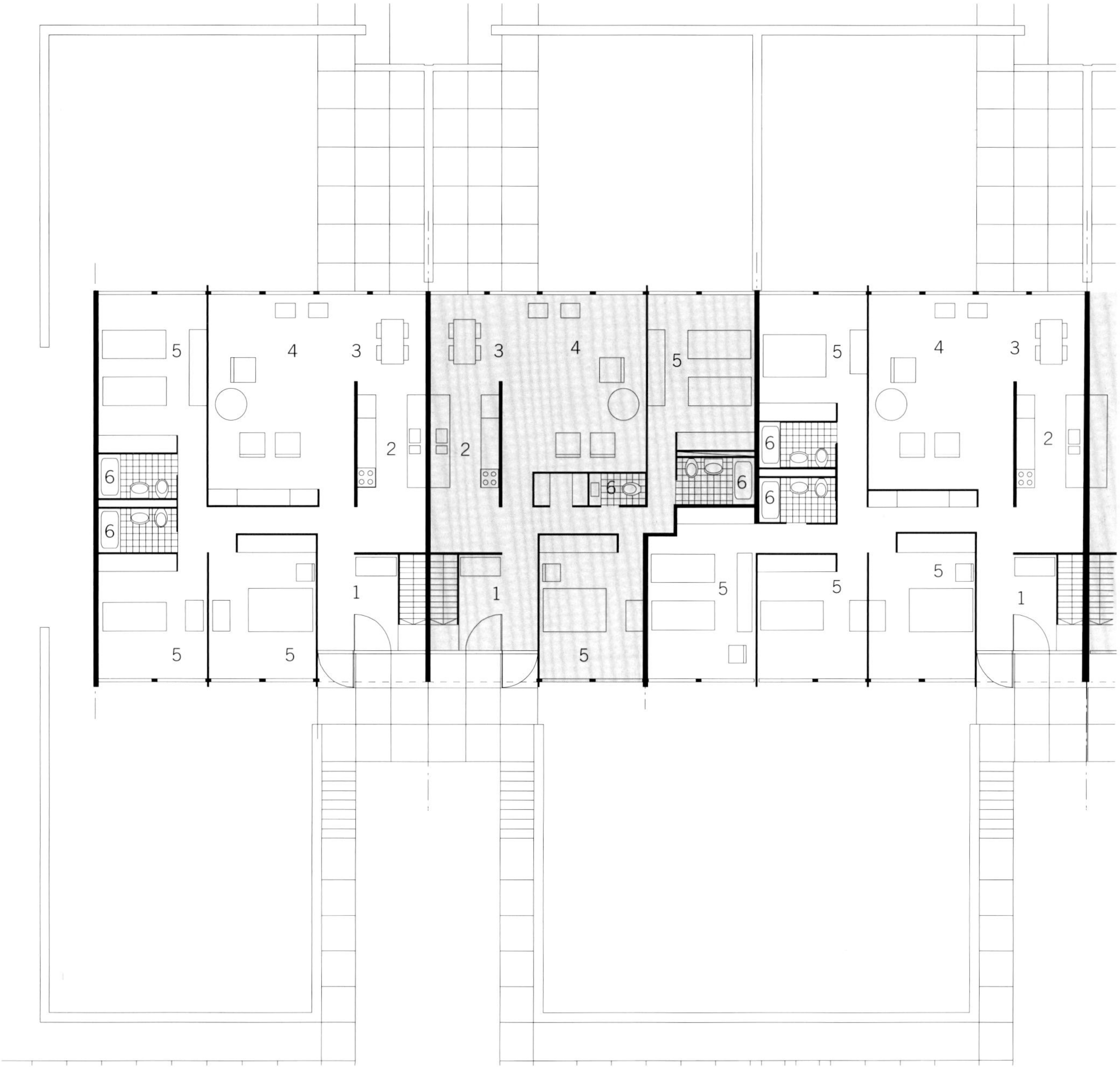

Peabody Terrace

Sert, Jackson & Gourley

Cambridge, Massachusetts, USA; 1964

When it was built in 1964, Harvard University's Peabody Terrace hall of residence received design awards and was much praised for its departure from the clear distinctions between low-rise and high-rise towers – achieved by combining the two forms. This complex of buildings was significant according to a 1974 appraisal published in *Progressive Architecture* because 'they made the new scale which everybody knew was coming seem acceptable'. Instead of Modernism's clarity of object and open space, the housing blocks are organized to form a series of shared open spaces at street level: courtyards are private but nevertheless maintain a certain permeability both to the surrounding streets and the river front.

The programme of 500 apartments, parking space for 300 cars, meetings rooms, a nursery school and playground was in principle to be tailored to the needs of married students, including those with families. To meet the economies necessary to build the scheme, Sert, Jackson & Gourley proposed, instead of the originally envisaged slab blocks, a standard module of six apartments that could be repeated across the whole scheme. The module is three bays wide and three storeys high. There is a staircase in the centre, and an access corridor connecting to the lifts on the middle floor only and connecting to other towers via bridges. An economical circulation system means two-thirds of the apartments occupy the full depth of the block and therefore have good daylighting and ventilation; this is perhaps less appropriate in a building where student tenants have small children and pushchairs, and are regularly moving in and out. The apartments are small – 3.43 metres (11 feet 3 inches) between separating walls – and have low (2.26-metre/7-foot 5-inch) ceilings, but are equipped with built-in cupboards, worktops and desks to maximize the amount of usable space. The walls were originally painted white, with the partitions to kitchens and bathrooms that protrude into the main space painted in bold blocks of colour. The façades are a key part of the overall design: floor-to-ceiling windows are distinct from red-and-green-painted ventilation openings, the corridors are on either north or east elevations, and balconies appear on the west- or south-facing elevation. Together with balcony overhangs on the south side and adjustable louvres on the west, which provide sun-shading, the richness and variety of the façades belies the standarized simplicity of the interior layouts behind.

1 Part plan typical floor with corridor 1:200

2 Part plan typical non-corridor floor 1:200

1 Access corridor
2 Stairs
3 Entrance/hall
4 Living
5 Kitchen
6 Bathroom
7 Bedroom
8 Balcony
9 Lifts
10 Study

Blues Point Tower

Harry Seidler and Associates

Sydney, Australia; 1961

When Blues Point Tower was built in 1961, it was, at 25 storeys, the tallest residential building in Sydney. It is conomically constructed with a concrete frame, and the apartments are small – 78 square metres (840 square feet) for the largest two-bed flat, and 31 square metres (330 square feet) for a studio. The tightly organized, almost square, plan has the vertical circulation in the centre, a concentric access corridor and, inside the apartments, all the bathrooms on the inside wall with mechanical ventilation systems. Each floor has seven apartments, and the top floor has a laundry and drying rooms. Instead of any projecting balconies, the living rooms have french windows that open full height, with external balustrades. The fire regulations, which required a minimum 1-metre (3-foot) depth of masonry between apartments, is met with ingenuity by a 90-degree rotation of alternate floor plans. This also gives the façades a distinctive and very unusual character, and contributes to the variety of different apartment types with differing outlooks and daylighting.

Blues Point Tower has attracted much attention and been the subject of much criticism since it was built, partly because of its location and partly because of Seidler's reputation. Its site – perhaps one of the most magnificent in the world, on the tip of McMahon Peninsula dominating views across Sydney Harbour – is designated parkland and therefore remains undeveloped, preserved in its natural state with dramatic rocky cliffs descending to the water's edge. The tower – which was never meant to be solitary but rather the first of a development, with a further ten or so buildings – is highly visible, directly across the harbour from Bennelong Point and Sydney Opera House. Given this location, it seems that Seidler's façade treatment was not merely the result of his rational approach to planning but an important aspect of the design. The form has considerable clarity, with a clear resolution of the top floors whose solid walls enclose the laundry and tank rooms. Seidler, who had studied in the UK and Canada before going to Harvard to study under Gropius, took courses with Josef Albers and worked with Oscar Niemeyer and Marcel Breuer. In practice in Sydney from 1948, he represented the introduction to Australia of a new architecture with a restrained aesthetic and a rational approach to design. Blues Point Tower clearly demonstrated this, at the time controversial, Europhile heritage, but more importantly it signalled the beginning of the shift towards high-density high-rise apartment living and away from the 'traditional' Sydney bungalow and its attendant increasing suburban sprawl.

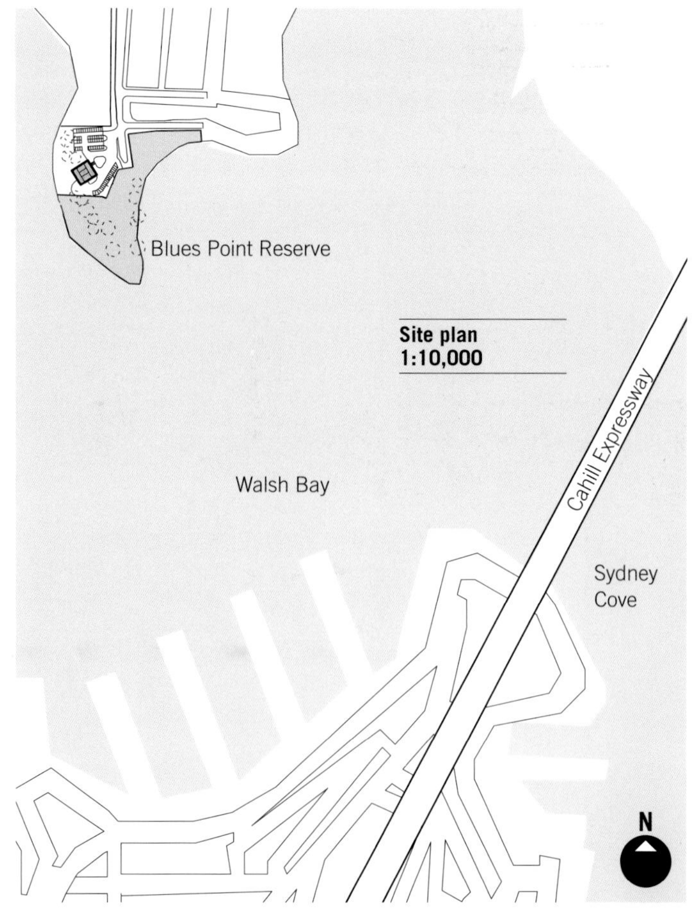

Opposite left: The tower seen from across the bay

Opposite right: Front façade

1

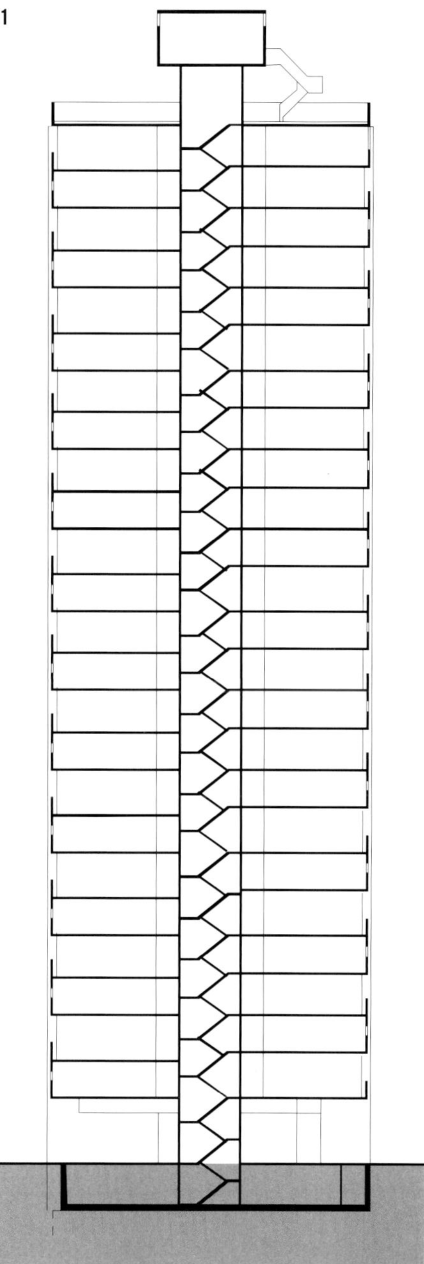

2

3

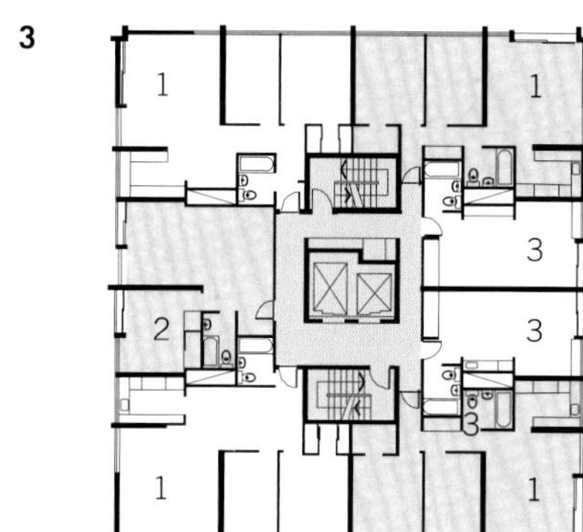

4

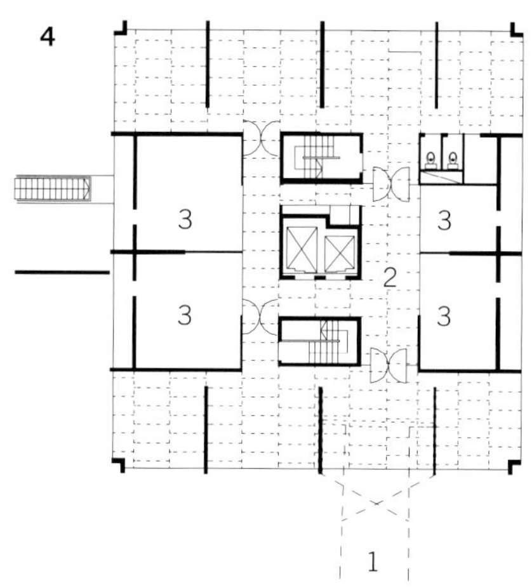

1 Section 1:500

2 Typical floor plan 1:200

1 Corridors and stairs
2 Entrance/hall
3 Kitchen
4 Living/dining
5 Bedroom
6 Bathroom
7 Closet

3 Plan at alternate floor levels 1:500

1 Two-bedroom flat
2 One-bedroom flat
3 Studio flat

4 Street-level plan 1:500

1 Entrance portico with canopy over
2 Lobby
3 Shop units

Bakkedraget Housing

Jørn Utzon, 1918–

Fredensborg, Denmark; 1963

Utzon had developed his ideas for the design of dwelling units as early as 1954, in a competition entry for the town centre of Elineberg submitted while he was working with Swedish architects Erik and Henry Andersson. These design proposals were for 14-storey blocks, with four apartments per floor. The apartments were aligned in a parallel row, orientated the same way towards balconies and views out to the surrounding landscape. Within each apartment the floor levels stepped down to varying degrees, in order to focus the view towards the ground rather than the sky. Most importantly for Utzon, the dwelling unit was the starting point for the design: 'by building up the town plan of the smallest possible unit, namely a flat, and by combining it with itself. This living group of towers gives significance to each flat.' This approach to the design of housing as a collection of individual units is also apparent in Utzon's designs for courtyard houses.

At Fredensborg, the courtyard space contained by two perpendicular wings within an almost square plan is conceived as the focus for the ordinary activities of family life. It is designed as a neutral space that can be occupied in a variety of different ways to suit the inhabitants. Without changing the basic nature of the house, the courtyard can be used as dining room, workshop, garden or playground for children. The two wings with windows overlooking the courtyard contain living space on one side and the bedrooms on the other. The exteriors of the houses, with austere brickwork and small windows, give little clue as to the activity behind. The design idea, which was intended to accommodate the changing needs of a growing family, was first developed for a housing competition in Skåne, and was then realized several years later as the Kingo Houses on a site in Helsingør before being developed for this scheme for retired workers at Fredensborg. Here, it includes several variations on the basic house type, with the addition of a terraced house based on an open-plan, double-height living space under a continuously sloping roof.

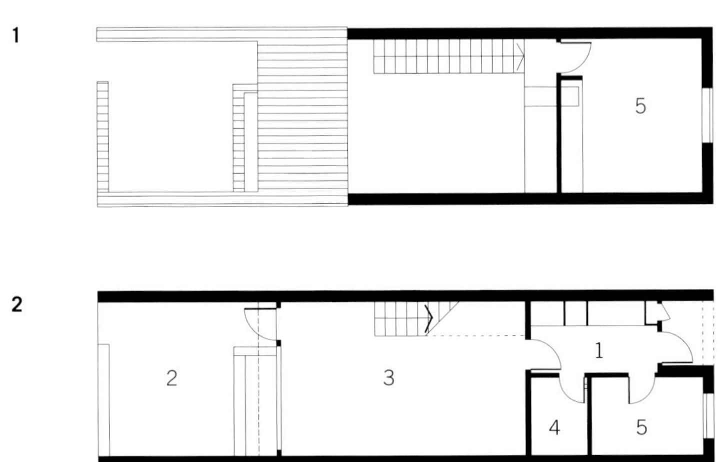

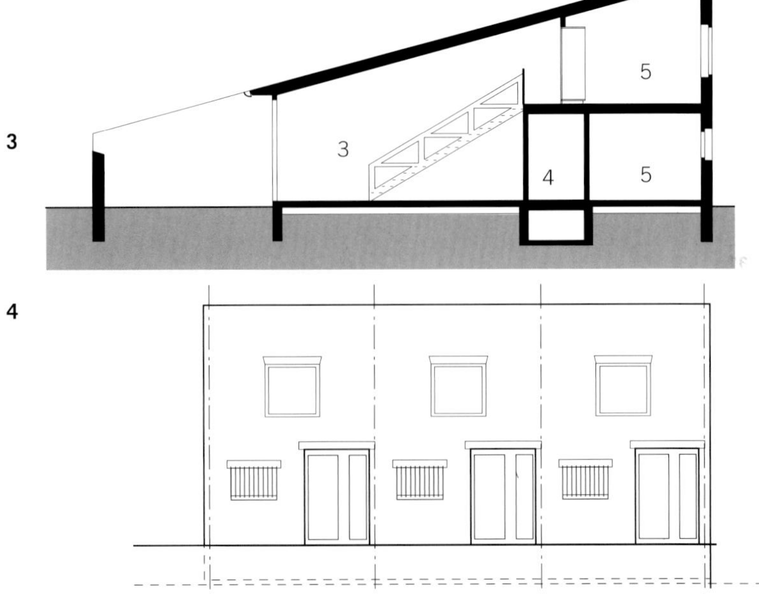

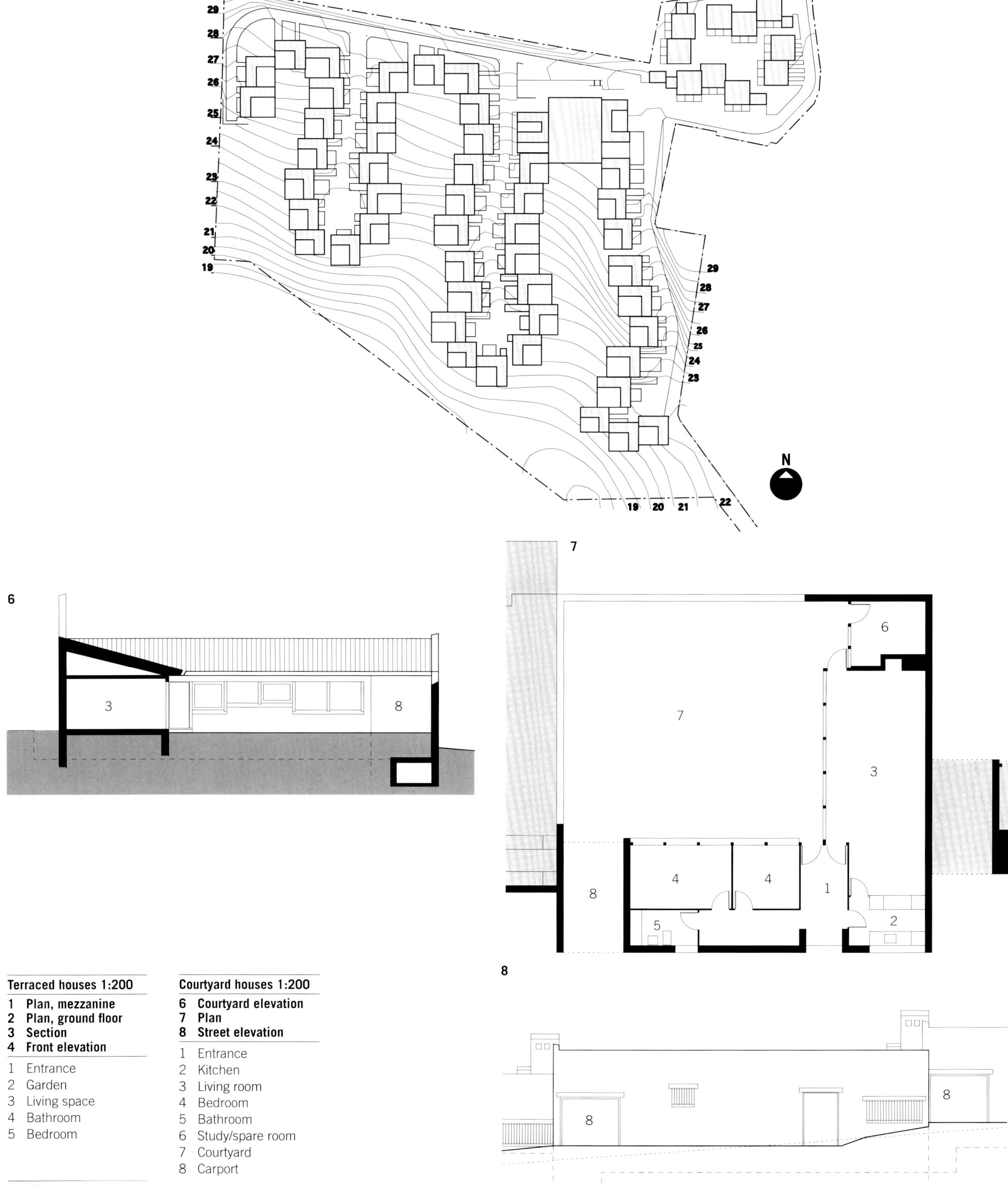

Terraced houses 1:200

1 Plan, mezzanine
2 Plan, ground floor
3 Section
4 Front elevation

1 Entrance
2 Garden
3 Living space
4 Bathroom
5 Bedroom

5 Site plan 1:2,500

Courtyard houses 1:200

6 Courtyard elevation
7 Plan
8 Street elevation

1 Entrance
2 Kitchen
3 Living room
4 Bedroom
5 Bathroom
6 Study/spare room
7 Courtyard
8 Carport

The Ryde

Phippen Randall and Parkes

Hatfield, UK; 1966

A group of 28 single-storey terraced houses fills a narrow strip of land sloping gently from north to south, with an access road along one side originally intended for individual plots. They were built as a cooperative venture by the Cockaigne Housing Society, founded in 1962 by the pioneering Michael Bailey who was determined to develop a new model for housing that would be more appropriate to contemporary needs in both functional and aesthetic terms. Built for owner occupation, The Ryde included a community house used for meetings and social events, a tennis court, playground and shared gardens and a flatlet for visitors. The houses sit across the slope, their floor levels stepping down the slope, and, unlike the two-storey pitched-roofed houses of the neighbourhood, they are barely visible from the outside. The single-storey buildings are just about higher than the surrounding shrubberies, and only projecting party walls and the dark-stained timber of the window and door frames are visible.

Inside, the party walls are a uniform 6.8 metres (22 feet 3 inches) apart, with the houses varying in depth between them according to their size. The houses are divided longitudinally with the living spaces on one side and the bedrooms and bathrooms arranged on the other. The bathrooms are all identical, and the bedrooms are one of two standard sizes. The partitions to the smaller bedrooms, which are intended to be flexible, can be opened up to the living spaces with wide sliding doors and folding screens. There are rooflights to bring light into the centre of the very deep plans and the larger houses have a central courtyard, which has full-height glazing all round.

Much thought has been paid to the interior fittings: there are wardrobes in all bedrooms and the entrance hall, and the partition between the kitchen and dining room is part cupboard/part work surface and serving hatch. The kitchen is also fitted with a service unit next to the front door with access from outside and inside. Meters can be read from outside; the dustbins, filled from the kitchen, can be picked up; and, at the time of its construction, the milkman would have been able to exchange bottles externally. Generally, the finishes and detailing are simple, the structural blockwork is painted and the timber partitions are varnished; doors and vertical sliding aluminium windows are framed in timber.

Site plan 1:2,500

1 Shared garden/ playground
2 Tennis court
3 Garages
4 Community house

Railway

The Ryde

N

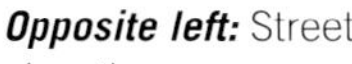

Opposite left: Street elevation

Opposite right: Garden elevation

1

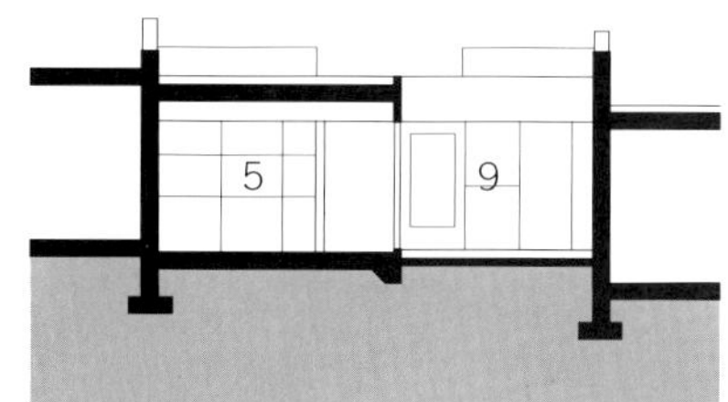

2

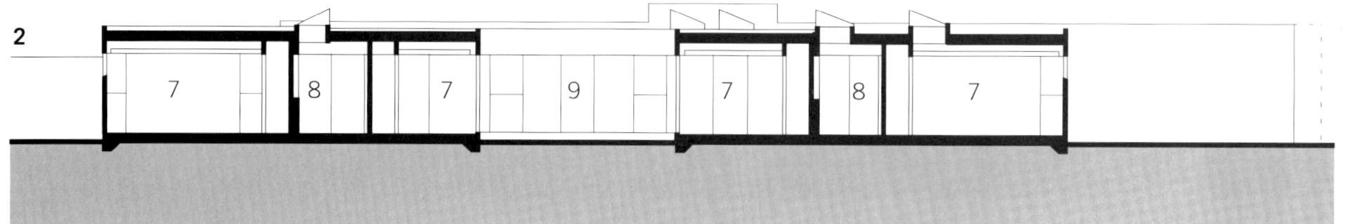

3

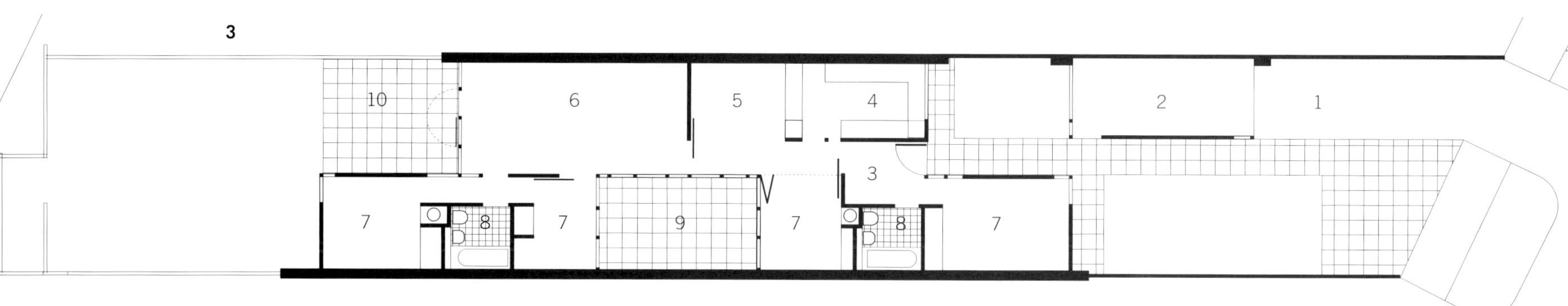

4

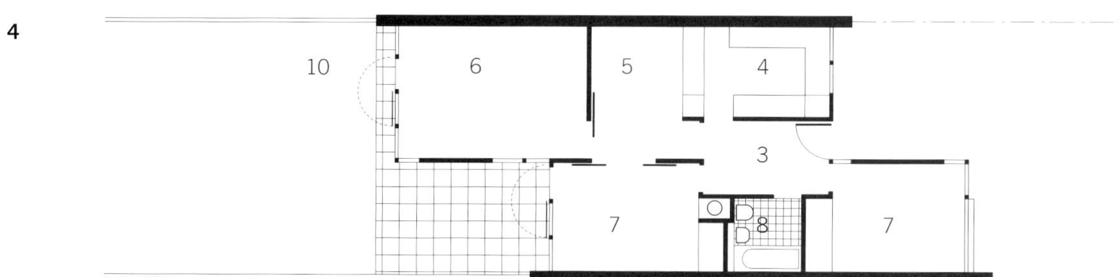

5

10
6
4
3
7
8

1 Cross-section 1:200

2 Long section of four-bedroom house 1:200

House plans 1:200

3 Plan of four-bedroom house
4 Plan of two-bedroom house
5 Plan of one-bedroom house

1 Driveway/parking
2 Garage
3 Entrance/hall
4 Kitchen
5 Dining
6 Living
7 Bedroom
8 Bathroom
9 Patio
10 Private garden

Habitat 67

Moshe Safdie, 1938–

Montreal, Canada; 1967

So striking was this experimental housing scheme that it became the symbol for the International Expo 67, of which it was a part. The concept had been developed at McGill University, and the Expo and the landfill peninsula site provided the ideal opportunity to build something so experimental. There is little in the project that relates to the conventions of housing in type, form or construction. The architect was more interested in exploring the application of modern technology – and especially mass production, particularly the methods of the motor-car industry. The dwellings were made from prefabricated units – concrete 'boxes' measuring 11.7 metres long x 5.3 metres wide x 3 metres high (38½ x 17½ x 10 feet) – which incorporated a one-piece moulded fibreglass bathroom unit and all the equipment, services and fittings. The units were then inserted into the main structure, but, seemingly in an ad hoc manner, loosely piled up one on top of the other. In fact they form three pyramidal structures, each with a lift core giving access to upper-level open decks or pedestrian streets, cranked in plan and connected via bridges to separate 'islands'. There is no recognizable 'façade', no obvious coherence to the composition and no clear hierarchy of space. Dwellings with two, three and four bedrooms, mostly on two levels with different layouts and sizes of apartments, are achieved through the combination of the standard units, often arranged in perpendicular fashion with many including double-height living spaces. All have terraces on the roof of the unit below.

The now familiar problems associated with prefabrication occurred in this project. Financially it was not successful, although it is possible that fabrication in greater numbers – only 354 of the originally planned 1,000 units were built – would have eventually resulted in a reduced cost per unit. The multiplicity of possibilities for combining the units in different ways led to more work on site and reduced the intended economy of using a standard unit. The installation was complicated partly due to the weight and size of the units and there were also criticisms of the level of prefabrication, which still left a good deal of work post-installation. The external access decks were not considered appropriate for the severe conditions of a Montreal winter.

Site plan
1:2,500

1

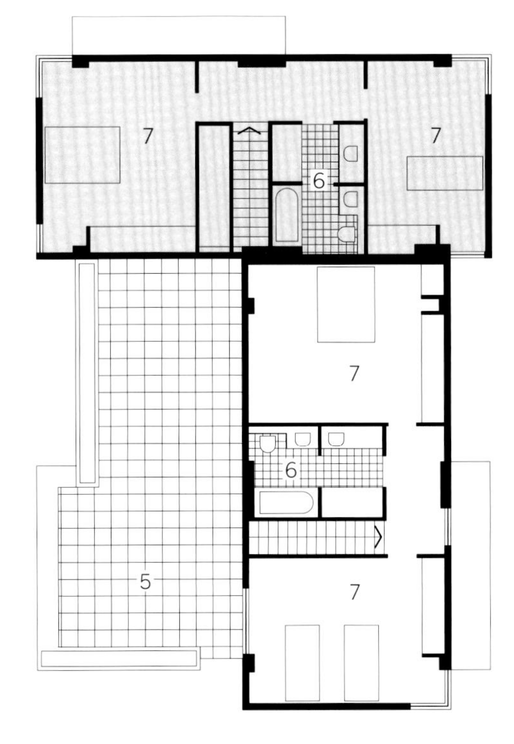

2

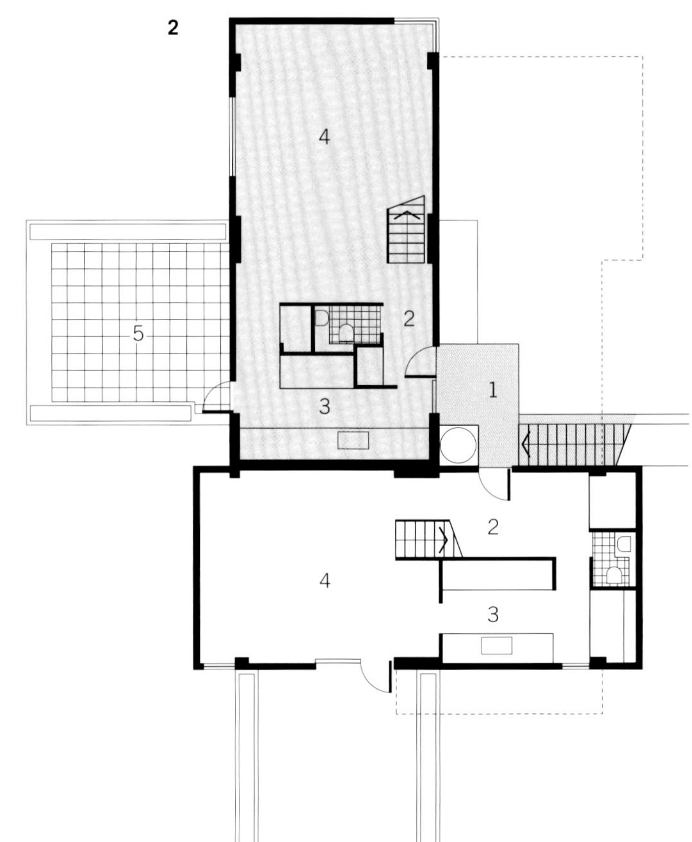

3

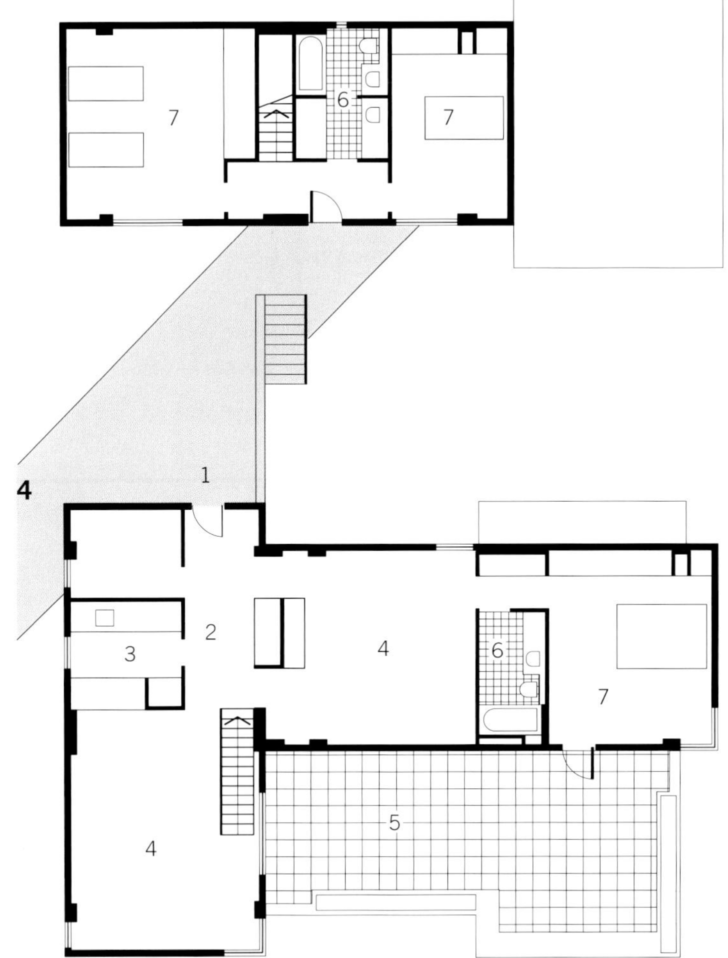

5

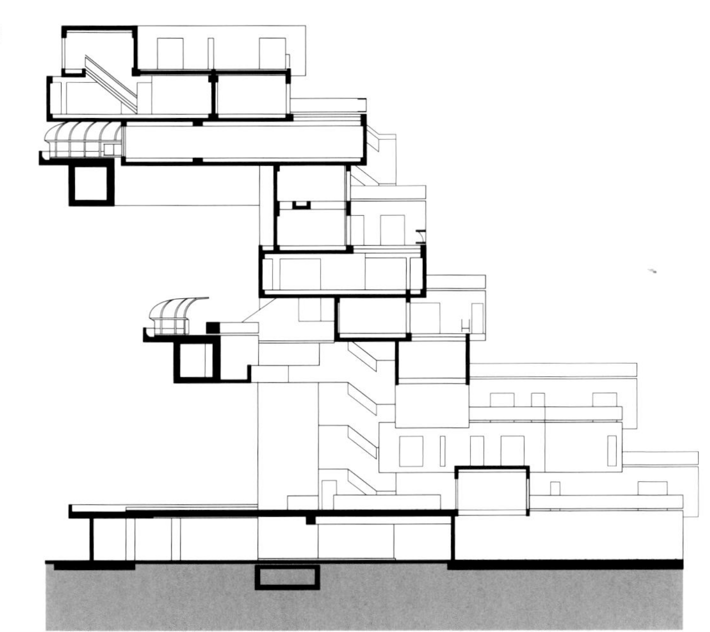

Typical apartment plans 1:200

1 Upper-level two-bedroom duplexes
2 Lower-level two-bedroom duplexes
3 Lower-level three-bedroom duplex
4 Upper-level three-bedroom duplex

1 Access gallery
2 Entrance/hall
3 Kitchen
4 Living/dining
5 Terrace
6 Bathroom
7 Bedroom

5 Part section1:500

Twin Parks Northwest Site 4

Prentice & Chan, Ohlhausen

New York, New York, USA; 1970

The Northwest Site 4 is one of two projects carried out by Prentice & Chan, Ohlhausen as part of a huge development project by the New York Urban Development Corporation across 13 different sites in the Twin Parks area of the Bronx. The architects' approach to the design of affordable housing in a poor and overcrowded neighbourhood is pragmatic. Site 5-11, their other project, has a U-shaped plan defining a new public open space, whereas the Site 4 building takes the simple form of a rectangular tower closing one side of the square. Sited at the top of a rocky hill, it is raised above the ground on pilotis which allow a pathway over the hill and down to the next street, providing a short cut through the block for pedestrians. Externally, the building has an austere appearance: there is no modulation of the surface, no projections, no balconies and no variation in the materials or textures of the surfaces. The windows, which are of just two basic sizes combined in different arrangements, contribute the only notion of decoration.

Inside the 19-storey tower, the architects have employed a more elaborate and unique approach to planning; the initial appearance is honeycomb-like. In the centre of the plan, two lifts and a main stair provide access to a central corridor which runs the full length of the plan on every third floor and partially on others. The apartments range in size from studios and one-bedroom units to five-bedroom flats, and comprise both single-level and duplex layouts. In a conventional manner, zones on either side of the central circulation space contain all private staircases and bathrooms and the living spaces are located adjacent to the external façades. The apartments were all planned to the then minimum space standards, and to increase living spaces the kitchens are often treated as part of, or at least accessed from, the living room. The plans repeat every third floor. Each third level has no access corridor, so that all the units extend the full depth of the block and are accessed from the floor above. Thus, although the rooms are small the apartments cover a large area in terms of internal circulation, with increased distance between the rooms and between rooms on different levels – all of which contributes to a feeling of space.

Section 1:500

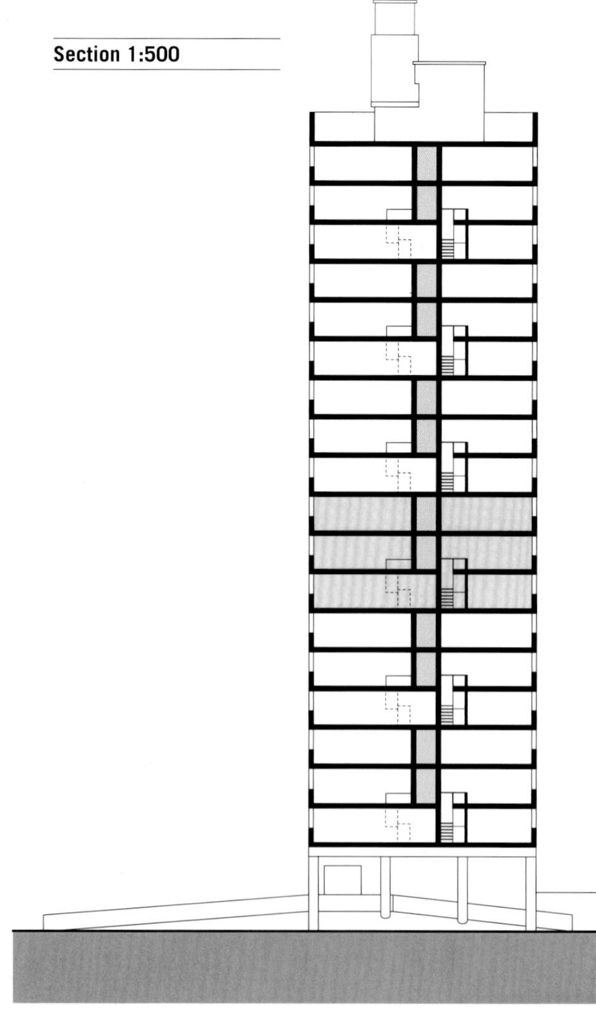

Floor plans 1:200

1 Upper-level floors 4,7,10,13,16 and 19

2 Middle-level floors 3, 6, 9,12 ,15 and 18

3 Lower-level floors 2, 5, 8,14 and 17

1 Corridors and stairs
2 Entrance/hall
3 Kitchen
4 Living room
5 Bedroom
6 Bathroom/WC
7 Studio flat
8 Stairs to lower/upper level of duplex
9 Store room

1

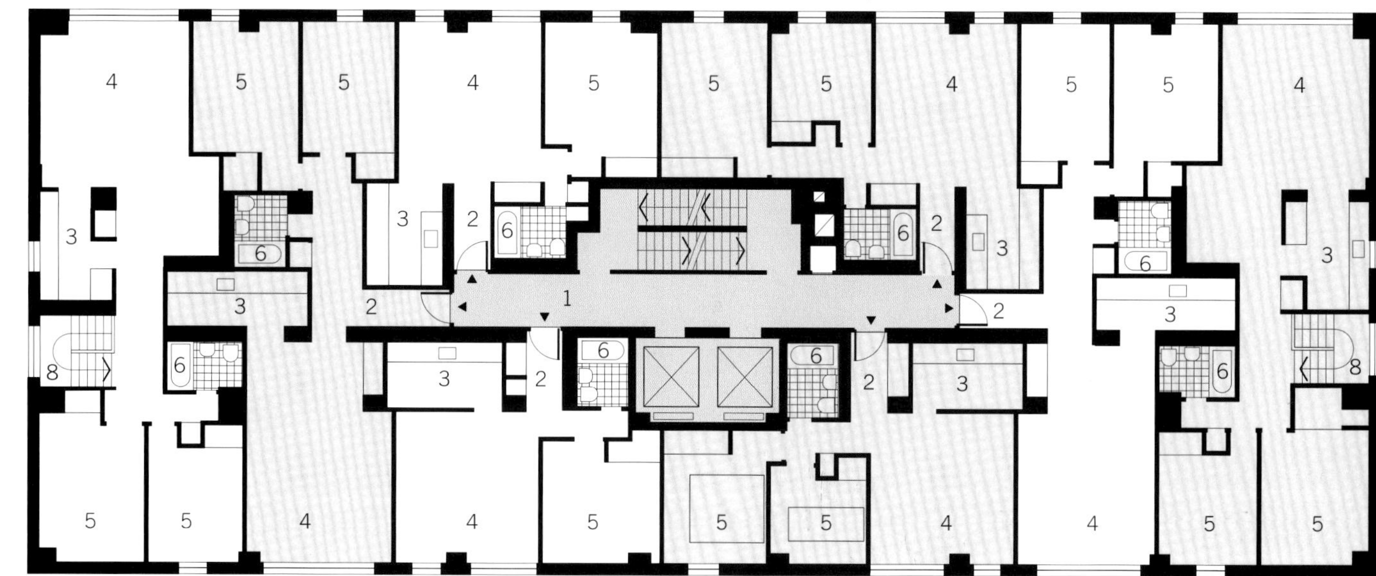

2

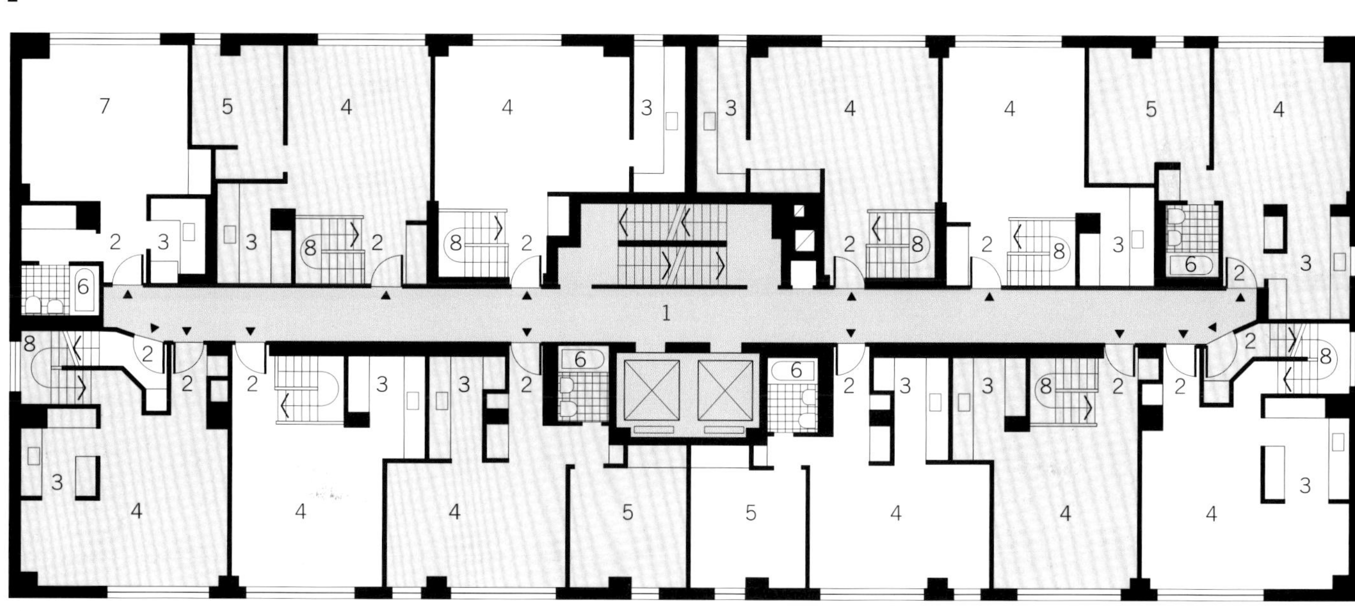

3

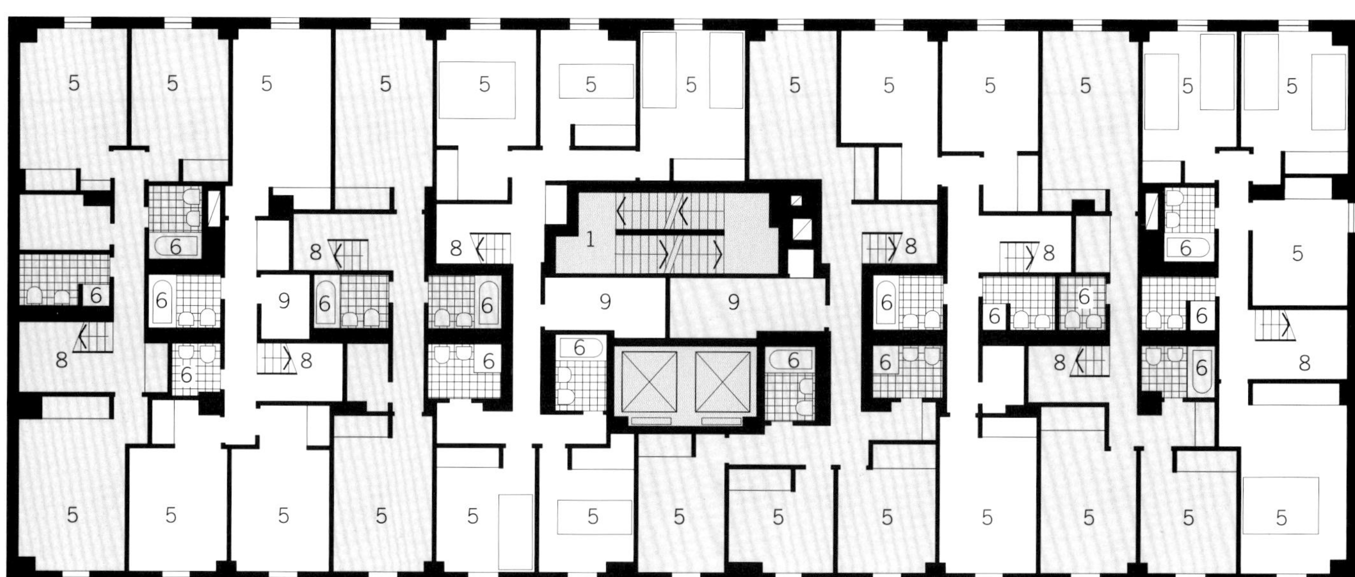

Left: Balfron Tower

Right: Trellick Tower

Balfron and Trellick Towers

Ernö Goldfinger, 1902–87

London, UK; 1968/1972

According to James Dunnatt and Gavin Stamp in *Works*, Goldfinger's distinct achievement in his post-war work is the expression of the frame. Described as having 'a rationalist and industrial conception of the world', Goldfinger had always considered the expression of structure and materials of key importance, as, for example, his earlier Willow Road terraced houses (1938) demonstrate. He used different modelling devices, such as recessed windows and projecting bays, but stopped short of a clear expression of the concrete frame. Other devices – the use of oversized steelwork sections, façades set back from the building line, or the pavement-edge use of large surfaces of plate glass – were all elements that had started to appear in his pre-war projects, for instance in the Abbott toyshop of 1936. Goldfinger also developed a concrete prefabrication system for use on London schools in the 1950s, with a regular grid of portal frames dominating the composition, and his Regents Park Road block of flats (1954) for a housing association had two apartments per floor and was constructed with a concrete frame. Goldfinger was also an advocate of choice, and with two flats per storey the use of a frame structure meant more flexibility in the interior layouts; bedrooms could be allocated to either flat, and tenants could choose between a small kitchen and a living/dining room or a kitchen/dining room and smaller living room.

Ernö Goldfinger's housing work dates back to the 1920s: his first designs for Philippeville in 1929 were exhibited at the CIAM 1933 conference, and his studies for kitchen designs were published in *L'Organistion Menagère* in 1928. He also published his design principles in *Planning your Home, Planning your Kitchen and Planning your Neighbourhood,* as packs of 20 cards. He designed his first daylit 'street-in-the-air' enclosed access corridors for his first local authority housing project, Abbots Langley, in 1956 for Watford Council. Intended to be an improvement on Le Corbusier's *rue intérieure*, it gave access on every third floor to a two-person flat and four-person apartments above and below. This nine-storey block, intended to maintain the open space and existing mature trees, was not acceptable to the council and was replaced in the revised built scheme with a four-storey block. The idea was thus not realized until the 1968 Balfron Tower in east London for the London County Council, which was effectively the prototype for the very similar Trellick Tower built in 1972, on the opposite side of the capital. The distinctive element is the lift tower, which is separated from the main block primarily for acoustic reasons and linked with bridges at every third floor level. The concrete surfaces, slit windows and the boiler rooms and chimneys cantilevering out at the top of the tower all contribute to its forbidding, fortress-like appearance. The footprint of both buildings is generally the same, but refinements to the design at Trellick include changes to the external proportions: four more storeys were added and the row of flats with 'pulpit' balconies, which introduces a horizontal break in the regular grid of the façade, was located higher up; the corner flats have windows and balconies on the south, main, façade; and the circulation tower is rotated to appear lighter in contrast to the main block. Refinements in technology included sophisticated electrical installations and double glazing fitted throughout as standard – important because of the nearby railway line. The interiors are spacious compared with other social-housing projects of the period, above the minimum Parker Morris standards in use in Britain at the time. There are two-person, four-person and six-person flats or maisonettes, with most extending the full depth of the block. The exceptionally wide structural bays, at 6.75 metres (22 feet 2 inches) with full-width balconies facing south, make the apartments appear very light, give a feeling of openness and afford spectacular views out.

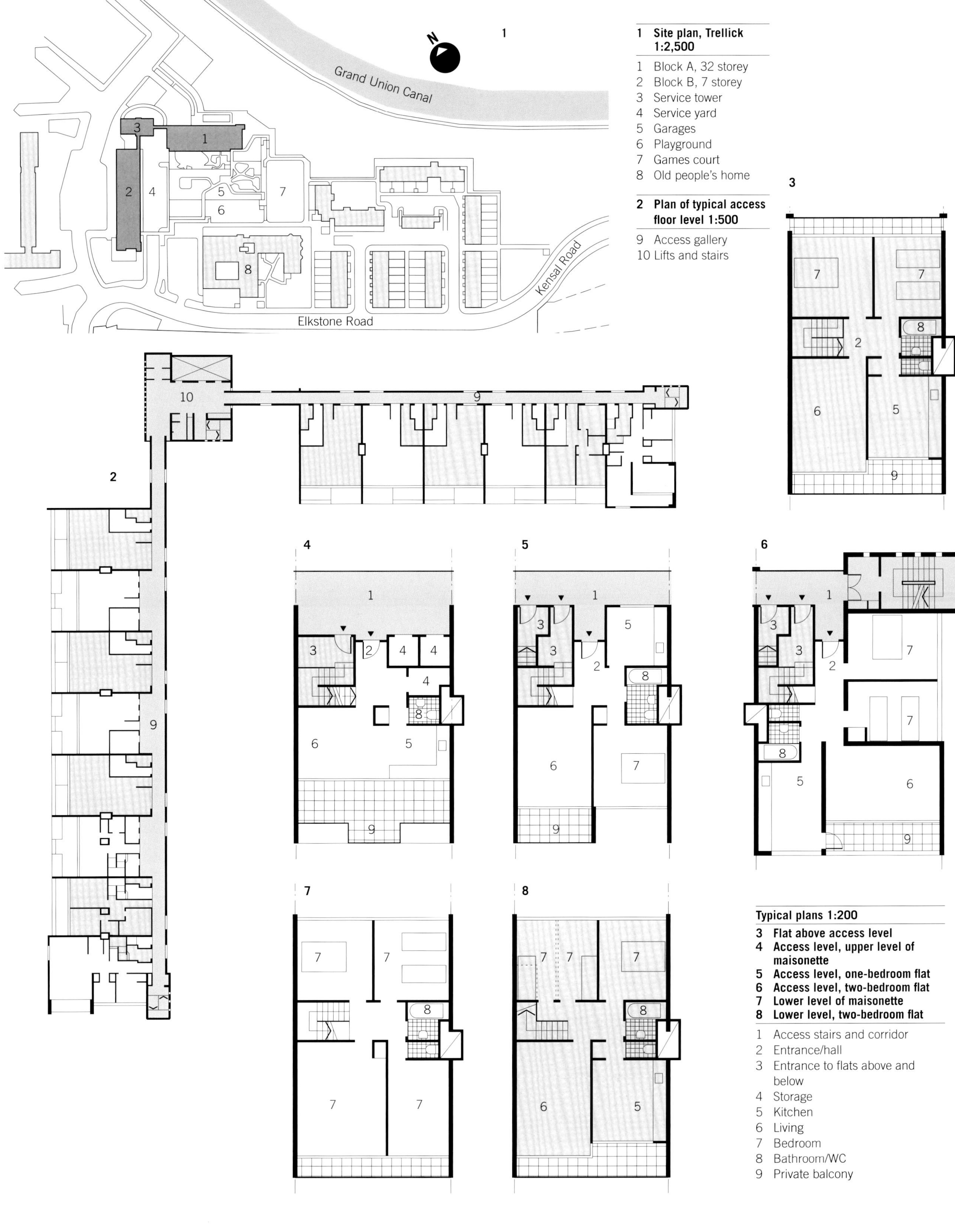

1 Site plan, Trellick 1:2,500

1 Block A, 32 storey
2 Block B, 7 storey
3 Service tower
4 Service yard
5 Garages
6 Playground
7 Games court
8 Old people's home

2 Plan of typical access floor level 1:500

9 Access gallery
10 Lifts and stairs

Typical plans 1:200

3 Flat above access level
4 Access level, upper level of maisonette
5 Access level, one-bedroom flat
6 Access level, two-bedroom flat
7 Lower level of maisonette
8 Lower level, two-bedroom flat

1 Access stairs and corridor
2 Entrance/hall
3 Entrance to flats above and below
4 Storage
5 Kitchen
6 Living
7 Bedroom
8 Bathroom/WC
9 Private balcony

Robin Hood Gardens

Alison and Peter Smithson, 1928–93/1923–2003

London, UK; 1972

The site, in London's East End, is particularly noisy, surrounded on three sides by major roads: to the east, the Blackwall tunnel motorway coming from the other side of the Thames; on the west, the main feeder road onto the Isle of Dogs; and, on its northern edge, the main A13 trunk road into central London. The layout, with two slab blocks running north–south on either side framing a large undulating green space in the centre, was a way to deal effectively with the noise and provide a tranquil open space for the residents. It was also an expression of the Smithsons' commitment to the idea of reclaiming the landscape, using new urban forms at a very different scale to the individual houses of the pre-war period in much of the UK. Their ambition is made clear in an extensive article published in *Architectural Design* in 1972, in which they state: 'at the new city scale making a garden should be like making a range of hills' and 'the approach to a house is the occupants' link with society as a whole … this is what really matters.'

They go on to describe the open access decks, which are located on the street side of both blocks as '… no mere balconies. Two women with prams can stop and talk without blocking the flow …' Furthermore, the entrance doors are arranged perpendicular to the deck, creating small spaces – 'pause-places' – a stoop for pot plants and flowers. Each of these entrance spaces leads to an upper or lower maisonette.

Kitchen/dining rooms are located at the entrance level, beyond the stairs which are perpendicular to the main axis of the flat. Above and below, the bedrooms are located on the 'quiet' side of each block, overlooking the central space, and the living rooms on the noisier street side.

At ground-floor level in both blocks, garden flats are directly accessible from the street side. On the other side, an open basement level has parking spaces under the buildings and beneath the edge of the central space. The 213 apartments were designed to the then-minimum UK Parker Morris space standards. Thought was given to how the spaces would be occupied – including such things as the possibility of moving cupboards in the kitchens and bedrooms, windows designed to facilitate cleaning from inside and the inclusion of amenities like laundry drying rooms, store rooms and incinerators.

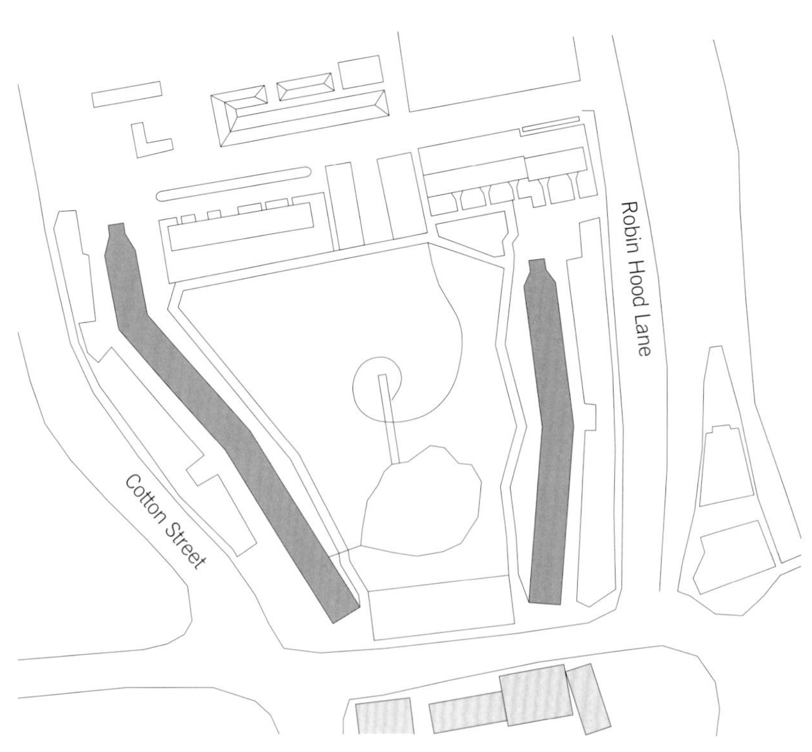

Site plan
1:2,500

Opposite left: East block

Opposite right: West block

1 Part section 1:200

1 Deck/access gallery
2 Entrance/hall
3 Kitchen
4 Bedroom
5 Living room
6 Flat at lower level
7 Garage
8 Grass
9 Service road

Plans of maisonettes 1:200

2 Lower-level plan
3 Deck/middle-level plan
4 Upper-level plan

1 Deck/access gallery
2 Entrance/hall
3 Kitchen
4 Bedroom
5 Living room

1

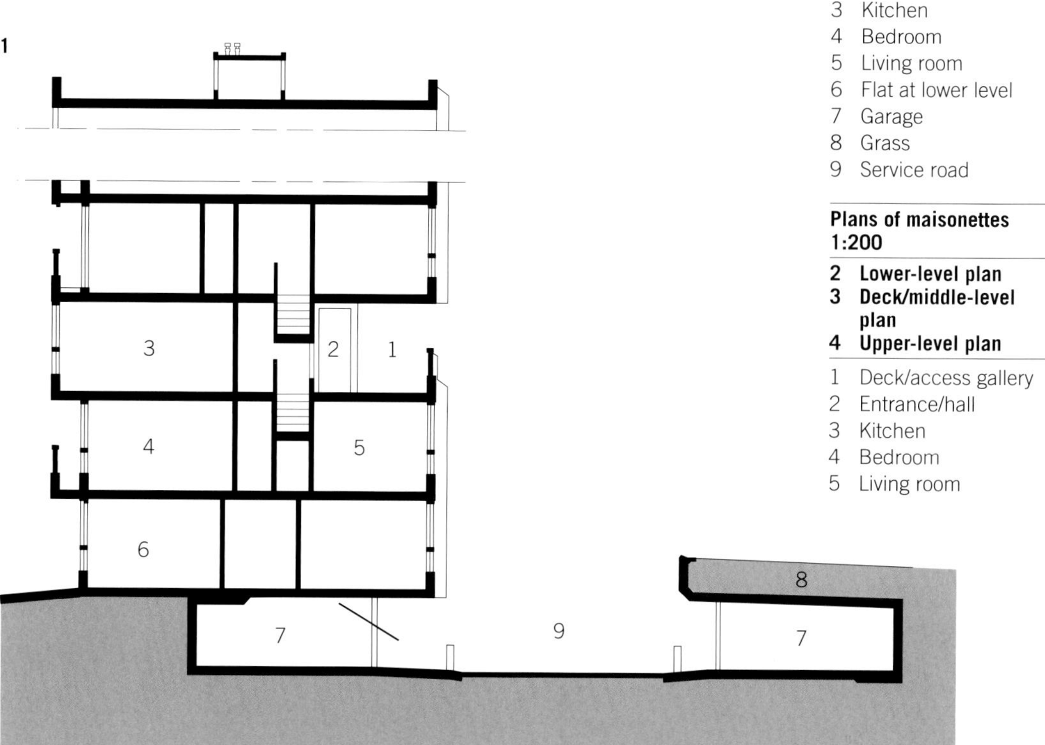

2

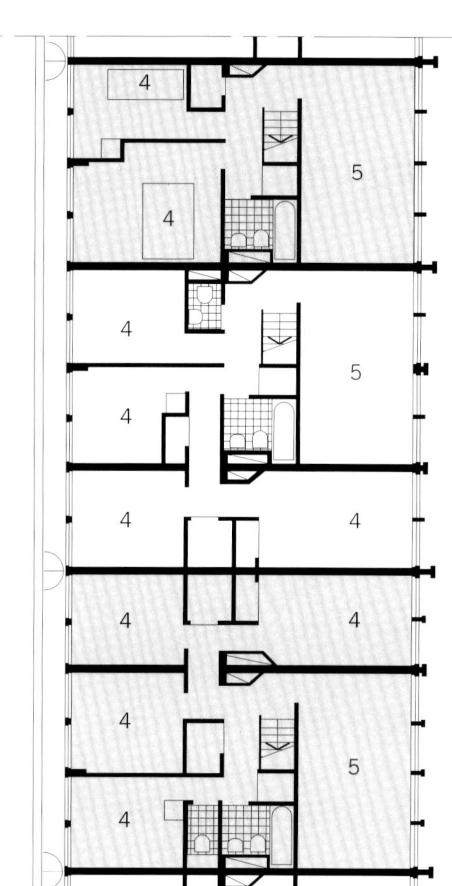

3

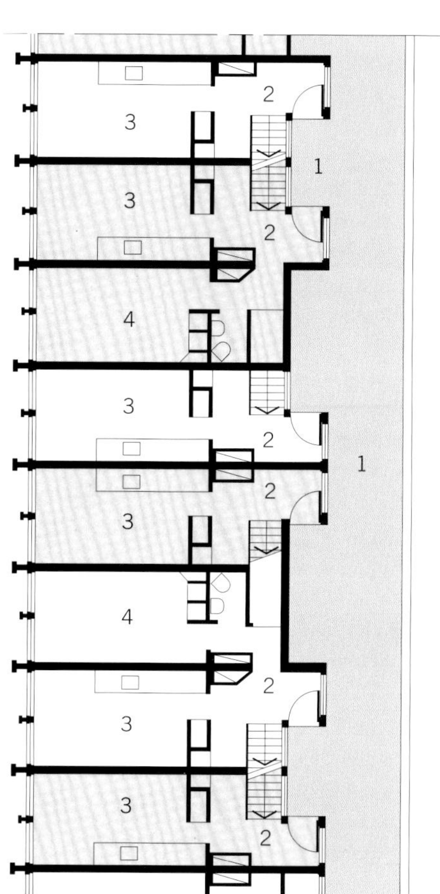

4

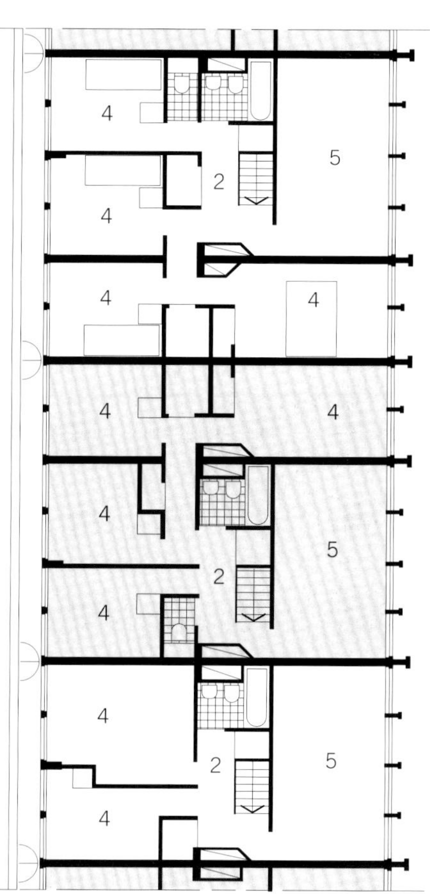

Nagakin Capsule Tower

Kisho Kurokawa, 1934–2007

Tokyo, Japan; 1971–72

The Nagakin Capsule tower is probably the most important work of the Japanese Metabolist group – a clear demonstration of their ideas that architecture should not be thought of as fixed or static, but should have the potential to grow or change over time. This notion is expressed here by Kurokawa through his use of capsules manufactured using non-traditional construction methods. The building can be thought of in two parts. One element is the fixed structural towers that contain the lifts, stairs and services and are constructed of steel and concrete. The second element, the habitable parts, is the individual 'pods': manufactured from lightweight steel in a factory and brought to site to be attached to the superstructure, they are more like pieces of equipment than dwellings. Intended for single people, many apartments were bought for use as pieds-à-terre by businessmen.

At street level there is an entrance lobby and multi-purpose hall, and access to the two towers via stairs and lifts. The first floor houses some commercial office space to cater for the large number of business occupants. As the capsules spiral around the towers, the entrances to the apartments are situated at each landing; the two towers are only connected to each other at the sixth-floor level, via a bridge. Inside, the capsules are fully fitted out with furniture and equipment. A bathroom unit is located in one corner of the space next to the entrance, and the bed space fits across the opposite end. The rest of the wall space is fitted with different kinds of storage units and optional fittings such as a freezer or audio-visual equipment, calculators and a desk. All the capsules are the same size, 2.5 x 4 metres (8 x 13 feet) in plan and 2.5 metres (8 feet) high, with some variation in layout depending on the location of the entrance. They are equipped with air conditioning as standard, and daylighting comes from the large, 1.3-metre (4-foot 3-inch) diameter windows in the end elevation.

Kurokawa also experimented with the use of capsules in other projects, notably Capsule House K in Mor-izumikyo, Nagano, in which four capsules are grouped around a fixed element containing a living space and atelier.

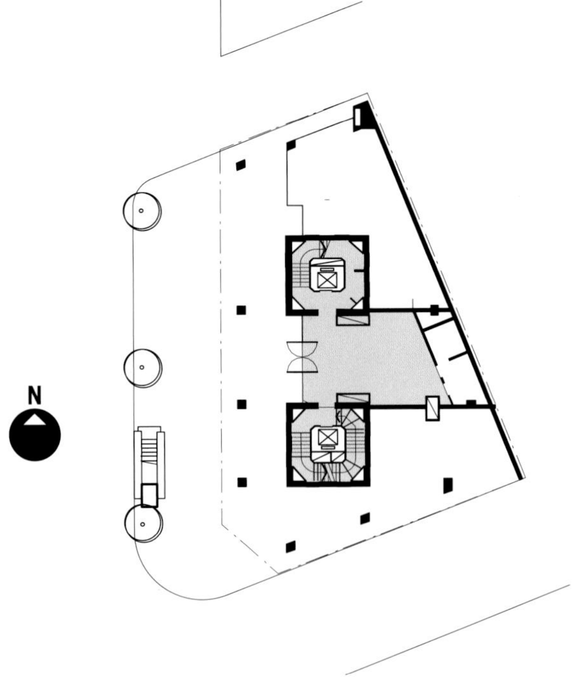

Ground-floor plan
1:500

1

1 **Elevation 1:500**

2 **Level 6 floor plan 1:200**

1 Circulation tower
2 Bridge connecting towers
3 Fire escape
4 Studio/pod

3 **Part floor plan 1:100**

2

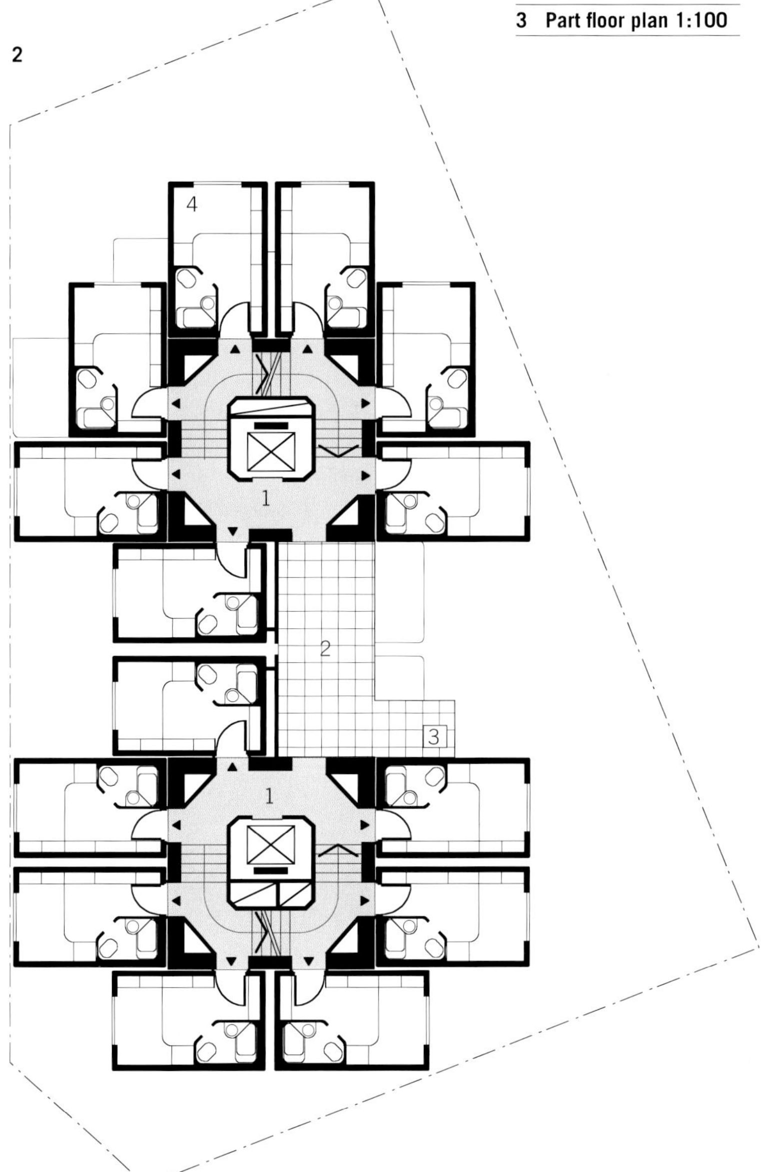

3

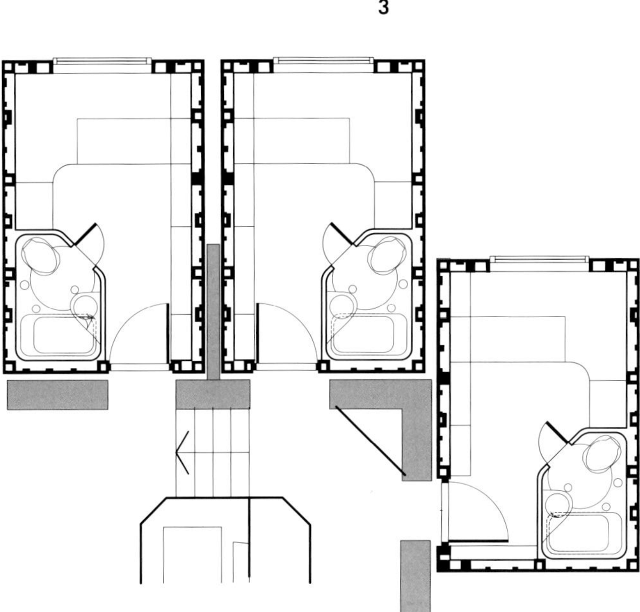

University Centre Housing

Giancarlo De Carlo, 1919–2005

Urbino, Italy; 1973–83

As a member of Team X (1956–77) alongside Jaap Bakema, Aldo van Eyck, the Smithsons, Georges Candilis and Shadrach Woods, De Carlo contributed to emerging ideas that saw architecture as part of a much broader discourse than hitherto, particularly within the context of life in the urban environment. He questioned many of what had become conventional approaches to the provision of housing and its design, particularly the idea of the minimum dwelling and economical production, stating at one point: 'we have a right to ask why housing should be as cheap as possible and not, for example, rather expensive.' For De Carlo, the theory of architecture and an understanding of historical context and contemporary society were key to developing architecture specific to a particular location – issues which were taken up in two journals he launched, the bilingual *Spazio e Società* (1978–2000) and the *International Laboratory of Architecture and Urban Design* (ILAUD, 1974–2004).

Among his best-known residential projects is the student housing at the university in Urbino, which is unlike his earlier work, which conforms largely to the ideals of CIAM. De Carlo's ideas about the importance of the relationship to the site and location, and the designing of organizational systems rather than visual or formal systems, were here developed over a decade in several phases.

Each phase of the Urbino project uses different formal arrangements, but all are based on the complexity of the interrelationships between people and the spaces between their dwellings – those used for socializing and moving around are seen to be as important as the private dwelling spaces.

The first scheme, the Collegio della Colle (1966), distributes individual student rooms in a garland-like fashion, connected by pathways leading to the central shared buildings. In developing the three further phases of the project, De Carlo saw this first element as the original centre of a city with new districts growing up around it, each, as if part of a larger city, with its own distinct local centre. The Collegio dell'Aquilone, closest to the centre of the later three colleges, uses a similar form, with curving plans following the contours of the hillside; in contrast, the Collegio della Tridente uses a strong geometric layout with three rectangular blocks radiating outwards from a central piazza. In section, the shared spaces overlap with three-storey high spaces and balconies overlooking the communal corridors.

The Collegio della Vela is more complex. With a prominent sectional design, its buildings are stepped in section following the slope of the hillside with planted roof terraces at every level. The circulation system is a warren of top-lit passageways and spiral staircases, offering no easy comprehension of the overall layout but demanding that visitors and occupants find their own routes as they would in a city. There are some similarities here with the Atelier 5 Halen estate (see pages 112–15) – most notably in the rectilinear concrete forms, terraces and dense planting but also in the whole approach to design, which focuses on the concept of settlement through a notion of historical evolution over time rather than on the design of the individual dwelling.

Opposite left: Collegio della Vela

Opposite right: Collegio dell'Aquilone

1

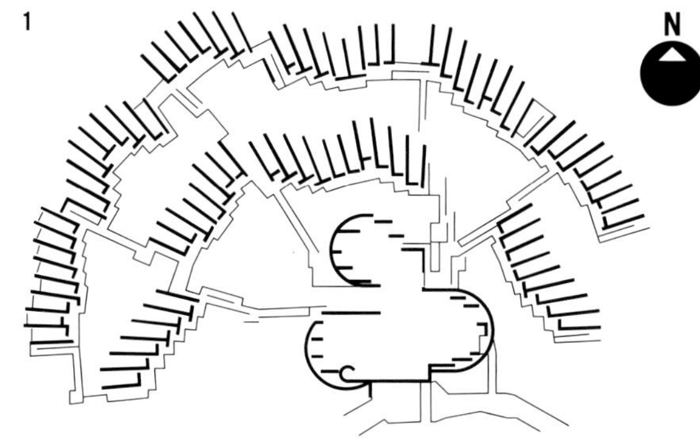

1 Collegio della Colle
Site layout 1:2,000

2

2 Collegio della Colle
Part typical plan
1:200

1 Corridors/stairs
2 Entrance/cupboards
3 Study/bedroom
4 Shower/WC

3

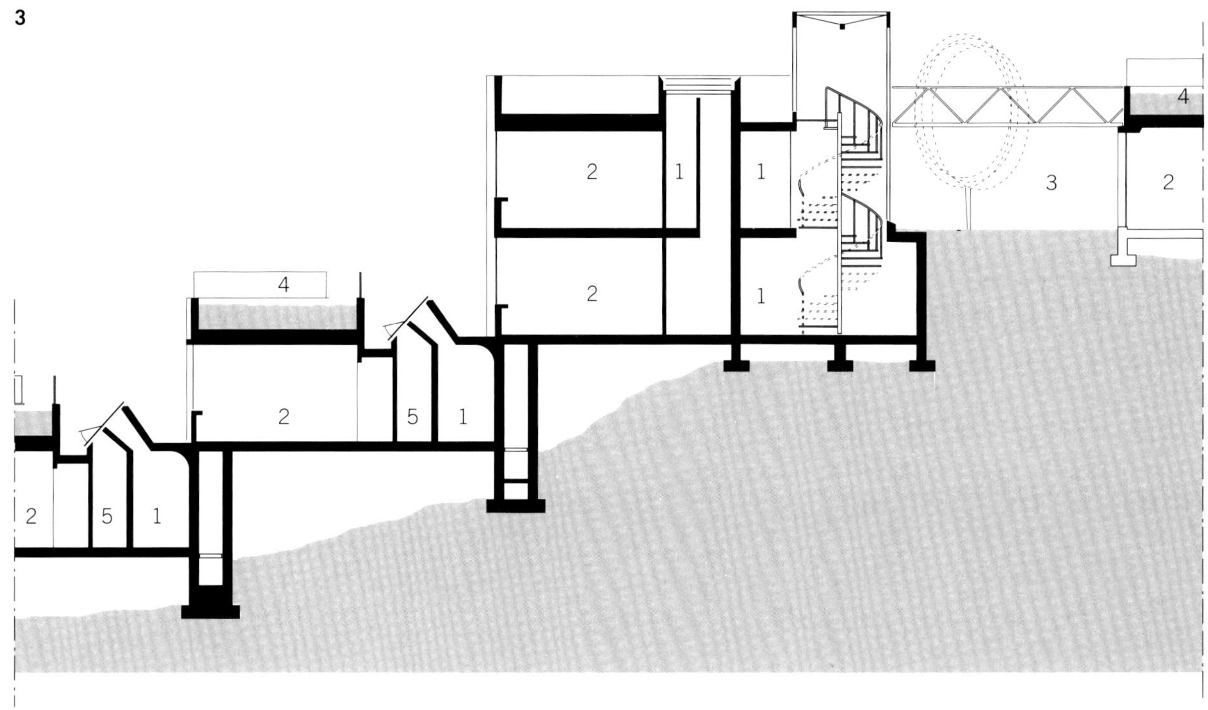

3 Collegio della Vela
Part typical section
1:200

1 Corridors/stairs
2 Bedroom
3 Garden
4 Roof garden
5 Service zone

Olympic Tower

Skidmore, Owings & Merrill

New York, New York, USA; 1976

With two floors of retail space, 17 storeys of offices and 30 floors of apartments, the Olympic Tower, in the Fifth Avenue retail district, was said to be New York City's first mixed-use building. By the early 1970s, as a result of earlier zoning legislation, New York city planners were considering ways to create or maintain lively city neighbourhoods with a mix of commercial, social and cultural activities. In midtown Manhattan, increasing numbers of office blocks were seen as a threat to the continued viability of Fifth Avenue as New York's historic shopping promenade and home of St Patrick's Cathedral, and incentives were introduced for developers who included retail and residential spaces as a part of their office developments. The Olympic went further, in order to take a fresh look at the kind of hotel services and facilities that could be included in a residential building: in addition to restaurants, it proposed a meals service for the flats, a concierge who could also help with travel arrangements, electronic security systems and an auxiliary emergency power generator. The subject of much publicity (mainly designed to boost sales), the 'Jet-set Unité for Manhattan' – as it was billed because its programme had so much in common with Le Corbusier's ideas for the vertical city – was, however, greeted with considerable, and probably justifiable, cynicism that the reality would be an 'ivory tower for the super rich'.

Despite popular criticism, the apartments sold rapidly. At street level, the apartments have a separate lobby from that of the offices. The lobby for offices is part of a double-height gallery forming a covered pedestrian street – described by the architects as a 'garden landscape', and including a waterfall – linking the entrances on 51st and 52nd Streets. The building makes no attempt to relate to its surroundings in terms of form, material or architectural composition, and without any set-backs the Fifth Avenue façade plunges uninterrupted down to street level. The individual apartments, with 2.7-metre (9-foot) high ceilings and floor-to-ceiling glazing throughout, have spectacular views across the city. Each floor houses eight very large one- and two-bedroom flats with baths, showers, WCs and cupboards lining the walls to the central corridor, and living rooms and bedrooms located adjacent to the façades. In the larger, corner apartments a dressing room connects bedroom and bathroom, and a kitchen located on the end is big enough to incorporate a small dining area.

Ground floor plan 1:1,000

1 Entrance to apartment building
2 Entrance to offices
3 Retail units

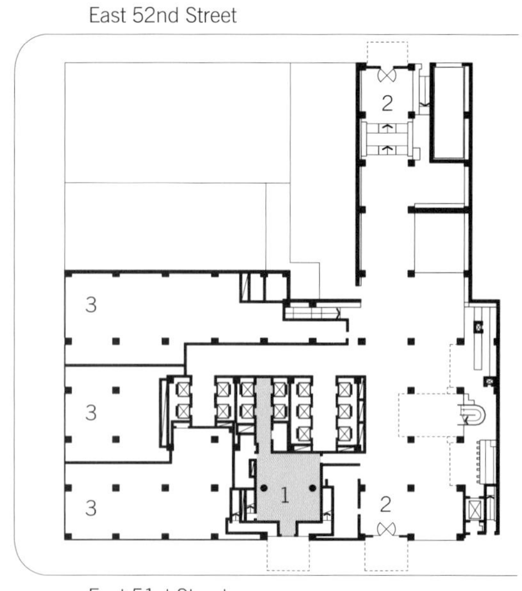

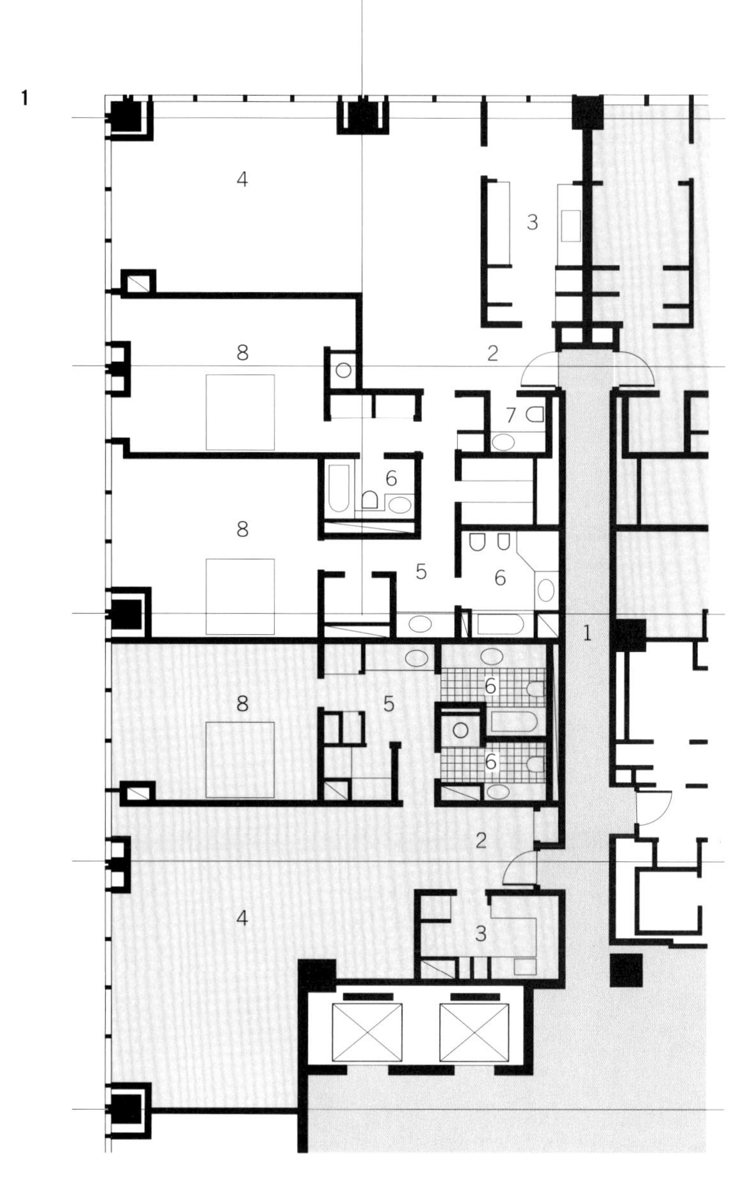

1 Part typical floor plan 1:200

1 Access corridor
2 Entrance gallery
3 Kitchen
4 Living/dining
5 Dressing room
6 Bathroom
7 Guest WC
8 Bedroom

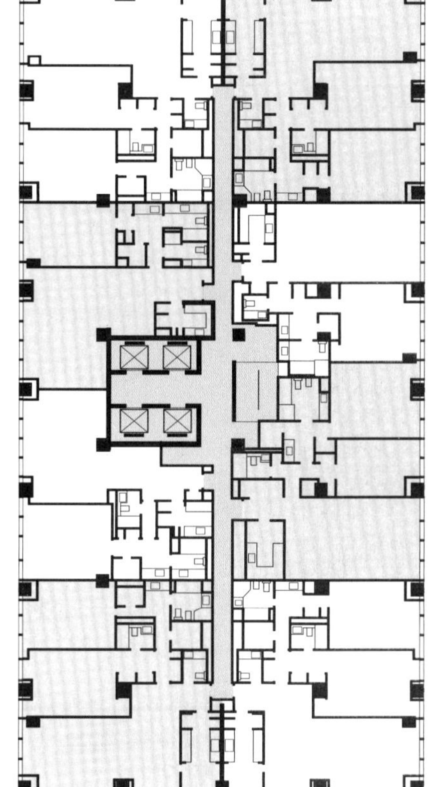

2 Typical floor plan 1:500

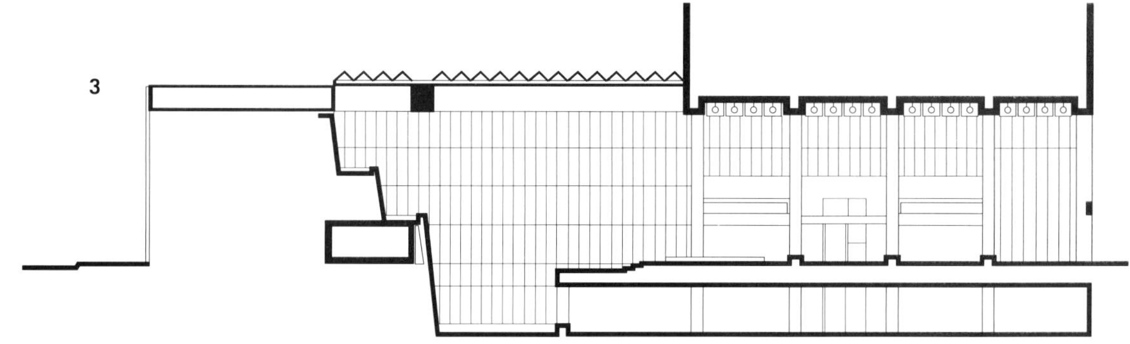

3 Section through ground floor 1:500

Walden 7

Ricardo Bofill, Taller de Arquitectura

Barcelona, Spain; 1974

The Walden 7 project was the first realization of the Taller's (studio's) ideas for a new kind of urban living, which had been explored first in an unsuccessful housing competition entry for Monaco and then at a more ambitious scale in La Ciudad en el Espacio (The City in Space) for Madrid. The concept – illustrated on the Monaco competition drawings with slogans, such as: 'time for each and time for all' and 'happiness is a cultural value' – proposed flexibility in the use of private space and a closer relationship between it and shared or public spaces. Dwellings were to be multi-functional and could be used for different activities: offices and shops were included, for example, and were clustered around public 'arenas' – spaces intended for activities such as basketball, judo or for cinema and sound-and-light projections. The individual could choose how to participate, either directly in the activities taking place or as a spectator. The multi-functional individual apartments were designed to be either closed off or easily combined with others to suit the changing needs of families over time.

The Walden 7 project, on the site of a disused cement works on the edge of Barcelona, made these ideas a reality. Described by the architects as a 'vertical labyrinth', the 446 dwellings are organized in towers around seven interior patios or courtyards. Externally, the façades are clad with red clay tiles; internally, the patios are clad with glazed ceramics, richly coloured and patterned. The voids within the blocks are filled with the curved forms of projecting balconies, and bridges that link the vertical circulation cores cross at different levels.

The roofscape includes two swimming pools, and at ground level there are bars and shops. The flats are based on a module, square in plan and measuring 30 square metres (323 square feet). Variations range from one single module up to four, and include duplex apartments. The most unusual feature of the apartments is a 'conversation pit' – a sunken area in the centre of the living space with, for example, a table on one side and bed on the other. In the single, or studio, module, the bath is positioned off the living space rather than enclosed in a separate room.

Location plan 1:10,000

1 Walden 7
2 Proposed phase 2
3 Site of cement works
4 South-west industrial district

1

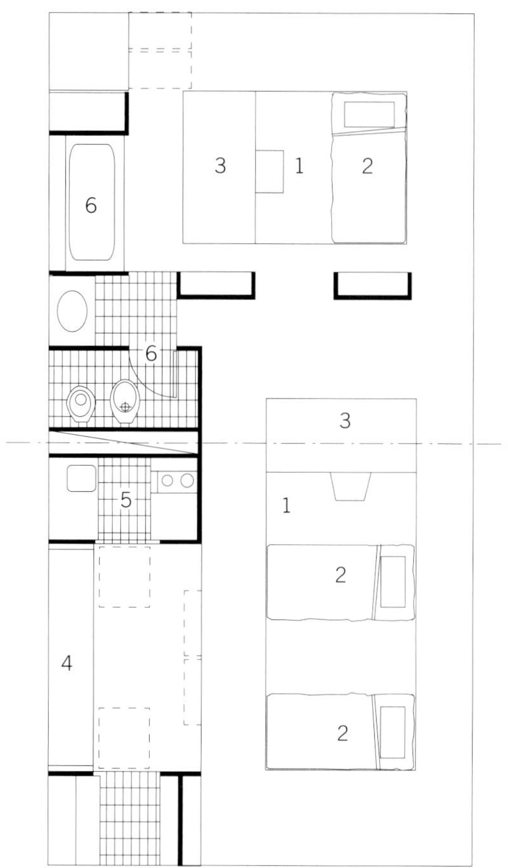

2

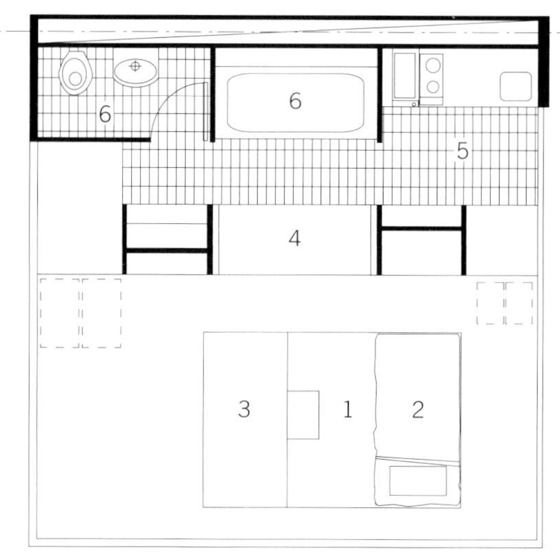

3

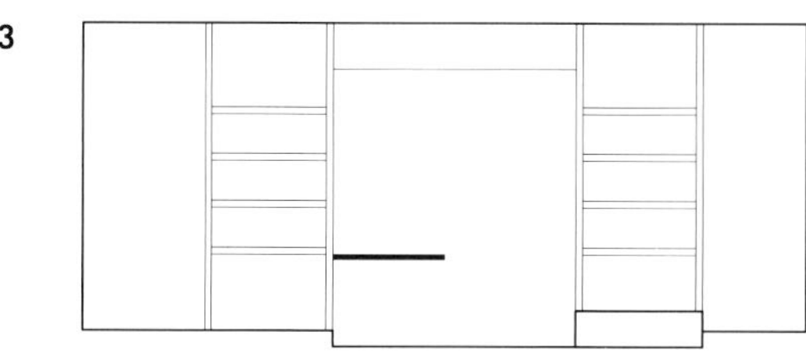

4

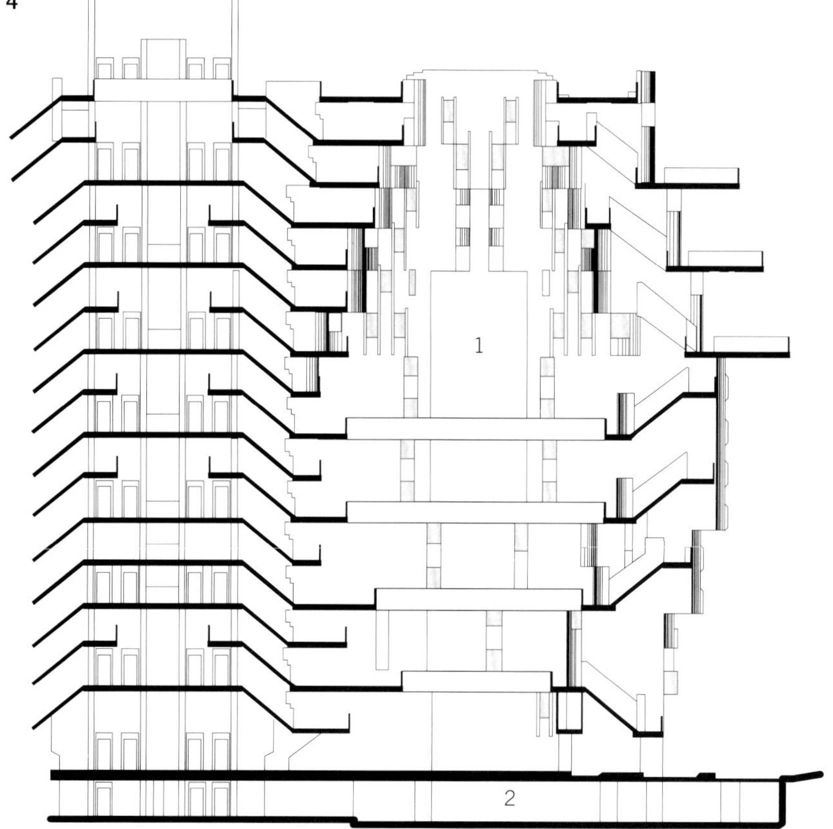

Plans of typical apartments 1:100

1 Three-bedroom flat
2 One-bedroom flat/ studio
3 Section/elevation of one-bedroom flat

1 Sunken floor
2 Divan
3 Movable table/ worktop
4 Fixed table/worktop
5 Kitchen
6 Bath/WC

4 Part typical section 1:500

1 Atrium
2 Basement parking

Far left: Street façade

Left: Interior of an apartment

Emmanuel Benaki Street Apartments

Atelier 66 (Suzanna Antonakakis, 1935– and Dimitris Antonakakis, 1933–)

Athens, Greece; 1973

The small block of four flats and office space on Emmanuel Benaki Street was built by a partnership of four tenants. The starting point was therefore the desires of the particular individuals and their families, rather than a set of given social conventions. This nevertheless led to the creation of a kind of five-point 'manifesto' for the design of the building – in the architects' words: 'not the conventional approach but another strategy.' Two of the points relate to the shared circulation space and the entrance, which is seen as an important space linking the street with the dwellings rather than a separation. A curving open stair is visible on the front façade, connecting the well-lit landing spaces visually with the street below and avoiding any narrow and dark shared corridors. The third point is that ambiguous and ill-defined outdoor spaces, which so easily become disused and uncared for, are to be avoided – replaced by a shared yard planted with trees and flowers. The other two points relate to the layout of the private spaces in the apartments themselves, the intermingling of inside and outside, and flexibility. Spaces are often open on both sides, with living rooms that stretch across the full depth of the plan and that have windows on both sides to allow light and ventilation throughout. The importance of flexibility in the use of space implies avoiding unnecessary divisions between private areas and space for guests, and the avoidance of spaces that are unusable because they are too small – especially the narrow balconies familiar in many housing schemes. Here, the balconies are spacious and linked to the living spaces in such a way that they can be seen to extend the space of the interior.

The section adds a further three-dimensional richness to the intricacies of the plans, with three of the four apartments extending to another floor level. The apartments on the third and fourth floors have a study/workroom at a different level: the fourth-floor apartment has its study in an attic surrounded by the roof terrace, while the third-floor unit has a study next to its entrance on the floor below. The first-floor apartment occupies two complete levels, with double-height living spaces in the centre crossed by a bridge-like corridor on the bedroom level which connects two staircases. Stairs also connect the balconies on both levels externally.

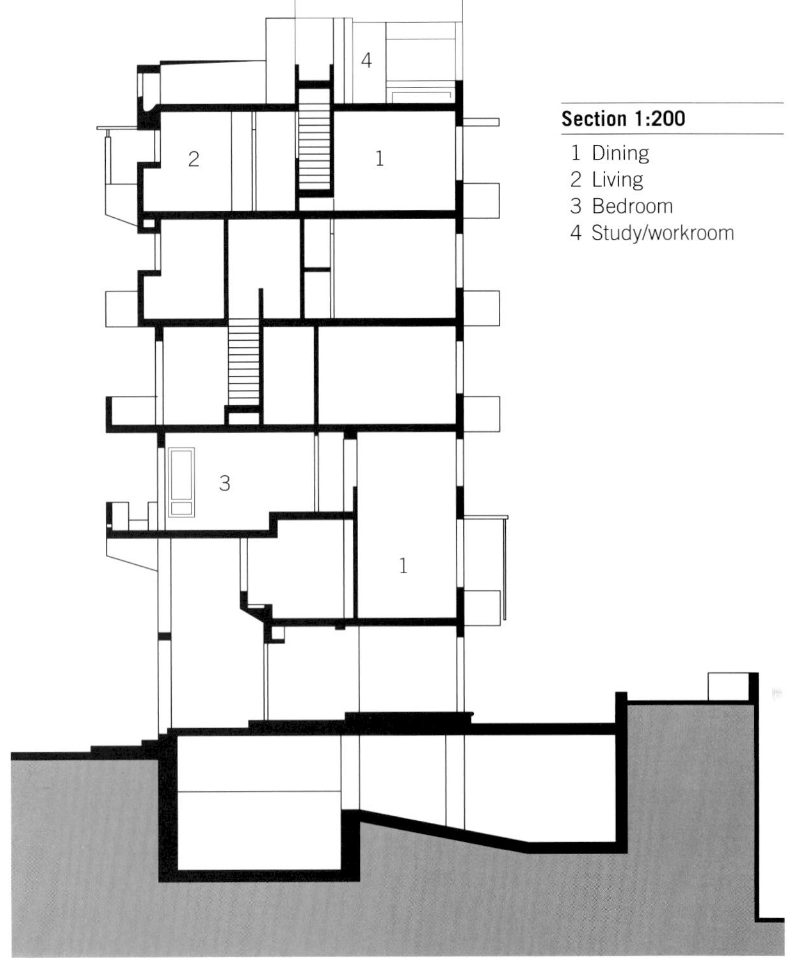

Section 1:200

1 Dining
2 Living
3 Bedroom
4 Study/workroom

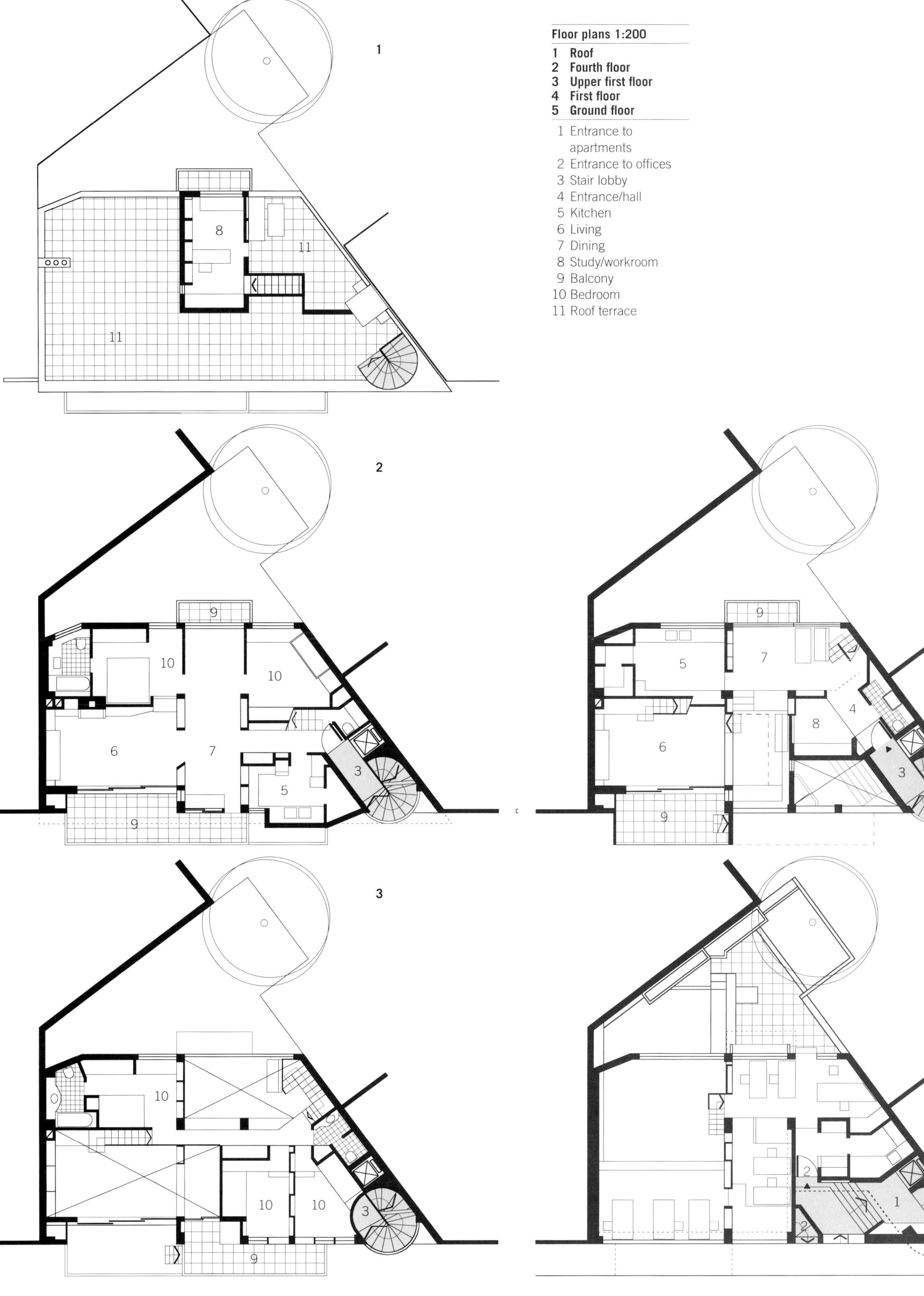

Floor plans 1:200

1 **Roof**
2 **Fourth floor**
3 **Upper first floor**
4 **First floor**
5 **Ground floor**

1 Entrance to apartments
2 Entrance to offices
3 Stair lobby
4 Entrance/hall
5 Kitchen
6 Living
7 Dining
8 Study/workroom
9 Balcony
10 Bedroom
11 Roof terrace

Housing on Calle Doña María Coronel

Cruz y Ortiz Arquitectos

Seville, Spain; 1976

In the Calle Doña María Coronel project Cruz y Ortiz transformed the traditional Sevillian patio into a continuously curving amorphous shape unrelated to the structure of the building. The living accommodation is organized in the residual spaces around the perimeter of this shape, and the courtyard also acts as a focus for activity: the main entrance into it from the street provides access both for pedestrians and for vehicles. This central feature was also a response to a requirement to leave 25 per cent of the land undeveloped, part of a local regeneration and urban development strategy to reduce overall population densities in the centre of Seville.

There are three apartments per floor, each with four rooms. The layout of each flat is tailor-made to fit the complex perimeter of the site. One apartment overlooks the street and the others have bedrooms and kitchens overlooking the courtyard and two small lightwells. Circulation spaces within the apartments include entrance hallways and separate lobbies leading to the bedrooms and bathrooms. There are no balconies, but in addition to the patio the roof level has a terrace accessible to all the residents. The patio itself is fitted with a fabric awning at roof level to reduce overheating in the summer.

Writing in the introduction to the monograph published by Princeton in 1996, Rafael Moneo describes Cruz and Ortiz's design of the Doña Maria Coronel courtyard as 'an act of outstanding courage' and part of their search to define an architecture that 'provides a single synthetic style'. Since completing this, their first, project, Cruz and Ortiz have gone on to design many other very different kinds of housing schemes as well as commercial and public buildings. Examples of these include the Carabanchel project (1989) in Madrid, which redefines the urban block with a series of three-storey high stepped forms; and the design of a new typology for a 1½-storey high single-family house for a development on the outskirts of the Andalusian mining village of Tharsis (1992). More recently, they have completed housing projects outside Spain – in Amsterdam, Rotterdam and Maastricht.

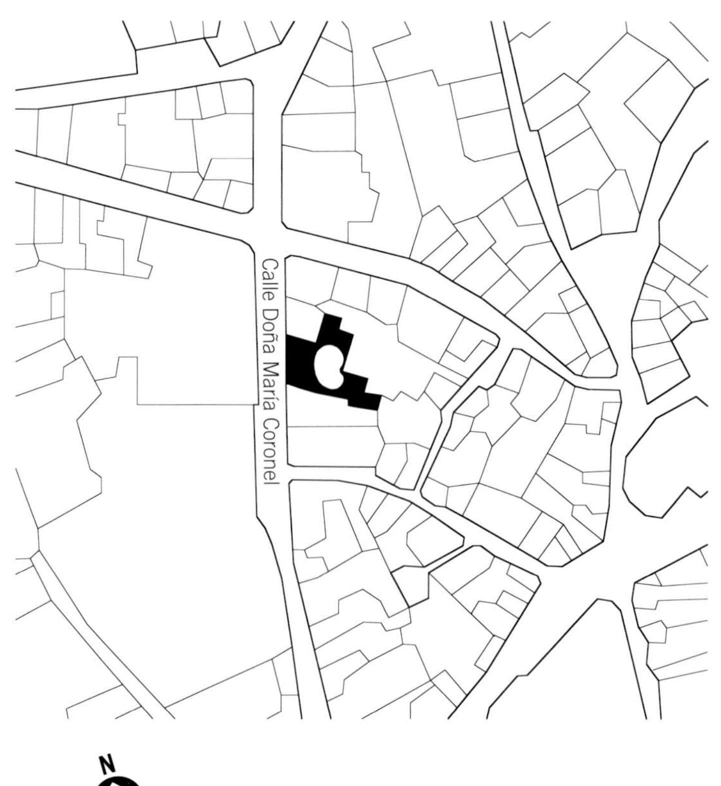

Site plan 1:2,500

Opposite left: Courtyard elevation

Opposite right: Internal courtyard

1

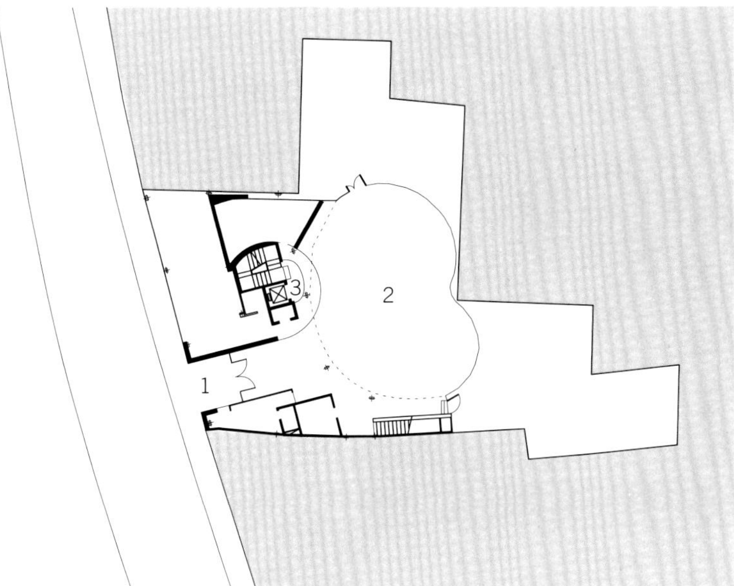

1 Ground-floor plan 1:500

1 Entrance from Calle Doña María Coronel
2 Patio
3 Lifts and stairs

2 Typical upper-floor plan 1:200

1 Patio/courtyard
2 Access stairs/lift
3 Entrance/hall
4 Kitchen
5 Living
6 Bedroom
7 Bathroom
8 Lightwell

2

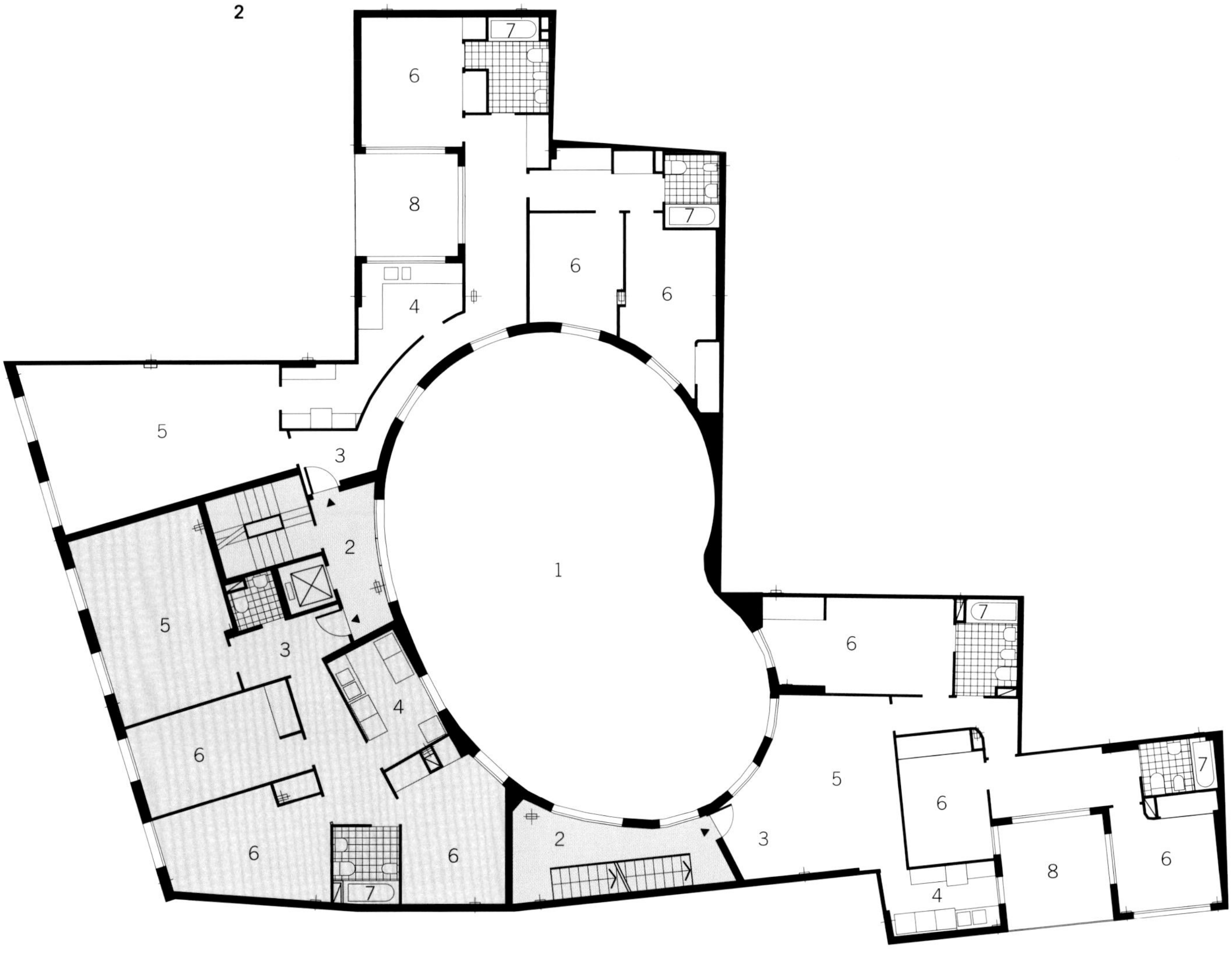

Gallaratese Housing

Aldo Rossi (1931–97) with Carlo Aymonino (1926–)

Milan, Italy; 1974

Aldo Rossi was associated with the Italian neo-Rationalists. He wrote the introduction to the catalogue of the exhibition of Rational architecture at the Milan Triennale in 1973, and was well known for his *The Architecture of the City* (1966). Rationalism's typological approach to design enables straightforward description, analysis and categorization through relationships to other things. However, it is important that the neo-Rationalists are distinguished from the early Rationalists and the Gruppo 7 of young architects in Milan during the Fascist period, whose approach to creating 'types' was intended to recreate the powerful national symbols associated with ancient Rome.

Rossi sought an autonomy for architecture – an escape from the functionalism of 1950s Modernism, which was considered too prescriptive and constrained by economics. He saw architecture as fundamental to the urban environment and used urban typologies – avenue, piazza, street – as models. The Gallaratese project, in collaboration with Carlo Aymonino, was an important step in finding fresh paradigms for much-needed housing developments. The initial site layout for the project was carried out with Aymonino. On a roughly triangular plot, three long rectangular buildings with central corridors, designed by Aymonino, radiated outwards from a semicircular amphitheatre and raised piazzas. Parallel to this central 'spine' is the fourth block, designed by Rossi. In direct contrast to the more usual 1950s Modernist approach of blocks standing isolated in open space, the architects here linked their blocks together, thus providing a natural community space at the junction of the blocks, which was designed to accommodate commercial space and public areas for shared use. The Aymonino blocks have complex modulated façades, painted in rich shades of brown and forming a contrasting backdrop to Rossi's starkly white, pristine, smooth block. The block is almost 200 metres long and 12 metres deep (650 x 40 feet), with 2-metre (6-foot 6-inch) wide access galleries; it follows a rigid 7.2-metre (24-foot) grid, the width of an apartment. A typical flat has a spacious entrance hall with cupboards, a large bathroom and, opposite, a small kitchen that gives onto the living space. A loggia is included on the opposite façade. At ground level, an arcade runs the length of the building.

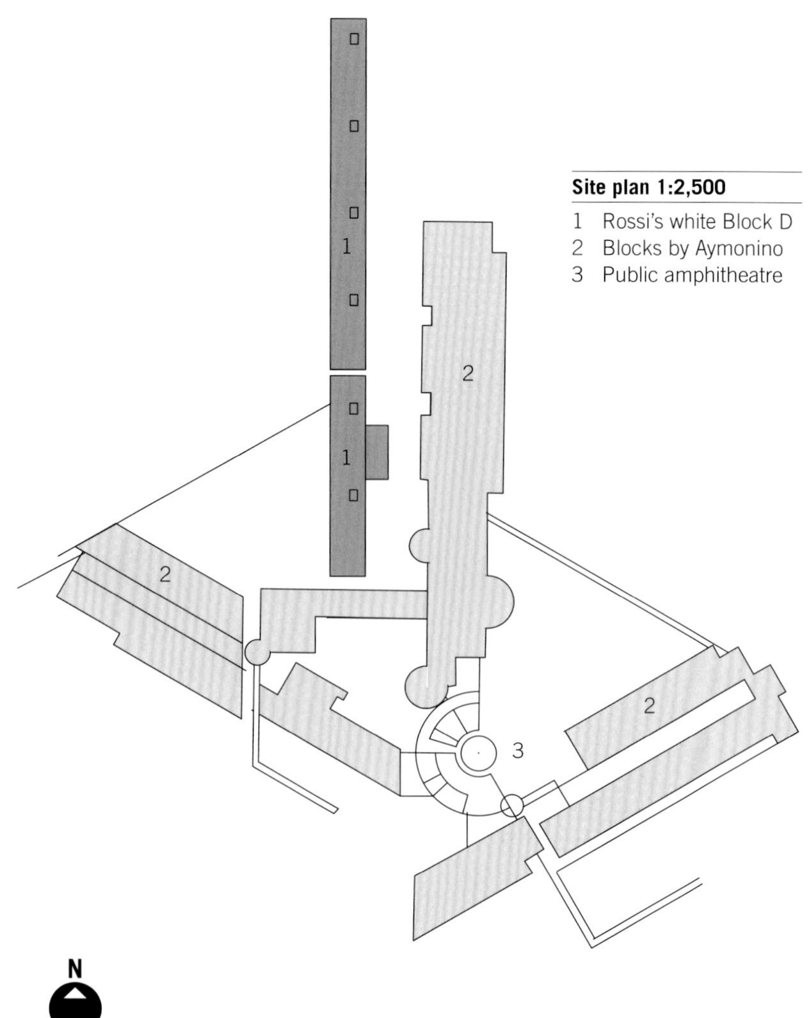

Site plan 1:2,500

1 Rossi's white Block D
2 Blocks by Aymonino
3 Public amphitheatre

1 Plan of typical one-bedroom apartments 1:200

1 Access gallery
2 Entrance/hall
3 Kitchen
4 Living
5 Bedroom
6 Bathroom
7 Loggia

2 West elevation 1:1000

3 Part east elevation 1:500

4 Part plan second-floor level 1:500

1 Access gallery
2 One-bedroom flat
3 Three-bedroom flat

1

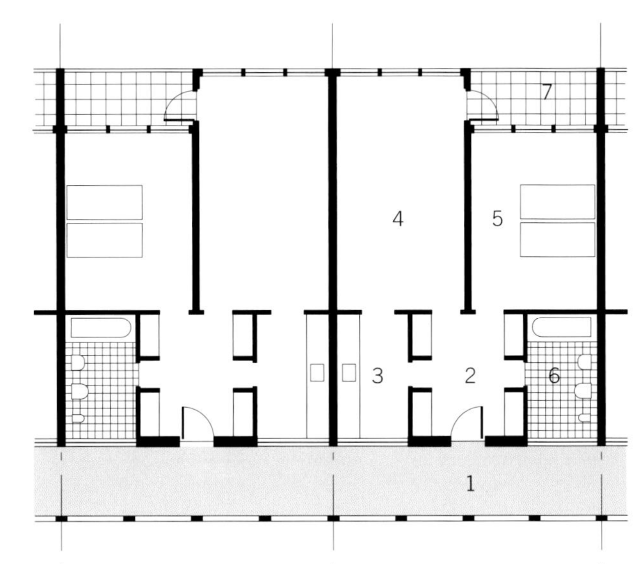

2

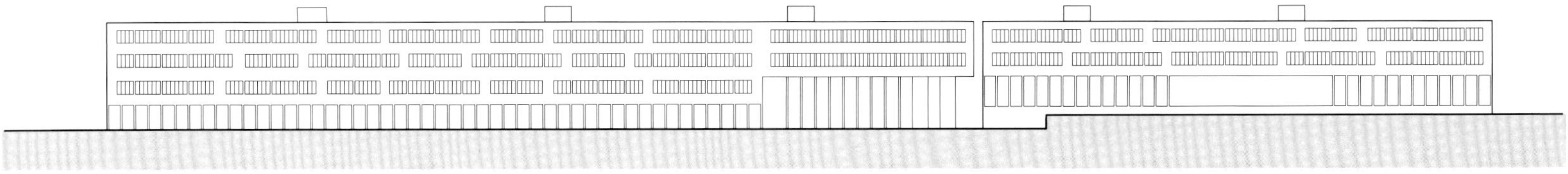

3

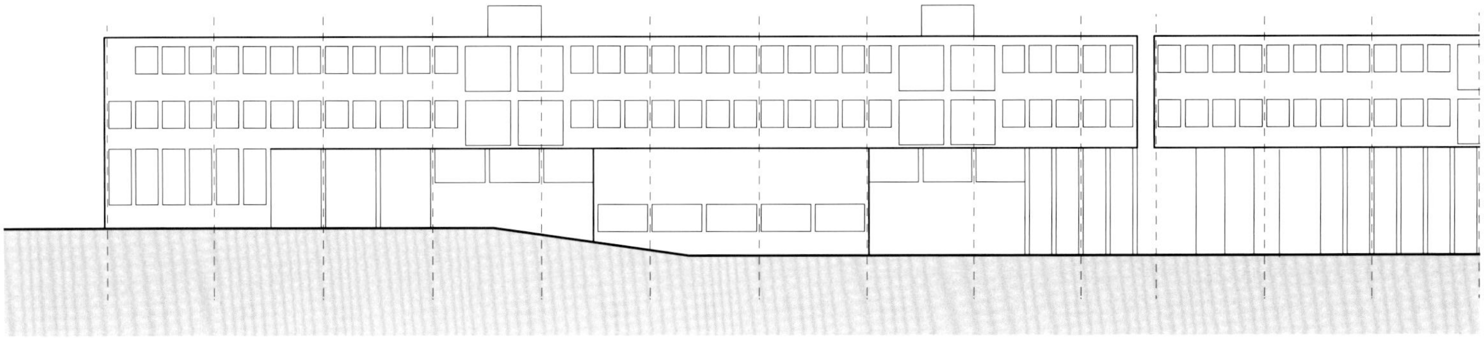

4

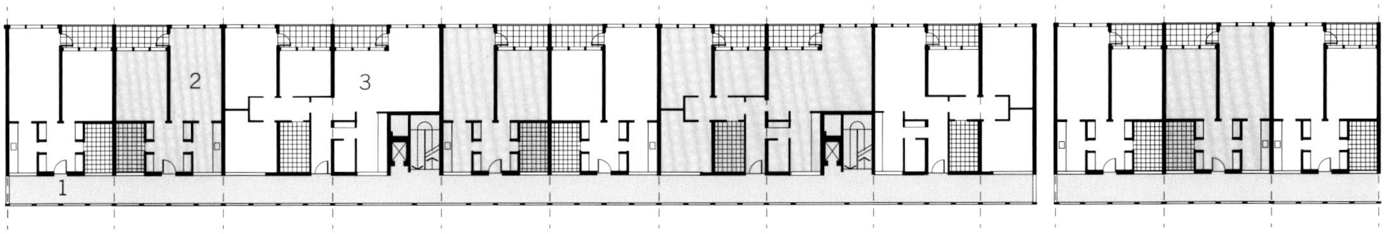

Quinta da Malagueira Housing

Álvaro Siza Vieira, 1933–

Évora, Portugal; 1977

This development is based on the unusual design of back-to-back terraced houses. Organized within identical rectangular plans, 12 metres (39 feet) deep and 8 metres (26 feet) wide, there are two basic patio-house types: one (type A) has a patio at the entrance on the street side, and the other (type B) has a patio at the back. The houses are laid out in parallel terraces, handed in pairs, back to back with 6-metre (19-foot 6-inch) wide roads between them. The uniformity of the design is broken up by the 'short cuts' of meandering pedestrian pathways, and the juxtaposition of the horizontality of the construction with the slope of the ground. The scheme is organized into several housing groups, with open park spaces between them.

Both house types have identical ground-floor plans, and the size of the dwellings is varied by the number of additional rooms at first-floor level. Sizes range from the one-bedroom single-level house with a large roof terrace to those houses with five bedrooms and two bathrooms on two levels. The patio, contained within the footprint of each house, provides daylight to the ground-floor rooms, and rooflights bring light and ventilation down to the bathrooms and other internal areas. From the street, the continuous wall surfaces of the façades are interrupted only by the entrance doors to the patios behind and by a minimal number of windows. Roof terraces are provided in all dwelling types, with the possibility for separate access from the patio. Flexibility is an intention of the scheme. The construction of the units, with the different options available, means that they can be extended at a later date. All the services – water, gas, electricity, TV and telephone cables – are ducted together at high level between the houses to facilitate variation, both at the time of construction and in possible future extensions. Situated on the outskirts of the town of Évora, in southern Portugal, the white-painted stucco finish and solid, low forms of these houses relate to the vernacular farm buildings of the Alentejo – in sharp contrast to the nearby 1960s and 1970s undistinguished concrete high-rises found in so many European suburbs.

1

2

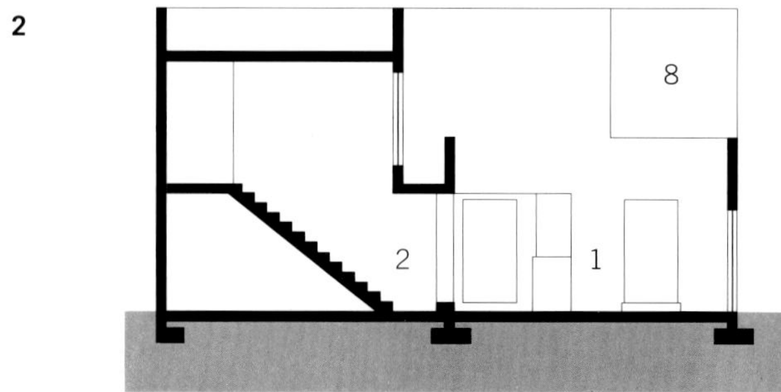

3

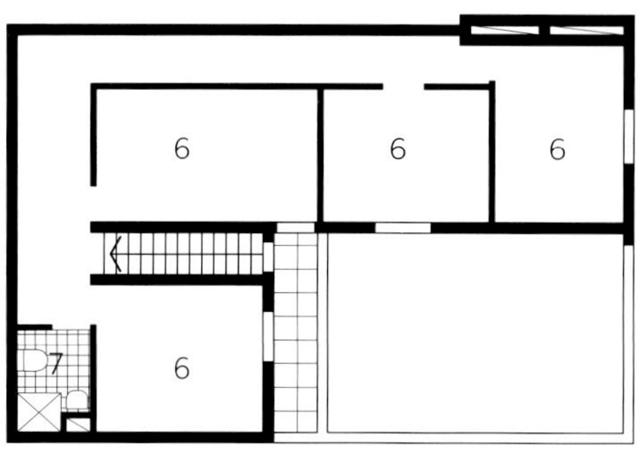

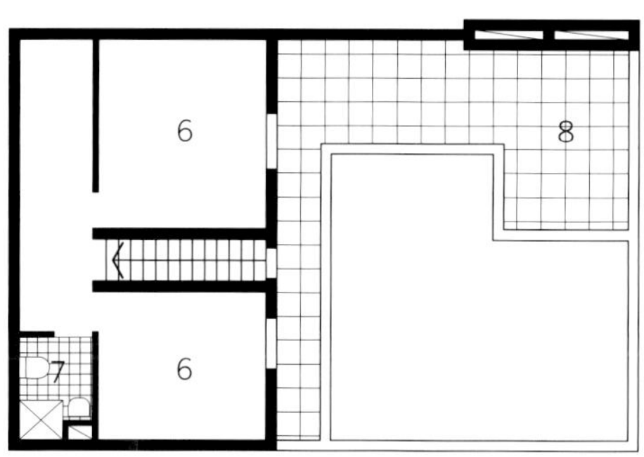

5

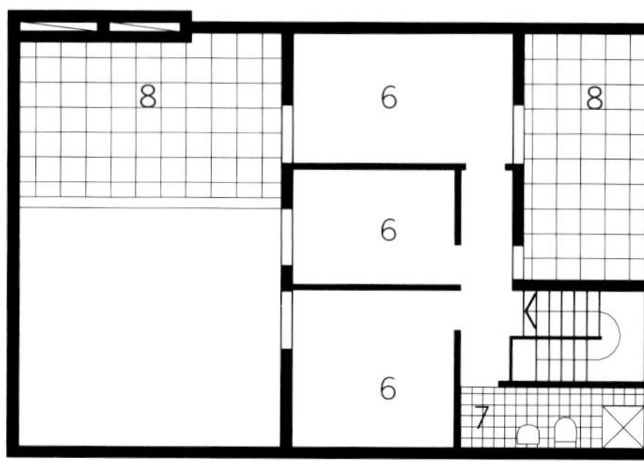

Plans of two courtyard houses 1:200

Type A courtyard at front

1 **Ground-floor plan**
2 **Section**
3 **Three variations of first-floor plan**
4 **First-floor roof terrace**

Type B courtyard at rear

5 **Three variations of first-floor plan**
6 **First-floor roof terrace**
7 **Ground-floor plan**
8 **Section**

1 Courtyard/patio
2 Entrance
3 Kitchen
4 Laundry
5 Living
6 Bedroom
7 Bathroom
8 Roof terrace

4

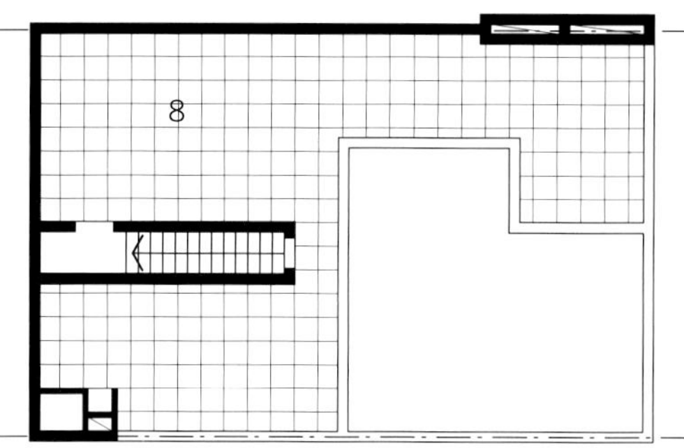

6

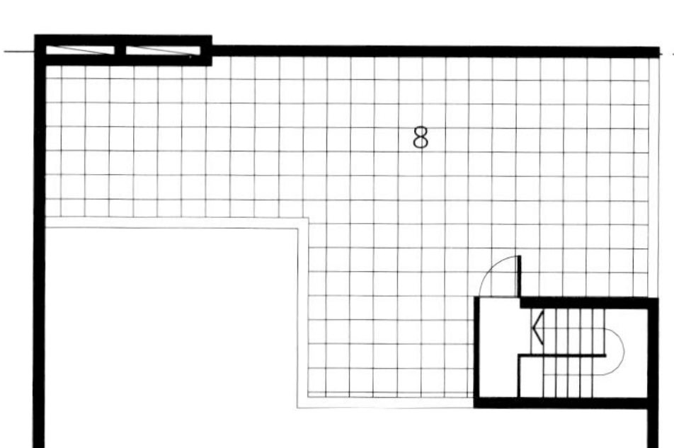

7

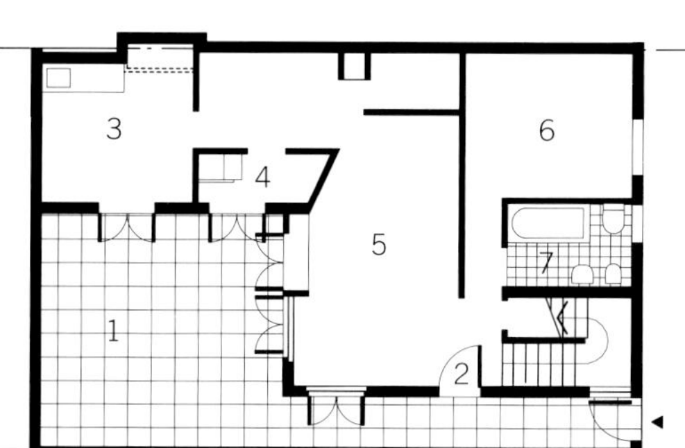

8

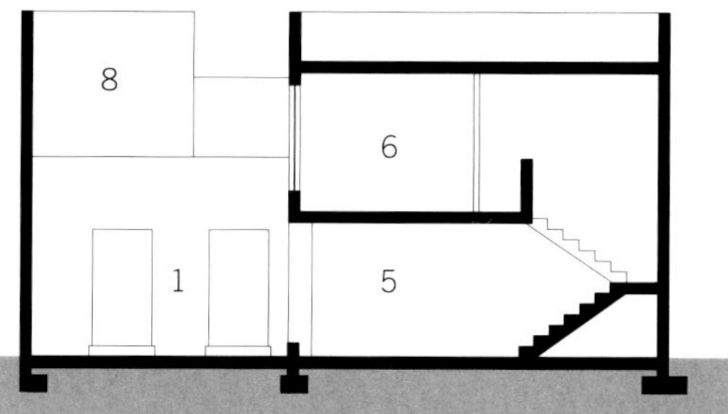

Post-Modernism

Left and above: **IBA Berlin residential blocks on Rauchstrasse, by Hans Hollein (left) and Rob Krier (above), both 1985**

During the 1980s, both West Germany and France were building large numbers of new housing projects. The work carried out to repair and rebuild Berlin as part of the **International Building Exhibition (IBA)**, under the directorship of Josef Paul Kleihues, was particularly influential at the time, bringing theories of housing design and urban planning to the fore. As part of the strategy to renew or to complete repairs to the bomb-damaged city, there were to be three different kinds of intervention in the existing urban fabric: urban reconstruction, city repair and gentle urban renewal. New urban models were to be developed, acknowledging both the forms of the traditional city and Modernism; in the words of Kleihues in the catalogue for the exhibition, the approach was to the 'city as an historical phenomenon'. The traditional city block, which Kleihues refers to as analogous 'with the pace of life and rhythm of urban space' was redefined and qualified as a constructed, continuous, divided block, and was to provide the formal structure for the international architects taking part. Peter Eisenman's **Corner Housing at Kochstrasse** (see pages 162–63), close to Checkpoint Charlie where until 1990 westerners crossed the border to the east, uses a clash of overlaying geometries to reveal the history and origins of the site. O. M. Ungers' **Housing on Lützowplatz** (see pages 164–65) is a more pragmatic approach to recreating an urban block, with a terrace facing the city and villas behind overlooking a shared garden.

In towns and cities across France, development continued in satellite towns and suburbs where there was no return to a nineteenth-century block model. Nevertheless, the architecture of Post-Modernism sought to replace what were by now thought of as the isolated, oversized and anonymous slabs of Modernism with buildings intended to create a sense of place and a sense of identity. To this end, architects abandoned the abstract idealism of Modernism's housing projects and its obsession with the perfect efficient plan, and sought a continuity with the past through historical reference, transferring their attention to the façade and to the visual power of form and surface. Henri Ciriani's **Noisy II Housing** scheme at Marne-la-Vallée (see pages 170–71) is just one of many schemes by architects specializing in housing design – among them Ricardo Bofill and Henri Gaudin – that sought to reinvent the urban environment in Paris's suburbs. Bofill's **Abraxas Housing**, also in Marne-la-Vallée, was completed three years after Noisy II. Within the existing city, Christian de Portzamparc's **Rue des Hautes Formes** housing (see pages 168–69) was highly innovative as a residential project that actually created urban space. It was also the first winner of the recently launched PAN (Programme d'Architecture Nouveau) competition, forerunner of the Europan housing competition which seeks to encourage an exchange of ideas as well as to build houses, and now operates across 20 EU countries. In southern France, Jean Nouvel et Associés' **Nemausus** project in Nîmes (see pages 178–79) takes a radical look at construction in order to provide more space per dwelling. By using basic industrial components and raw building materials, no finishes and no decorations, Nouvel substantially

reduced the cost of the development, with the result that each apartment can be much larger than those in comparable social housing projects.

In England a similar Post-Modern approach saw a return to the street as the physical and social organizing element of the city. In London, Jeremy and Fenella Dixon's **St Mark's Road Housing** scheme (see pages 166–67), followed by a second scheme by the same architects in Ashmill Street, took cues from the surrounding nineteenth-century terraced houses, demonstrating how the 'traditional' London house could be reinvented – at a different, smaller scale reminiscent of early twentieth-century cottages – in a modern form to provide a sense of place. Another unusual version of the terrace-house type – back-to-backs – is used in the **Pence Place** scheme by Gwathmey Siegel in Columbus, Indiana (see pages 180–81), where pedestrian streets and front gardens separate the interlocked parallel rows of houses.

Byker Wall in Newcastle (see pages 174–75), by the British-born Swedish-based architect Ralph Erskine, was to be the last of England's large-scale, local-government-funded social housing schemes, completed in 1982. It is as well known for its colourful high wall of flats encircling the perimeter as for its 'community architecture' credentials, which saw architects permanently

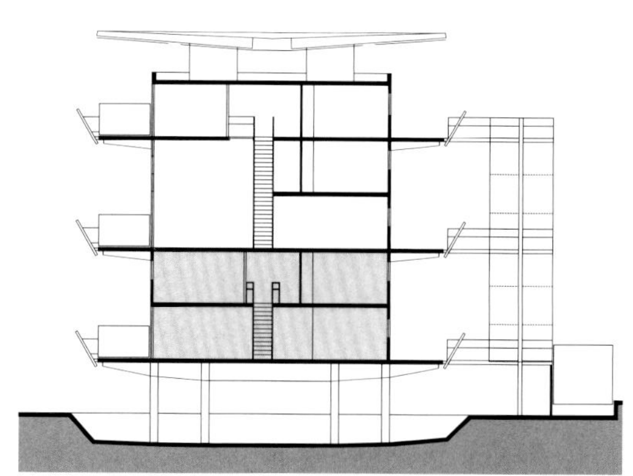

located on the site during construction and the participation of residents at all stages in the design process.

While this period saw the re-examination of tower and slab-block models for social housing, in less dense urban environments they continued to provide a model for the luxury market. In Sydney, Australia, Harry Seidler and Associates' 43-storey **Horizon Apartments** tower (see pages 190–91) with its small footprint was seen as preferable to the space required by a low-rise building. Similarly, in American cities with lower densities high-rise luxury condominiums have become commonplace as a residential building type. Arquitectonica's **Atlantis Condominium** in Miami (see pages 172–73) is generally recognized as being the first of this new brash type, opening the way for the many others that have followed.

A decade later, Arquitectonica also contributed a building to the **Nexus World** development in Fukuoka, Japan, alongside buildings by Portzamparc, Rem Koolhaas, Mark Mack and Steven Holl (see pages 186–87). Mack's scheme, like Holl's, has cleverly designed plans with split levels, double-height volumes and sliding panels, but it is the only one finished with brightly coloured surfaces reminiscent of traditional Japanese architecture.

Opposite top left: **Abraxas Housing**

Opposite top right: **Atlantis Condominium**

Opposite left: **Byker Wall**

Above left: **Nexus World development**

Above right: **Nemausus, section**

Corner Housing at Kochstrasse

Eisenman Robertson Architects

Berlin, Germany; 1982–86

This social housing project occupies what was a prominent site in Berlin. It sits on the corner of Friedrichstrasse, the main avenue running north–south but cut off by the Berlin Wall, and Kochstrasse, the last perpendicular street before Checkpoint Charlie. The significance of this location to the history of the particular geography of Berlin was key to Peter Eisenman and Jacquelin Robertson's design approach. This project was also part of the contemporary theoretical critique of Modernism, which focused on its seeming inability to deal with history and the idea of a sense of place. Post-Modernist architects called on the idea of memory through the use of symbol but Eisenman and Robertson were seeking another approach, referred to in the project submission as 'anti memory' – an approach, most easily likened to archaeology, that employed the traces, remnants or absence of earlier structures as abstract tools with which to develop form.

The building is clearly related to its particular site. The geometry of the ground plan is a response to the existing conditions: the street plan of Berlin. Overlaid on the street gird is the Mercator Grid (the UTM), which uses longitude and latitude to map the curving surface of the globe – which here, coincidentally, is at 3.3 degrees to the street grid. This 'other' abstract geometry is made visible in the central section of the building, which appears twisted away from the main street front but contained within the conforming top and bottom sections. This clash of geometries appears in plan in angled partitions and tapering internal spaces. The positions of walls are related both to found structures (those that site excavations revealed) and imagined structures, and the material is Berlin brick. The project also envisaged a grid of limestone walls and included promenade spaces for the contemplation of 'history' in all its senses.

Budgetary constraints limited the scope of the final scheme somewhat and meant that only this first phase of the project, which was originally intended to extend to fill the whole city block, was constructed.

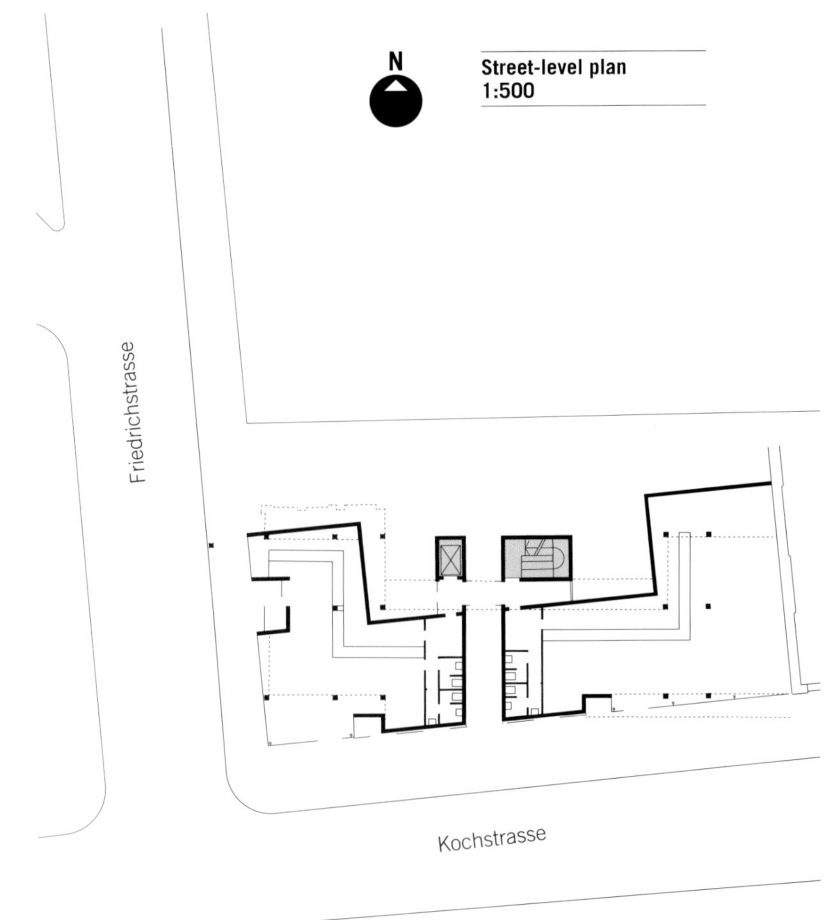

Street-level plan
1:500

1 Typical floor plan 1:200

1 Common circulation
2 External access galleries
3 Entrance/hall
4 Kitchen
5 Living room
6 Bathroom
7 Bedroom
8 Balcony

Plans of attic duplex 1:500

2 Upper-level plan

3 Lower-level plan

4 Section 1:500

Housing on Lützowplatz

O. M. Ungers, 1926–2007

Berlin, Germany; 1979–83

Lützowplatz had been destroyed by a new traffic planning scheme, implemented after the Second World War, that widened the roads to the west and south leaving the square as little more than an oversized roundabout. In addition, only a few fragments of the original buildings that formed the perimeter of the square remained. Ungers' housing design sets out to address the coherence of the square by reinstating one side of it, to the west. The form of the housing, the location of certain rooms, and the section were all developed in response to the site conditions, particularly the traffic flow and noise levels of what has become a very busy traffic intersection.

The housing, in two parts, forms the perimeter of a 'new' city block. Along the east side a continuous façade forms a buffer to the traffic, behind which five 'villas' form the other punctuated boundary. Circulation routes cross the site parallel to the edge block running north to south. On the west side, in the centre of the larger city block, a street provides access for car parking and was envisaged as a play street for local children. Between the two a pedestrian pathway meanders between the gardens. The main block has the staircases and kitchens on the street side with the living rooms overlooking the quieter internal side of the block. The lower maisonettes have private gardens and the section is stepped, giving the upper dwellings roof terraces. The villas in the middle of the block follow the same design principles, containing two pairs of maisonettes each with the staircases facing the parking street, and the roof terraces and living rooms overlooking the central garden area. The overall form of the scheme recalls many European terraced housing schemes with parallel party walls and façades following the street, but here the usual consistency of roofline is broken. The pitched roofs appear only over the villas and intermittently on the edge block, replaced by a stepped section and flat roof terraces; and the use of one standard-size square window for almost all of the spaces replaces the more traditional visual hierarchy.

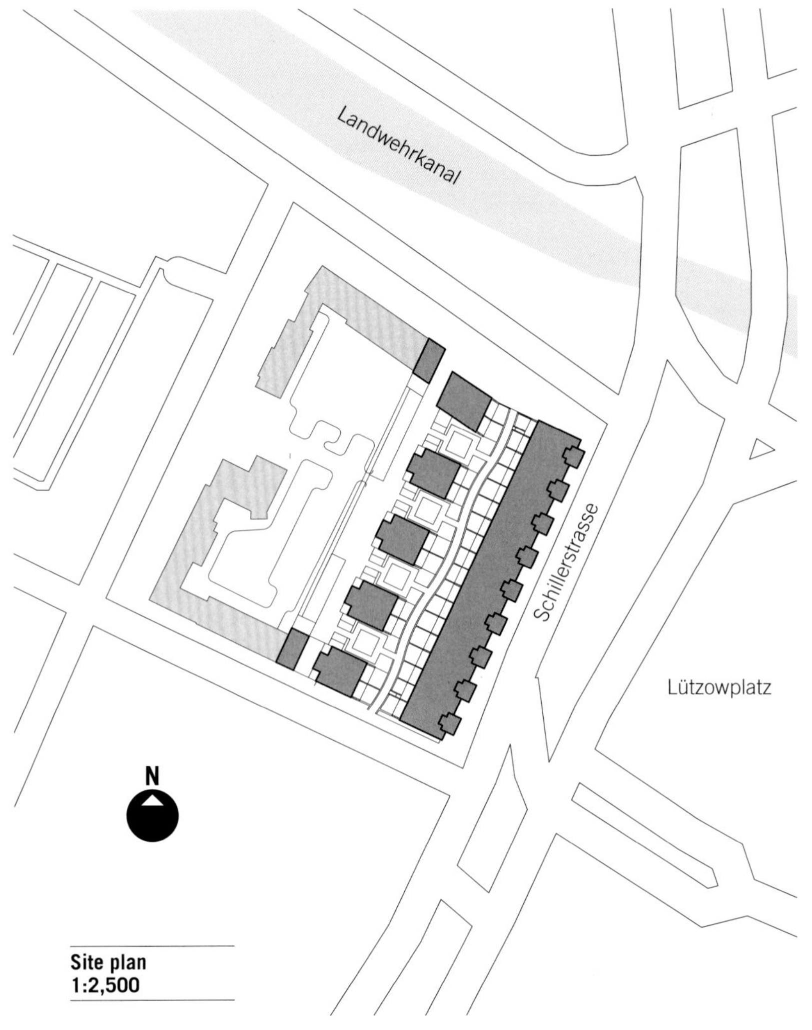

Site plan
1:2,500

1

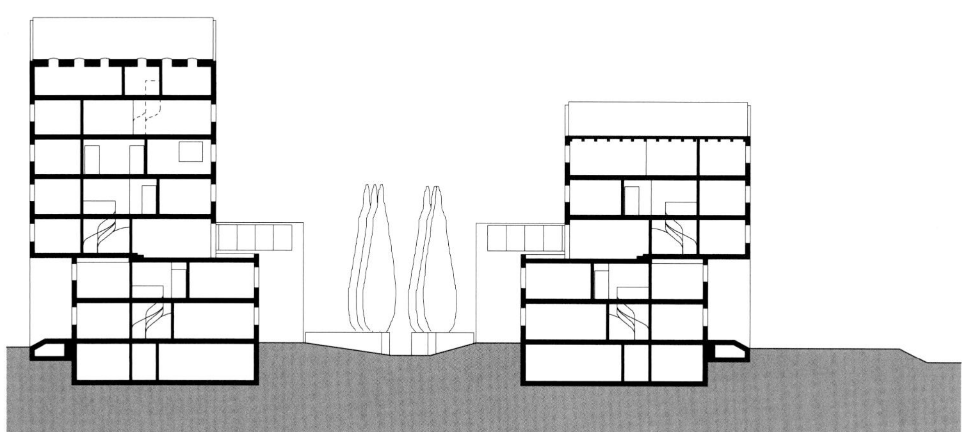

1	Section 1:500
2	Part plan ground floor 1:500
3	Part plan first floor 1:500
4	Elevation to Lützowplatz 1:500

2

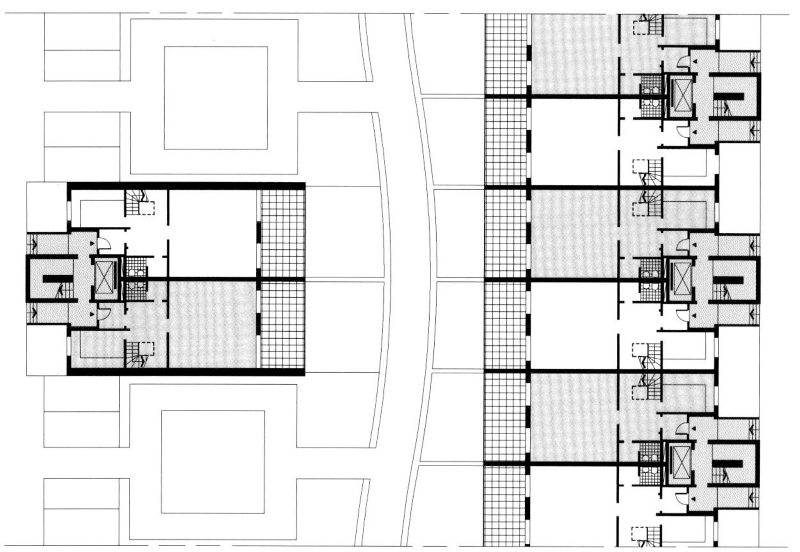

3

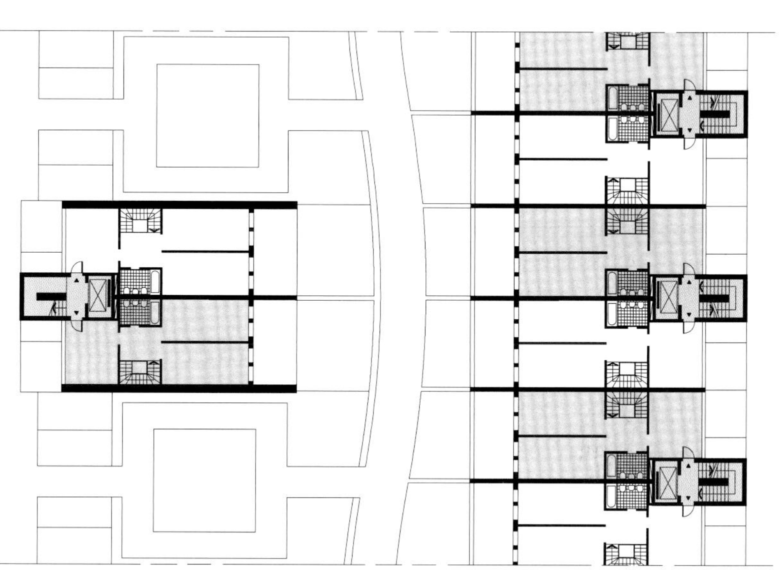

4

Far left: Street view looking south

Left: Front elevation

St Mark's Road Housing

Jeremy and Fenella Dixon, 1939– /1938–

London, UK; 1979

The most important aspect of this project is not the plan itself but the typology – the terraced house – that created, in Jeremy Dixon's words, 'continuous street space with appropriate facades that distinguished architecturally between "public fronts" and private backs'. In England, public dislike of the tower and slab blocks of the 1960s and 1970s very often focused on their lack of privacy and ill-defined or bleak open spaces; the latter belonging not quite to the public realm of street or city square nor to the clearly private domain of front gardens or backyards. The St Mark's Road social housing scheme confidently returns to the site context in order to inform its design, and draws on the traditional street pattern and the rich history and typology of the very English terraced house.

The St Mark's Road dwellings have simple, 'traditional' London terraced-house plans, with a room at front and back, windows to the street or gardens and the staircase located in the central, darkest, part of the plan. In place of the common form of the half-width rear extension, the plan recedes at the top-floor level to form a roof terrace. The narrow houses are paired, giving an impression from the outside of greater size in response to the larger scale of the dwellings in the immediate surroundings, and they are approached by stairs that lead up to the entrance half a level above the street. The floor beneath the houses, half a level below the street, is occupied by double-width single-aspect flats. Visually, the repeated façades use a variety of elements reminiscent of familiar Victorian houses – embellishments such as corbels, finials and patterned brickwork – but reinterpreted using contemporary materials as well as abstracted grids. The terraces are angled in plan, resolved with protruding bays at the entrances and meet at the corner of the street with a small block of flats. Jeremy and Fenella Dixon completed the later Ashmill Street scheme (1984), which similarly reinterprets aspects of terraced housing design using a very London vocabulary of white stucco and red brick complete with metal railings to the street.

Site plan
1:1,000

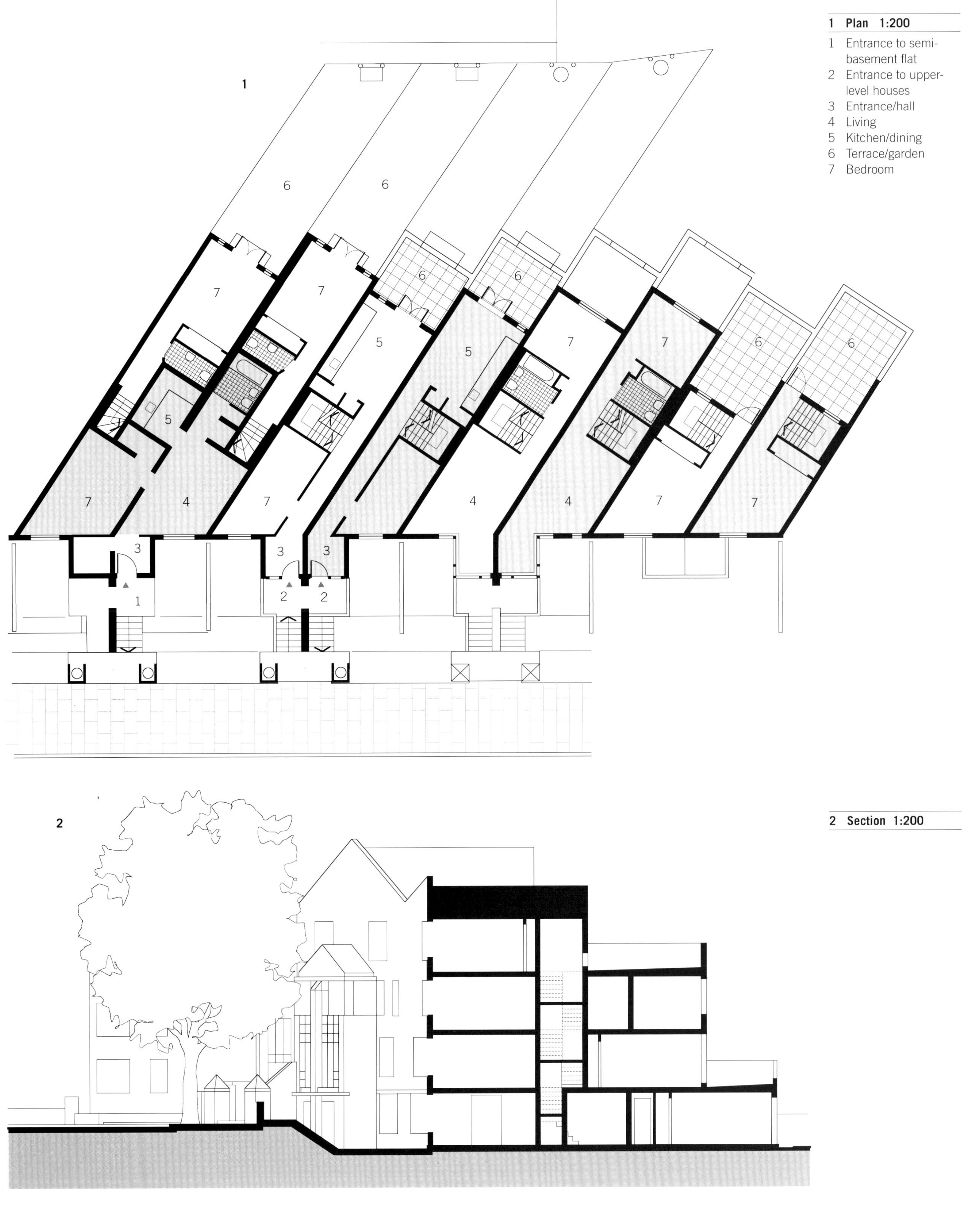

1 Plan 1:200

1 Entrance to semi-basement flat
2 Entrance to upper-level houses
3 Entrance/hall
4 Living
5 Kitchen/dining
6 Terrace/garden
7 Bedroom

2 Section 1:200

Rue des Hautes Formes

Christian de Portzamparc and Georgia Benamo, 1944– /

Paris, France; 1975–79

This project came about as the result of a 1975 competition run by the city of Paris' social housing department, the RIVP (Régie Immobilière de la Ville de Paris), under the direction of Michel Lombardini as part of the innovative PAN (Programme d'Architecture Nouvelle), or New Architecture Programme. Two towers had originally been planned for the rather difficult site in the run-down 13th arrondissement, but the novel approach of Portzamparc and Benamo was to be heralded as a turning point in the design of modern residential buildings. According to France's professional architecture journal, *AMC Le Moniteur Architecture*, it was one of the four most important housing projects built since the Second World War. Instead of isolated towers or, alternatively, infill blocks aligned with the streets, the scheme uses a series of seven different buildings to create its own urban spaces. The narrow street opens up to form a small square, around which are grouped the tall slender forms of the buildings. Archways and beams connect the buildings at cornice level, signalling that they belong to one overall scheme, and, at ground-floor level, arcades integrate the buildings with the street.

Out of a total of 210 dwellings there are 18 different variations. The small footprint of each block means fewer front doors per landing – often just two – and reduced internal circulation space. The composition of the façades reflects the varied internal layouts, and the architects have used a huge number of different window designs to create yet further variation in the quality of the internal spaces and different relationships with the street. Most apartments have windows facing at least two, and often three or more, directions, which can take the form of small rectangles up to full height and which might be recessed to form a loggia or provide access to a balcony. The avoidance of any obvious symmetrical arrangement in the forms or the façades is part of a deliberate attempt to humanize the impact of such a large architectural project, to make an architectural landscape that will contribute both to the scale and intimacy of the dwelling and to the public space as part of the wider urban area.

Site plan
1:2,500

1

1 Typical upper-floor plan 1:200

2 Partial ground-floor plan 1:200

1 Access/stairs
2 Entrance/hall
3 Kitchen
4 Living
5 Bedroom
6 Bathroom
7 Store room

2

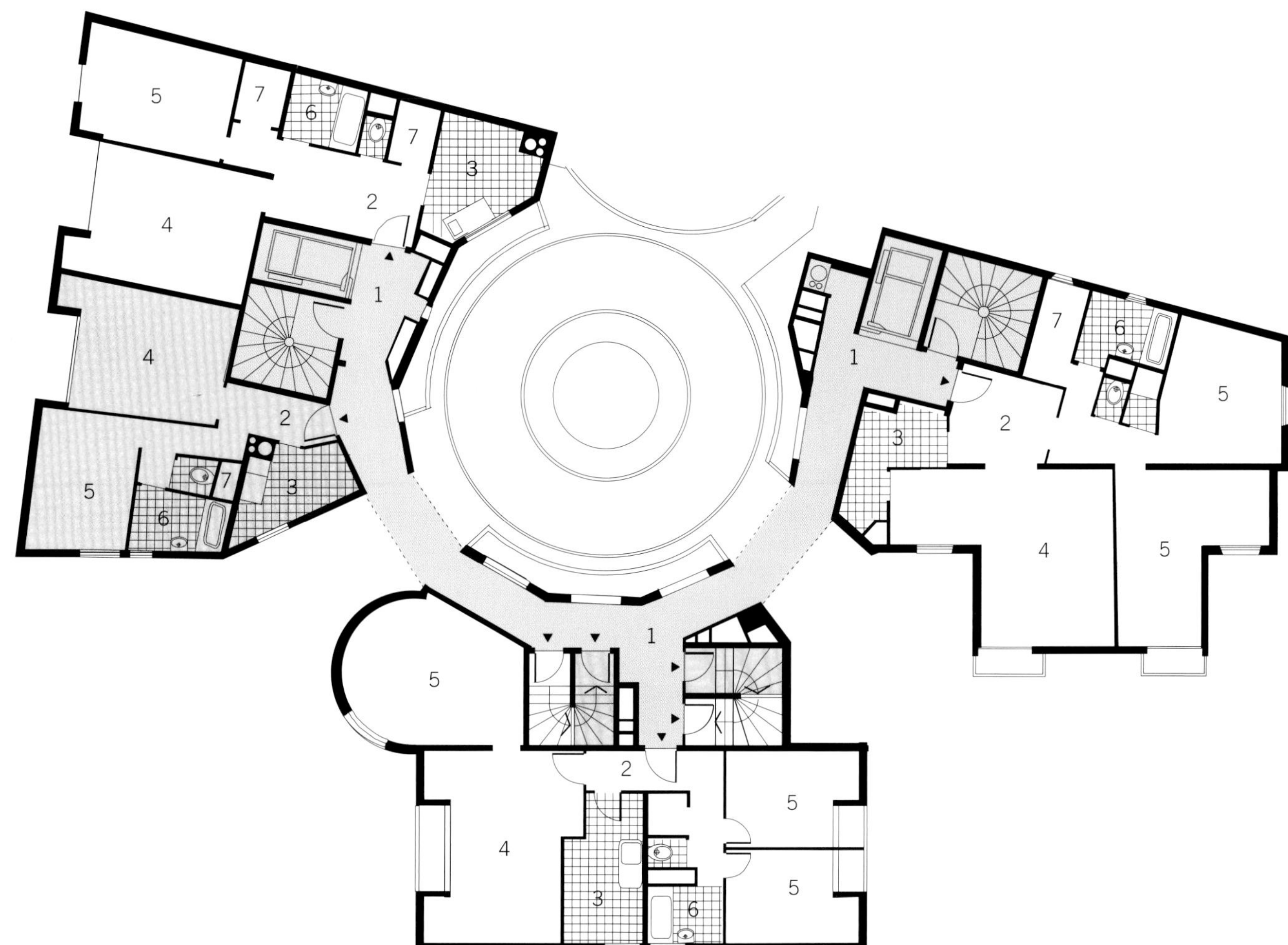

Noisy II Housing

Henri Ciriani, 1936–

Marne-la-Vallée, France; 1980

In much of Europe, and in France particularly, the New Town building programmes of the 1970s centred on major competitions and generated much debate on the nature of urban space. They prompted a re-evaluation of the Modernist 'blocks', which, existing as they did independently of any built or natural landscape, were blamed for the demise of urban space. Some New Town planners simply returned to pre-Modernist ideas, but others, of which Ciriani was one, believed that there was a way to develop a new kind of urban space using Modernism's principles. At Noisy, he used a Modernist form – the linear block – but related it to the specific location of its site in the new town of Marne-la-Vallée. Ciriani described the difficulty of designing in the emptiness of a new town – without the constraints of any existing surrounding buildings, unhindered by small parcels of land – as a problem of scale: the realm of the urban type that lies between housing and citywide morphology, which he called an 'urban piece'.

The urban piece in Noisy is built around a road junction – a T-shaped composition with one long block facing north on the main road, forming a main street with the building opposite, and two shorter perpendicular bocks on the south side. The intersection of these two blocks is marked by a vast portico, which frames the entrance into the buildings. Once past the main block, there is an open square to one side and a series of stepped terraces that break up the mass of the buildings. The block is organized as a series of individual towers, each with a central stairwell and circulation space, with the apartments laid out four per floor, one in each corner. Each has a projecting balcony, one above the other, forming a distinctive element on the façades. Here again, while using the Modernist form of the block Ciriani has modulated the façade specifically to allow sunlight into the different rooms and also as part of its visual composition, which is highly coloured and refers both to elements of classical composition and to the more prosaic but familiar dark-green paint of metropolitan Paris.

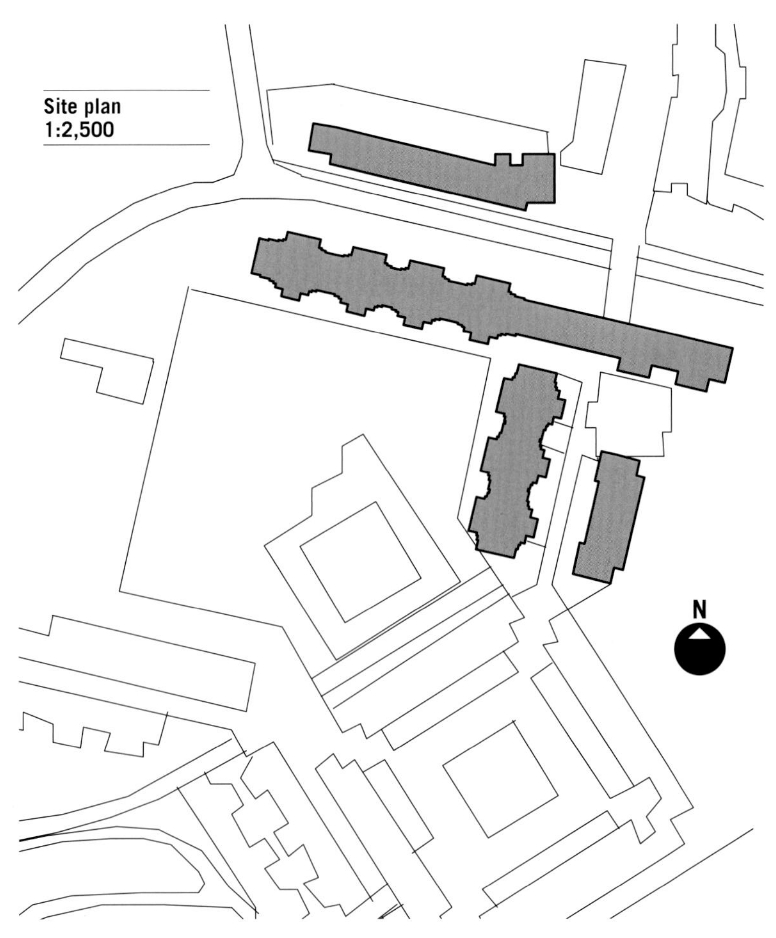

1

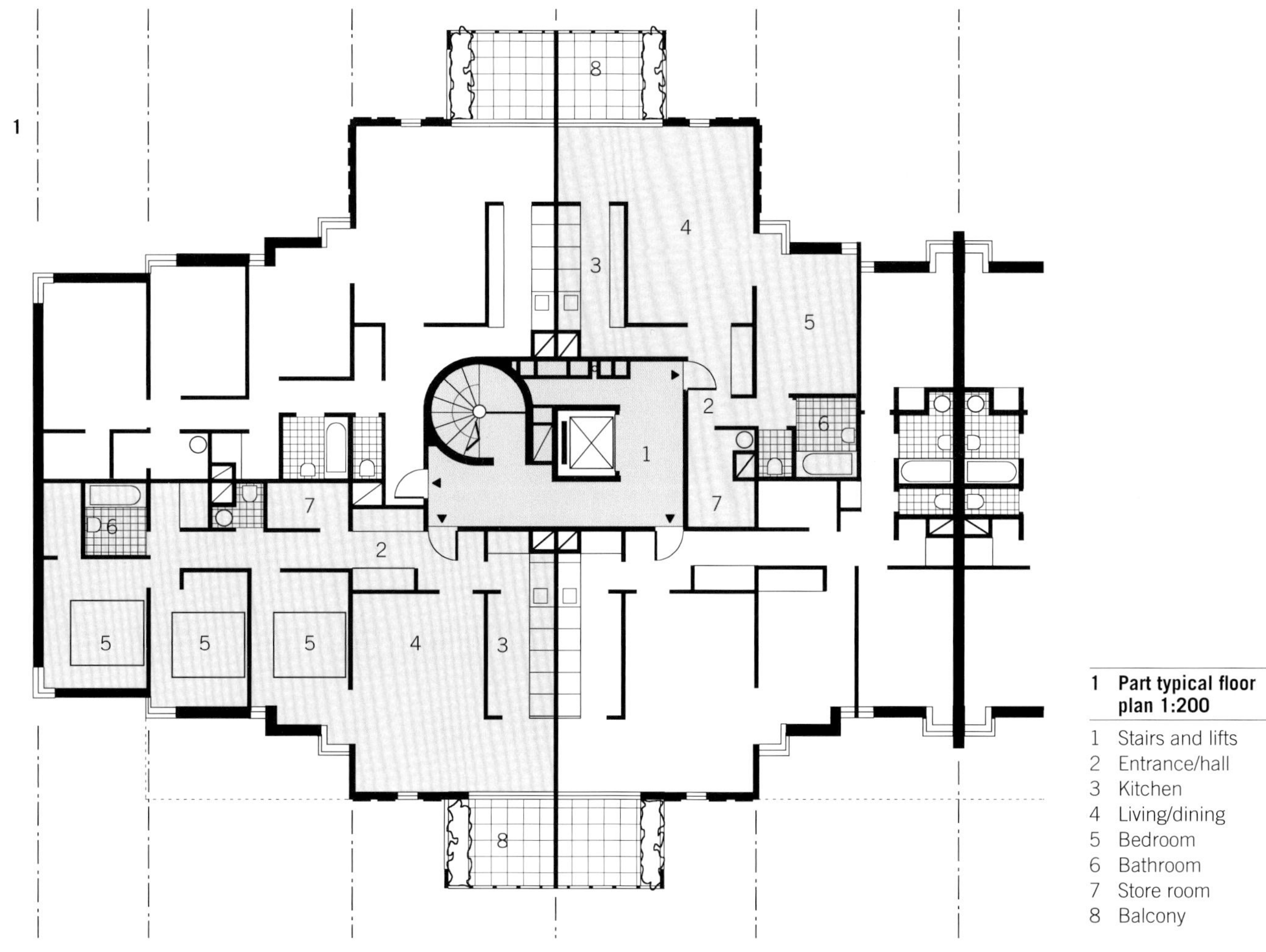

1 Part typical floor plan 1:200

1 Stairs and lifts
2 Entrance/hall
3 Kitchen
4 Living/dining
5 Bedroom
6 Bathroom
7 Store room
8 Balcony

2 Section looking south 1:200

2

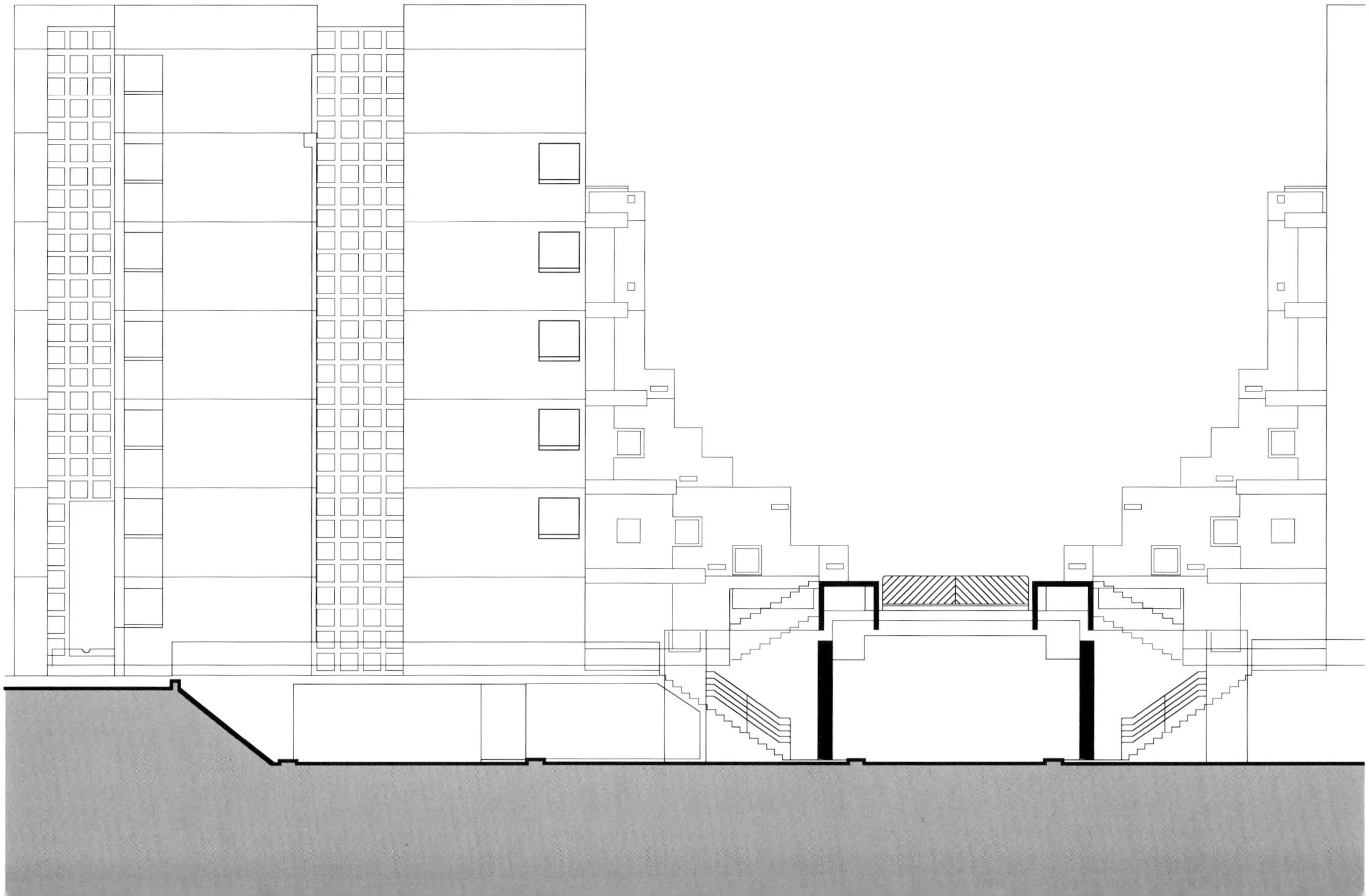

Atlantis Condominium

Arquitectonica

Miami, Florida, USA; 1982

Laurinda Spear and Bernardo Fort-Brescia, the principals at Arquitectonica, have had an enormous impact on Miami's architecture – not only by contributing a substantial number of buildings in a short space of time but also by designing in their own version of Post-Modern classicism, which has become identified with the city. The Atlantis condominium, built relatively early in their careers, established their capability as practitioners and has become probably the best known of their apartment buildings.

From the starting point of a relatively simple rectangular form – the 91-metre x 11-metre (300- x 37-foot) slab sits perpendicular to Biscayne Bay and the road, aligned east–west – there are playful interventions. At the bay end, the slab is curved to make a nautical reference and on the street side a red triangle sits on the roof, referring to the urban rooftop form. Yellow triangular balconies protrude from the north (entrance) façade, and most startling of all is the 'sky court' – a four-storey high square hole in the middle of the block. Behind it a cube (11 x 11 x 11 metres/37 x 37 x 37 feet), in the same yellow as that painted on the walls of the sky court, sits at an angle to the main building as if it were the missing piece lying where it happened to fall. It houses a gym and squash court, while paved gardens, a tennis court and a lap pool angled parallel to the bay complete the layout at ground level. The north façade is fully glazed with reflective glass and the south façade has a dramatic blue masonry supergrid in front of the balconies, its wide frame and angled dividers contributing to the sun-shading.

Inside, the lobby continues the same play with Platonic shapes and scale, mixing the structural with the non-structural to achieve its sculptural effect. Columns – both circular and triangular, some structural and some merely disguising ducts and pipework – are oversized and used to emphasize the entrance area, to demarcate the desk and to frame seating areas. Above six duplex apartments with private patios at the lower levels, there are 90 flats on the upper floors, with six apartments per floor served by two lift cores. All the apartments have windows facing south, with the larger ones facing both north and south. All the residents have access to the surreal sky court, which has become a symbol of Miami's own new tropical Modernism.

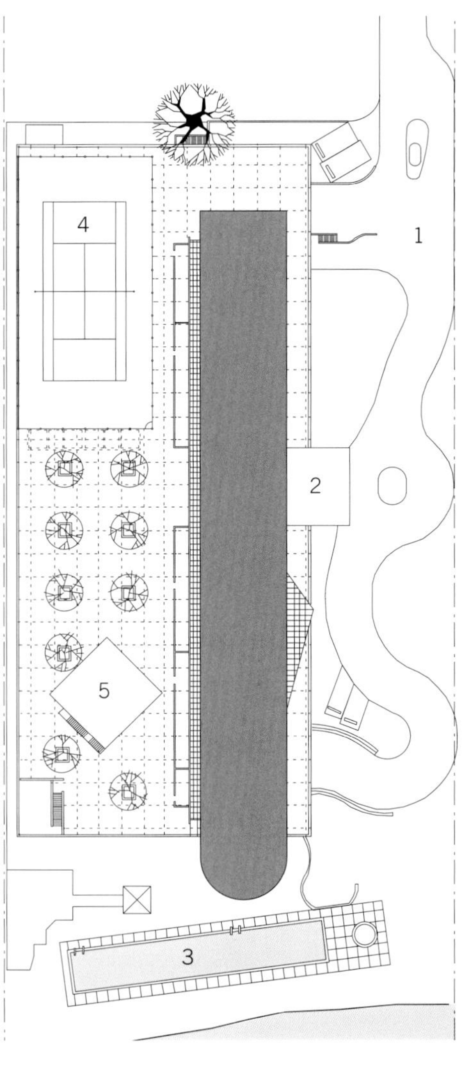

Site plan
1:1,000

1 Access driveway
2 Entrance
3 Pool
4 Tennis courts
5 Gym and squash courts

1

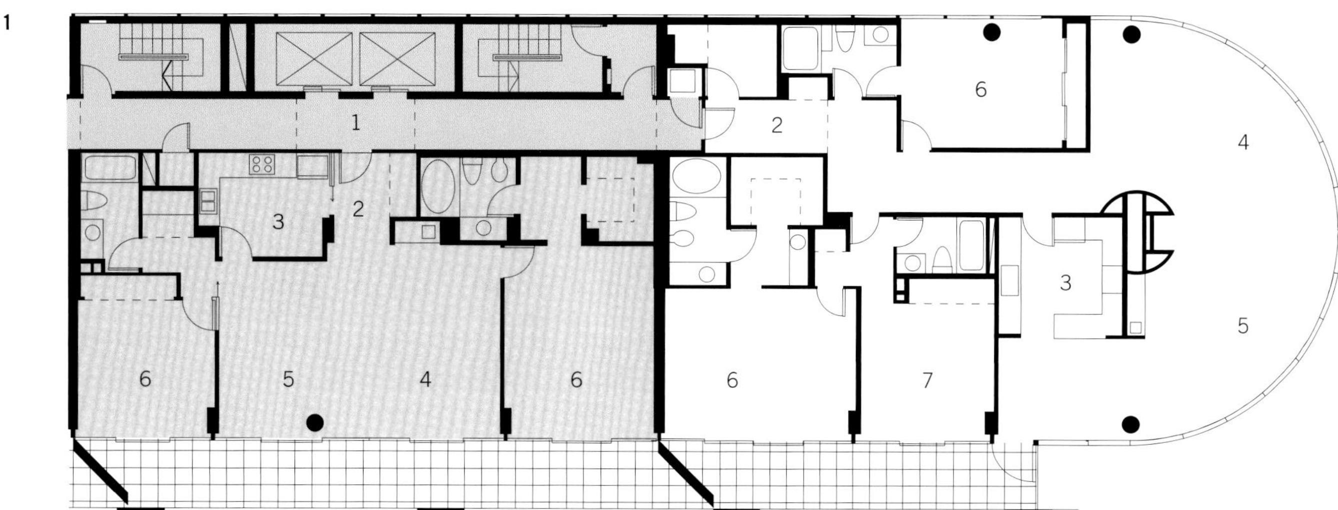

2

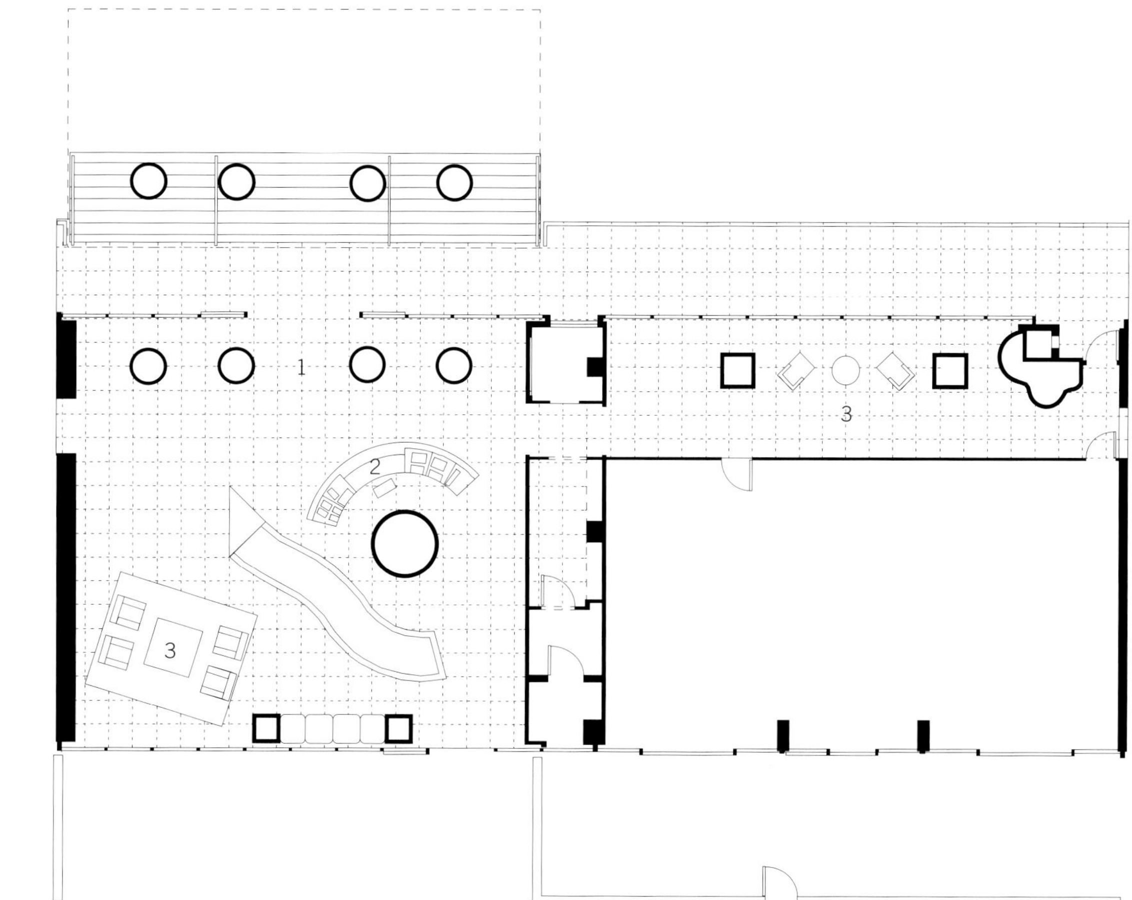

1 Part plan of typical floor 1:200

1 Access corridor
2 Entrance
3 Kitchen
4 Living
5 Dining
6 Bedroom
7 Study/bedroom

2 Plan of lobby 1:200

1 Entrance
2 Reception
3 Lobby/seating area

Byker Wall

Ralph Erskine, 1914–2005, and Vernon Gracie & Associates

Newcastle-upon-Tyne, UK; 1968–82

Ralph Erskine and Vernon Gracie & Associates' redevelopment scheme for the Byker district in Newcastle, which rehoused local residents from their condemned brick terraces, is as important for the way in which it was carried out as for the resulting architecture. The architects' approach was to consider the social aspects of housing and to see the redevelopment as a way to serve the local community. They started with a pilot group of 48 houses, following intense consultation with volunteer residents to establish the framework for the design. They then remained in residence, with an office on the site for the rest of the design and construction period, engaging the local residents in the redesign of their own community. The architects' 'open door policy', their 'plan of intent' rather than a more intimidating or alienating master plan, and their exhaustive consultation made this a model of 'community architecture'.

The 'Byker Wall' is the key feature that gives the development its identity: a long curvilinear block that meanders along the northern edge of the site. The Modernist version of the long sinuous form as a housing type appears first in Le Corbusier's 1930s proposals for Algiers as dramatic sweeping viaducts following the curves of the coastline, and then in built form in Affonso Eduardo Reidy's Pedregulho project (see pages 86–87) as a backdrop to the estate following the contours of the sloping ground. At Byker, in part 'to provide a recognizable physical form' – like all the typologies used by Erskine – and to make it easy for residents to orientate themselves, it was proposed as a functional solution to the problems presented by excessive noise from the adjacent metro line and a planned new motorway, which was subsequently not built. The Byker Wall contains mainly smaller dwellings intended for families or individuals without children. Sheltered behind it, two-storey and split-level timber-framed family houses, which make up 80 per cent of the scheme, are laid out along small streets in an attempt to recreate the neighbourhood scale of the original community. Perpendicular 'link blocks', with maisonettes at lower levels and smaller units above, make the physical and visual connection between the wall and the smaller-scale dwellings. Visually, the powerful form and solidity of the wall's brickwork is offset by the addition of highly detailed surfaces of colourful lightweight stained timber, which have an almost 'DIY' aesthetic.

1

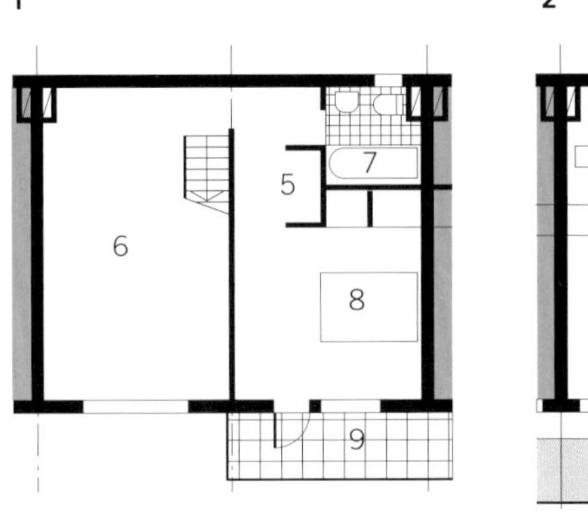

2

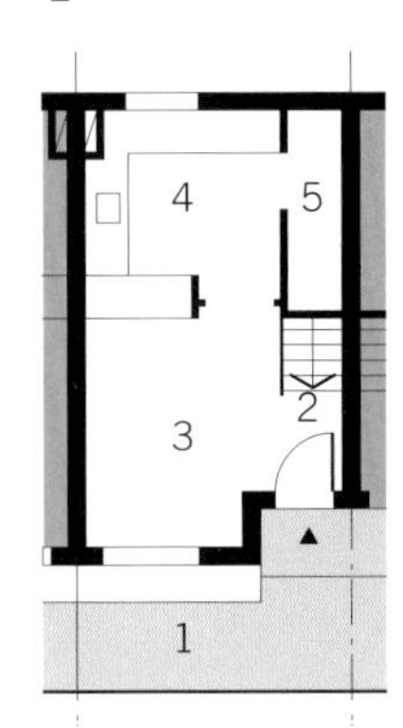

Perimeter block, plans of two-person maisonette 1:200

1 Lower level
2 Upper level

1 Access gallery
2 Entrance/hall
3 Dining room
4 Kitchen
5 Store room
6 Living rooom
7 Bathroom
8 Bedroom
9 Balcony

Opposite left: Perimeter block

Opposite right: Detail of timber balconies

3

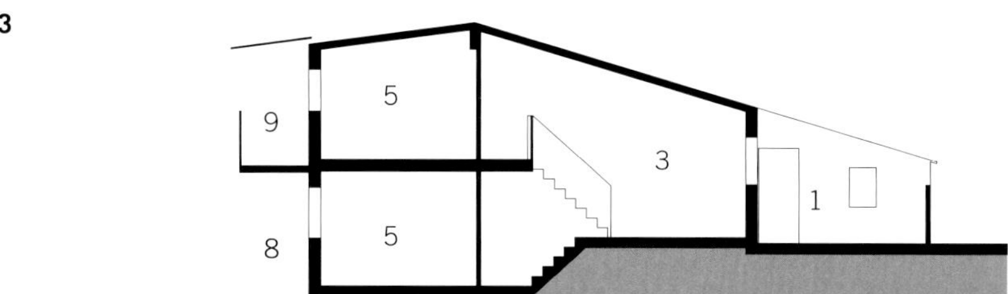

Houses, plans and section 1:200

3 Section
4 Upper floor
5 Lower floor

1 Front garden
2 Entrance/hall
3 Dining room
4 Kitchen
5 Bedroom
6 Bathroom
7 Store room
8 Garden
9 Balcony
10 Living room

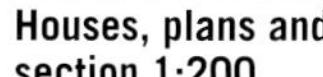

4

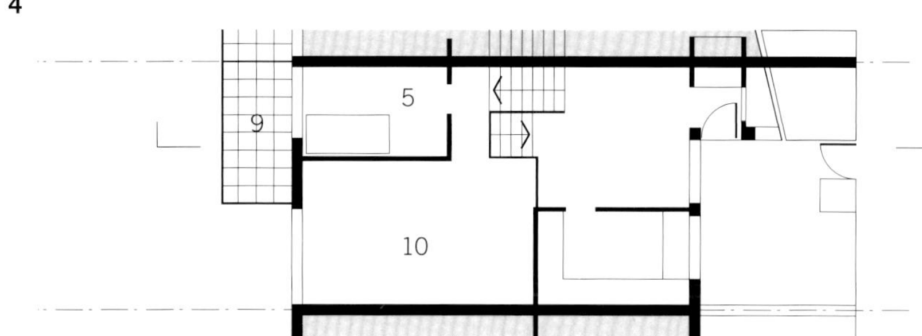

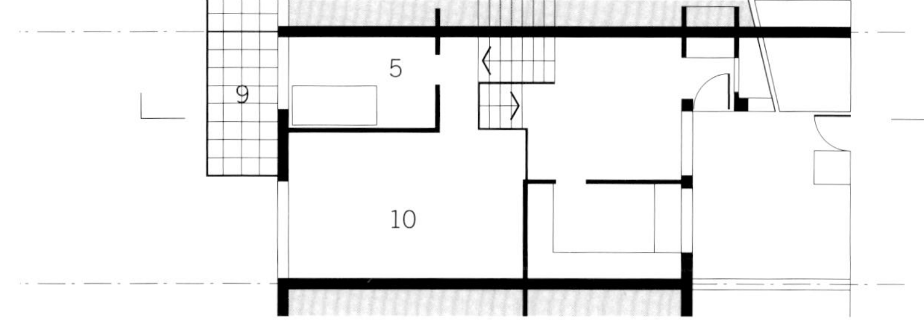

5

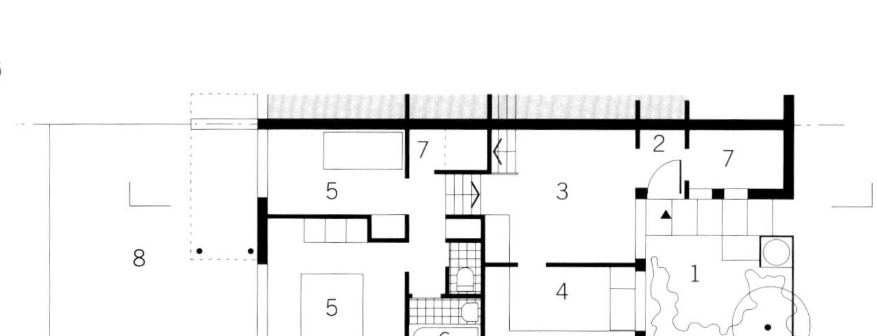

6

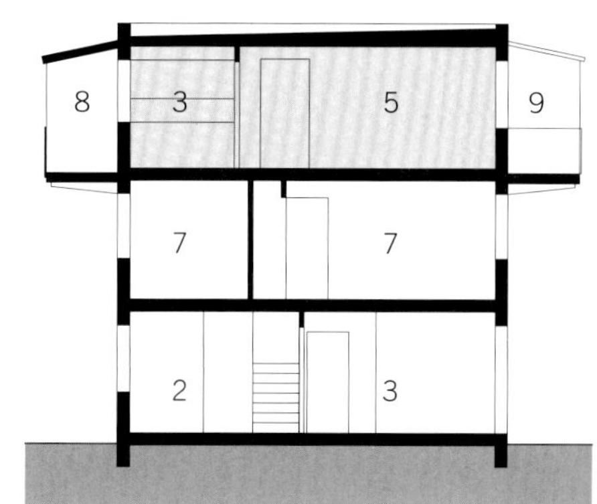

Link block two-person flat and five-person maisonette 1:200

6 Section
7 Second floor
8 First floor
9 Ground floor

1 Entrance/hall
2 Dining room
3 Kitchen
4 Store room
5 Living
6 Bathroom/WC
7 Bedroom
8 Access gallery
9 Private balcony

7

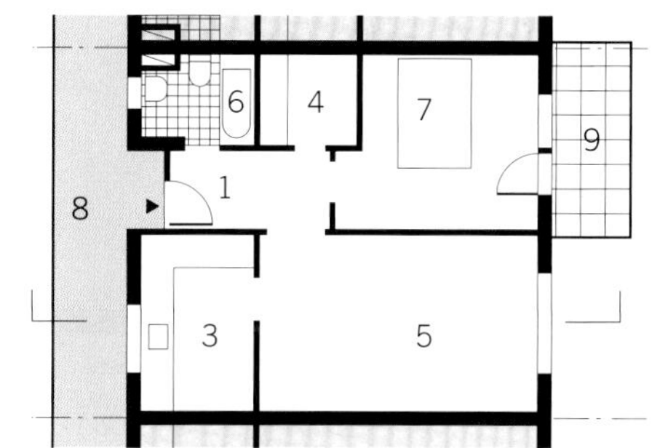

8

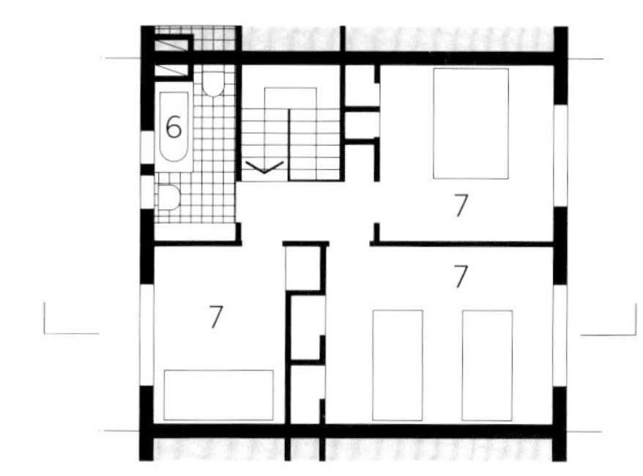

9

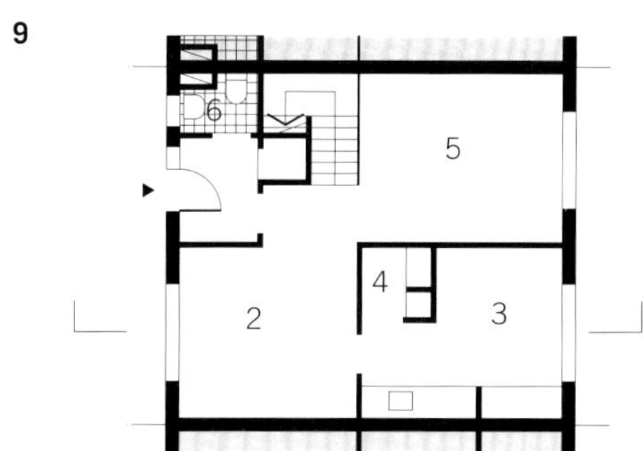

Housing for the Elderly

Steidle + Partner

Berlin, Germany; 1982–87

As part of the refurbishment and extension of an existing structure, the architect has constructed an independent new building with a similar-sized footprint parallel to the existing building, and linked to it with a covered atrium space. A further parallel strip forms a communal garden space that includes allotments. Uniquely, the atrium is not used just as a bridging device to link the old with the new – it is treated as a social space, conceived as a new kind of courtyard that works at every floor level. Ramps with a gradient of 6 degrees form the main circulation system, meandering from one end of the atrium to the other with intermittent landings and stopping places that punctuate the routes.

The existing building has been converted into mostly two- or three-bedroom family-sized flats with independent entrances from the rear; and, in the central part, there are smaller, one-bedroom flats for the elderly which can be accessed from the ramps. The new block is divided into three separate 'towers', with four flats on each floor with shared entrance landings. The flats in the new block, all one-bedroom units for the elderly, are roughly triangular in plan with a 45-degree diagonal wall to the living space separating each pair. The bathroom and kitchen are arranged along one side of the resulting L-shape, with the bedroom, which opens off the living space, on the other. Each flat has a small loggia on its external façade. Windows to the bathroom and kitchens that overlook the atrium are fitted with sliding shutters for privacy.

The use of ramps means a reduced dependency on lifts, ease of linking the different floor levels in the existing buildings with those in the new, and also that all the apartments are fully accessible for wheelchair users. The design of the atrium, with exposed steel framework and glazed roof space, is intended to be conservatory-like and, importantly, a social space that can be occupied by neighbours who might stop and talk or just watch the activity of other residents.

Site plan
1:2,500

Opposite left: New building

Opposite right: Side elevation with atrium to the right

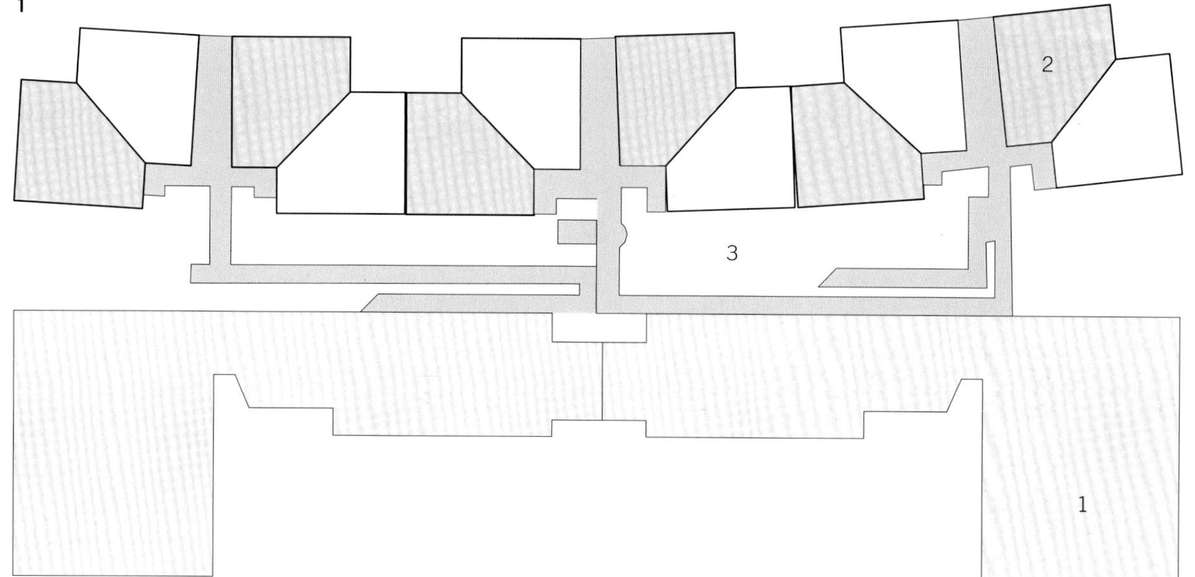

1 Outline plan 1:500

1 Existing building
2 New apartment block
3 Atrium with access ramps

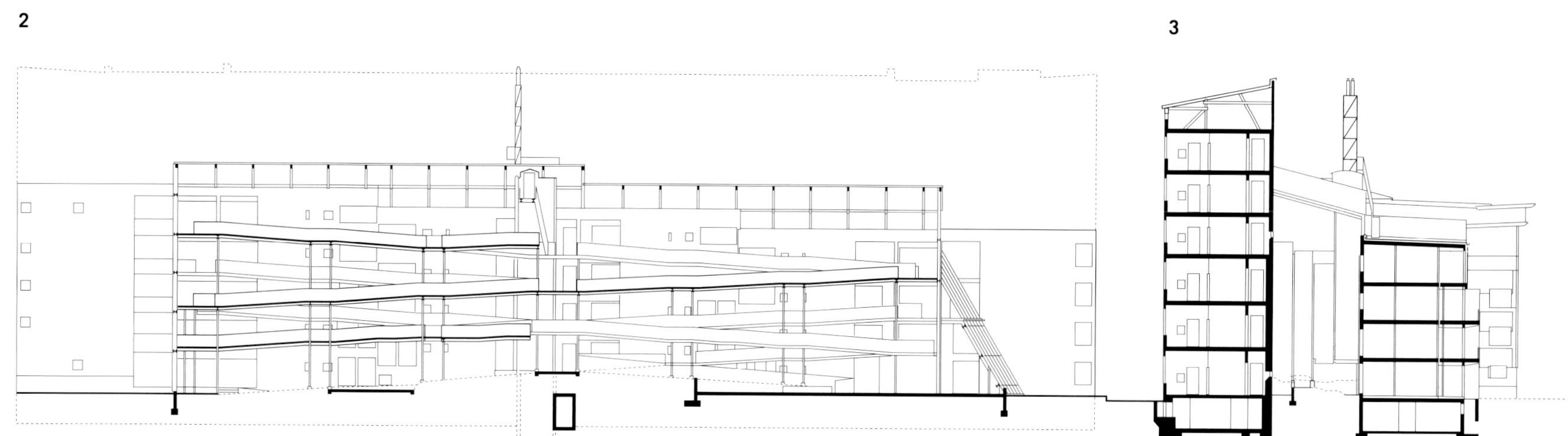

2 Long section through atrium 1:500

3 Cross-section 1:500

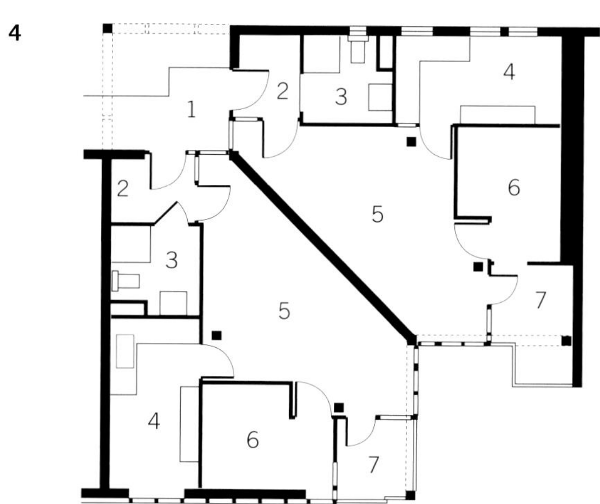

4 Plan of typical apartments 1:200

1 Access balcony
2 Entrance/hall
3 Shower/wet room
4 Kitchen
5 Living
6 Bedroom
7 Loggia/winter garden

***Far left*:** North façade

Left: Interior with garage doors opening onto terrace

Nemausus

Jean Nouvel et Associés with Jean-Marc Ibos, Frédéric Chambon and Jean-Rémi Nègre

Nîmes, France; 1985–88

Unusually, the two blocks comprising this scheme are laid out orientated east–west, so that one façade faces almost due north and the other almost due south. What might initially appear an inappropriate arrangement in the hot climate of southern France makes sense in relation to the layout of the apartments, which all stretch the full depth of the block, and the arrangement of their balconies. On the north side there are access balconies, and on the south side identical balconies are divided to provide a private outdoor space for each apartment. The two blocks, which have a simple concrete-frame structure with columns and dividing walls every 5 metres (16 feet 6 inches), are raised up on pilotis above a partly sunken ground level that accommodates shaded, but not enclosed, car parking.

The appearance of the blocks and the nature and type of materials used are not the familiar ones of domestic building – instead, the architects have sought to create a different kind of domestic experience. An impression that the building is insubstantial or lightweight, floating above its pilotis, is given by the extensive use of perforated metalwork balustrading and balcony decks and staircases – all of which are reminiscent of nautical detailing. In place of regular french windows or more high-tech aluminium sliding patio doors, the south-facing façades are fitted with full-height folding garage doors that incorporate glazed panels. Most of the internal partitions, including those to the bedrooms, are fully glazed – something that would be more familiar in an office context. This material innovation is also part of the project's spatial experiment, and the architects insisted on making savings in the materials and finishes in order to maximize the amount of space in the apartments. The 114 units comprise 17 different dwelling types, including duplex and triple apartments as well as single-storey flats. The fixed elements of bathrooms, WCs and kitchen fixtures are generally conceived as blocks within the extended space of the apartments; in only the smallest flats are they arranged conventionally, along one of the party walls. Internally, the use of openwork stairs, landings and bridges across the double-height spaces allows for good levels of daylight and clear views right from the entrance out to the balcony on the opposite façade.

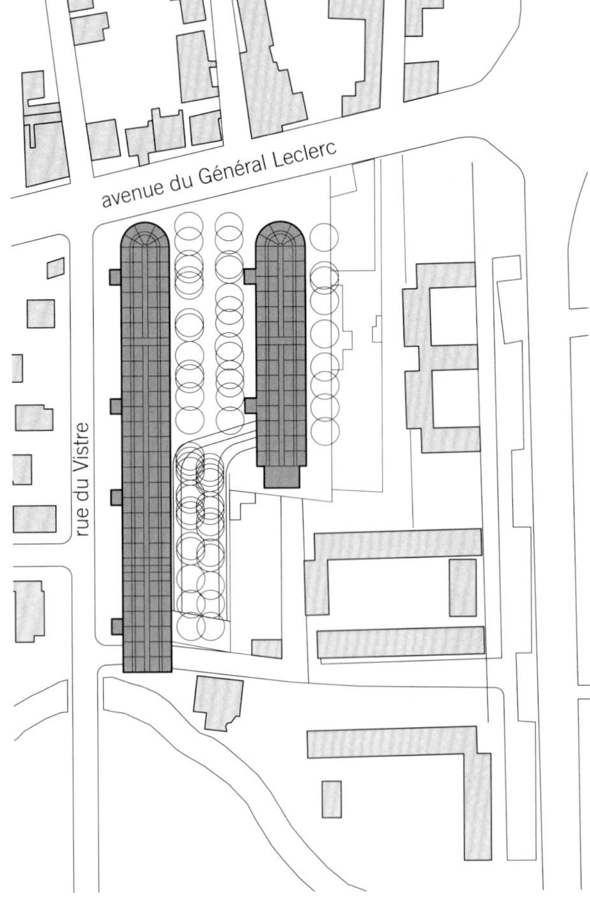

Site plan 1:2,500

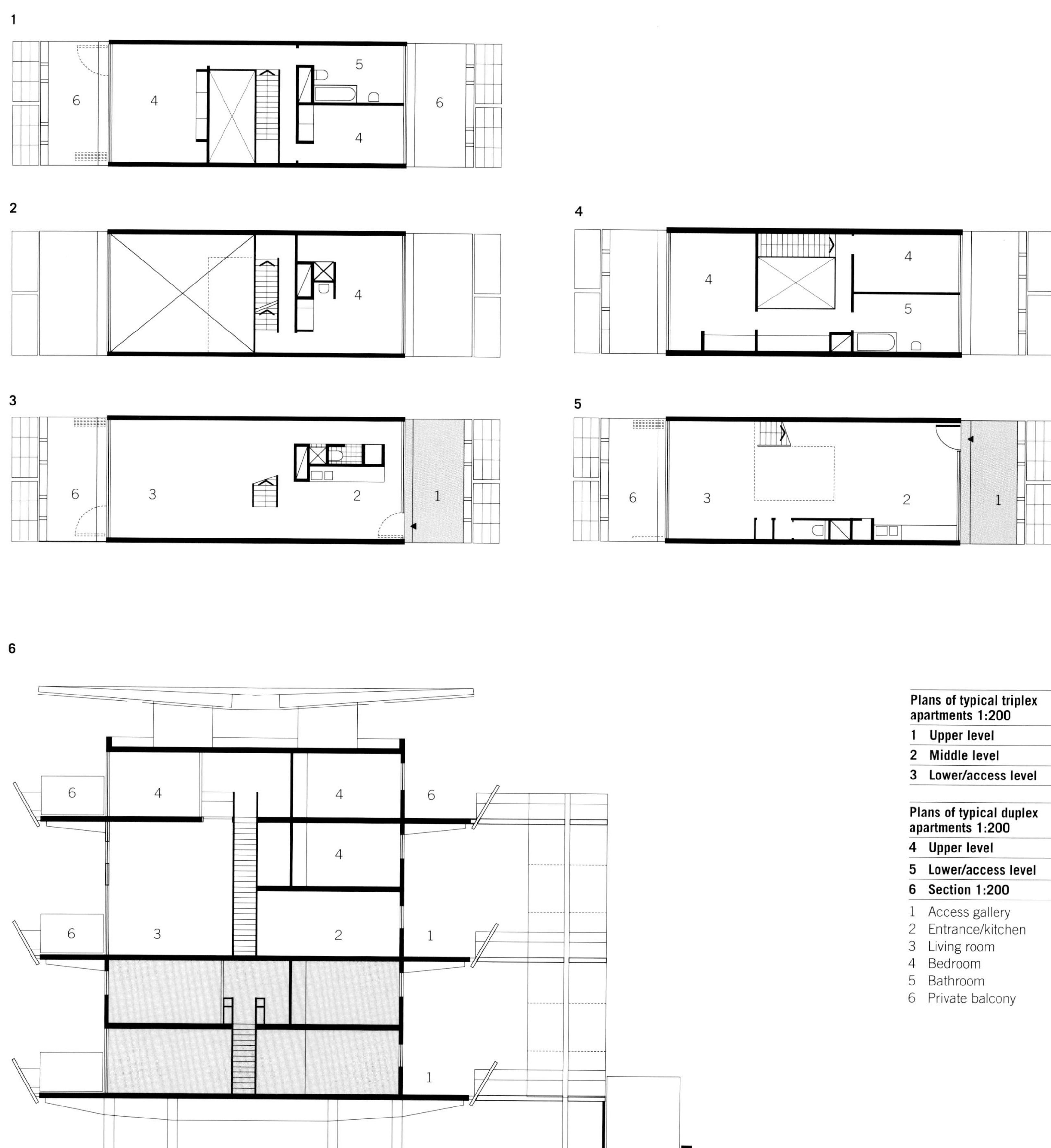

Plans of typical triplex apartments 1:200

1 Upper level

2 Middle level

3 Lower/access level

Plans of typical duplex apartments 1:200

4 Upper level

5 Lower/access level

6 Section 1:200

1 Access gallery
2 Entrance/kitchen
3 Living room
4 Bedroom
5 Bathroom
6 Private balcony

Pence Place

Gwathmey Siegel & Associates

Columbus, Indiana, USA; 1984

Back-to-back terraced houses are a rarity. To set out to design a housing scheme where each house has three shared walls and only one external façade vastly reduces costly external-wall construction and makes this an economical way to build. As a result, however, adequate daylighting and ventilation can be problematic, but in this two-storey version Gwathmey Siegel have found an innovative solution. An openable clerestory window is positioned at the top of the oversailing pitched roof, bringing air and daylight into the back of the plan above the staircase.

The plan of the houses is simple, with, on the ground floor, a living room with kitchen in one corner, a hallway and cloakroom; and, on the first floor, three bedrooms along the width of the house and an internal bathroom on the back wall. There are two houses adapted for wheelchair users – larger, with a deeper plan and additional bedrooms on the lower floor – and also a community building with offices and common room. On a triangular site next to a railway line, the 40 houses that make up the scheme are arranged in parallel rows and accessed from pedestrian pathways. The car parking is separately laid out along one side. Another aspect of the back-to-back typology is gardens at the front of the houses rather than the more private rear. Both the front door and the living rooms open directly onto these front 'yards', or courtyard gardens, which are enclosed with cedar clapboard fences that incorporate a storage structure. Similar attention to detail has been carried out across the whole site, with planters screening the parking rows, screens around the rubbish bins and several small-scale children's play areas in the spaces between the terraces.

Site plan
1:2,500

1 Parking
2 Children's play space
3 Refuse bins

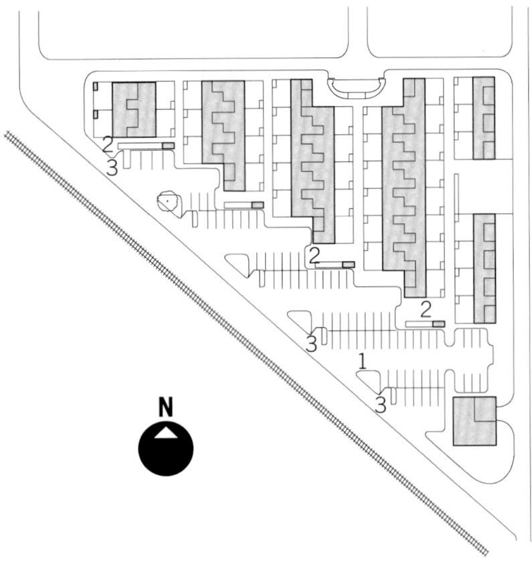

Opposite left: Pedestrian entrance to the scheme

Opposite right: Parking with children's play area beyond

Plans of typical houses 1:200

1 First-floor plan
2 Ground-floor plan

3 Section

1 Front yard
2 Storage
3 Entrance/hall
4 Laundry
5 Kitchen
6 Living/dining
7 Bathrooom/WC
8 Bedroom

1

2

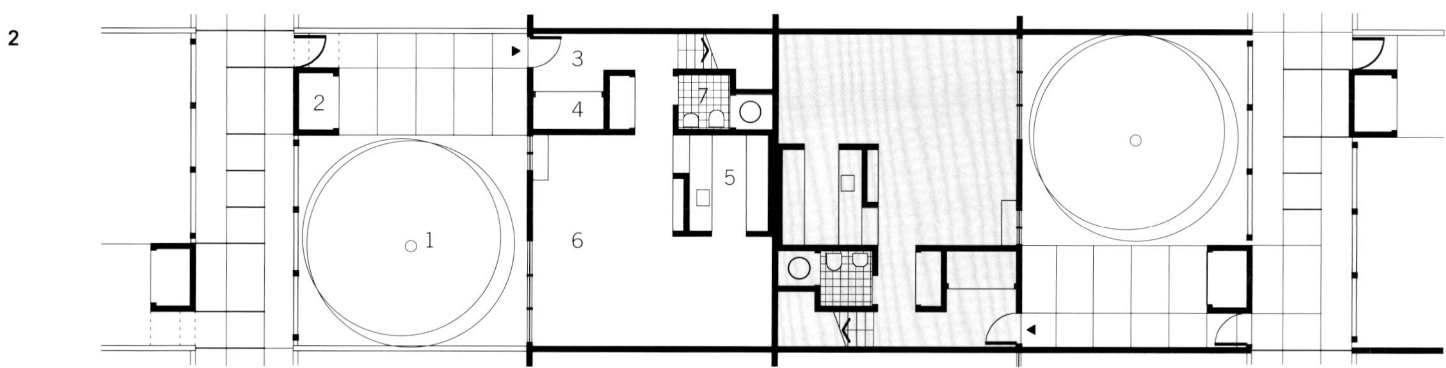

3

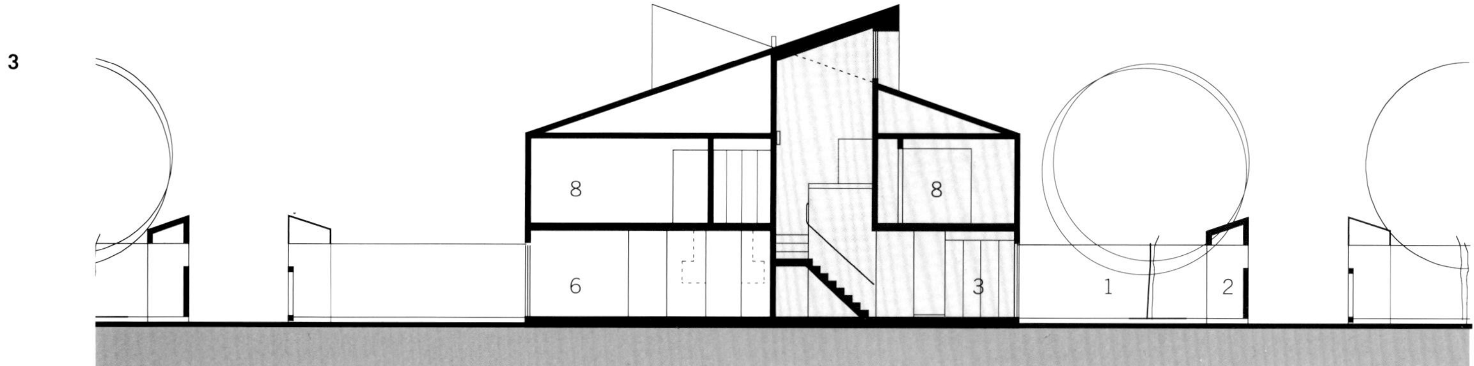

IJ-Plein Housing

OMA

Amsterdam, The Netherlands; 1988

OMA were responsible for the master plan of the whole site, a former shipyard north of the river IJ opposite Amsterdam's central district, with a total provision of 1,375 dwellings, public space, playgrounds, a school and shops. The master plan sets out buildings in rows of parallel blocks of different heights in a triangular configuration, with an open space at the centre on the eastern side and, on the western side, three rows of urban villas. Their original scheme had proposed a high-rise development in order to increase the density and create a new skyline, but this was blocked by local residents.

OMA then designed in detail the two parallel blocks on the farthest eastern edge of the site. The longer of the two is raised over a podium, which functions as both a storage space for bicycles and a dyke. The space in front on the water's edge accommodates car parking and was intended for small shop-pavilions; at one end, a triangular form houses a community centre. The blocks provide a variety of different dwelling types and sizes with fairly simple layouts: kitchens mostly within living spaces, bathrooms and store rooms located in the central area of the plan and habitable rooms with balconies on the external walls to benefit from natural light and ventilation. Glazing is used extensively, both for outside walls and for internal partitions, in order to bring borrowed light deep into the plan and to contribute to a sense of lightness and spaciousness. The most innovative element of the layouts is the treatment of the circulation spaces and access to the dwellings. Staircases are arranged horizontally rather than vertically in order to cascade through the floors – laterally in the smaller block and perpendicularly in the longer block, shifting the position of the landings on each floor level. Daylight is brought into the stairwells through skylights and the open access gallery at the top-floor level.

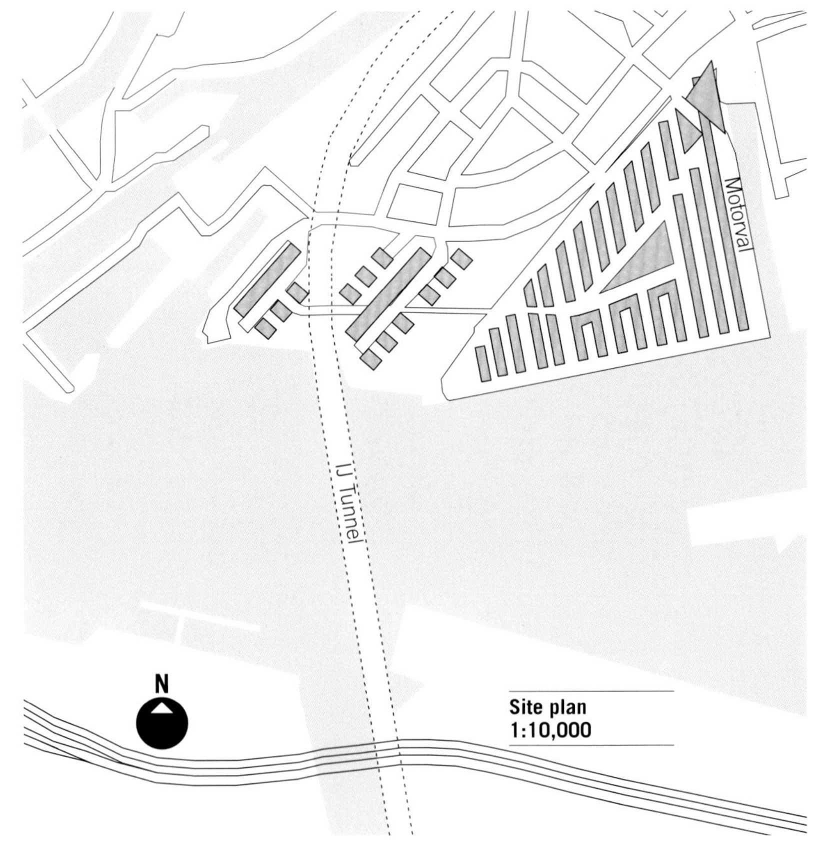

Site plan
1:10,000

1

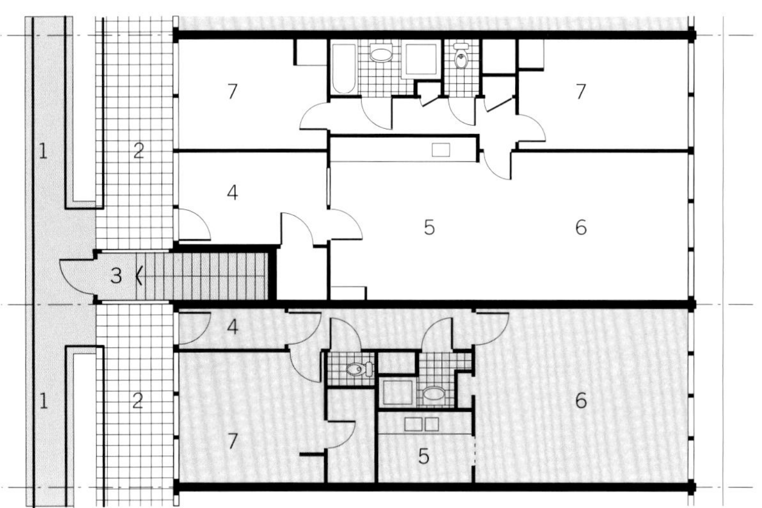

Typical apartment plans 1:200

1 Flats in long block level 4

2 Flats in long block level 3

1 Access gallery
2 Balcony
3 Stairs/access
4 Entrance/hall
5 Kitchen
6 Living
7 Bedroom

2

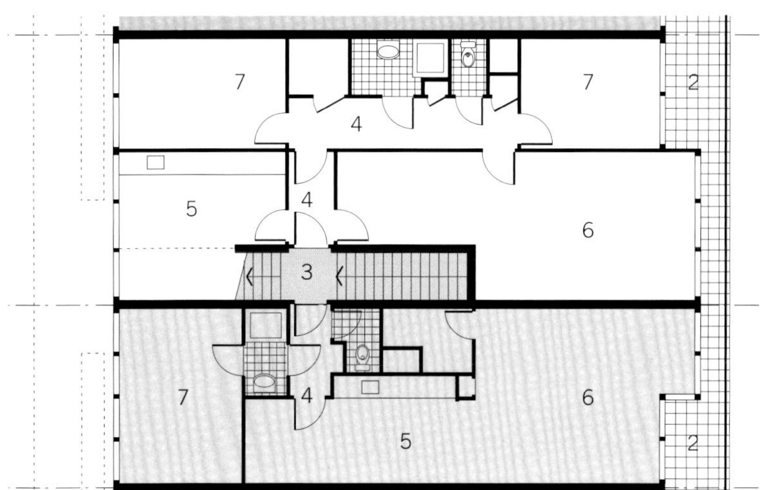

3

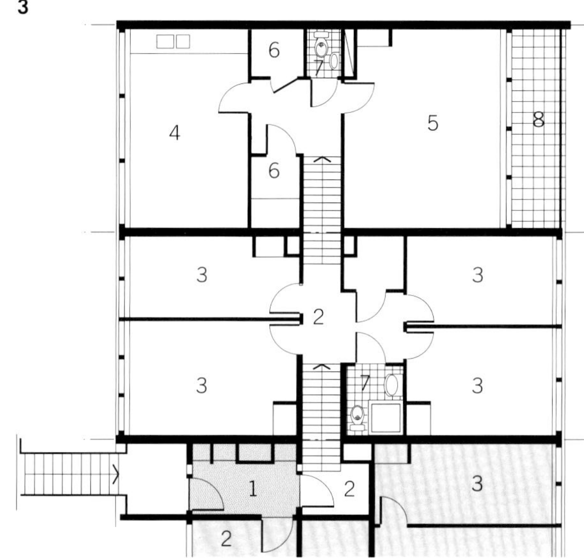

3 Short block maisonette levels 3 and 4

1 Porch
2 Entrance/hall
3 Bedroom
4 Kitchen/dining
5 Living
6 Store room
7 WC/shower
8 Balcony

Spiral House

Zvi Hecker, 1931–

Ramat Gan, Israel; 1990

According to Zvi Hecker, 'A building is based on the precision of an idea on which variations are made. With the Spiral House, the idea itself is very simple, therefore the variations can be very complex.' The idea in the Spiral House is to base the form of the building on a spiral staircase. The plan geometry is developed within a circular outline overlaid with a 16-pointed star. Each level is rotated 22.5 degrees in plan, and the single apartment on every floor has an outside terrace on the roof of the 'step' below. The roof terraces are outward-facing – open to the sky and views – while, on the opposite side of the building, the corridors, entrances and spiral staircases are located in the shadier underside of the steps. Between the two is a shared interior courtyard. The building sits on a hillside in Ramat Gan to the north-east of the Tel Aviv metropolitan region.

The use of geometry as the basis for design is evident in much of Hecker's work, and in his partnership with Alfred Neuman and Elder Sharon from 1959 to 1964. The Dubiner House, across the road from the Spiral House, was built in 1963 and is a larger apartment block in which the architect first explored the complexities of polyhedral geometry in a stepped section. For Hecker, the construction process is a part of the ongoing process of design and should not preclude changes on site. Living opposite in the Dubiner House, he was able to be closely involved with the progress of the construction work on the Spiral House, where intervention on site included using stone tiling externally and experimenting with different textures for the particularly expressive concrete finishes.

The building, both in form and material, recalls traditional Arab villages. In form, the stepped terrace, where the roof is used as part of the living space for the apartments, and the grouping of the living spaces around an interior courtyard are familiar arrangements, and the use of inexpensive, readily available materials is in line with the local building environment.

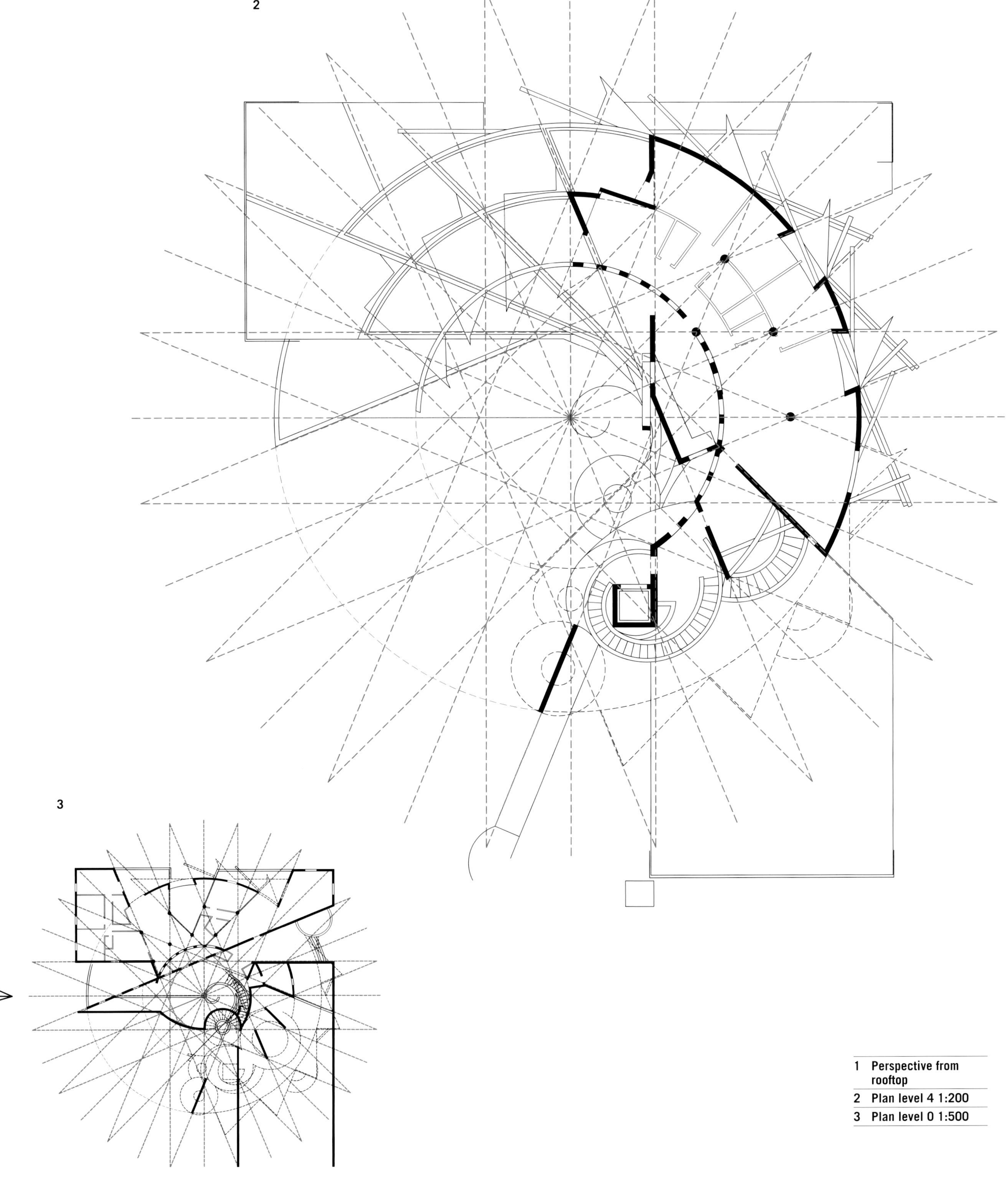

1 Perspective from rooftop
2 Plan level 4 1:200
3 Plan level 0 1:500

Nexus World Housing

Steven Holl Architects

Fukuoka, Japan; 1991

This block of 28 apartments is part of the Nexus World housing development, a project for middle-income families in the Kashii district of Fukuoka, the provincial capital of Kyushu, Japan. The master plan for the development, which aimed to find a new urban 'lifestyle', defined an urban block with twin 120-metre (395-foot) high towers at the centre and individual blocks a maximum of five storeys high around the perimeter. The overall plan and the towers were designed by Arata Isozaki, and along with one local architect, Osamu Ishiyama, five internationally renowned non-Japanese architects were invited to contribute building projects. Besides Steven Holl Architects, projects have been completed by Oscar Tusquets, Christian de Portzamparc, Mark Mack and OMA. As an experimental project, Nexus World set out to provide a wide variety of different dwelling types and to explore the possibility of a new urban form for housing.

Steven Holl Architects' building sets out to explore the experience of space rather than form. It follows the curving edge of the street on the south side of the urban block. At ground level, retail units have a continuous façade on the street side with covered courtyard-like spaces at the rear. On the upper-floor levels this arrangement is reversed, and the four resulting void spaces appear on the street side of the building to afford the apartments maximum sunlight. These voids are flooded with reflecting pools to preserve their emptiness and assert their presence through shimmering reflections on the surrounding surfaces, both inside and outside the apartments.

Access to the apartments is on the north, inside the block, via external staircases with a central access gallery on the first floor and an open access gallery on the top level. The experience of the journey rather than an efficient use of space determines the design of the circulation spaces; as well as the provision of external front doors, views across the water courts and north–side voids from the lower-level walkway, a sense of suspension over the park and the sky view from the top are all seen as a part of the understanding of a 'passage through space'. The apartments are generally either maisonettes or duplexes, extending across the full depth of the plan and into the 'fingers' that define the void spaces. Key to the internal layouts is the idea of flexibility for the residents, both daily and over the longer term. Folding panels allow spaces to be altered easily in order to be used variously as living spaces or bedrooms, and, over time, rooms can be added or subtracted to accommodate changing needs in a changing family. Within the apartments, labyrinthine corridors and level changes seemingly extend the space of the dwellings.

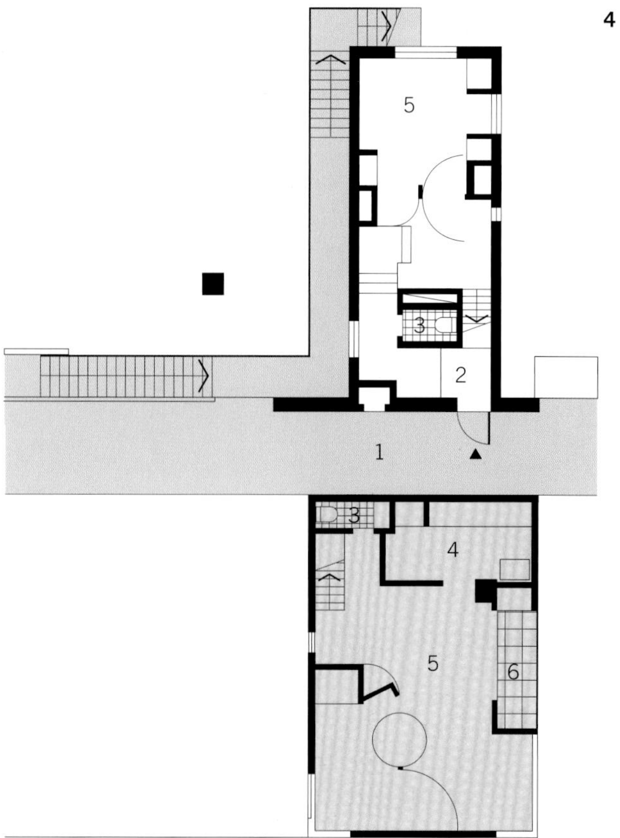

Opposite left: Street elevation

Opposite right: Multi-level interior

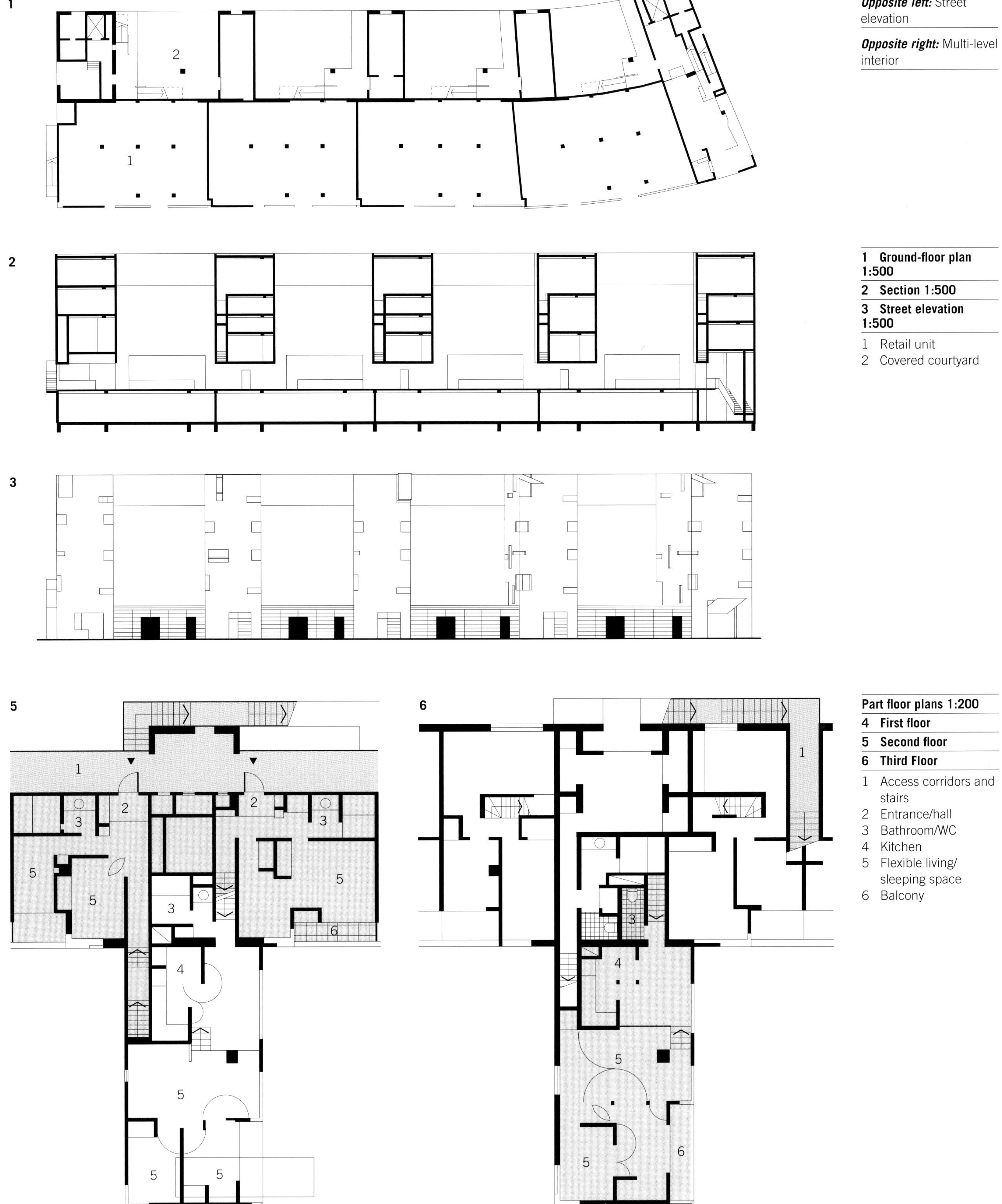

1 Ground-floor plan 1:500

2 Section 1:500

3 Street elevation 1:500

1 Retail unit
2 Covered courtyard

Part floor plans 1:200

4 First floor

5 Second floor

6 Third Floor

1 Access corridors and stairs
2 Entrance/hall
3 Bathroom/WC
4 Kitchen
5 Flexible living/ sleeping space
6 Balcony

Far left: View of central courtyard

Left: Façade facing service yard

Rue de Meaux Housing

Renzo Piano Building Workshop

Paris, France; 1991

Instead of recreating the traditional street pattern, with linear blocks and rear service yards, the Renzo Piano Building Workshop has here created a courtyard scheme, a design that is closely related to the scale and proportion of the surroundings but which has a distinct urban form. On the rue de Meaux, three blocks fill the gaps between existing buildings and follow the street frontage. They are separated by narrow pedestrian pathways, which give access to the planted courtyard space behind. At approximately 100 metres by 60 metres (330 x 200 feet) overall, the central block of the three closes one short edge (approximately 60 metres/200 feet long), while the two buildings on either side continue to form the long sides of the courtyard (approx 105 metres/345 feet in length). There are retail units at street level, ramps down to the car parking – which extends underneath the buildings – and access gates to covered service roads and parking areas for municipal vehicles, all of which forms a two-storey plinth to the residential parts of the building. In the long blocks, roughly aligned north–south, flats occupy the full depth with rooms overlooking the courtyard and outward. The courtyard elevations have strong vertical elements, with set-backs on the outward-facing façades that form a series of roof terraces. The stairs and lifts are located on the façade, on the courtyard side, and serve two flats per landing. In the blocks on the street, and at the opposite end of the development, a greater depth means that the circulation is located in the centre, with apartments (generally smaller ones) on either side with windows facing in one direction.

As well as the courtyard form – outside the norm for Paris's social housing department, the RIVP (Régie Immobilière de la Ville de Paris) – the scheme also employs an experimental cladding system, one of the few prefabricated systems to be successfully applied to housing construction. Renzo Piano Building Workshop had, in fact, designed the system for their 1990 office extension to the IRCAM building (phase 1: 1971–77) next door to the Pompidou Centre, and they adapted it for the rue de Meaux scheme. Based on a visible concrete-framed structure, the cladding system has a regular GRC 'frame' or square grid of 900 x 900 mm (35 x 35 inches) with visible thin fins, 30 x 300 mm (1¼ x 12 inches) deep, within which solid panels formed with terracotta tiles to a module of 400 x 200 mm (15¾ x 8 inches) are clipped into position. The size of these panels sets up the dimensions of the rooms within the apartments, with living rooms being generally four modules wide and bedrooms being three. There are 40 apartment types, including duplexes at the upper levels. Most have roof terraces or incorporate loggias, and, as is common in much French planning, access to the bedrooms is from the living spaces.

There are just two kinds of plants in the courtyard: a fragrant honeysuckle, which forms a dense green carpet in vivid contrast to the rich red terracotta; and slender silver birch trees, whose fragile trailing leaves provide some privacy at upper levels without blocking out the light.

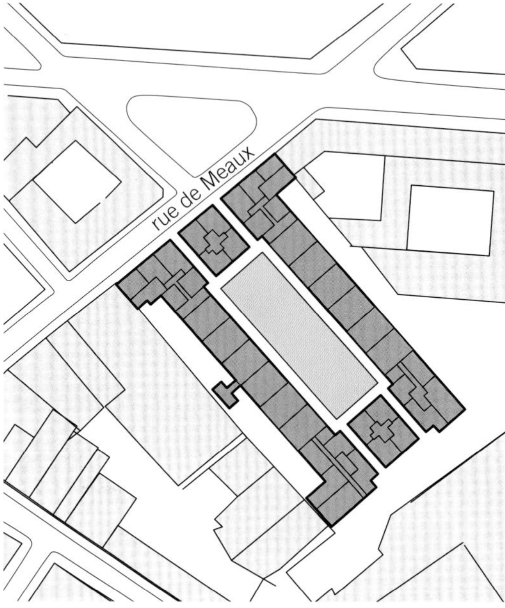

Site plan
1:2,500

1 Plan of typical two-bedroom apartment 1:200

2 Plan of upper level of three-bedroom duplex apartment 1:200

1 Shared circulation
2 Kitchen
3 Living room
4 Bedroom
5 Bathroom
6 Loggia
7 Terrace
8 Winter garden

1

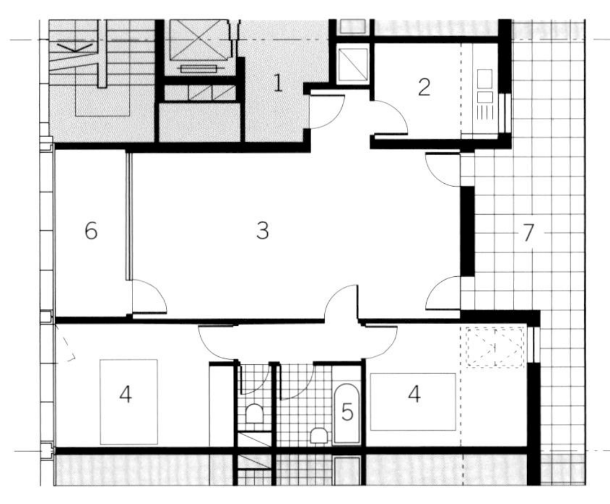

2

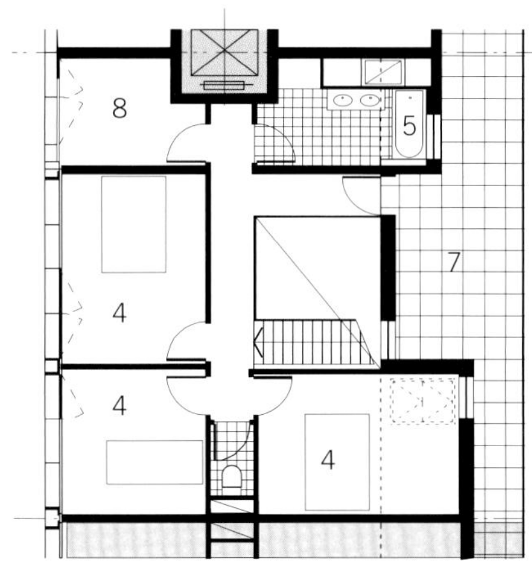

3

3 Elevation 1:500

4 Section 1:500

1 Central courtyard
2 Parking
3 Service access

4

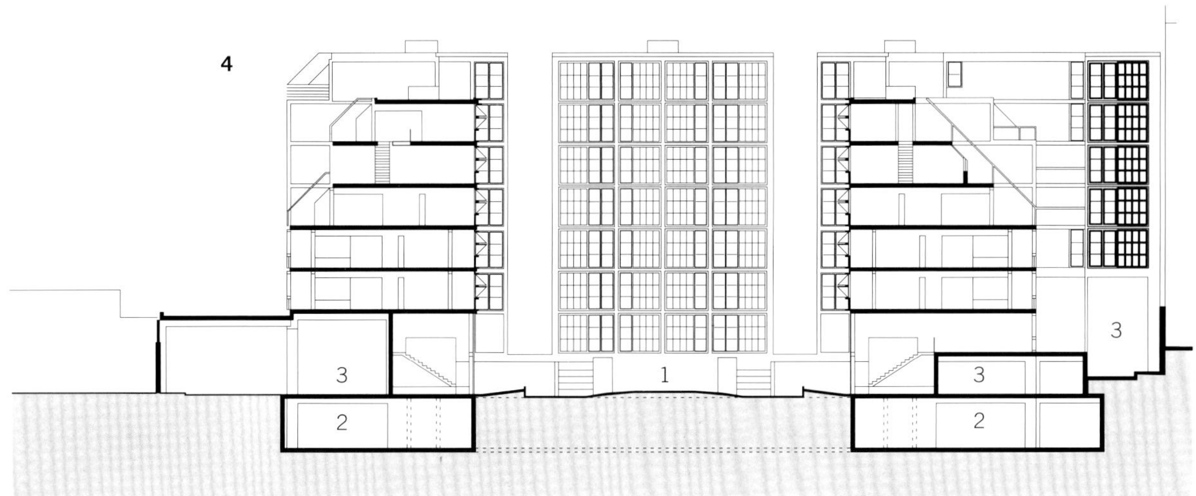

Horizon Apartments

Harry Seidler and Associates

Sydney, Australia; 1998

Harry Seidler (1923–2006) was probably Australia's best known, internationally recognized architect, in practice since 1948 and responsible for some of the landmark buildings in Australia's principal cities. In Sydney, his Australia Square Tower was the nation's first skyscraper. It was the tallest lightweight concrete building in the world at the time it was built, in the late 1960s, and it led to many other similar commercial buildings in the following decades. Seidler's work in the residential sector – both on individual houses and Modernist tower blocks – continued in parallel but was initially less well received, and took some time to be considered acceptable in the Australian context (see Blues Point Tower, pages 128–29).

The plan of the 43-storey-high Horizon Apartments – roughly a quarter-circle – is divided into radiating segments to form the individual apartments. There are five per floor at the lower levels and four per floor from the 31st to the 41st storeys, with penthouses on the top two floors. The curved balconies, cantilevering outwards and extending the segment lines, give the building its particular character. Starting from the need to provide space for a table and chairs, the curve varies in depth from 1.2 to 3.5 metres (4 to 11 feet 6 inches) and is reversed on alternate floors, contributing to a greater sense of space and a less rigid appearance. The balconies are generally orientated to the north-east, with spectacular views across Sydney Harbour, its bridge and the opera house. The upper levels have larger apartments and fewer balconies. Some units have a degree of inbuilt flexibility, with removable dividing walls between bedrooms; all have full-height faceted glazing between the radiating fins of the structural dividing walls, protected from the sun by balcony overhangs and exterior awnings.

At the lower levels the scheme includes low-rise split-level apartments and facilities for all the residents: car parking, a swimming pool and a tennis court. In recent years, Seidler and Associates have built two more housing blocks, North Apartments and Cove Apartments, both with similar curvilinear balconies.

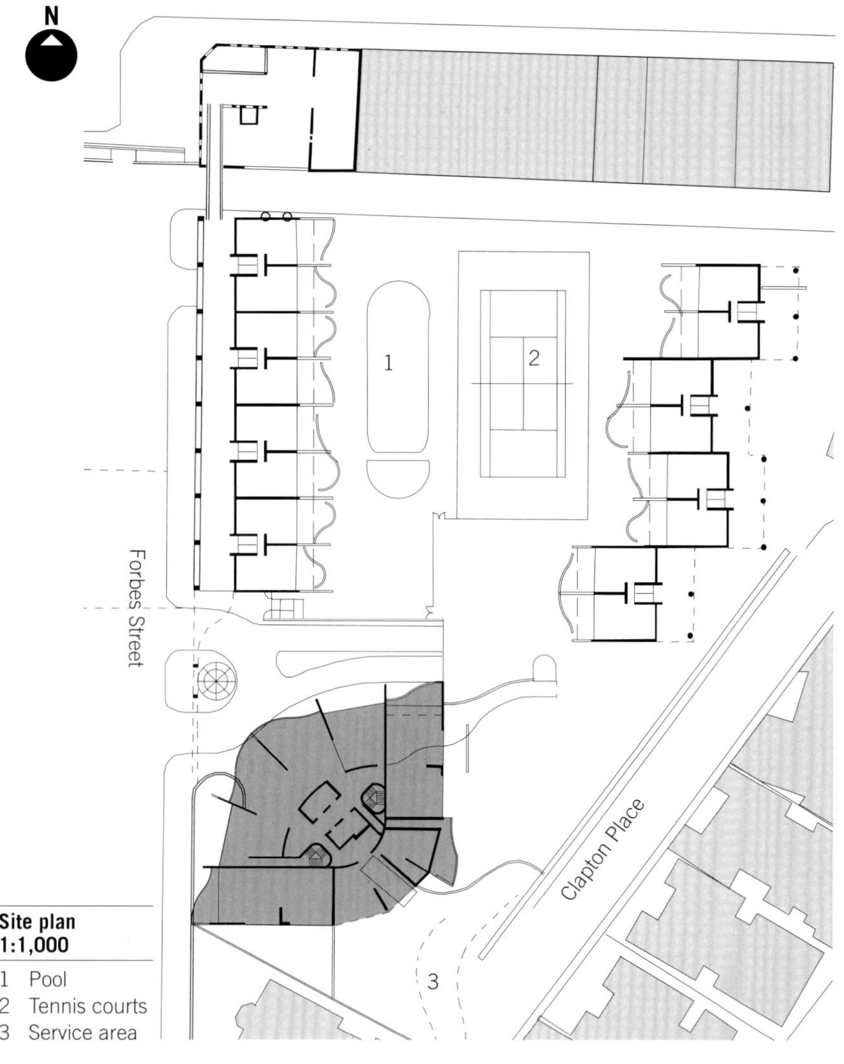

Site plan
1:1,000

1 Pool
2 Tennis courts
3 Service area

Opposite left: Exterior facing north

Opposite right: Curved cantilevered balconies

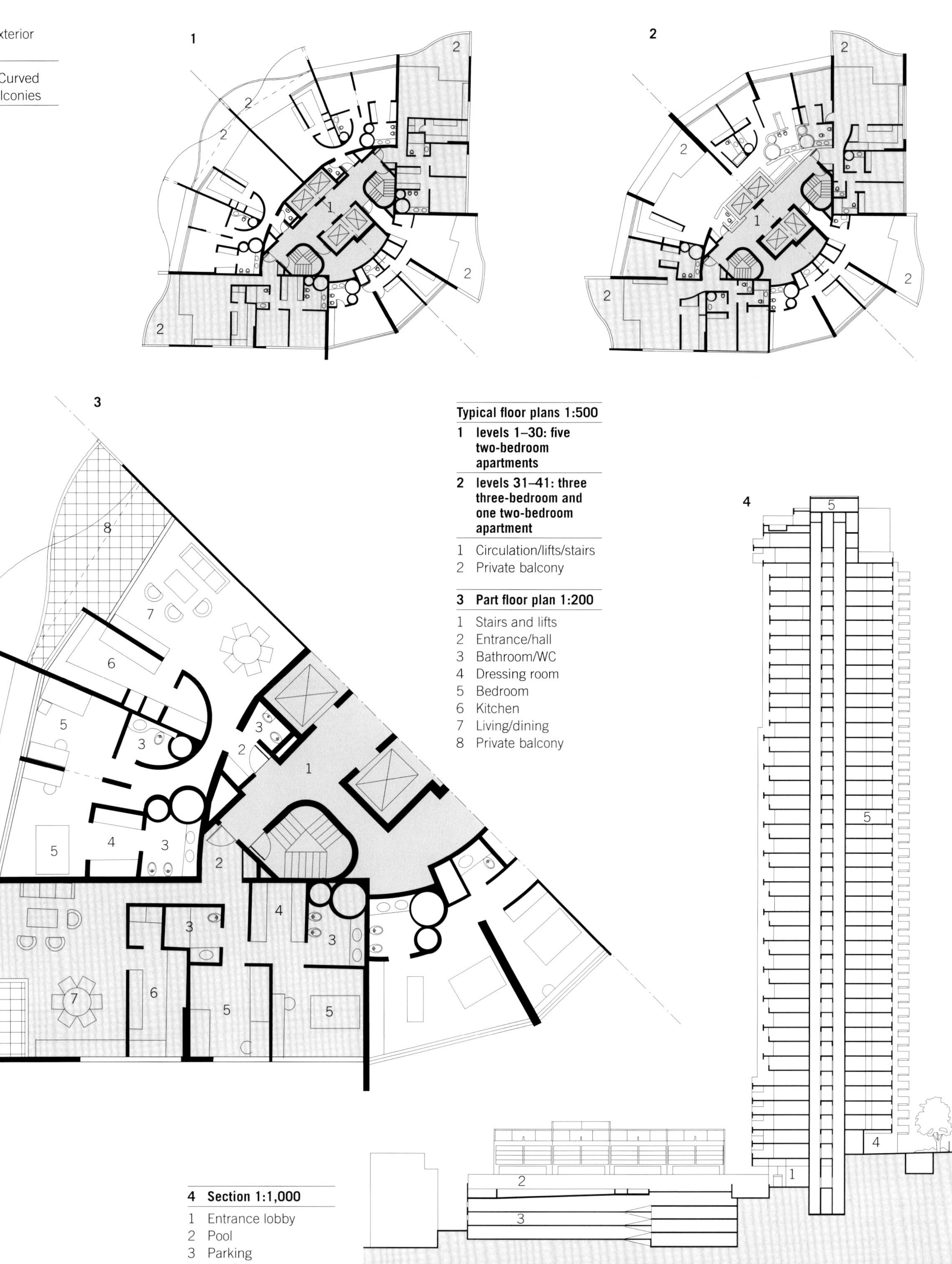

Typical floor plans 1:500

1 levels 1–30: five two-bedroom apartments

2 levels 31–41: three three-bedroom and one two-bedroom apartment

1 Circulation/lifts/stairs
2 Private balcony

3 Part floor plan 1:200

1 Stairs and lifts
2 Entrance/hall
3 Bathroom/WC
4 Dressing room
5 Bedroom
6 Kitchen
7 Living/dining
8 Private balcony

4 Section 1:1,000

1 Entrance lobby
2 Pool
3 Parking
4 Service area
5 Plant and maintenance

Contemporary Interpretations

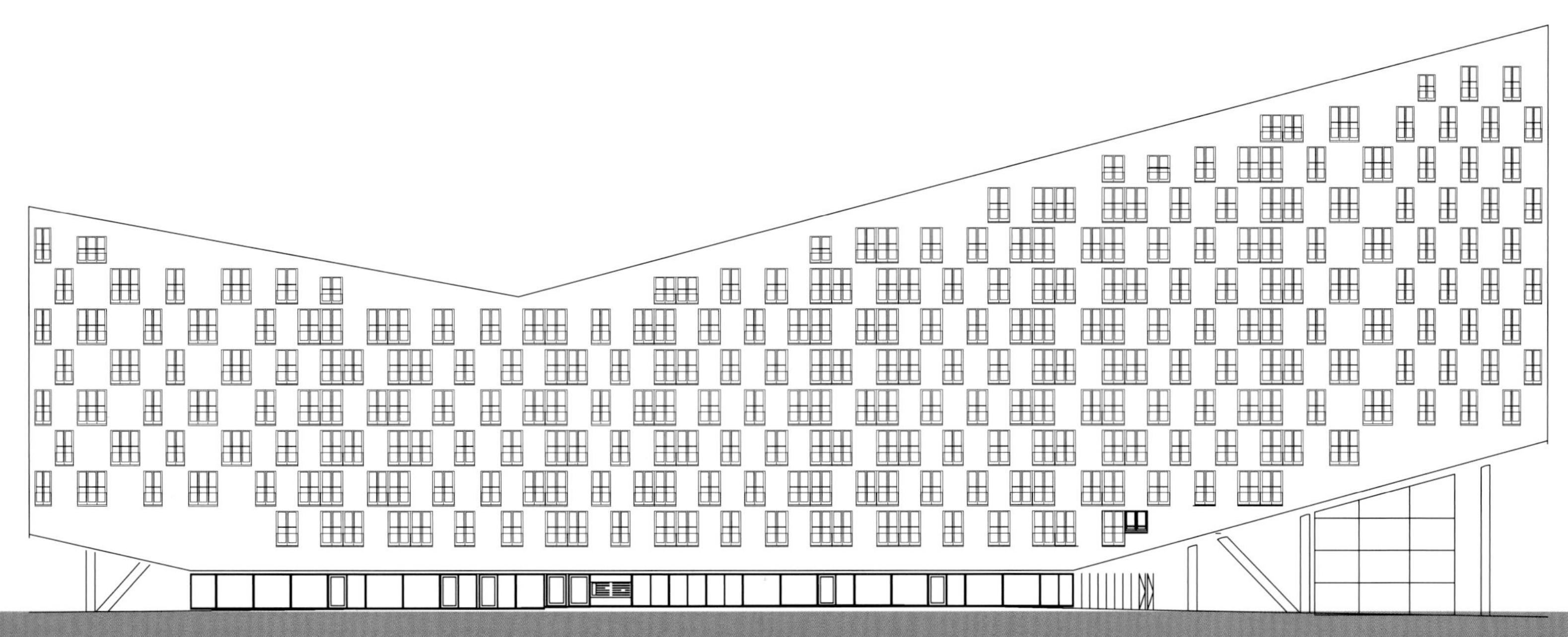

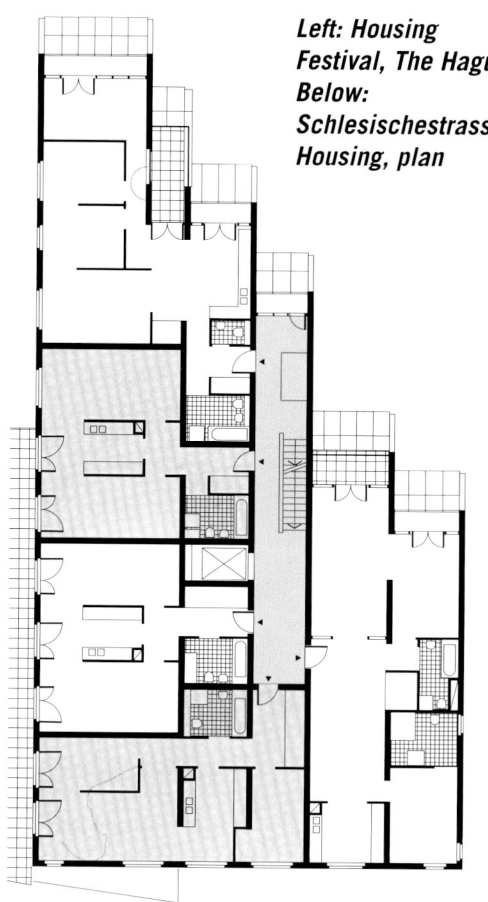

Left: Housing Festival, The Hague
Below: Schlesischestrasse Housing, plan

In much of Europe and the USA in the 1990s and the first few years of the twenty-first century, housing projects are more often part of urban 'regeneration' projects than the 'development' programmes of the 1920s and 1930s or the 'expansion' and reconstruction programmes of the post-war decades. Projects on infill and brownfield sites that require interventions into pre-existing urban landscapes demand a different approach to design: one based on a response to the immediate neighbourhood and local geography. The unifying effect of buildings with just one repeated plan-type is no longer considered desirable in communities with a diverse population – instead, a wide range of dwelling types is now preferred. The biggest impact has probably come from changes in construction, largely as a result of rapidly changing legislation reflecting concerns about reductions in energy consumption and the potential effects of global warming and climate change. Flexibility (argued for by Modernists) is now recognized as an important aspect of design – whether diurnal or seasonal; focused on the life of the family within the dwelling; in the longer term, over time to accommodate the different needs of a growing family; or, longer-term still, to allow for reconstruction of the interior in a reconfiguration of apartments over many years to accommodate changing tenants. Within this more complex 'landscape', architects continue to experiment with new planning arrangements, new urban forms and reinterpretations of traditional and modern typologies.

The **Housing Festival in The Hague**, built over 15 years between 1987 and 2003, was planned by Kees Christiaanse of KCAP to demonstrate the broadest range of housing types and is clearly organized in a linear strip in three groups: low, medium and high-rise. KCAP's own scheme in the high-rise section, **Kavel 25** (see pages 196–97), is described as a 'toppled tower' – a new way of looking at a slab block that includes a reworking of Le Corbusier's Unité duplexes and shared open spaces within its overall volume. The more rational, organizational approach of Volker Giencke's and Léon Wohlhage Wernik's schemes are clear from their plans (respectively: **Carl-Spitzweg-Gasse** in Graz – pages 198–99 – and **Schlesischestrasse Housing**, Berlin – pages 200–201). Both use a parallel zoning system to organize the spaces of their projects – with identifiable zones for circulation, bathrooms and services, and habitable spaces – but with very different results. In one project, the circulation and service zones are clearly articulated on the exterior; in the other, the zones are concealed within the homogeneous form of the block. The

Far left: **Kitagata Housing, interior of double-height living space**

Left: **Mirador Apartments, upper-level access corridor**

very narrow slab of SANAA's **Kitagata Housing** building (see pages 206–7), at only 7.3 metres (24 feet) wide, interprets the apartment building as a collection of rooms. Between access galleries on one side and a continuous verandah on the other, a series of identical rooms, each 4.8 x 2.6 metres (15 feet 9 inches x 8 feet 6 inches) in size, are arranged in parallel strips and only need to be combined in different ways to provide a variety of interlocking flats and maisonettes.

The 'superblocks' of MVRDV's **Silodam** in Amsterdam (see pages 202–5), followed by their **Mirador Apartments** project in Madrid (see pages 222–25), set out to provide a variety of different sizes and types of apartment. Conceived as 'suburbs' or 'mini-neighbourhoods', they are 'collided' together in groups of different plan-types – an arrangement clearly recognizable from the outside. The more recent Mirador project goes beyond the ideas expressed in Le Corbusier's Unité d'Habitation – the notion of the 'vertical garden city' that attempts to provide the infrastructure of a small town or suburb in one building – to contain a 'sky plaza': a public open space integrated at high level within the building.

The façade clearly plays an important role in the architecture of contemporary housing projects. The balconies or roof spaces for drying clothes, found in many early social housing schemes, have now disappeared to be replaced by a variety of verandahs, loggias and winter gardens, fulfilling several functions at once. At Walter Menteth's **Consort Road Housing** scheme in Peckham, London (see pages 226–27), fully glazed and operable verandahs act as noise barriers, provide a thermal buffer and add flexibility to the plan with an additional area that can be occupied as part of the living space in the summer. In Ian Moore Architects' **Liverpool Street Housing** project in Sydney (see pages 220–21), deep loggias behind perforated brises-soleil act similarly as a buffer against the heat and intense Australian sunlight. The use of screening devices also provides privacy and partially enclosed additional space in both Herzog and de Meuron's backlands **Rue des Suisses Housing** scheme in

Paris (see pages 210–211) and in FOA's **Carabanchel 16 Housing** in Madrid (see pages 228–29).

Alongside the development of new forms, architects continue to employ enduring and traditional typologies. A simplified version of the terrace appears in S333's **Schots 1 + 2** project in the Netherlands (see pages 212–215), with two-, three- and four-storey houses under a continuously sloping cornice line at roof level forming a linear edge enclosing a new kind of semi-private urban space. In England, Proctor and Matthews' **Abode** scheme in Harlow (2003) uses a highly modulated façade with verandahs, screens and porches – a very different kind of architecture to that of the Schots project, but equally concerned as much with the design of the external streetscape as with the individual houses. The patio or courtyard house is reworked by Souto Moura Arquitectos in the **Courtyard Houses** at Matosinhos (see pages 208–9), Portugal, at large scale with two enclosed courtyards and an enclosed garden. The **Yerba Buena Lofts** project in San Francisco (see pages 216–217) by Stanley Saitowitz/Natoma Architects takes a warehouse model as the basis for a very deep plan with double-height volumes and low mezzanines.

In terms of the interior 'layouts', for most of these projects the flexibility associated with undifferentiated spaces is a key element in their plan layouts. 'Loft-like' duplexes similar to those of the Corbusian Unité, with kitchens and bathrooms grouped above and below mezzanines, are a common type, appearing in several of these schemes. Sliding doors and partitions that allow spaces to be separated or joined are also a common feature. While the size of apartments has remained largely unchanged, many contemporary projects reflect the diversity of activities indulged in by their occupants with a return to plans that include just one shared space – the kitchen and living room combined – in order to provide more 'bedrooms': the all-important private or individual spaces.

Above left: **Yerba Buena Lofts, interior of a small unit**

Above right: **Yerba Buena Lofts, Shipley Street exterior**

Opposite: **Abode housing scheme**

Far left: Front façade

Left: External stair in one of the voids

Kavel 25

KCAP

The Hague, The Netherlands; 1992

Kavel (or Plot) 25 is part of the housing exhibition of some 550 units by 45 different architects that was built in the Hague between 1987 and 2003. The site, a strip of land along the Dedemsvaartweg 1,500 metres long by 30 metres wide (5,000 x 100 feet), lies between a road and a ditch, on the edge of a pre-war housing project designed by W. M. Dudok. The overall urban plan, conceived by Kees Christiaanse of KCAP, divided this strip into three zones between main intersecting roads, each one dedicated to a different typology: low-, medium- and high-rise buildings. Participating architects included, in the Netherlands, MVRDV, OMA, Mecanoo and Fritz van Dongen; and internationally, Steven Holl Architects and Arquitectonica from the USA, Henri Ciriani from France and Josep Lluís Mateo of MAP Arquitectos from Spain. Initially conceived as a festival to mark the 200,000th dwelling to be built since the beginning of the Netherlands' post-war reconstruction plan, it inevitably found itself compared to the early Modernist housing exhibitions of the 1920s – the Weissenhof in Stuttgart, the Werkbund in Vienna (see pages 48–51 and 60–63) and the Baba exhibition in Prague – and to the later, more politically driven, Berlin exhibitions of 1957 (such as the Hansaviertel projects, see pages 106–9) and the 1984 IBA (see page 159). It has perhaps been most successful in practical terms in providing much-needed housing and showcasing contemporary ideas, although it may be too soon to assess any impact on theory or contemporary architectural discourse.

Plot 25 is in the high-rise section of the strip and referred to by the architects as a 'toppled tower'. It is raised off the ground on pilotis and has two large voids carved out of its rectilinear volume to comply with the requirements for transparency. These voids, sometimes occupied by stairs and with landings passing through them, become intermediate spaces between the private space of the individual dwellings and the public realm of the street outside. Apartments are on six levels above the open ground floor. The first floor has single-storey flats, which occupy one and a half bays of the structural grid, with an external gallery access; and the fifth floor has double-width single-storey units. Otherwise, the apartments are Corbusian duplexes with central access corridors on the third and fifth floors. The two voids are surrounded by the entrances to the dwellings – acting as foyer spaces – and separate the block into a recognizable middle section and two ends.

1

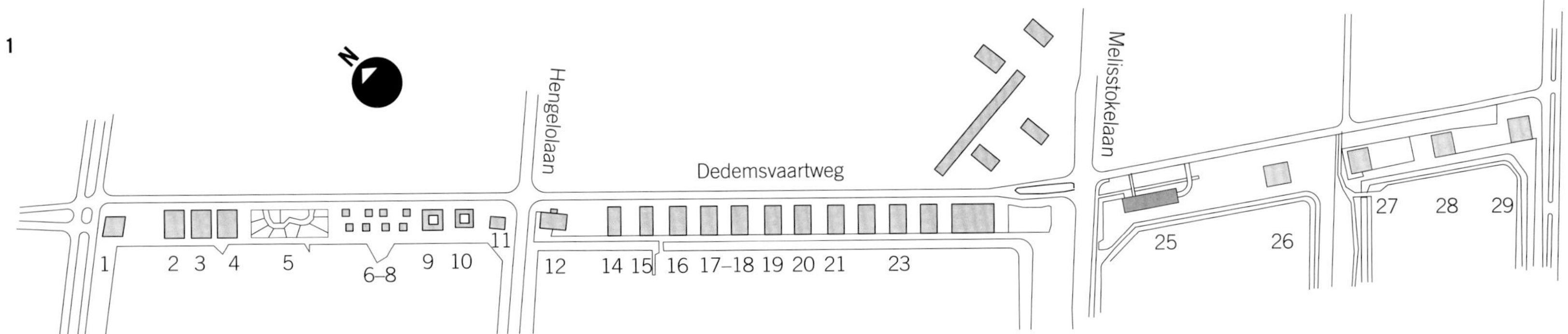

2

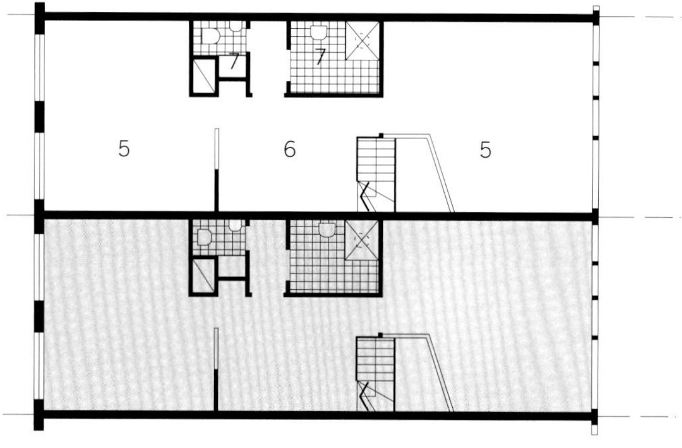

4

3

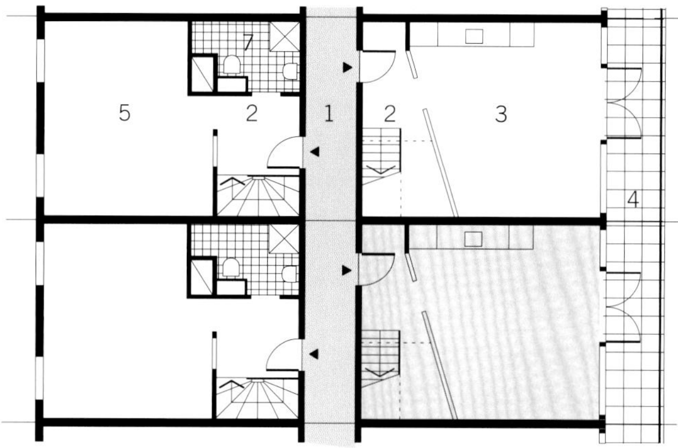

1 Site plan 1:7,500

Names of architects:
1 Kingma Roorda architecten, 2 Oosterhuis.nl, 3 Mecanoo architecten, 4 DKV architecten, 5 Galis Architektenburo, SCALA Architecten, atelier PRO Tet Metzelaar, MVRDV, Jeroen Huijsinga architect, Splinter Architecten, Architectenbureau Victor Mani, Arconiko architecten, Aerts Architectenbureau ir., Geurst & Schulze architecten, 6–8 Henri Ciriani Architecte, Franklin D. Israel Design Associates, MACK Architect(s), Hariri & Hariri, Steven Holl Architects, Stefano de Martino, Andrew MacNair, 9 Vera Yanovshtchinsky architecten, 10 Groep 5 van der Ven, 11 Chiel van der Stelt architect/vormgever, 12 Archipelontwerpers, 14 Van Herk & De Kleijn Architecten 15 Geurst & Schulze architecten, 16 de Architekten Cie., 17+18 Engel + Zillich Architekten, 19 Franklin D. Israel Design Associates, 20 MAP Arquitectos, 21 Stéphane Beel Architecten, 23 Edith Girard Architecte, 25 KCAP, 26 Architectenbureau Marlies Rohmer, 27 Henri Ciriani Architecte, 28 Arquitectonica, 29 Roelf Steenhuis Architekten

Plans of duplex levels 4 and 5 1:200

2 Upper level

3 Entrance level

4 Plan of typical flat, First floor 1:200

1 Access gallery
2 Entrance/hall
3 Kitchen/dining
4 Balcony
5 Bedroom
6 Living
7 Bathroom/WC
8 Storage

5

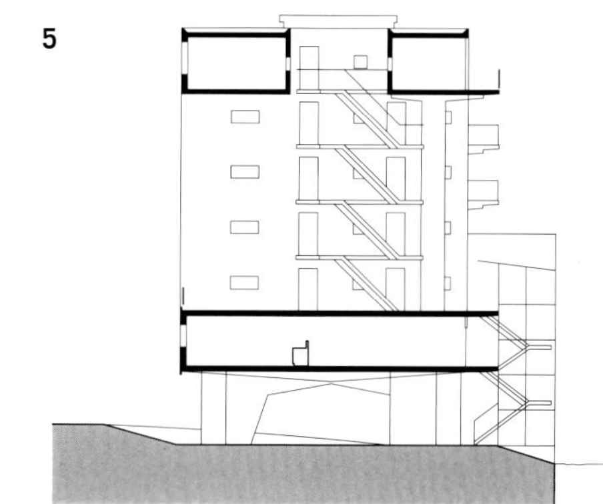

6

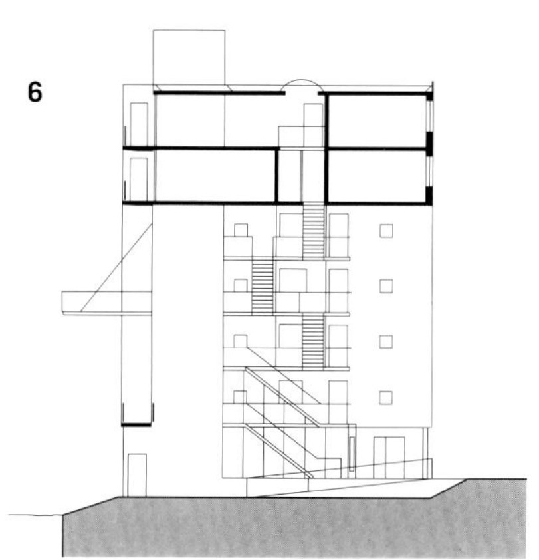

Sections 1:500

5 Section through upper void

6 Section through lower void

Carl-Spitzweg-Gasse Housing

Volker Giencke, 1947–

Graz, Austria; 1992–94

The plans of the two blocks that make up this scheme of 49 dwellings, can be read as a series of parallel zones from front to back. On the north side, there are prominent, open, steel access staircases that rise up perpendicular to the plan underneath oversailing roofs. From the landings, which generally lead to one apartment only, projections from the main façade house the vertical service runs, the entrance lobbies, cloakrooms and bathrooms. Within the main block, most apartments occupy two bays of a 6-metre (20-foot) wide structural grid which varies in depth from 5 metres to 7.5 metres (16 feet 6 inches to 24 feet 6 inches). On the south side, balconies and loggias vary the size and nature of the apartments. The design of the four-storey section avoids lifts by organizing the lower two levels as flats and the upper two as maisonettes. The flats, generally with two bedrooms, all have large balconies. The kitchens vary in size and layout – sometimes located within the living space, which extends the full depth of the plan; sometimes, more conventionally, enclosed as a separate room. The maisonettes, which have three bedrooms, have a small loggia at the lower level, a balcony at the upper level and, in addition, a shared roof terrace that extends the full length of the block.

The approach to the design – a rigorously organized regular concrete-framed structure embellished with metalwork stairs, oversailing roofs to screen the balconies, and exposed staircases – recalls early Modernist designs that focused on function and materials. The site arrangement, too, has more in common with early Modernism than with later developments. Rather than following street lines, the two blocks are arranged to take advantage of the sunlight and to provide a communal garden. Careful consideration of the privacy of the dwellings, particularly those on the ground floor, is evident in the additional depth and the raised level, which forms a plinth above the natural ground level and which also allows natural light and ventilation into the basements. Curved ramps give easy access for bikes and prams, and intermittent broad flights of steps invite use for sitting out.

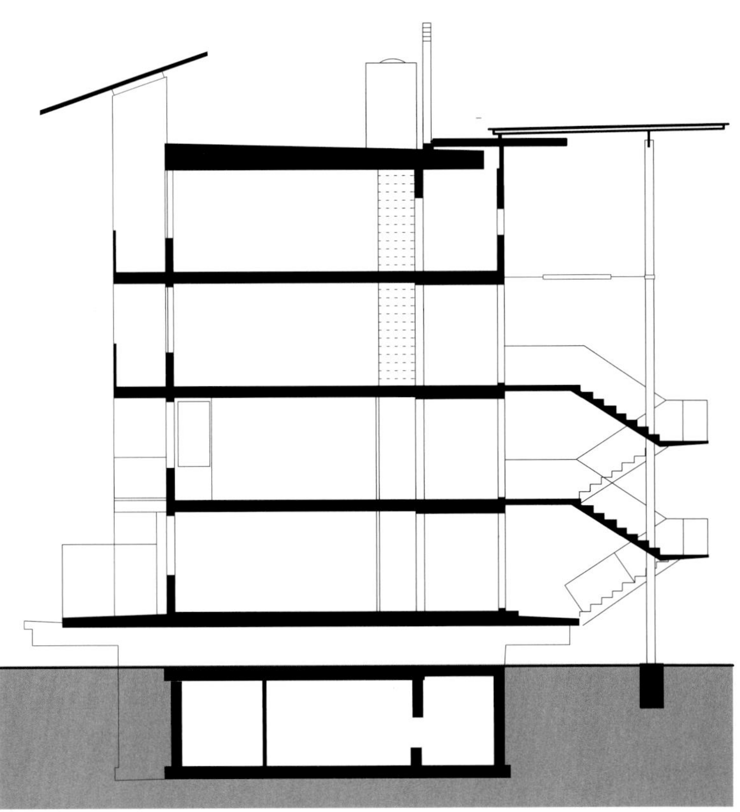

Section 1:200

Opposite left: North elevation with access stairs

Opposite right: South elevation with balconies and loggias

Part floor plans 1:200

1 Roof plan
2 Third-floor plan
3 Second-floor plan
4 First-floor plan
5 Ground-floor plan

1 External stair
2 Entrance/hall
3 Bathroom/WC
4 Kitchen
5 Living room
6 Bedroom
7 Balcony/terrace

1

7

2

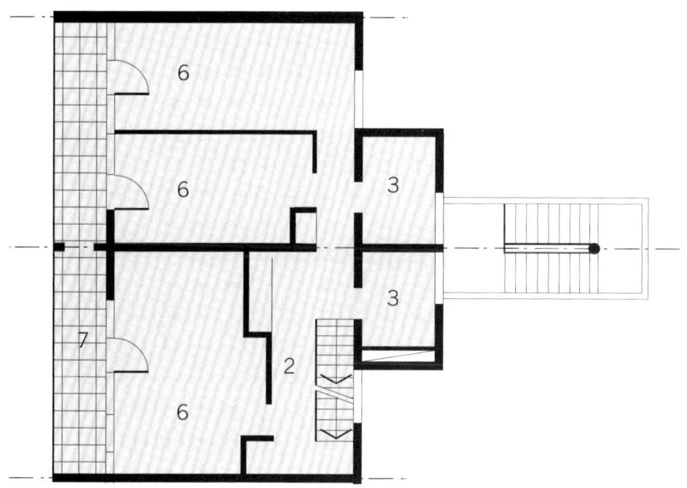

4

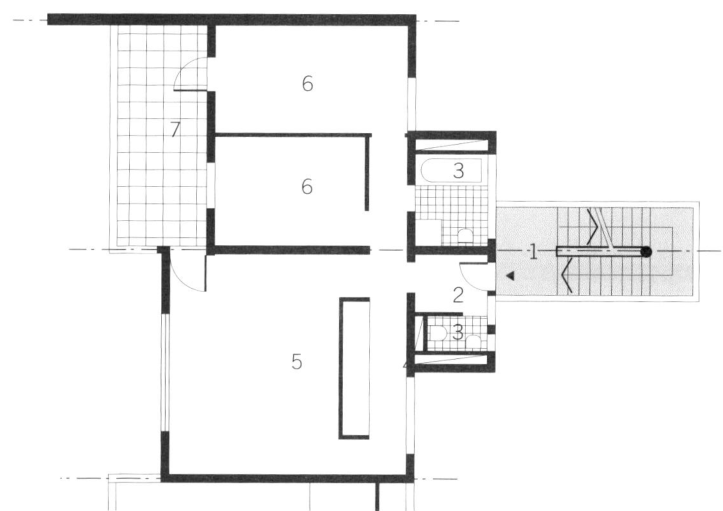

3

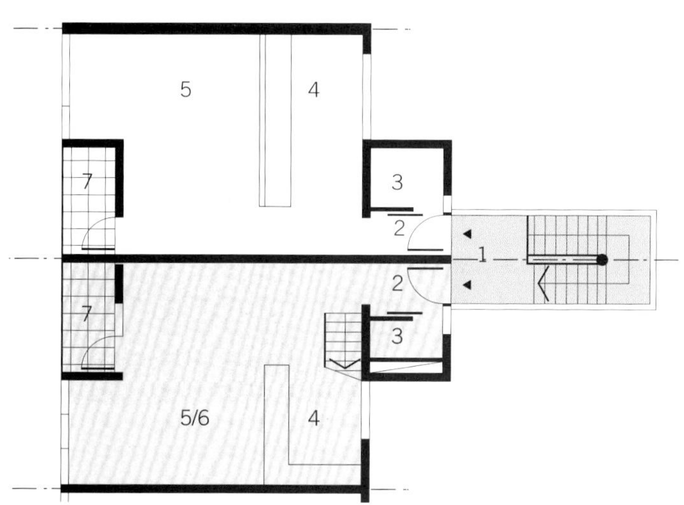

5

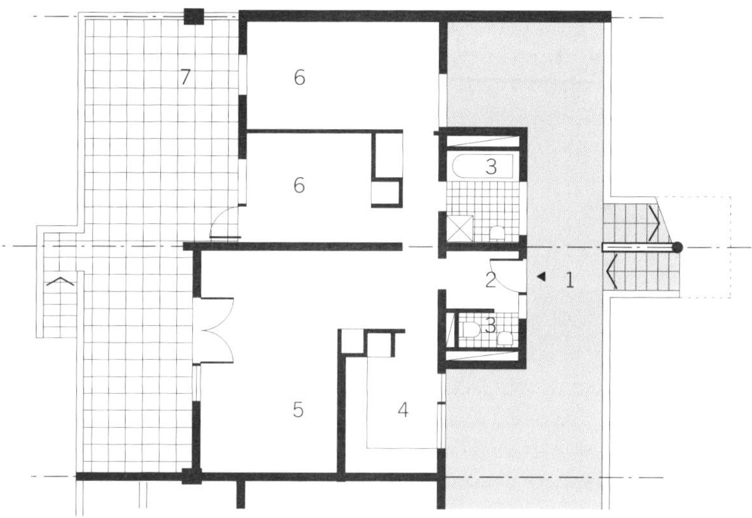

Schlesischestrasse Housing

Léon Wohlhage Wernik Architekten

Berlin, Germany; 1994

Rather than follow the alignment of the existing façades on this infill site on the south-east corner of a city block, the architects have designed a free-standing building. The street edge forms a right-angled masonry structure, punctuated with a regular grid of window openings at the upper levels above ground-level commercial spaces – at first glance, a common conventional arrangement. However, on the other two sides the simple rectangular form of the block disintegrates – a result of the architects' intention to create an apartment building that would be both flexible and environmentally sustainable. The street façades on the north and east sides are of dense masonry construction to provide high levels of thermal and acoustic insulation. On the south-facing side, the dramatically inclined glazing means a benefit from solar gain via winter gardens at every level, and the stepping-back in plan towards the open space at the back avoids overshadowing and brings sunlight and daylight into the apartments.

Internally, the building is conceived as a series of zones, parallel to the long street edge. Living spaces with windows line this street elevation, then comes a narrower band of service spaces – bathrooms, cupboards and entrance hall – next to the linear strip of the shared circulation space, with stairs and lift. On the other side of this circulation zone, a further two 'strips' of accommodation form a larger apartment. The smaller flats have a shared balcony along the length of the street and the larger flats on the south side have, in addition to a private balcony, either one or two winter gardens behind the inclined glazing. The architects have tried to avoid the limitations of minimum space standards by designing flexible internal layouts. There is little differentiation in room size and type, and, typically, wide sliding doors mean that rooms can interconnect, allowing the occupants some choice between a more conventional separation of spaces and a more open-plan environment. The winter gardens, along with extra insulation in the masonry façades, contribute to an economical maintenance and efficient energy consumption.

Site plan
1:2,500

Opposite left: Street elevation

Opposite right: Rear elevation

1

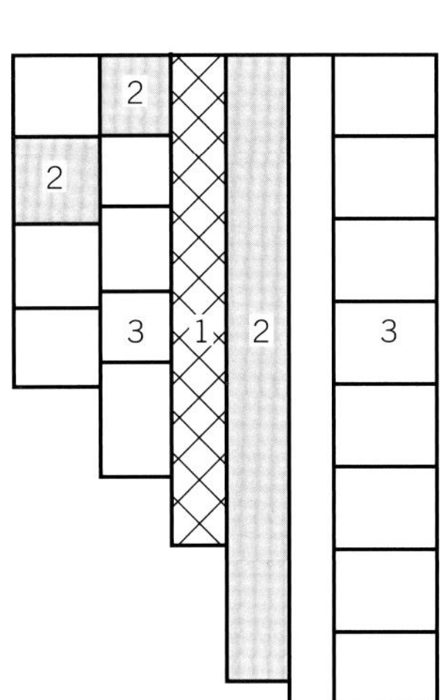

2

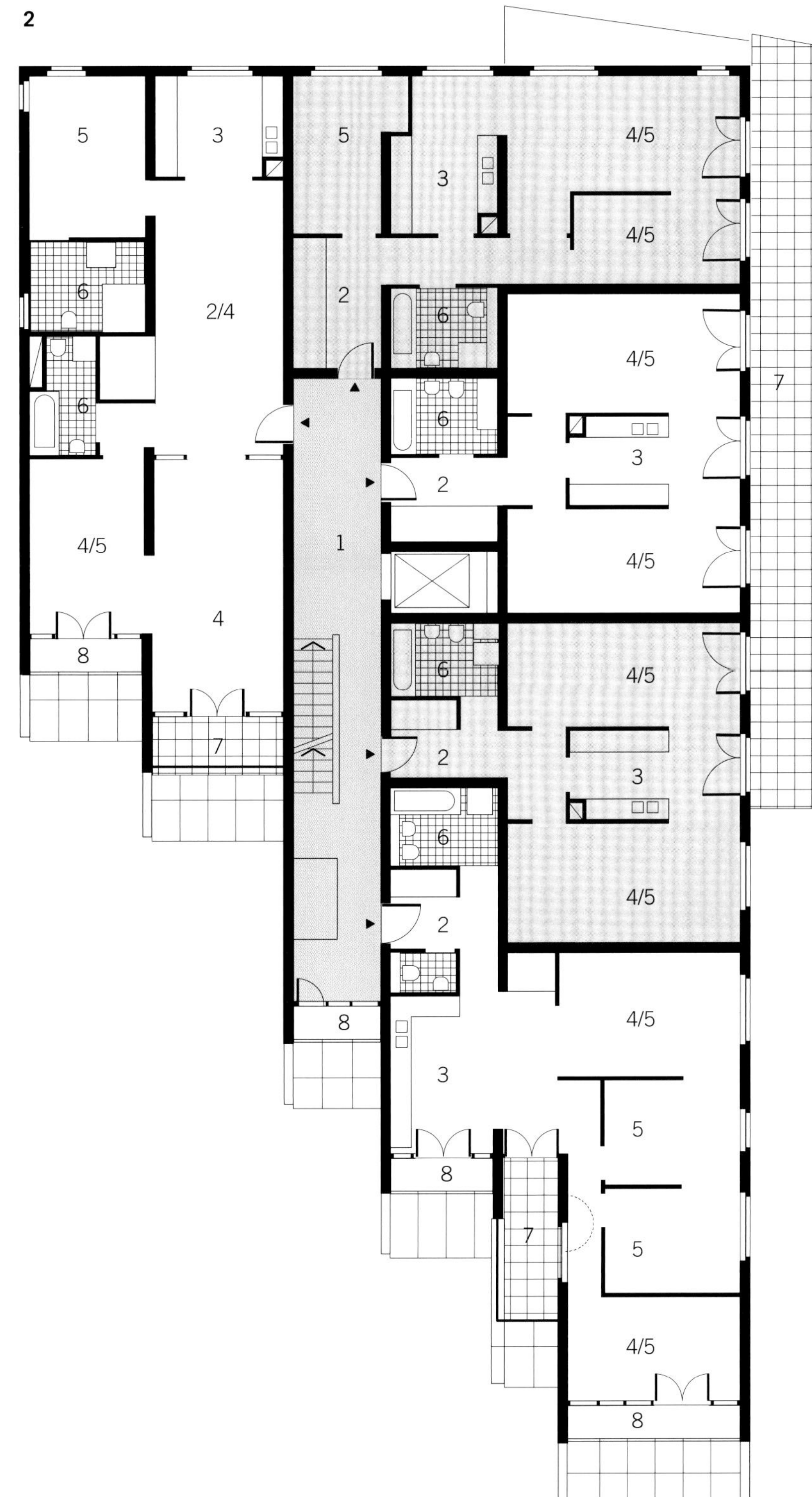

Organizational diagram

1 Central circulation
2 Services
3 Flexible living spaces

Typical floor plan 1:200

1 Access stairs and corridor
2 Entrance/hall
3 Kitchen
4 Living/dining
5 Bedroom
6 Bathroom
7 Balcony
8 Winter garden

Silodam

MVRDV

Amsterdam, The Netherlands; 2002

The massive, 2,600-square-metre (28,000-square-foot) Silodam housing block, sitting on the end of a pier in Amsterdam's harbour, is popularly likened to a cargo ship, laden with brightly coloured steel containers and towering above the surroundings. The seemingly random façades, a collision of different colours and styles, in part results from MVRDV's intention to avoid the usual horizontal stratification and create a three-dimensional version of urban space. Within an overall rectilinear form ten storeys high, 120 metres (400 feet) long and 20 metres (65 feet) deep, the apartments are grouped, between four and eight together, by type (15 types in all). Each group is visible on the exterior of the building via the differing colours and textures of a variety of materials and construction – clearly identifiable from the outside as a series of 'neighbourhoods'. The scheme includes commercial space, which was originally intended to have been dispersed throughout different parts of the building as part of the overall three-dimensional composition – rather than the more usual horizontal zone at street level, separating residential accommodation above from commercial below. A roof-level terrace is accessible by residents, there is mooring space for small boats available underneath the building, and there is also a restaurant and a public space: a large open deck with spectacular views over the harbour.

The apartments are not only different in size and colour, but are also distinguished by the varying placement of the interior walls which can be moved and replaced by future inhabitants. The different apartment types are either the full or half-depth of the block – between 6 and 15 metres (20 and 50 feet) wide – and contain single-, double- or triple-height spaces. Some are split on both sides of the block with spaces overlooking the water on one side and, on a different level, spaces looking towards the city on the other side. Façades are generally developed to include loggias, some extending to two storeys high. The architecture makes an important contribution through its social compostion to new ideas of diversity in housing, with mixed tenure and the greatest possible number of different types of dwelling together in one building to promote the widest variety of inhabitants.

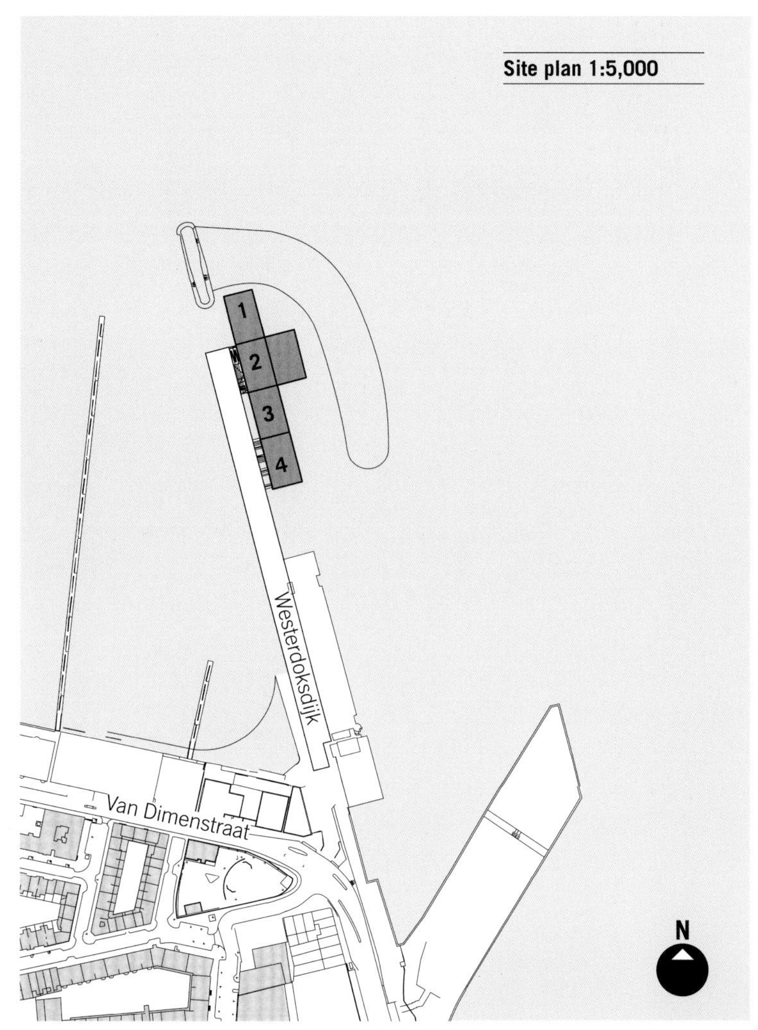

1

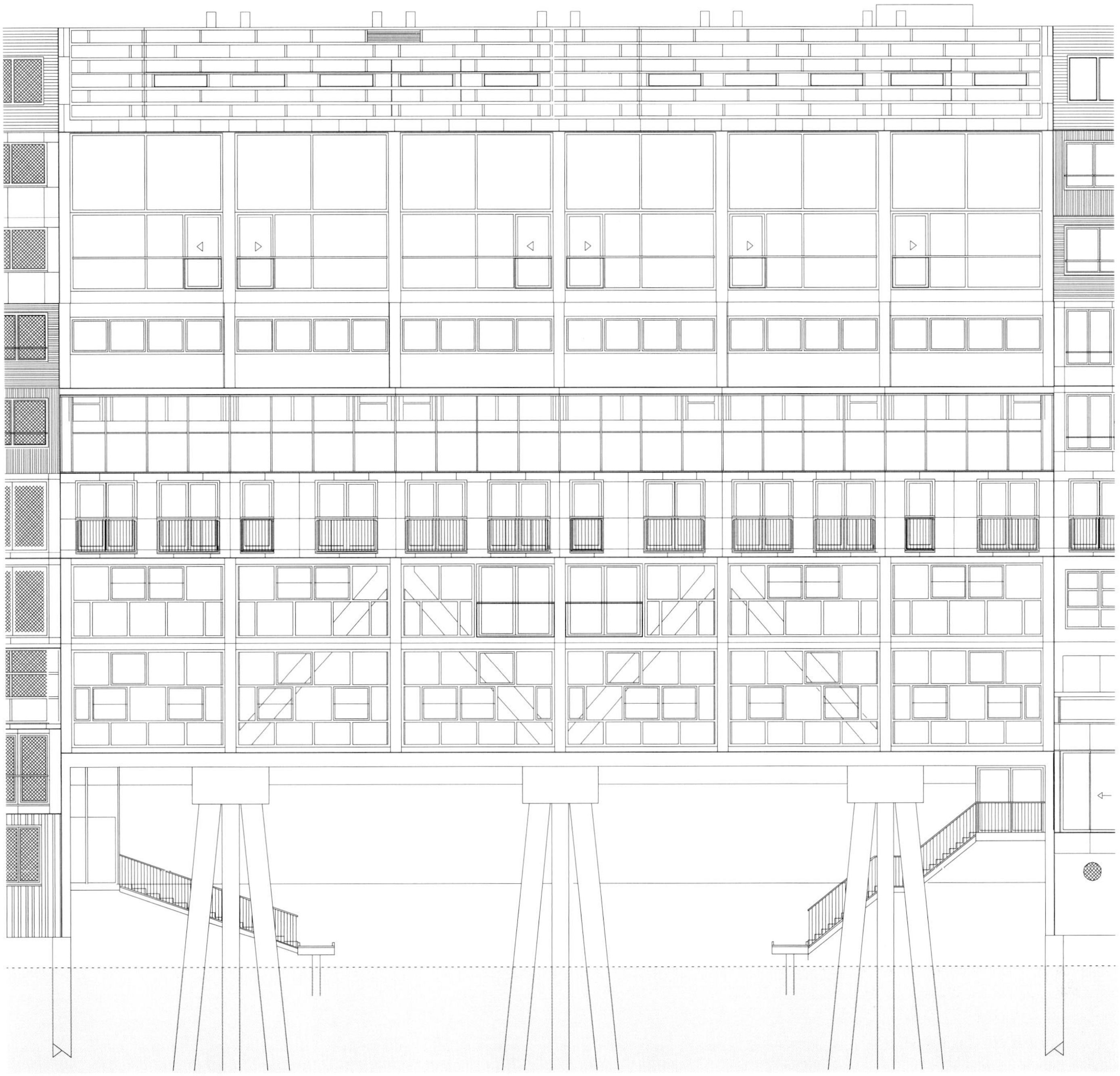

2

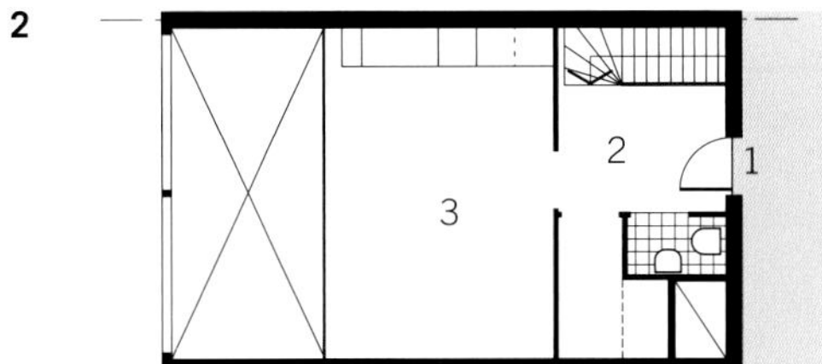

3

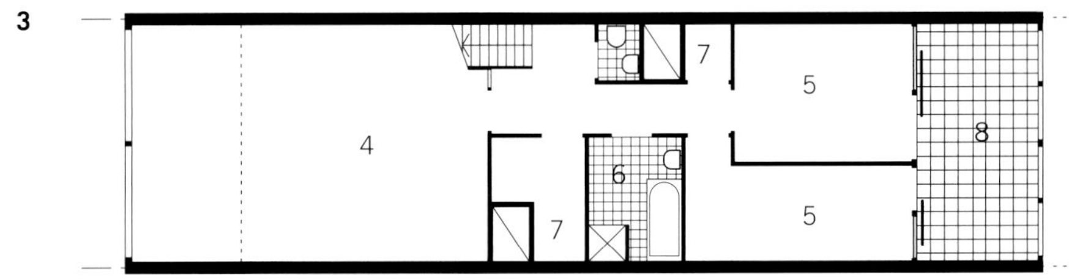

1 East elevation, Block 3 1:200

Type plans 1:200

Interlocking 'Unité', Block 3

2 Upper-level plan (level 7)

3 Lower-level plan (level 6)

1 Access corridor
2 Entrance/hall
3 Kitchen
4 Living
5 Bedroom
6 Bathroom/WC
7 Utility/store room
8 Terrace/patio

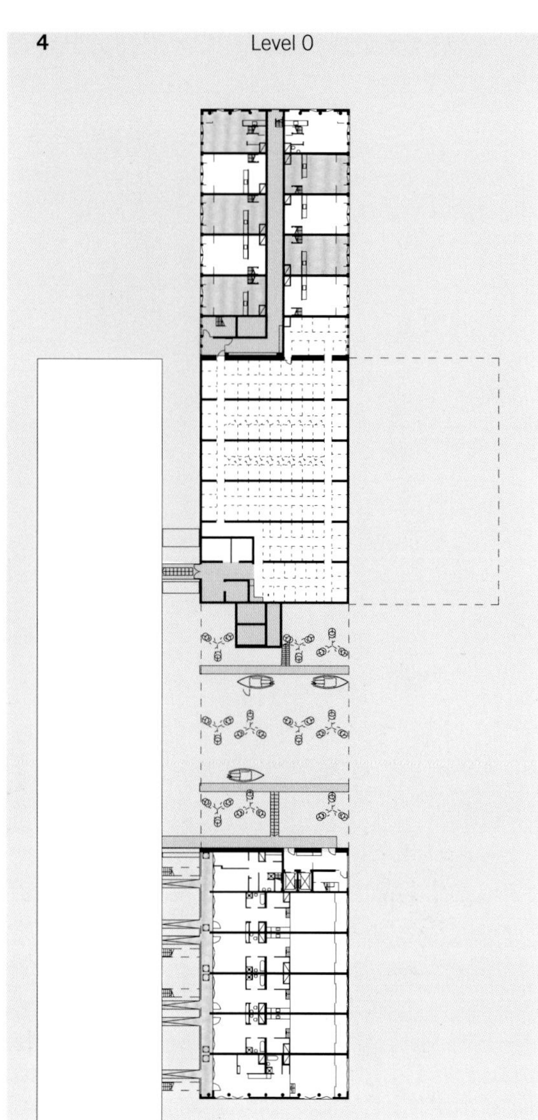

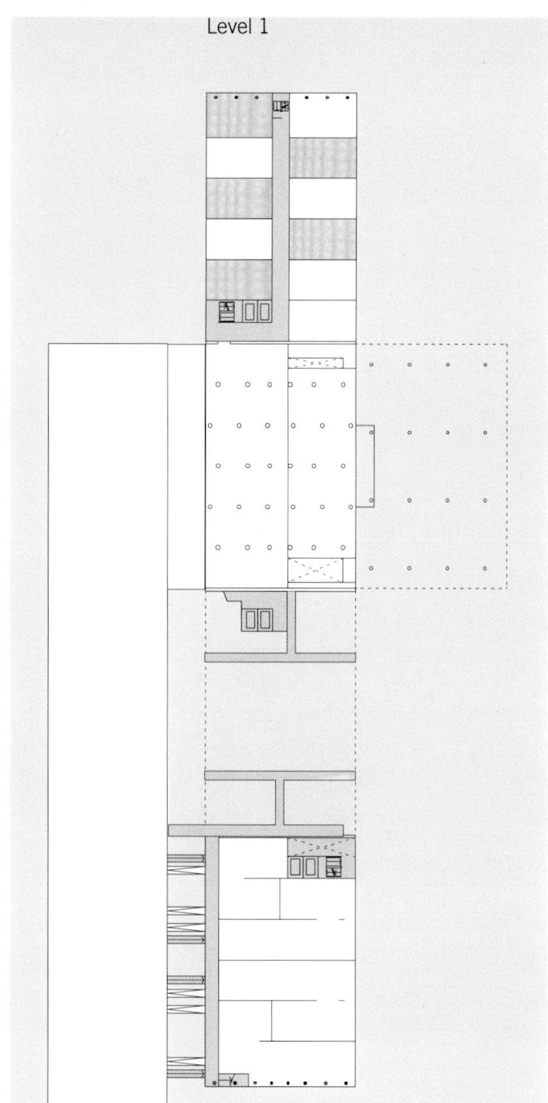

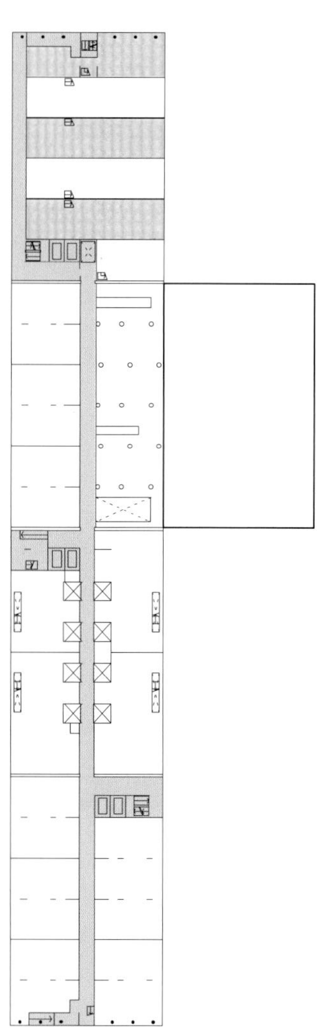

4 Floor plans 1:500

Type plans 1:200

Venetian single-aspect duplex, Block 1

5 Upper level (level 1)

6 Lower level (level 0)

Valerius full-depth duplex, Block 1

7 Upper level (level 3)

8 Lower level (level 2)

1 Access corridor
2 Entrance/hall
3 Kitchen
4 Living
5 Bedroom
6 Bathroom/WC
7 Utility/store room
8 Terrace/patio

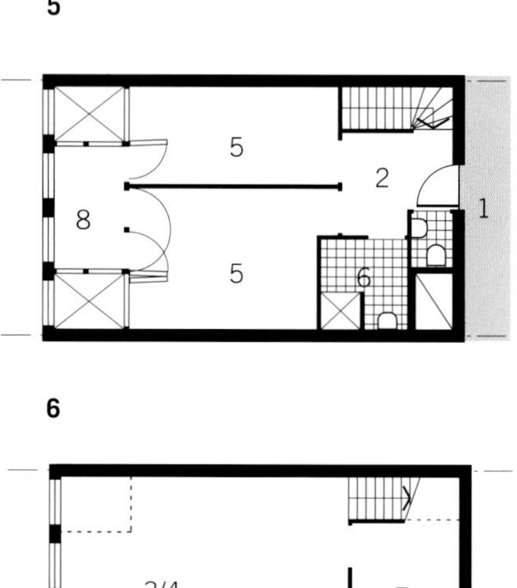

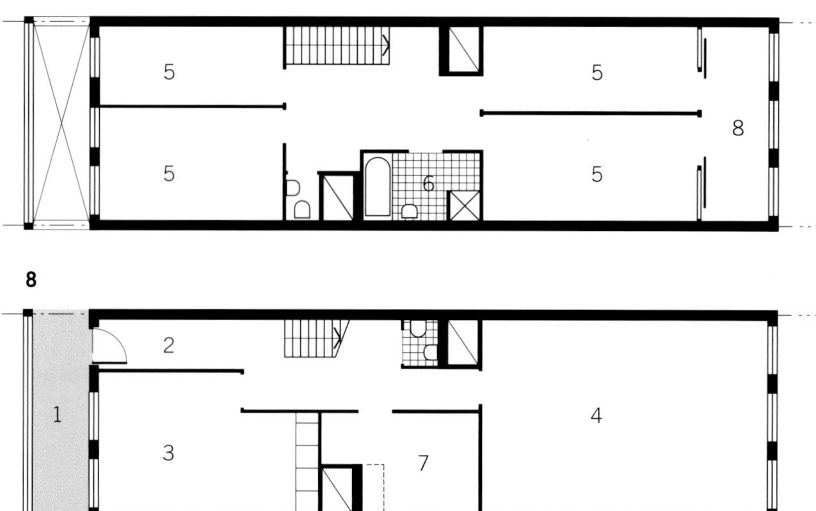

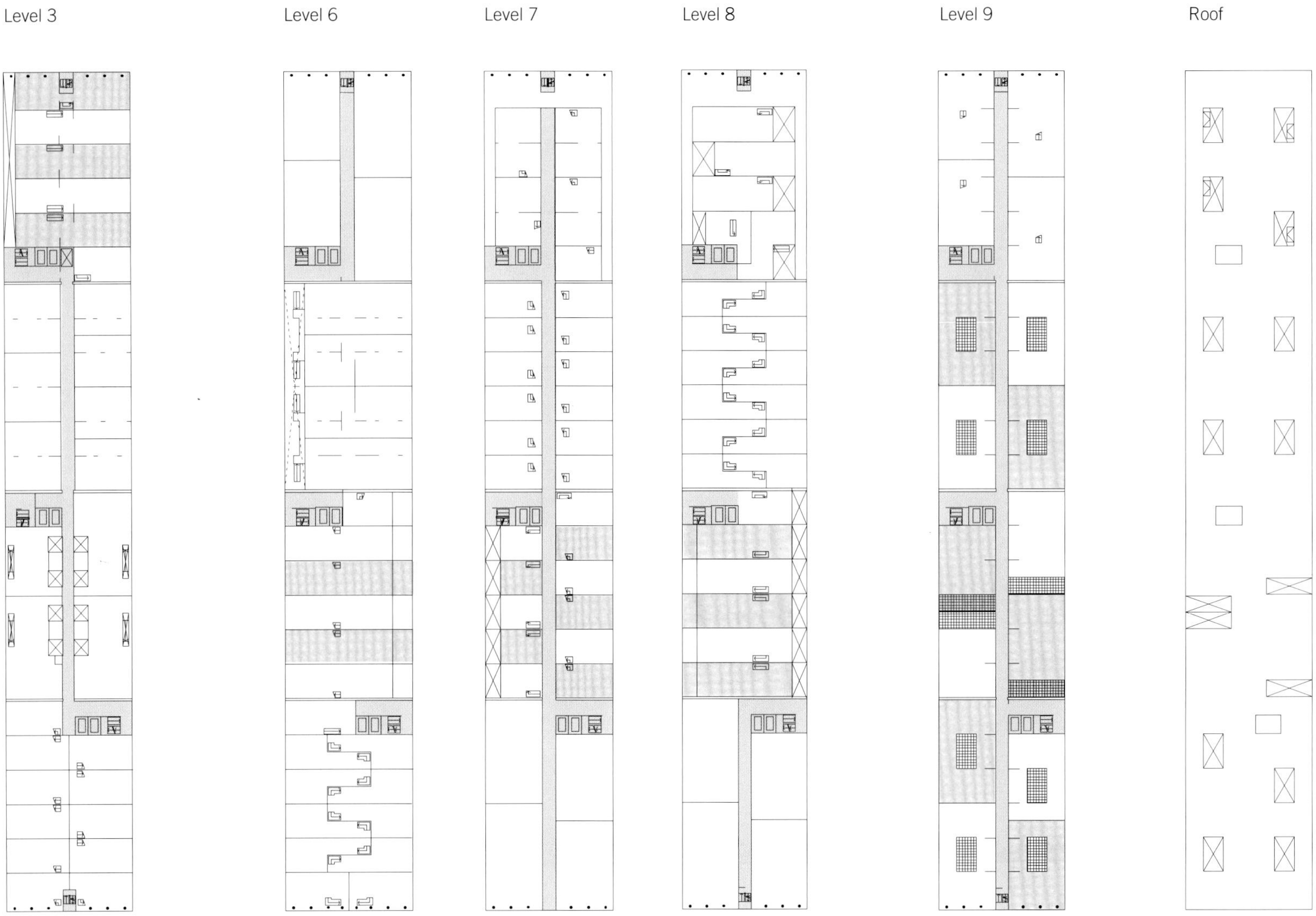

Level 3 Level 6 Level 7 Level 8 Level 9 Roof

Type plans 1:200

9 Patio, Blocks 2 and 4 (level 9)

10 Penthouse, Block 3 (level 9)

1 Access corridor
2 Entrance/hall
3 Kitchen
4 Living
5 Bedroom
6 Bathroom/WC
7 Utility/store room
8 Terrace/patio

9

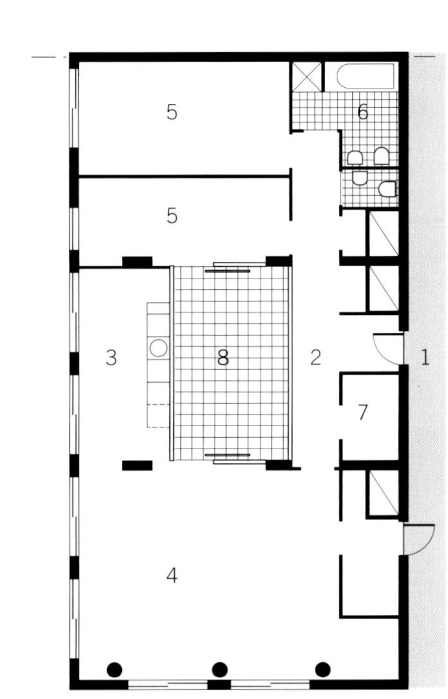

10

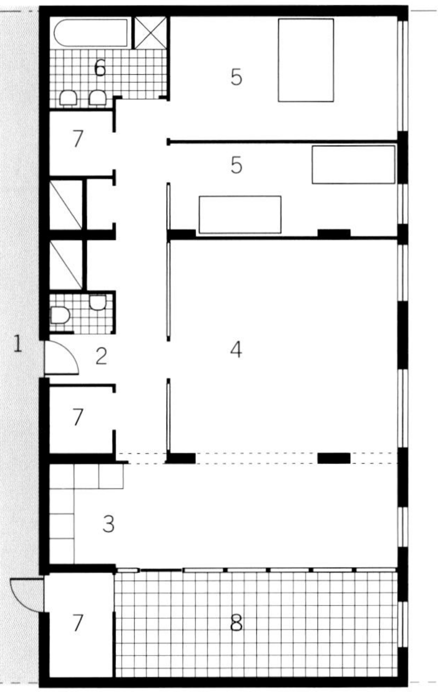

Sejima Wing, Kitagata Housing

Kazuyo Sejima and Ryue Nishizawa/SANAA

Kitagata, Japan; 1994–2000

In Kazuyo Sejima's own words, 'collective housing today is not just for families but a place where people live in all kinds of collective ways. In other words, the base unit is not an apartment but a single room.' Accordingly, the wing designed by her practice at the Kitagata site in Gifu prefecture takes the idea of the single room as its starting point. Four different types of room are identified: a bedroom or private room; a living/dining room, which includes kitchen fittings; a tatami (or Japanese-style) room; and a terrace (or open room). Each has different characteristics. The bedrooms, the most private spaces, are always paired and grouped with a shower room and WC at one end. The terrace extends the full depth of the block and is open to the elements. The living space is sometimes double height, incorporating a stair at one end, and sometimes has bridges and balconies linked to adjacent spaces at the upper level. Each of the rooms is the same size (2.6 x 4.8 metres/8 feet 6 inches x by 15 feet 9 inches) and they are arranged in rows. A variety of dwelling types is achieved by combining the rooms in different ways. The smallest apartment has just four rooms, the largest seven.

This arrangement of rooms in a strictly linear manner is made possible by the addition of a continuous corridor-like verandah space on the south side of the block. Almost fully glazed, the verandah, in combination with the open terraces, gives the block an overall appearance of transparency, and contrary to normal expectations of privacy the inhabitants are highly visible. On the opposite side of the building, the access balconies at every level and the staircases are also exposed to the elements and highly visible. Instead of the empty corridor – interrupted at intervals by the conventional 'front door' to each apartment, which signals activity – here there are doors to each of the rooms. Not only does this change the nature of the structure of the dwelling – as the occupants can come and go independently of the shared spaces within the dwelling – but the 'public' space of the access corridor becomes the lobby for every room.

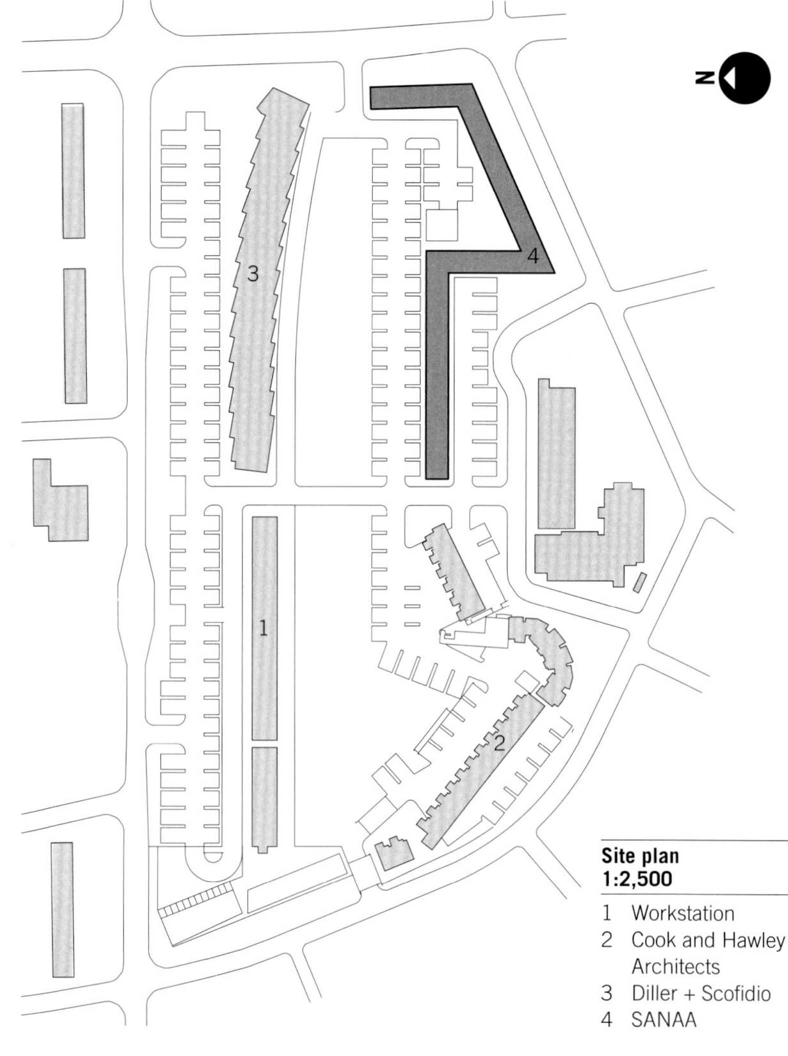

Site plan
1:2,500

1 Workstation
2 Cook and Hawley Architects
3 Diller + Scofidio
4 SANAA

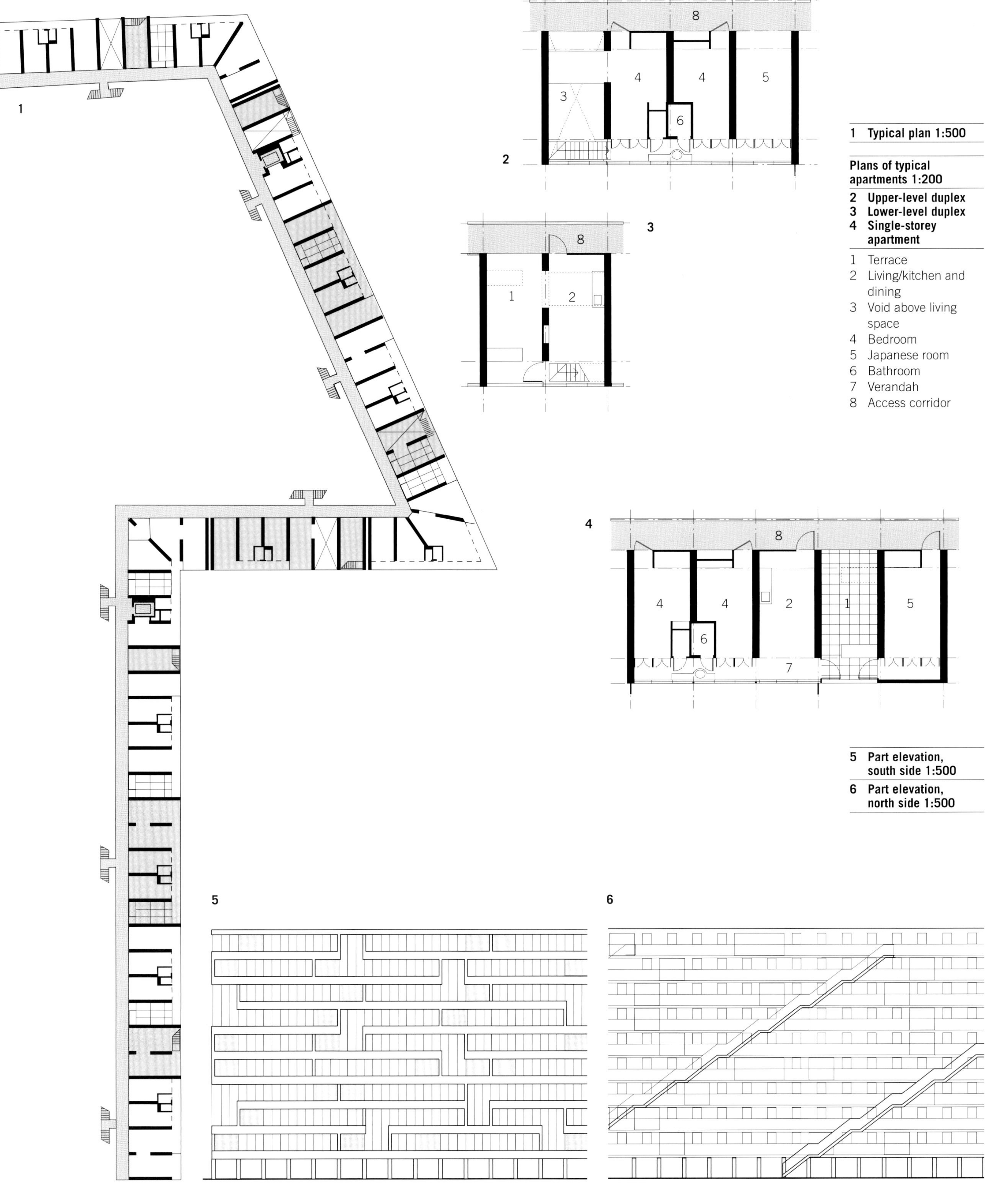

1 **Typical plan 1:500**

Plans of typical apartments 1:200

2 **Upper-level duplex**
3 **Lower-level duplex**
4 **Single-storey apartment**

1 Terrace
2 Living/kitchen and dining
3 Void above living space
4 Bedroom
5 Japanese room
6 Bathroom
7 Verandah
8 Access corridor

5 **Part elevation, south side 1:500**

6 **Part elevation, north side 1:500**

Courtyard Houses

Souto Moura Arquitectos

Matosinhos, Portugal; 1999

This is a small row of dwellings built on the site of what was once the large vegetable garden of an old villa. The courtyard houses are single-storey, retaining a low profile close to the ground and maintaining the views from the old villa across the landscaped gardens and out to the harbour beyond. The nine identical terraced houses are constructed within a simple rectangular plot, orientated roughly north–south, staggered in two groups and unified by continuous oversailing flat concrete roof planes in three parallel strips.

The dwellings, each with four bedrooms and bathrooms as well as a garage, are large – 12 metres wide by 28 metres long (39 x 92 feet). The organization of the plan is focused on the interior, with a series of interconnected inside and outside spaces. The houses all have a paved courtyard in the middle of the plan, a second smaller courtyard at the entrance, and, at the rear, a garden enclosed by the same concrete walls forms a third 'courtyard' space. At the end of the larger gardens a pool is included, with shower and laundry facilities beyond.

The courtyards are key to bringing daylight into such a deep plan. From the entrance, a private hallway leads to the bedrooms at the front of the house and a wider corridor leads to the back of the dwelling, where the main living space and kitchen have full-height south-facing glazed doors that open onto the garden. One of the bedrooms has a window to the entrance courtyard and the other three, in the middle of the plan, have windows onto the central courtyard. The central courtyard also has a window onto a study space located off the hallway, and another that brings additional light into the rear of the living space.

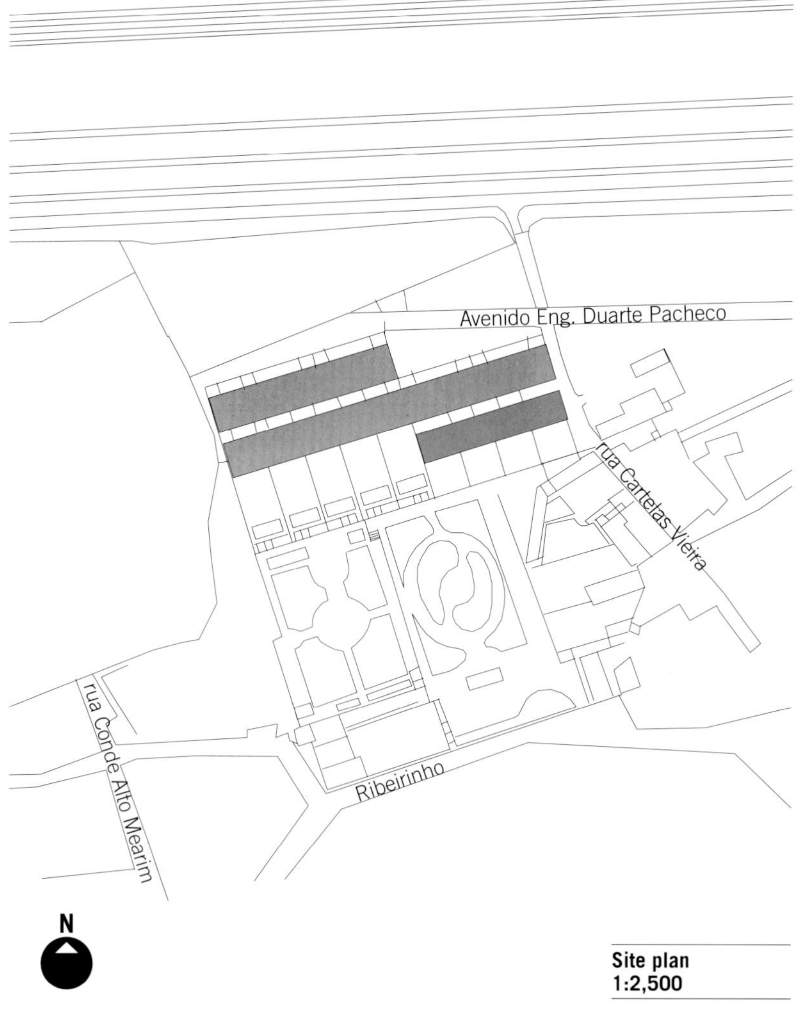

Site plan
1:2,500

1 Section 1:200

2 Plan 1:200

1 Courtyard
2 Entrance
3 Kitchen
4 Living/dining
5 Bedroom
6 Garage
7 Pool

1

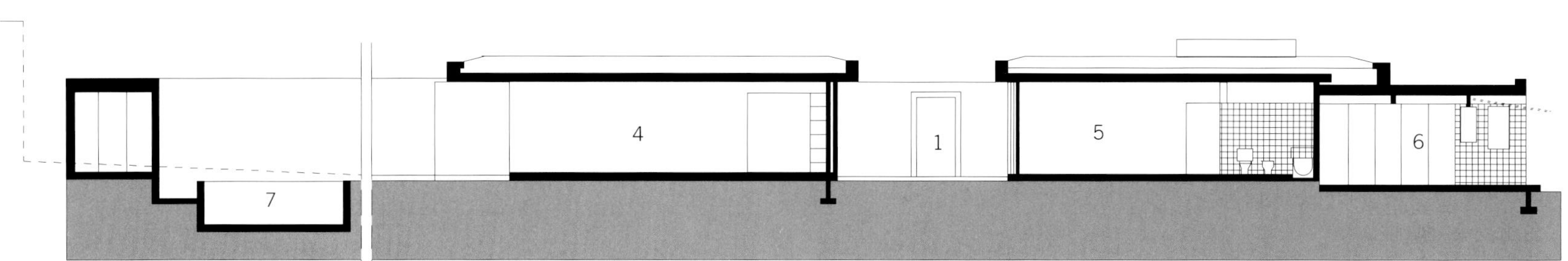

2

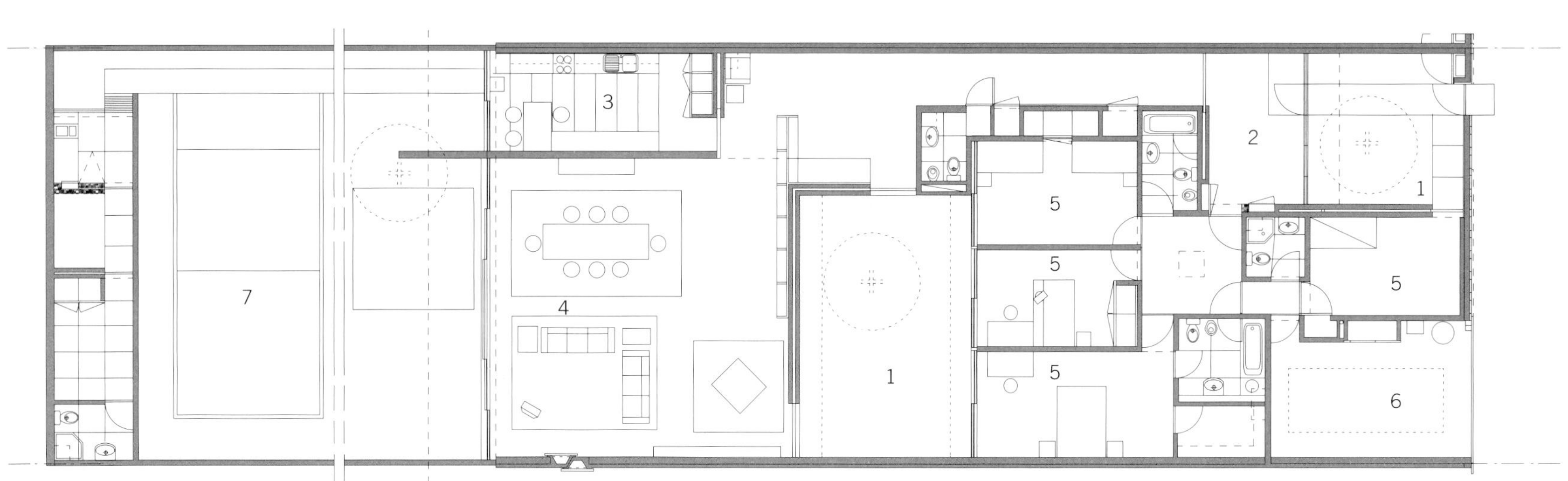

Far left**:** Narrow balconies along façade of central block

Left: Louvred façade of infill block on rue des Suisses

Rue des Suisses Housing

Herzog & de Meuron

Paris, France; 2000

Although a relatively small project, with around 60 dwellings and 50 car-parking spaces, there are three distinct elements to this scheme. Two gaps in the perimeter of the block, on rues des Suisses and Jonquoy, are infilled with blocks seven storeys high and of a similar depth in plan to the existing buildings. In the middle of the block, in a newly defined semi-public courtyard space, there is a three-storey block of flats and two separate small houses, two storeys high. The two perimeter blocks have a central core of stair and lift, and their apartments are organized one per floor in the smaller block and three or four per floor in the larger. In contrast to the neighbouring brick-and-stucco façades, aluminium shutters cover the entire surface of the glazing, floor to ceiling at every level – and are modulated only at the top floor, which is set back in line with the adjacent mansard roof. Parts of the façade are angled in plan, parallel to the widened internal access corridor and leading towards the entrance passageway. This somewhat austere façade is animated by the movement of the opening and closing of the shutters, reflecting the activities of the inhabitants.

Shutters on the façade of the centre block, this time of horizontal slatted timber, mean that it, too, is not static but changes to suit the residents' needs for shading or desire for privacy. Directly behind the shutters each apartment has a narrow balcony along its entire length, accessible from each of the rooms, which are arranged in a line behind glazed timber screens. On the opposite side, a corridor connects the rooms and becomes part of the living space at one end. On the ground floor, there are single-storey projections which enclose private courtyards, and on the top floor the apartments are reduced in width to provide roof terraces.

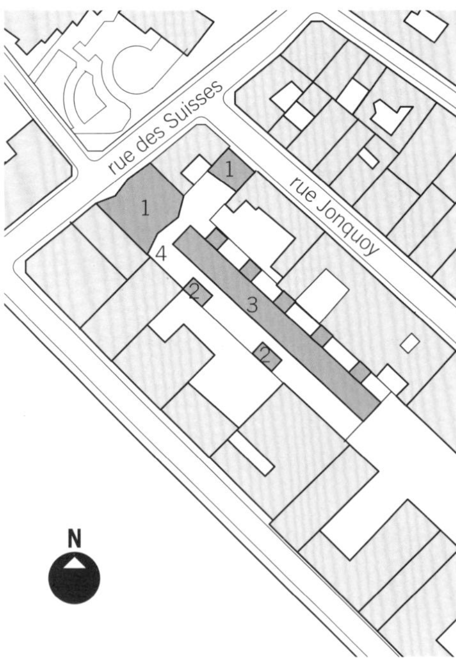

Site plan
1:1,000

1 Infill blocks on street fronts
2 Two-storey houses
3 Main three-storey block
4 Shared courtyard

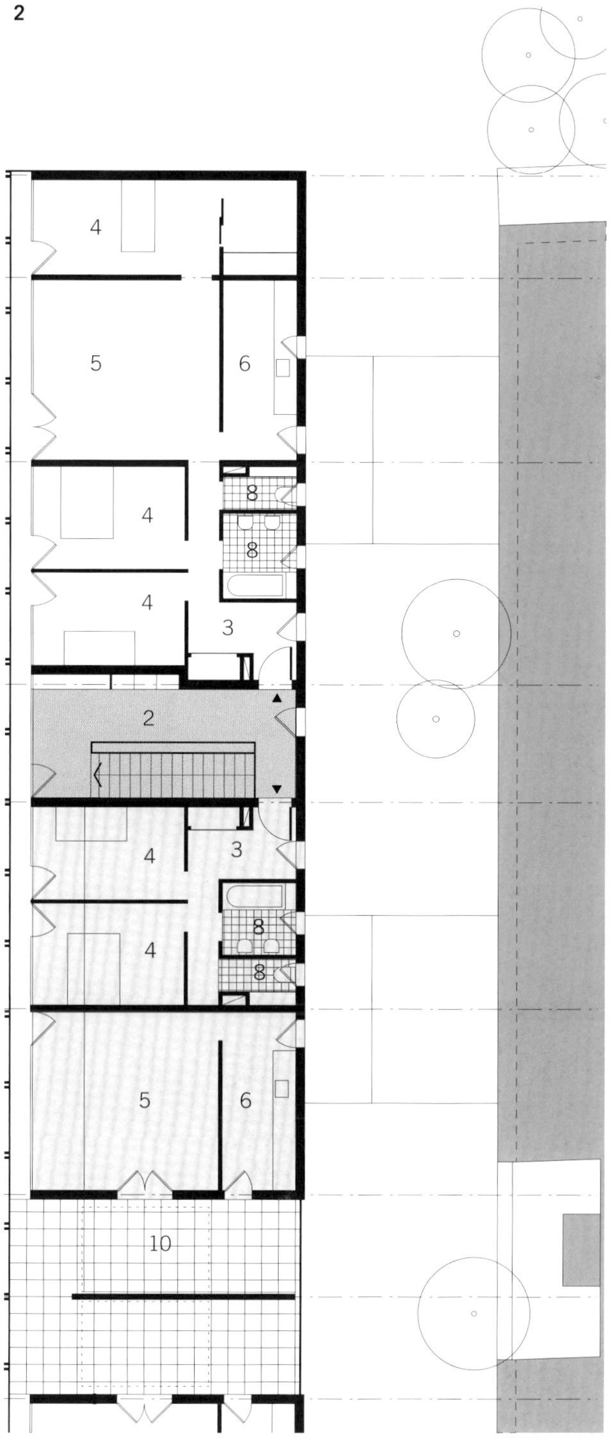

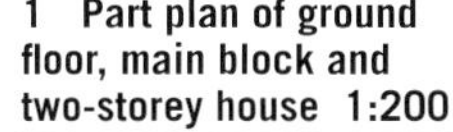

1 Part plan of ground floor, main block and two-storey house 1:200

2 Part plan of second floor, main block 1:200

1 Covered balcony
2 Stair lobby
3 Entrance/hall
4 Bedroom
5 Living room
6 Kitchen
7 Utility
8 Bathroom/WC
9 Private garden
10 Roof terrace

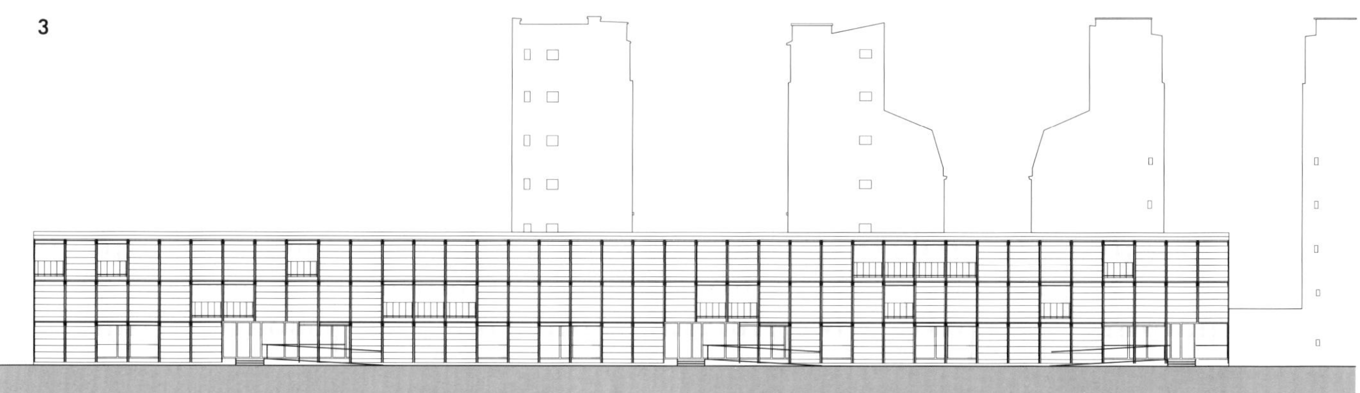

3 Elevation 1:500

Schots 1 + 2

S333 Architecture + Urbanism

Groningen, The Netherlands; 2002

S333's two buildings, Schots 1 + 2, form part of a much larger urban regeneration project won in the Europan Competition of 1993. Although part of the same scheme, the two parts – one, individual terraced houses; the other, an eight-storey block – have a very different visual appearance in terms of both form and cladding materials. Linked by an underground car park, yet separated at ground level by a central pedestrian street lined with commercial spaces, the two elements of this scheme eschew any familiar, regular pattern of road networks and city blocks in favour of a more fluid composition that proposes new hybrids of external spaces. On one side, the combination of cranked terraces and a gradually rising ground plane interspersed with broad steps forms a series of courtyard-like spaces behind and above the shop units. As a result, a large proportion of the terraced houses, which vary from two to four storeys in height, have their own front doors onto the quieter spaces away from the busy shopping thoroughfare. On the opposite side, both the flat roofs and vertical surfaces of the blocks of flats are conceived as part of a 'constructed natural landscape'. The flat roofs have either a gravel surface or are planted with meadow grasses, and training wires and watering systems for planting are incorporated on some of the façades.

The programme includes a wide variety of accommodation intended to provide for the elderly, students and lone parents as well as families. All of the housing types are for rent, with a 30 per cent social housing element. The internal layouts of the flats and houses follow a similar design approach, are compact and have minimal provision for the likes of cupboards and other fittings, and only some apartments have utility spaces. The terraced houses are 5 metres (16 feet 6 inches) wide, have an efficient stair with winders top and bottom and bathrooms located in the centre of the plan to maximize the size of the living areas at both front and back. Sheltered behind the continuously sloping roofline, some of the houses have a roof terrace. In the apartments, the bathrooms and kitchens are similarly located in the central, darkest part of the plan. Bedrooms are situated on either side of a central hallway leading to the full-width living space. Many of the living spaces have fully glazed façades with french windows, and some include small loggias.

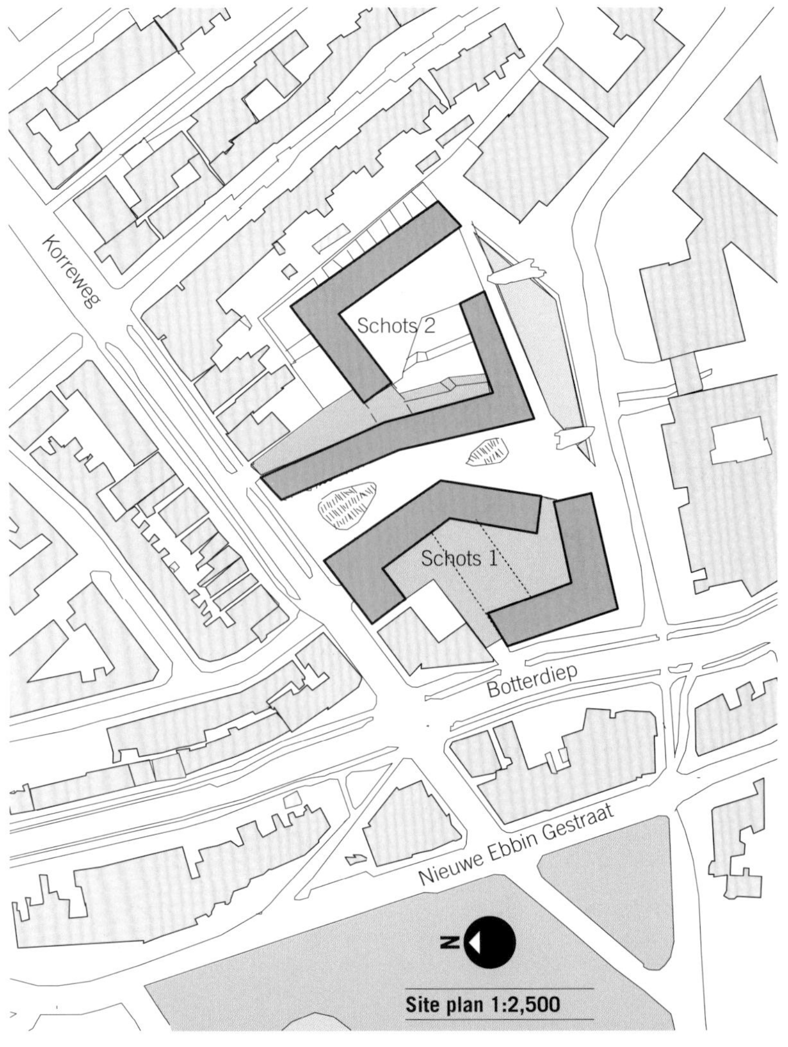

Site plan 1:2,500

Opposite left: Schots 2

Opposite right: Schots 1

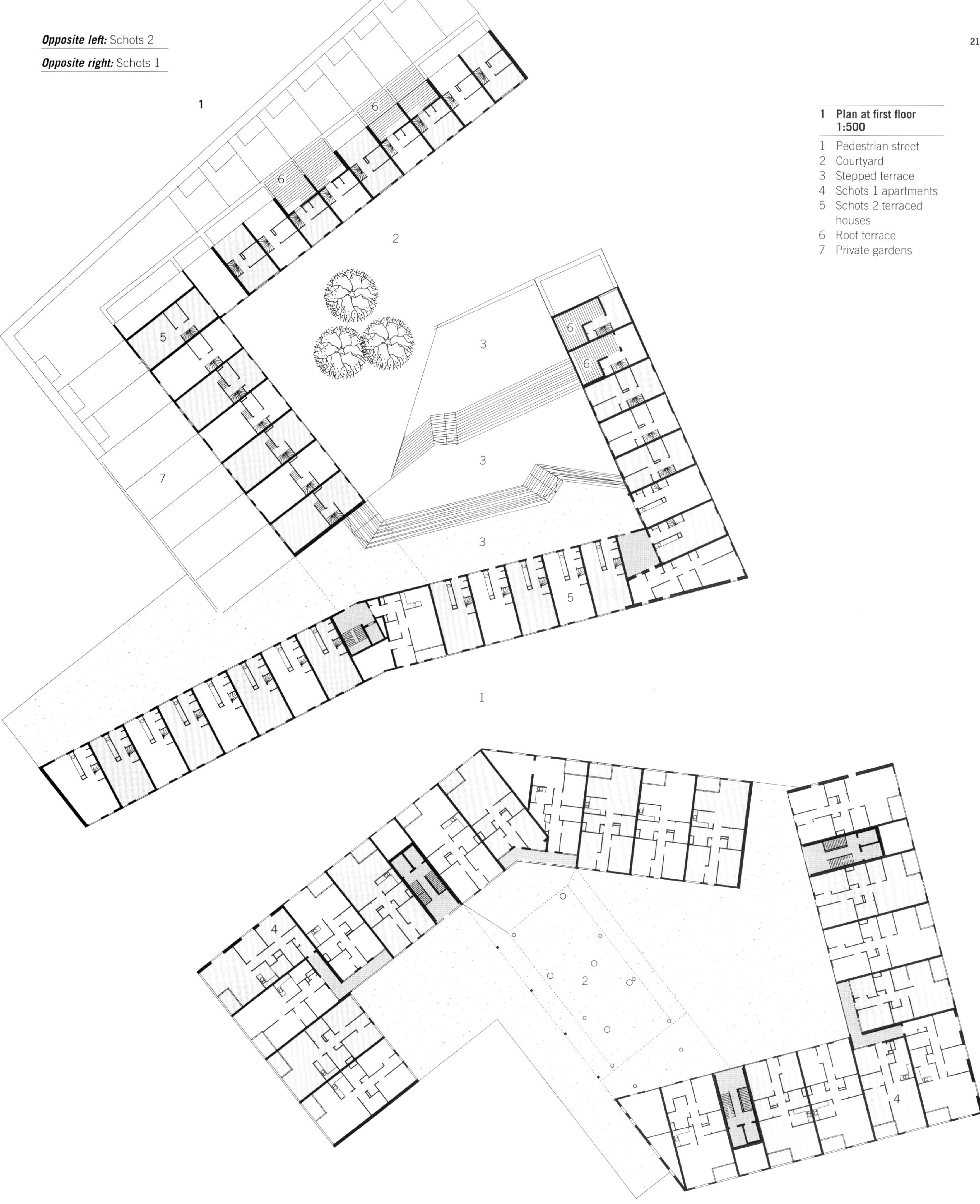

1 Plan at first floor 1:500

1 Pedestrian street
2 Courtyard
3 Stepped terrace
4 Schots 1 apartments
5 Schots 2 terraced houses
6 Roof terrace
7 Private gardens

Three-storey terraced houses 1:200

2 Second-floor plan
3 First-floor plan
4 Ground-floor plan
5 Second-floor plan
6 First-floor plan
7 Ground-floor plan

1 Entrance/hall
2 Kitchen
3 Living/dining
4 Bathroom/WC/ shower
5 Bedroom
6 Laundry
7 Study
8 Roof terrace

Two-storey terraced houses 1:200

8 First-floor plan
9 Ground-floor plan

1 Entrance/hall
2 Kitchen
3 Living/dining
4 Bathroom/WC/ shower
5 Bedroom
6 Study

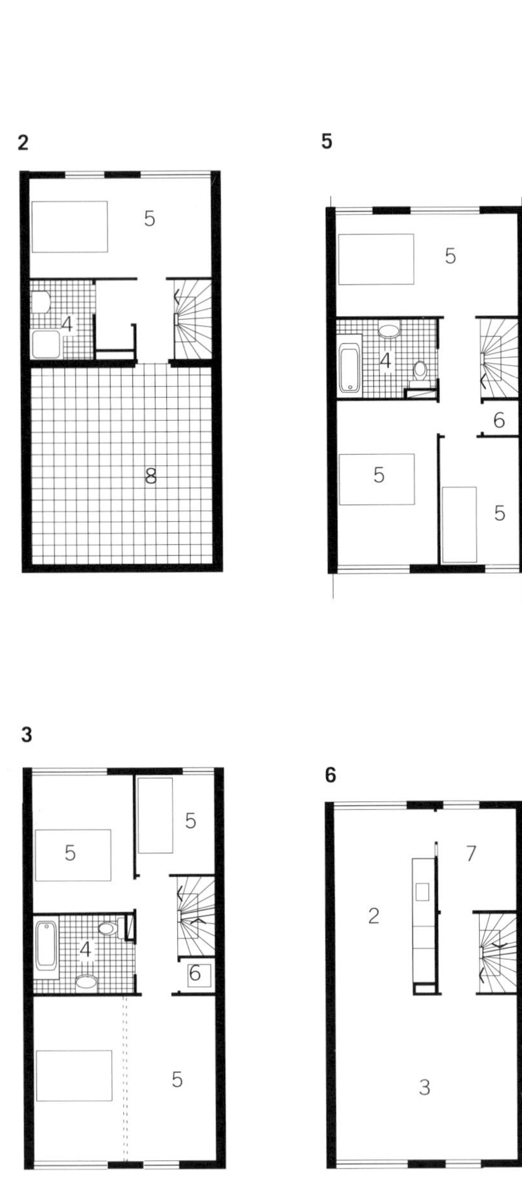

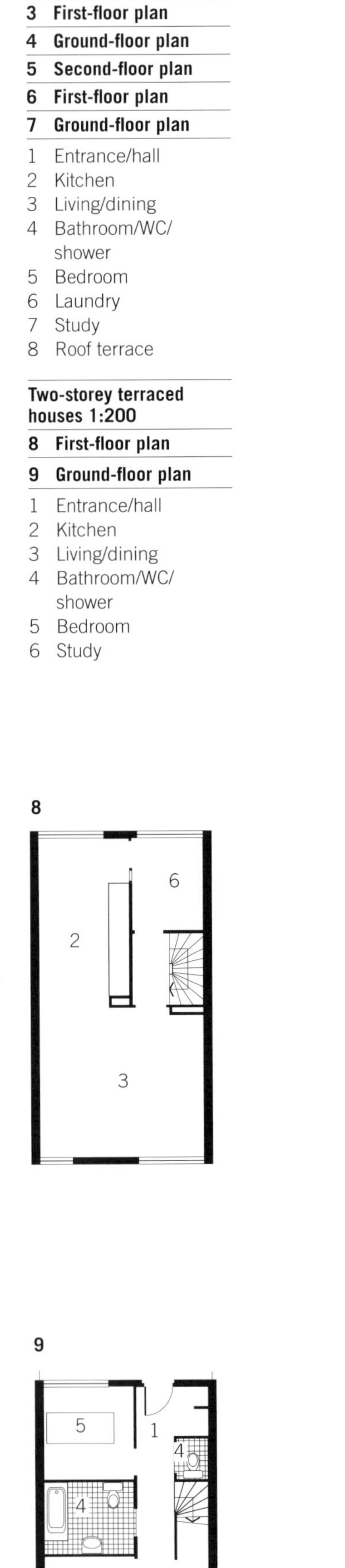

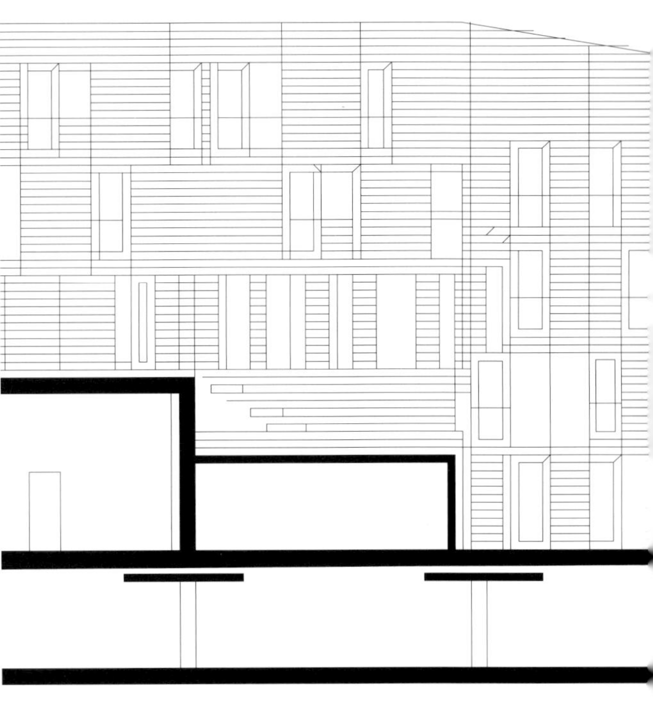

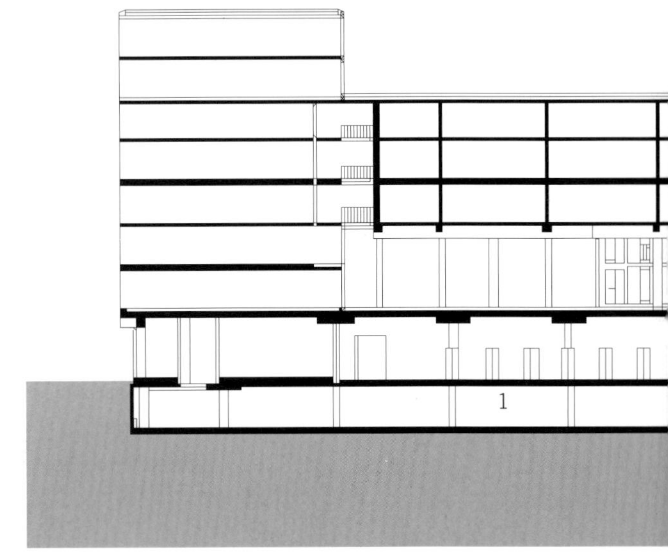

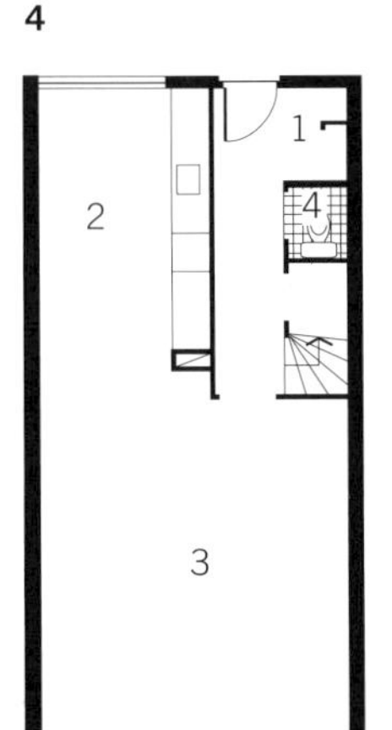

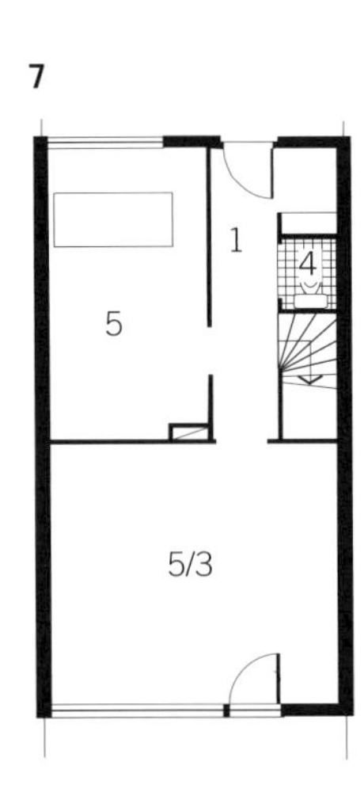

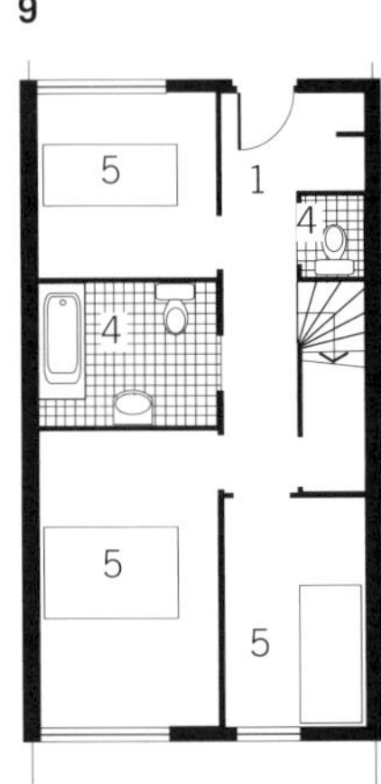

10

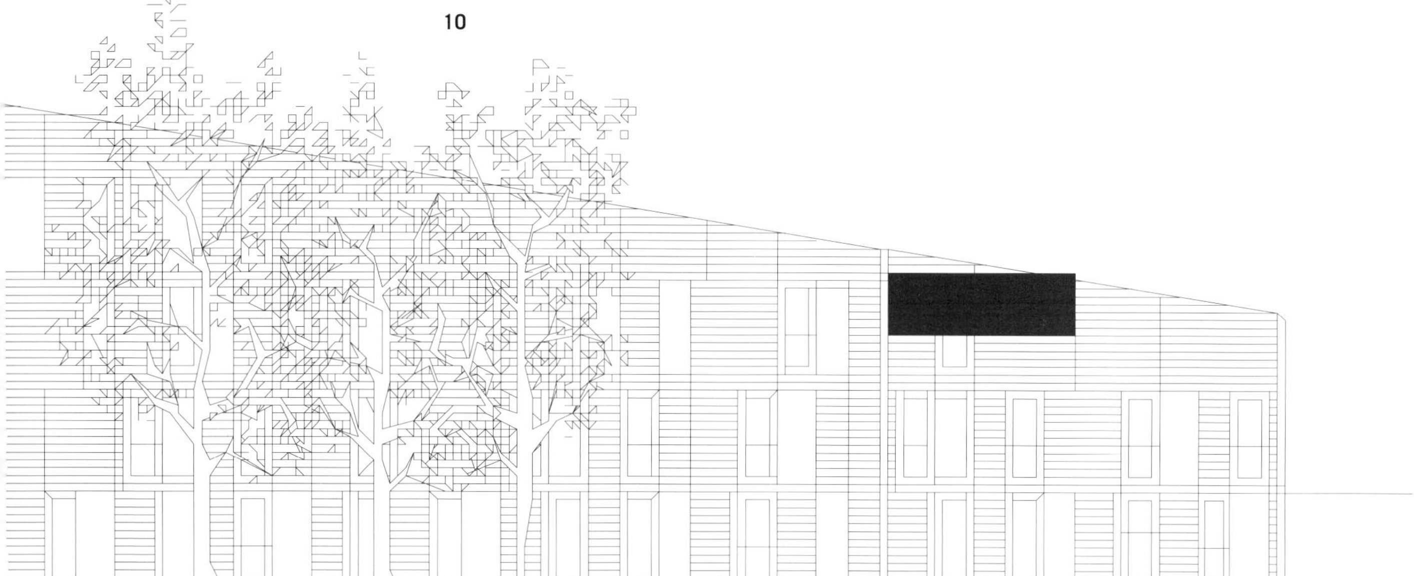

10 Part elevation of terraced houses 1:200

11 Section 1:500

1 Parking
2 Pedestrian street
3 Commercial and retail spaces
4 Flats (Schots 1)
5 Terraced houses (Schots 2)

11

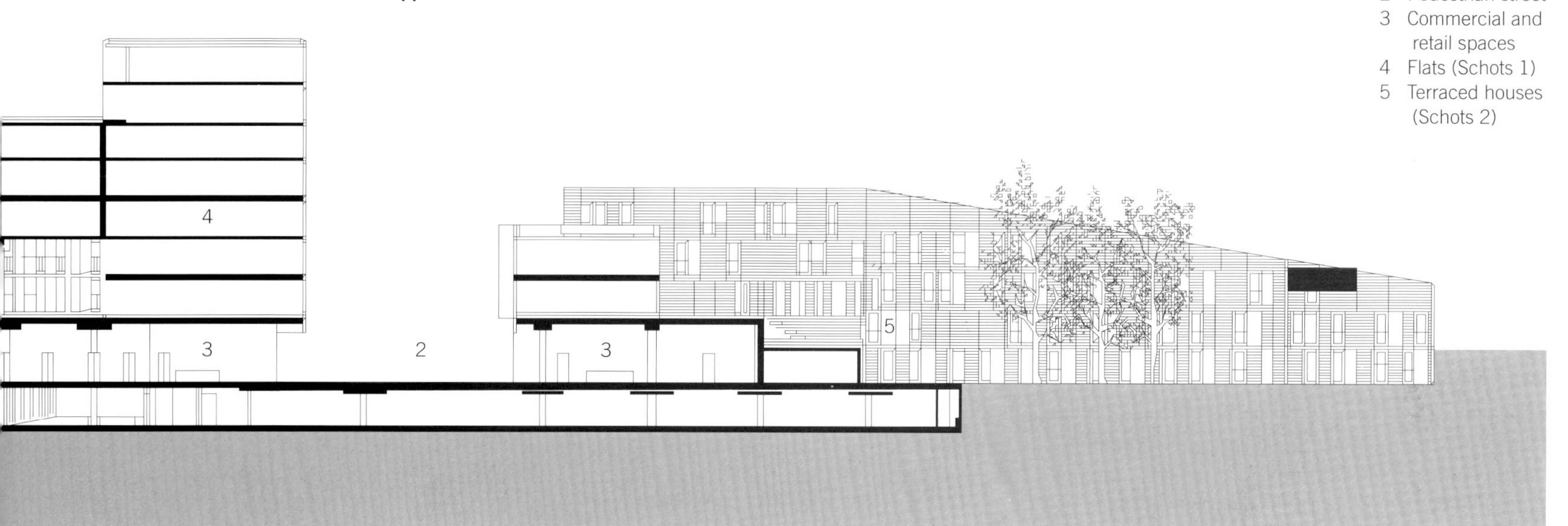

12

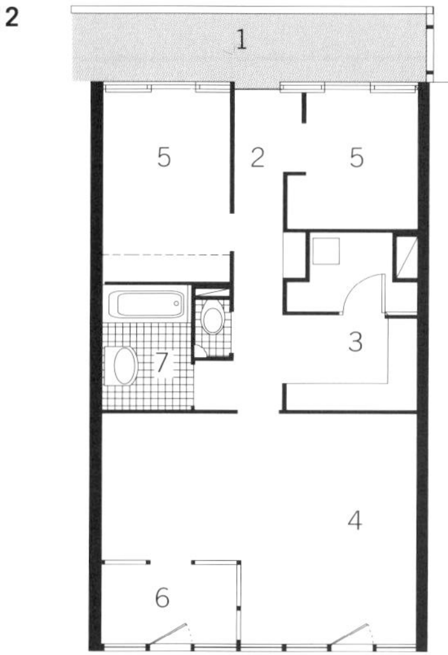

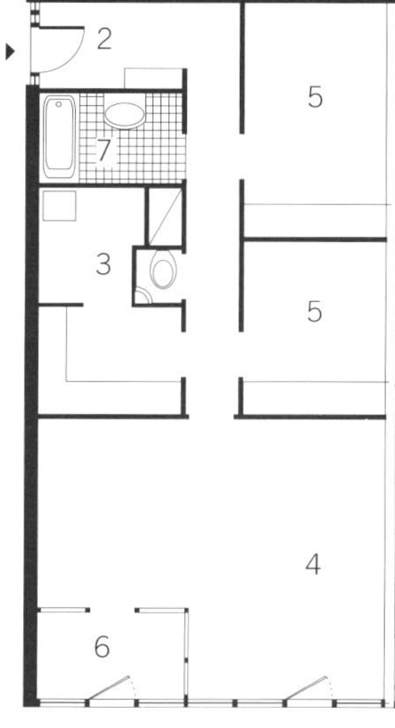

12 Plans of typical apartments 1:200

1 Access corridor
2 Entrance/hall
3 Kitchen
4 Living/dining
5 Bedroom
6 Loggia
7 Bathroom

Far left: Folsom Street façade

Left: Double-height living space

Yerba Buena Lofts

Stanley Saitowitz/Natoma Architects, Inc.

San Francisco, California, USA; 2002

The Yerba Buena Lofts follow a typical loft or warehouse design – low floor-to-ceiling heights, a very deep plan and a narrow structural grid. All of this is made habitable by the use of mezzanine floors and double-height living spaces with fully glazed façades which bring daylight into the deep plans. All the 200 units are rectangular in plan; they have a uniform width of 4.9 metres (16 feet) and their depths vary in plan from 15 to 20 metres (50 to 65 feet) to include the overall depth of the plan and the extent of the mezzanine. Generally the entrance, bathrooms and storage spaces are underneath the lower ceiling of the mezzanine. The kitchens are organized as part of the living space, along one wall or partially enclosing the staircase. Most of the apartments have a small balcony formed as a result of the 'crenellated' façade: the full-height glazing is stepped in plan to form these balconies, which have translucent glazing to the elevation between the visible thin concrete planes of the structure.

The building occupies the whole depth of the city block, with the dark central spaces on the lower four levels occupied by car parking. The block steps back at this point, to relate better to the domestic scale of Shipley Street on the south side, and deeper apartments take up the space on the upper-floor levels. The utilitarian nature of a loft (or warehouse) is echoed in the materials and finishes used as well as the simplicity of the form. The concrete construction is visible on the façade, where the very thin 'fin' columns, 2.4 metres (8 feet) deep and 35.5 cm (14 inches) thick, form a regular, clearly visible 'eggcrate' structure with steel-framed full-height glazing. The edges of these fins and the ends of the concrete floor slabs are exposed, and where they meet at the façade they form the underlying square (visual) grid which defines each unit, and within which translucent and transparent glazing is organized on different planes to provide the balconies. Inside the apartments the concrete is left bare, defining the area adjacent to the façade and forming a double-height loggia.

SIte plan 1:2,500

Typical apartment plans 1:200

1 Type 1 mezzanine
2 Type 1 lower level
3 Type 2 mezzanine
4 Type 2 lower level

1 Entrance
2 Bathroom/WC
3 Den
4 Kitchen
5 Double-height living space
6 Bedroom
7 Dressing room/laundry
8 Void over living space
9 Loggia

5 Section 1:500

1 Parking
2 Roof terraces
3 Central circulation corridor and lifts

6 Elevation on Folsom Street 1:500

1

3

2

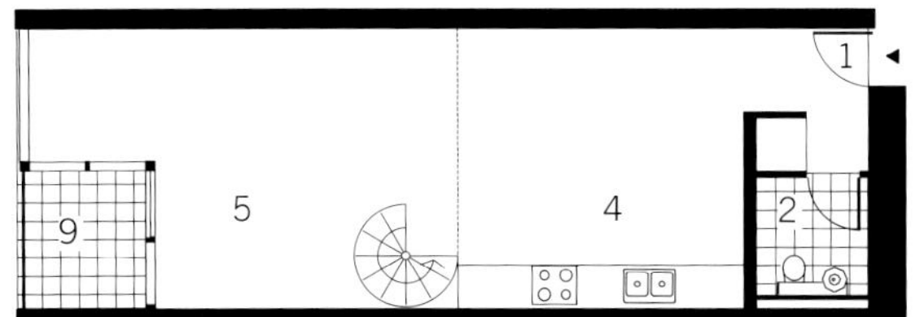

4

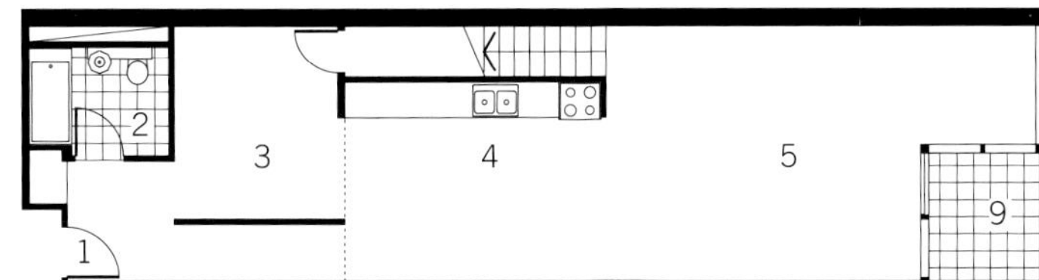

5

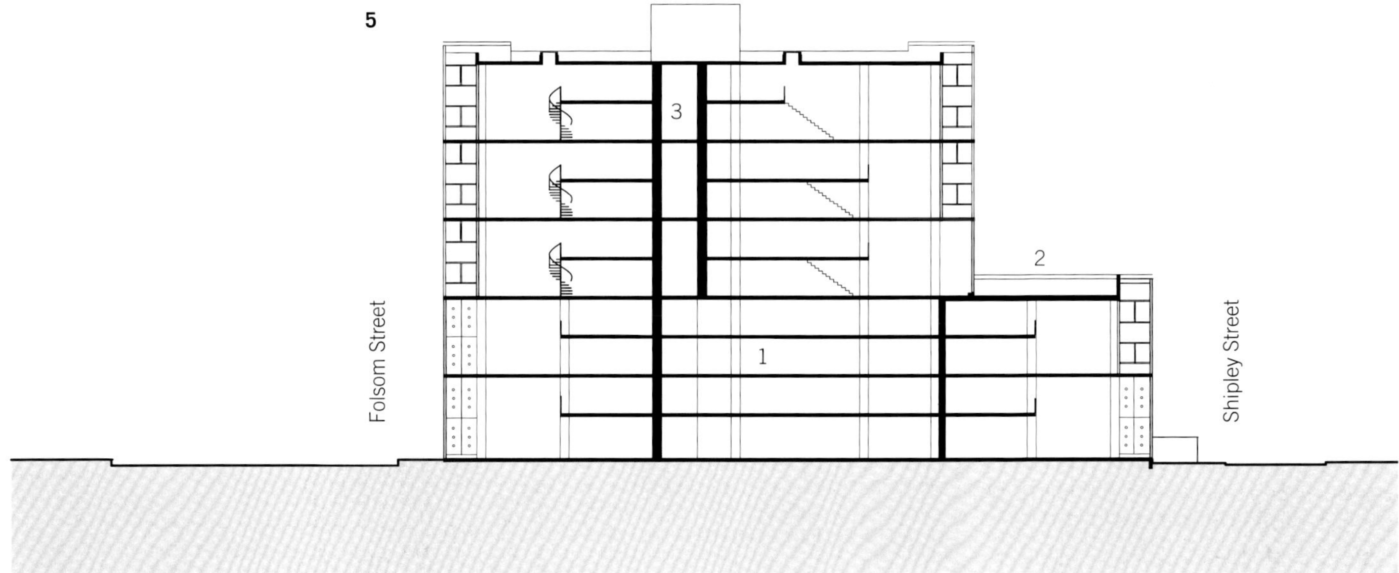

6

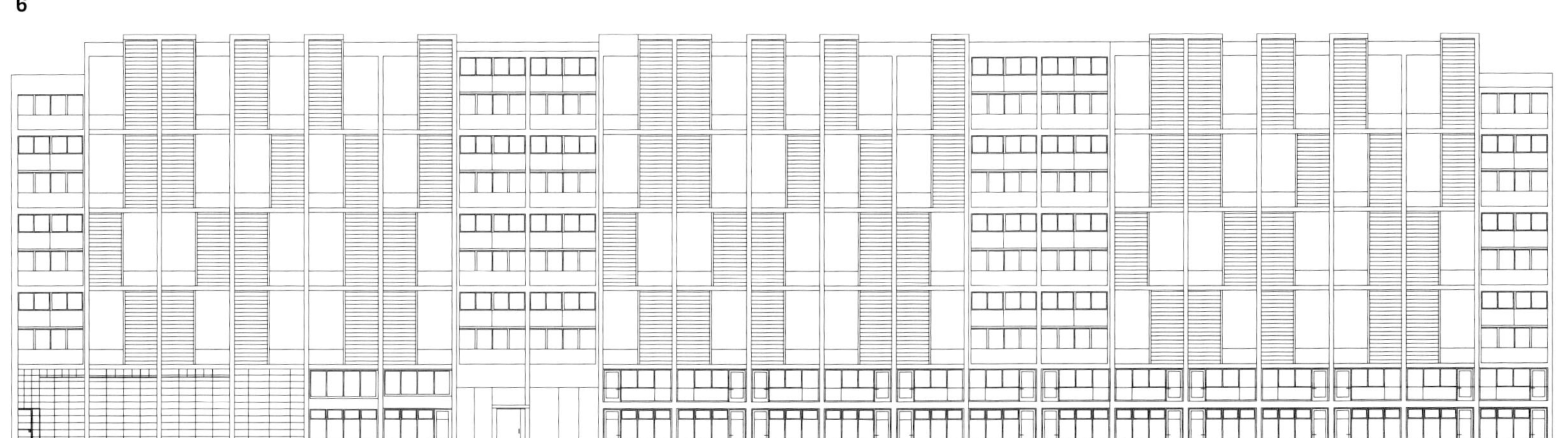

Far left: The zinc-clad block

Left: Courtyard elevation

The Whale

de Architekten Cie.

Amsterdam, The Netherlands; 2000

The Borneo Sporenburg development, completed in 2000, occupies a redundant dockland area located to the east of Amsterdam. The master plan, by Adriaan Geuze and West 8, connects the two peninsulas of the docks with three new bridges and covers the whole area with a grid of long, rectangular parallel blocks of low-rise dwellings punctuated with three large 'sculptural' blocks. The architecture of the dwellings is based on the patio-house and is an attempt to reinvent the traditional Dutch canalside house. In order to maintain a coherent whole while providing variety, West 8 worked closely with the series of different architects commissioned to design the dwellings – including OMA, Neutelings Riedijk Architects, UN Studio and Enric Miralles.

De Architekten Cie.'s Whale, one of the three high-rise blocks, is a significant landmark within the area, highly visible because of both its great size in comparison to the surrounding terraced housing and its surface of shimmering zinc cladding. It has a 50 x 100-metre (165 x 330-foot) footprint, the same size as a typical city 'Berlage block' in the south of Amsterdam, but contains twice as many apartments. The simple form of the rectangular closed block is modified by the simple device of lifting the sides to make a sloping roofline and allowing access underneath the block at ground level. Floor plans are, therefore, not repeated but different at every level with a wide variety of apartment sizes and types, particularly in the upper and lower corners. Ground and basement levels have commercial spaces and car parking. The courtyard, which is more accessible and therefore more public, is overlooked by access corridors at alternate levels, and the apartments from a variety of different angles. The flats also have winter gardens on their exterior edges, affording views out across the city and the IJ river.

De Architekten Cie. used the courtyard form again in a smaller private development of 40 apartments in the Botania district of Amsterdam (2002). Here there is a more conventional rectangular exterior with a roof punctuated by sunken courtyards, and the main interior courtyard space is dramatically divided by apartments, stepped one above the other, spanning the full 33-metre (108-foot) width of the block.

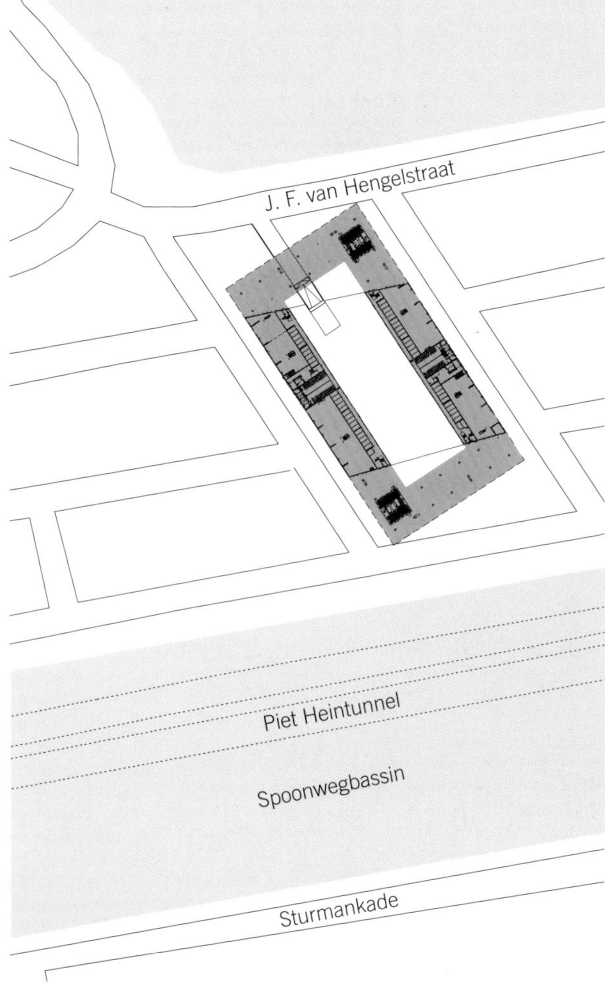

Site plan 1:2,500

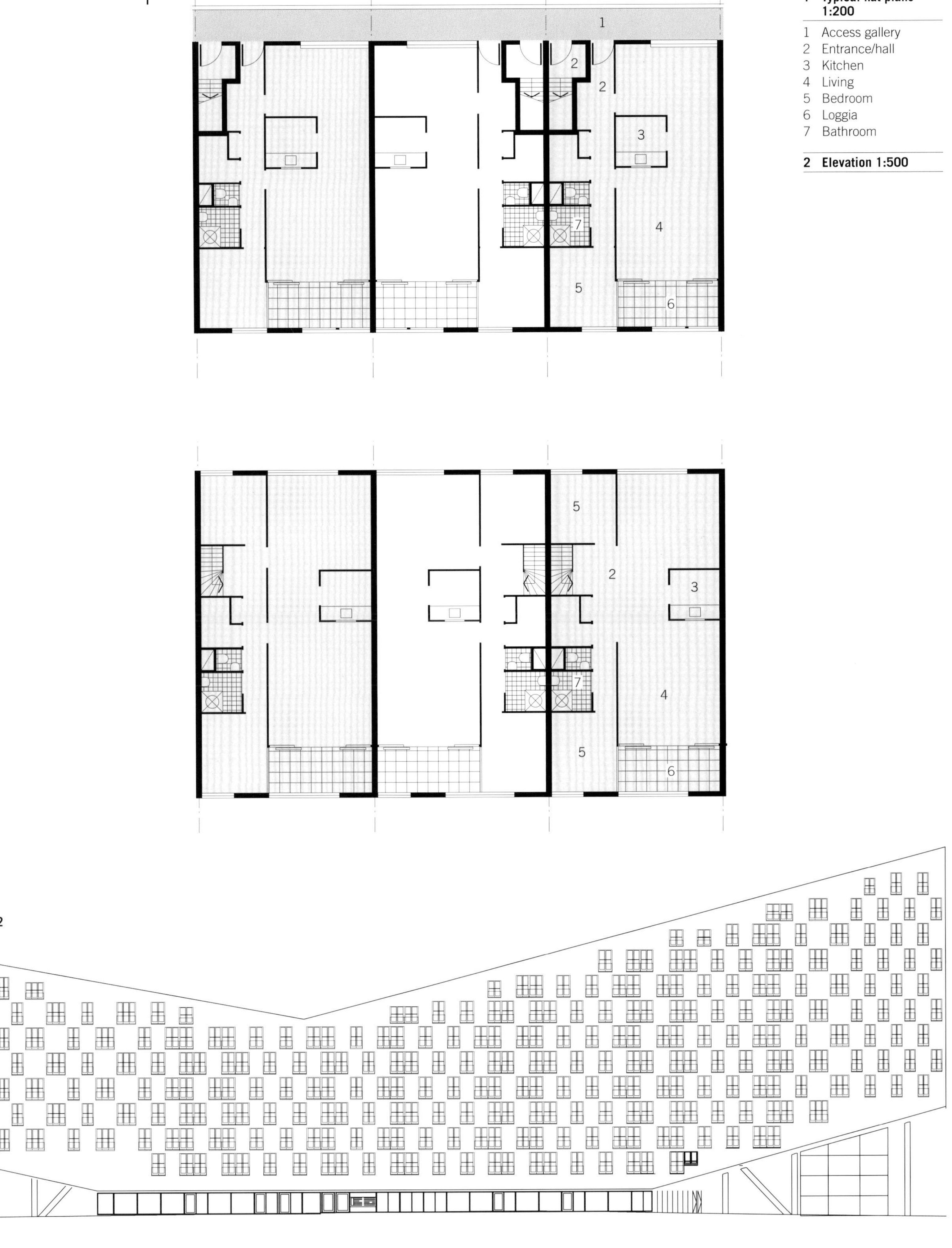

1 Typical flat plans 1:200

1 Access gallery
2 Entrance/hall
3 Kitchen
4 Living
5 Bedroom
6 Loggia
7 Bathroom

2 Elevation 1:500

Liverpool Street Housing

Ian Moore Architects

Sydney, Australia; 2004

This block in Sydney, Australia, is one of a series of apartment buildings by the same architect. The Grid, Barcom Avenue and Kings Lane are all projects by Ian Moore Architects that demonstrate a similar approach to the design of apartment buildings. They all have in common simple rectilinear structures, unfussy detailing, solid colours and spacious open planning with natural ventilation and large balconies. Ian Moore Architects' reputation was established with the completion of the Altair project: a large block of 139 flats on a difficult site above the Kings Cross Tunnel and with streets on three sides, which won them several design awards in 2002. There, within a slim rectilinear structure, the architects created flexible living units – most facing north, with those behind the lifts and stair shafts having views on three sides. The need for air conditioning was eliminated through a design that provided natural cross-ventilation and very deep balconies. The Altair building is set above a podium level that houses shared facilities, including a lap pool and a children's play space.

The Liverpool Street project sits on a corner, completing the end of a block, and forms an L-shaped plan around an existing two-storey building. The L is divided into two distinct parts, with the vertical circulation, stairs, lift and service shafts located where the two wings meet. The base of the building is made up of five double-height commercial units at street level that extend half the depth of the main block. The upper floors have a central corridor on alternate levels, providing access to a single-aspect flat on one side and the lower level of a Unité-type duplex on the other. Loggias extend the full width of the apartments on both north and south elevations; those on the east side have balconies extending beyond the façade, almost the full depth of the block.

The building is highly visible from the street, with the smaller wing standing out in a distinctive orange colour. All the façades have louvred shutters, remote controlled to provide shading from the sunlight, which give a varied texture to the otherwise undecorated surfaces.

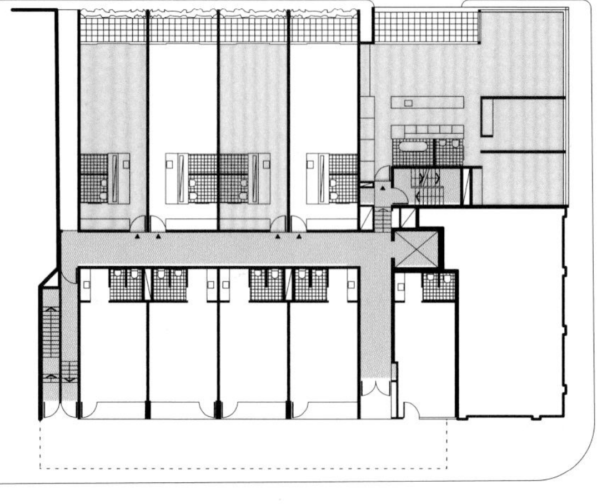

Plan at ground floor 1:500

1

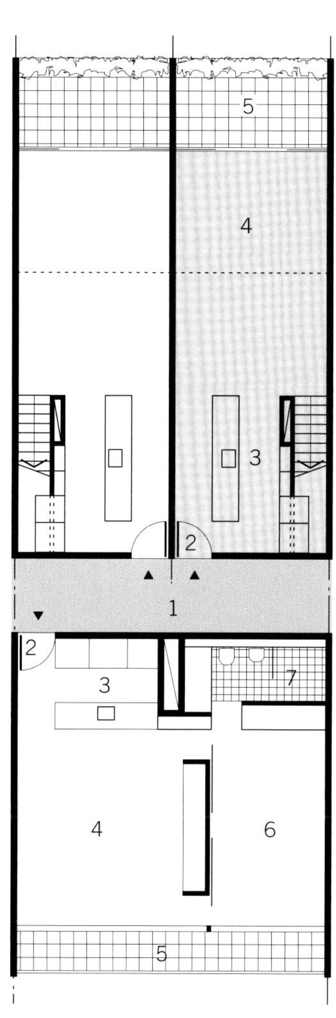

2

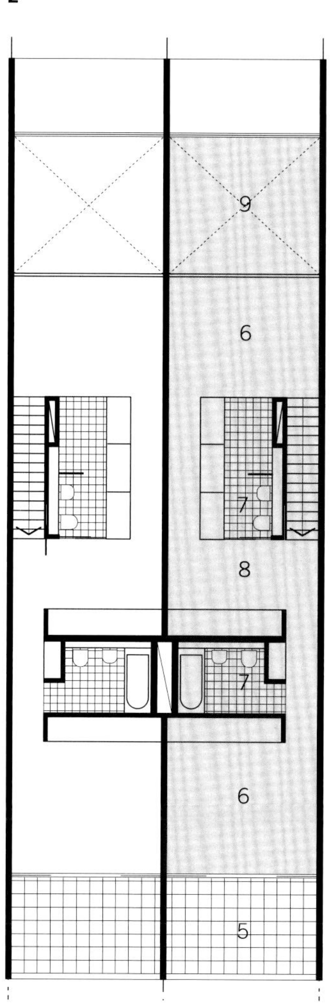

Typical apartment plans 1:200

1 Lower-level duplex and typical flat plan

2 Mezzanine level

1 Access corridor
2 Entrance
3 Kitchen
4 Double-height living space
5 Balcony
6 Bedroom
7 Bathroom
8 Study
9 Void over living space

3 Elevation Liverpool Street 1:500

4 Rear elevation 1:500

5 Section 1:500

3 4

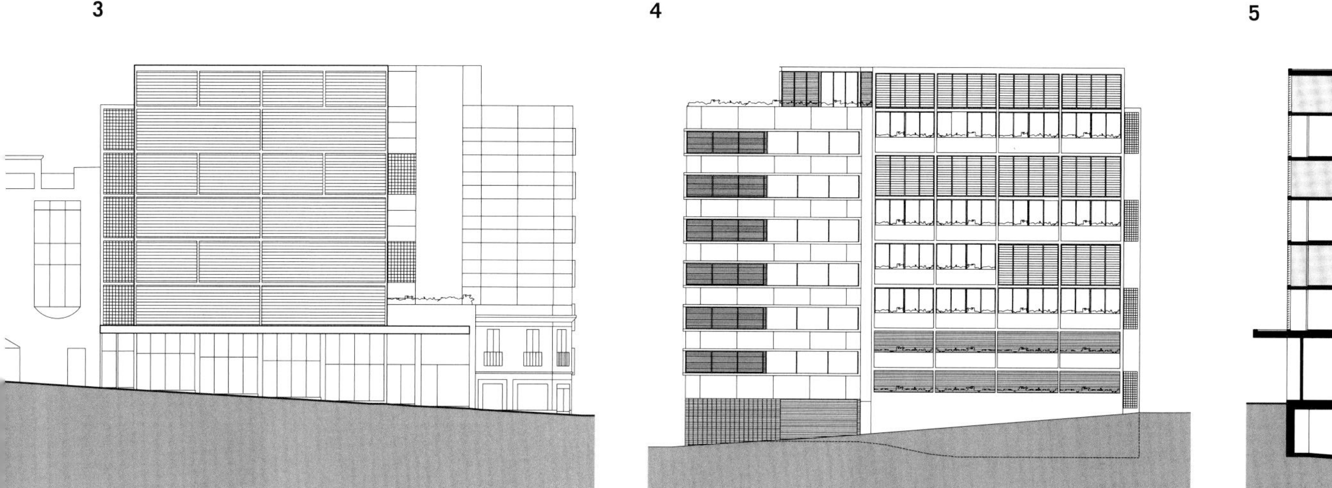

5

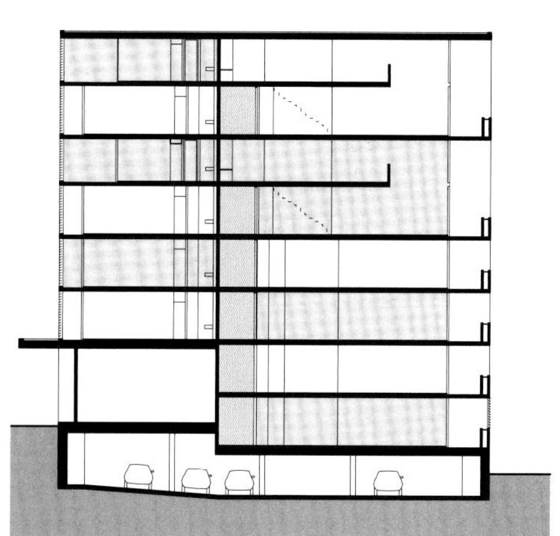

Mirador Apartments

MVRDV + Blanca Lleó

Madrid, Spain; 2004

The Mirador is a further development of MVRDV's 2002 Silodam housing scheme in Amsterdam (see pages 202–5) – a ten-storey high rectangular block, within which different dwelling types are grouped together in 'mini-neighbourhoods'. The new 21-storey form – that MVRDV have termed the 'superblock' – is similarly made up of smaller blocks fitted together, clearly distinguishable on the elevations and conceptually treated like a series of suburbs. The analogy with urban space is continued, with the architects' description of the circulation as 'vertical streets', and, 12 storeys up, a five-storey high void is cut through the block and conceived of as a 'sky plaza': a part of public open space that belongs to the urban landscape.

The vast size and scale of this building makes it highly visible and provides the neighbourhood both with its own landmark and with a piece of residential architecture 'elevated' to the scale of the city. The easily recognizable mini-neighbourhoods are intended to deal with the need for identity and belonging, considered to be of particular importance, in addition to which the architects claim that they 'aim to emphasise what are the unquestionable values of the inhabitant's space: surface area, light, facilities and views'.

The overall form, rectangular in plan, is divided into three parts – two end blocks and a central section. Internal shared circulation is minimal. Vertical circulation cores are located in the end blocks, serving generally either two or three flats per landing at one end and flats and duplexes at the other. Two further vertical circulation shafts are located in the central section, serving two double-aspect flats per landing up to the eighth floor. Above this, the apartments in the central section are all either duplexes or triplexes and are accessed from the two end blocks via central internal corridors on the 11th, 18th and 19th floors. A wide range of different apartment types and variations are developed according to their aspect and location in the block. Common elements include open-plan living spaces, within which kitchens are located – some equipped with sliding partitions so that they may be left open or closed off – and stairways leading to bedroom floors, often at the lower levels of the flats. Baths and showers are provided in a multiplicity of configurations, not always with WCs – and unconventionally, within bedrooms, in alcoves or behind sliding partitions. Most of the apartments have private outside spaces, generally loggias recessed within the overall volume and conceived of as an extension of the living space or kitchen. Duplexes on the 19th and 20th floors have external terraces at roof level, accessible via open stairways that visibly criss-cross the double-height access corridor.

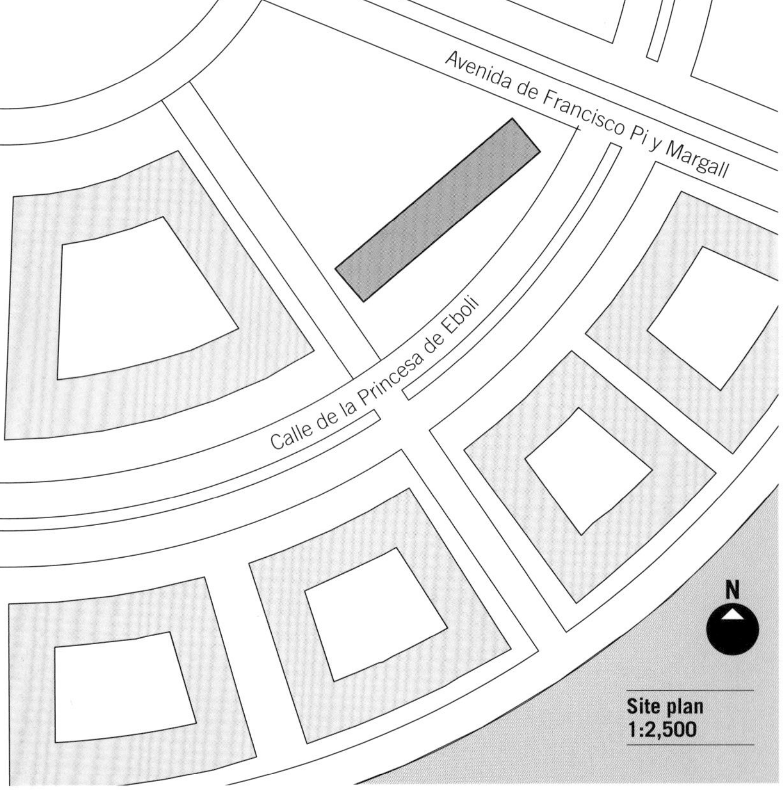

Site plan
1:2,500

Opposite left: South elevation

Opposite right: The five-storey high 'sky plaza'

1 Cross-section 1:500

2 Plans of typical apartments on floors 2–11 end block 1:200

1 Entrance/hall
2 Kitchen
3 Living/dining
4 Bedroom
5 Bathroom/shower/ WC
6 Loggia
7 Storage

1

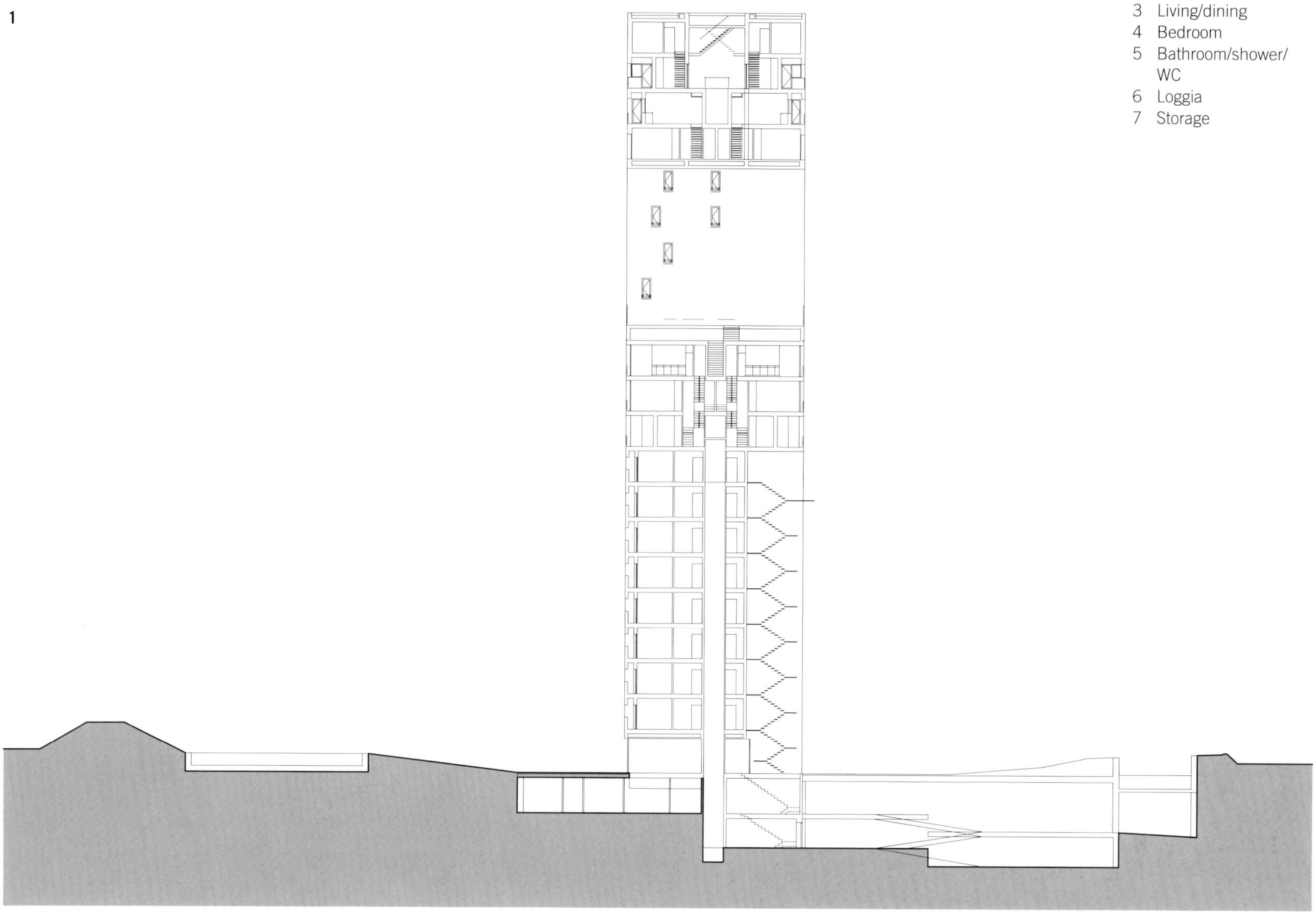

2

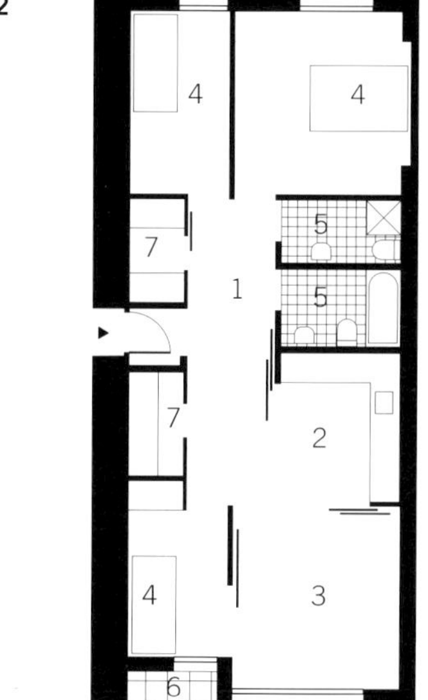

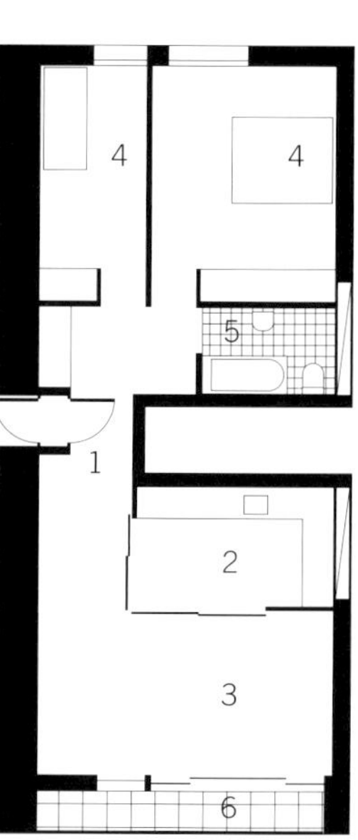

3

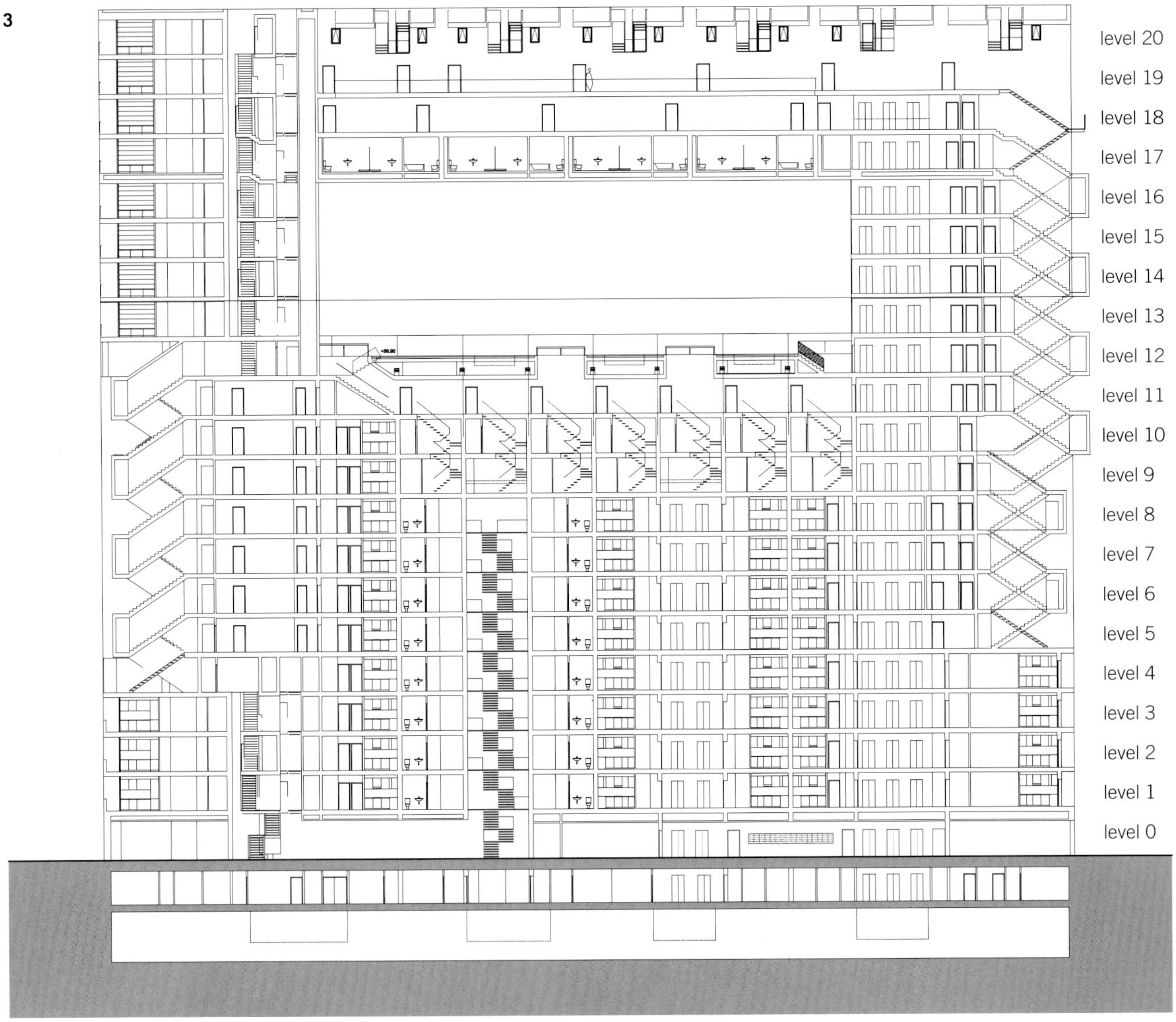

level 20
level 19
level 18
level 17
level 16
level 15
level 14
level 13
level 12
level 11
level 10
level 9
level 8
level 7
level 6
level 5
level 4
level 3
level 2
level 1
level 0

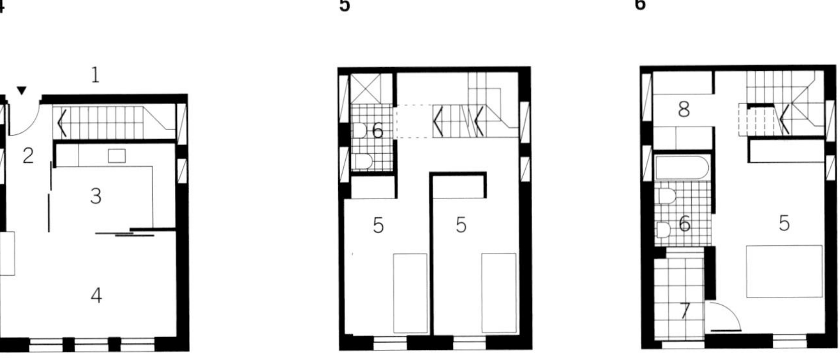

3 Long section 1:500

Plans of triplexes on floors 9, 10 and 11 1:200

4 Upper floor/access level 11
5 Middle floor, level 10
6 Lower floor, level 9

1 Access corridor
2 Entrance/hall
3 Kitchen
4 Living/dining
5 Bedroom
6 Bathroom/shower/WC
7 Loggia
8 Storage

7

7 Floor plans 1:500

Consort Road Housing

Walter Menteth Architects

London, UK; 2007

The scheme combines a row of nine three-storey terraced houses with, at either end, a four- and a six-storey high block. The buildings follow the line of the road, reinforcing the importance of the street, which has been improved with wider pavements and tree-planting. At the rear, the space between the buildings and the railway contains private gardens for the houses and a small number of parking spaces. In the block closest to the railway, the circulation space is located at the rear, behind a glazed curtain wall that provides a buffer to the noise and disruption of the railway and surrounding activities. Contributions to enhanced environmental quality include planted roofs and gabion walls to encourage vegetation, nesting boxes to encourage small birds, photovoltaic arrays to generate electricity, a combined heat-and-power unit to provide base heating and 'whole house' mechanical ventilation with heat recovery for lower CO_2 emissions.

Environmental and social sustainability were also key to the design of the layouts of the houses and flats themselves, which have been used as an example of good practice in terms of flexibility. The three-storey, four-bedroom houses are a response to the growing demand in London for larger family homes. The main living space occupies the whole of the ground floor, a large open area with fitted kitchen units at one end and glazed doors onto the garden at the other. On the first floor, either of the two equal-sized rooms overlooking the garden or the street can be used as a second 'living' room that might, for example, be a children's playroom or a study. The second flight of stairs that, unusually, rises in line with rather than above the first flight, leaves space for two bedrooms at the front and one at the rear on the second floor. In the blocks at either end, the flats, either one or two bedroom, also allow for some flexibility in how the different rooms are used. Wide sliding doors between the living room and bedroom means that the spaces can be thrown together or closed off. Winter gardens on the street side provide extra space, which can be occupied during the summer months and which, for those facing south or west, can provide some passive solar gain for home heating and an acoustic buffer to the road.

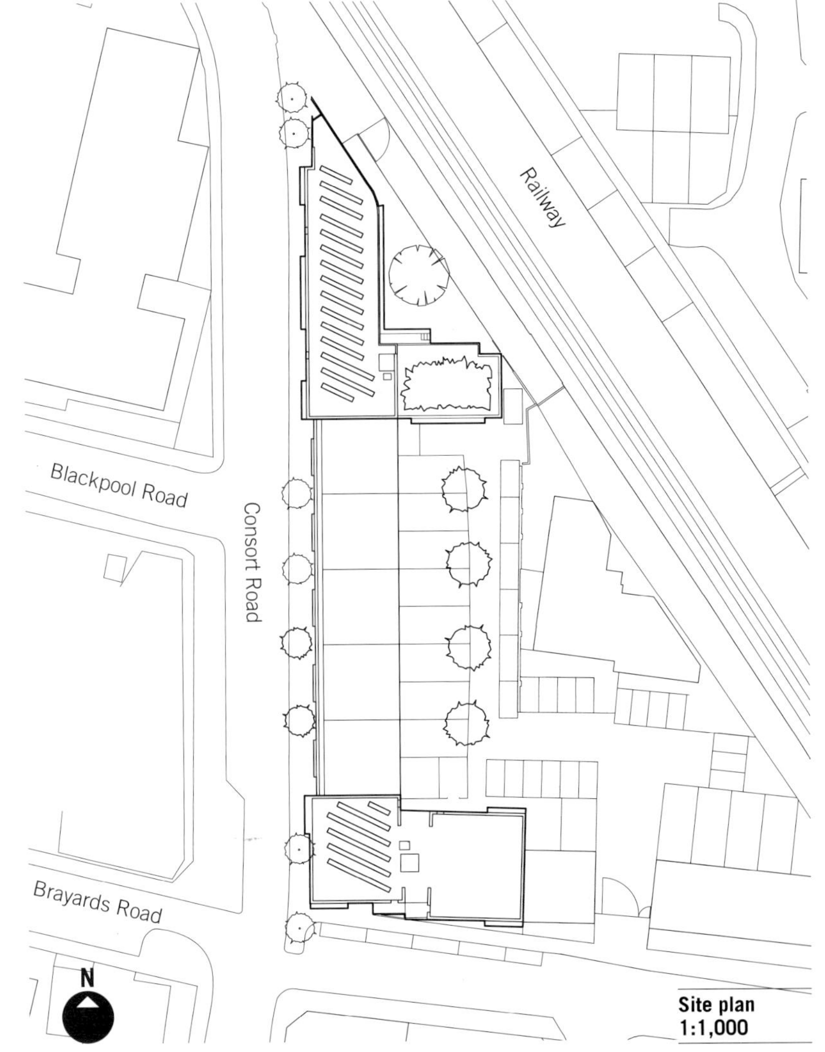

Site plan
1:1,000

Opposite left: North corner of the six-storey block

Opposite right: Terraced houses

1 Plans of typical flats 1:200

1 Access corridor
2 Entrance/hall
3 Living room
4 Winter garden
5 Bedroom
6 Kitchen
7 Bathroom

Terraced house plans 1:200

2 Second-floor plan
3 First-floor plan
4 Ground-floor plan

1 Front porch/area
2 Entrance
3 WC/shower
4 Kitchen
5 Living room
6 Private garden
7 Bedroom
8 Bathroom
9 Store

5 Elevation on Consort Road 1:500

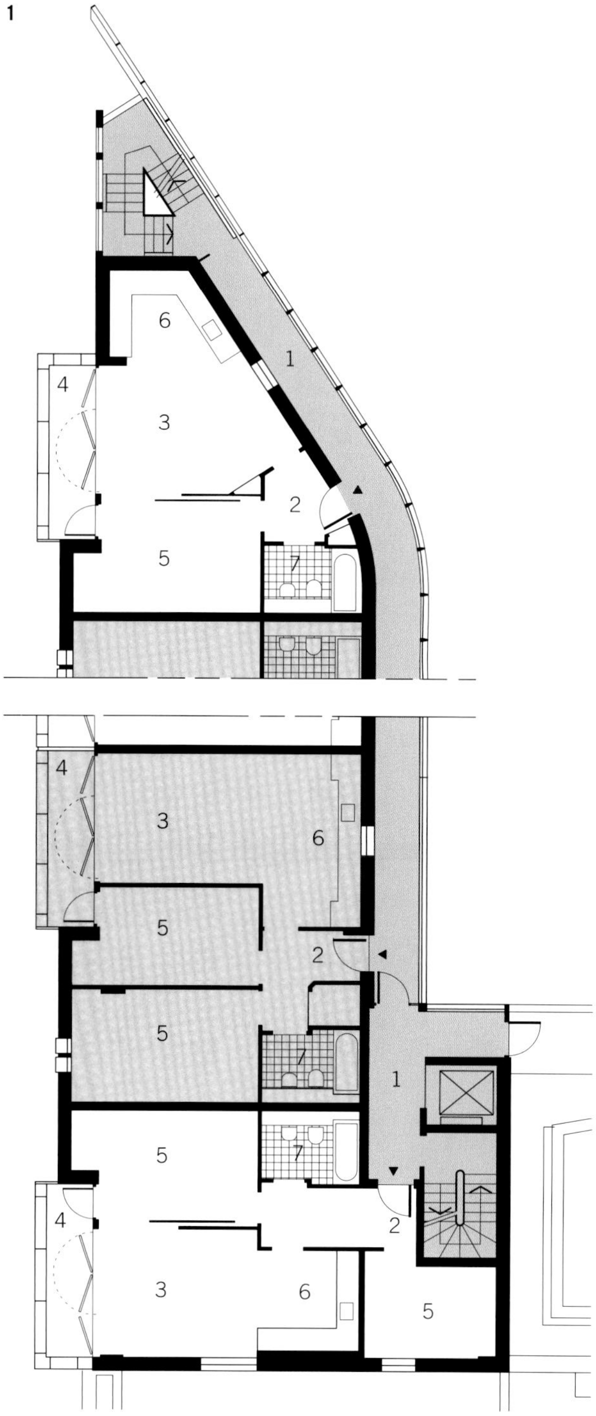

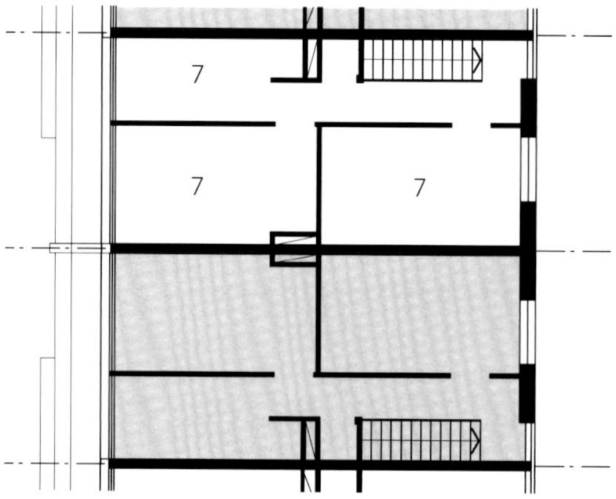

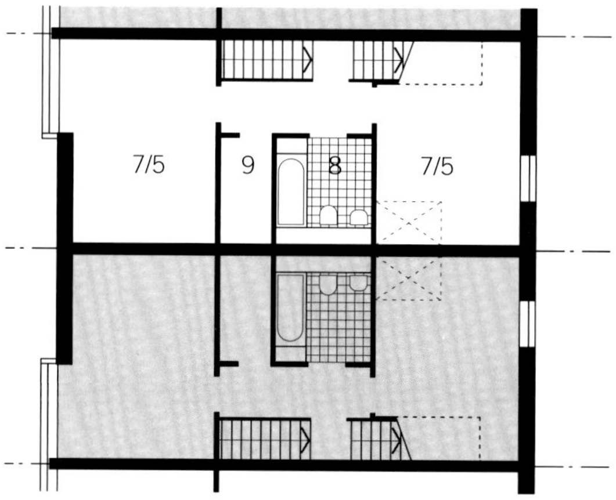

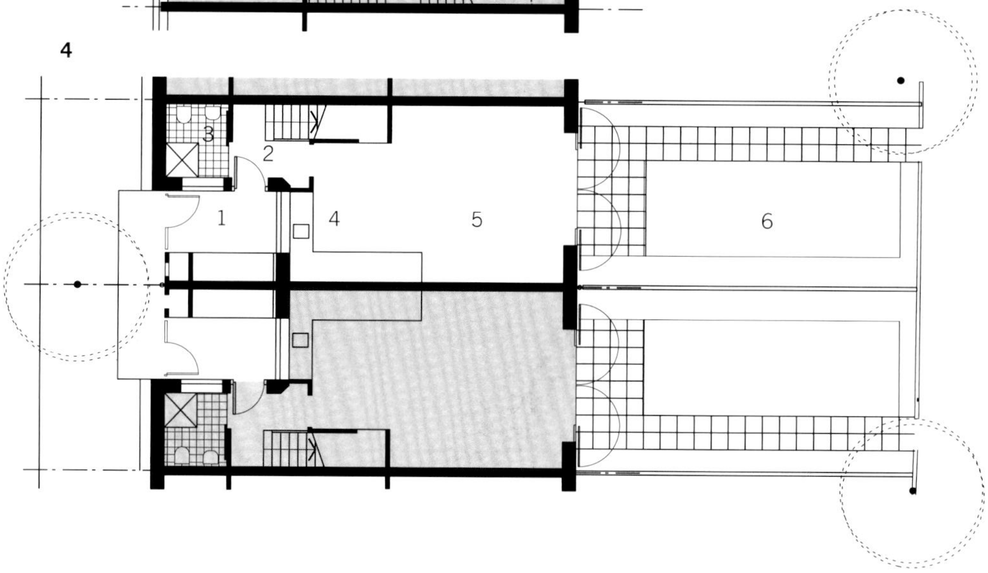

5

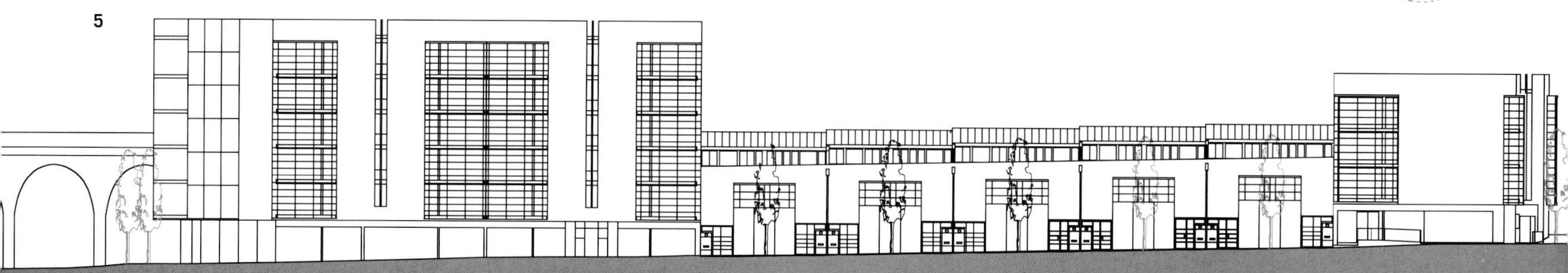

Carabanchel 16 Housing

Foreign Office Architects

Madrid, Spain; 2007

For Foreign Office Architects (FOA), the key to this project was their desire to find an innovative sustainable approach to the provision of social housing in line with the usual constraints of budget, and requirements for numbers and types of units. The resulting block is rectangular in plan, 100 metres (328 feet) long and orientated north–south. It sits on one edge of its site, leaving the rest of the plot open to provide some garden space for the residents; under this space which the car parking is buried below a sloping planted surface. The project uses solar water-heating panels, located on the roof of the block, and natural stack ventilation to internal bathrooms and kitchens – although, at the developer's insistence, air conditioning is also provided.

The individual flats typically stretch the full depth of the block between parallel structural walls, and have a double orientation, east and west, at either end. The relatively narrow 'tube-like' space of each apartment is therefore free of any structural elements. The 13.4-metre (44-foot) width of the building is extended at both ends by 1.5-metre (5-foot) deep terraces, which run the full length of the block. The façades themselves are fully glazed, and the terraces are enclosed with sliding and folding screens made of bamboo. The screens provide shading from the strong sunlight, and residents can open them up in different configurations in order to use the terraces as part of the internal space of the flats.

FOA dismiss contemporary concerns about identity, differentiation and the possibilities for customization on the basis that these constitute a 'rural or bourgeois' attitude that persists in identifying an individual with their house. Instead, they propose that part of the choice, and an advantage, of urban living lies in the possibility of anonymity. This argument is used to justify the architects' refusal to include what they refer to as 'cosmetic contortions' at the expense of quality of construction and space. Instead, their stated aim is to 'provide the maximum amount of space, flexibility and quality to the residences, and to erase the visibility of the units and their differences into a single volume with a homogeneous skin able to incorporate a gradation of possibilities not dependent on the architect's vision but as an effect of the inhabitants' choice.'

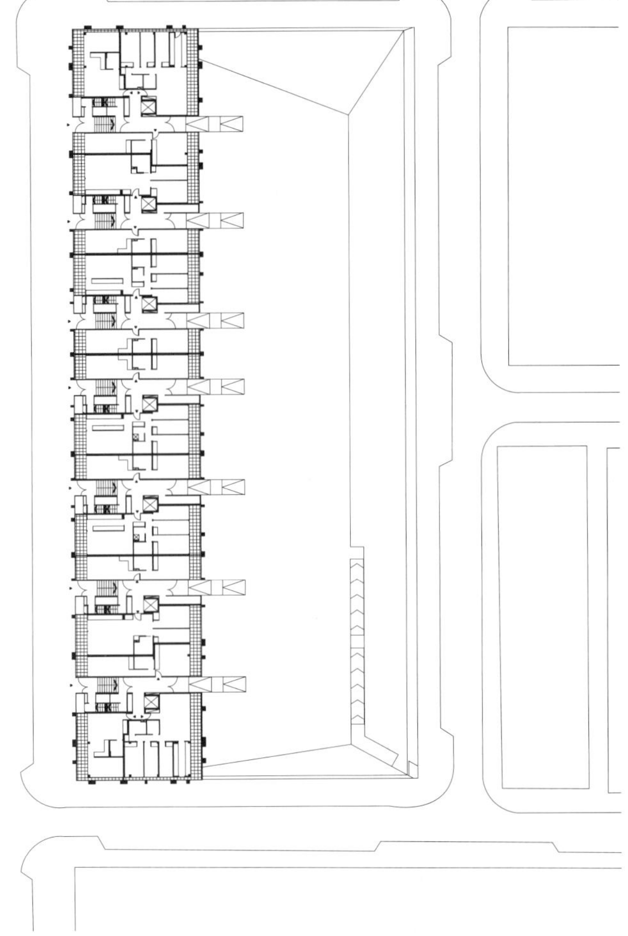

Block plan 1:1,000

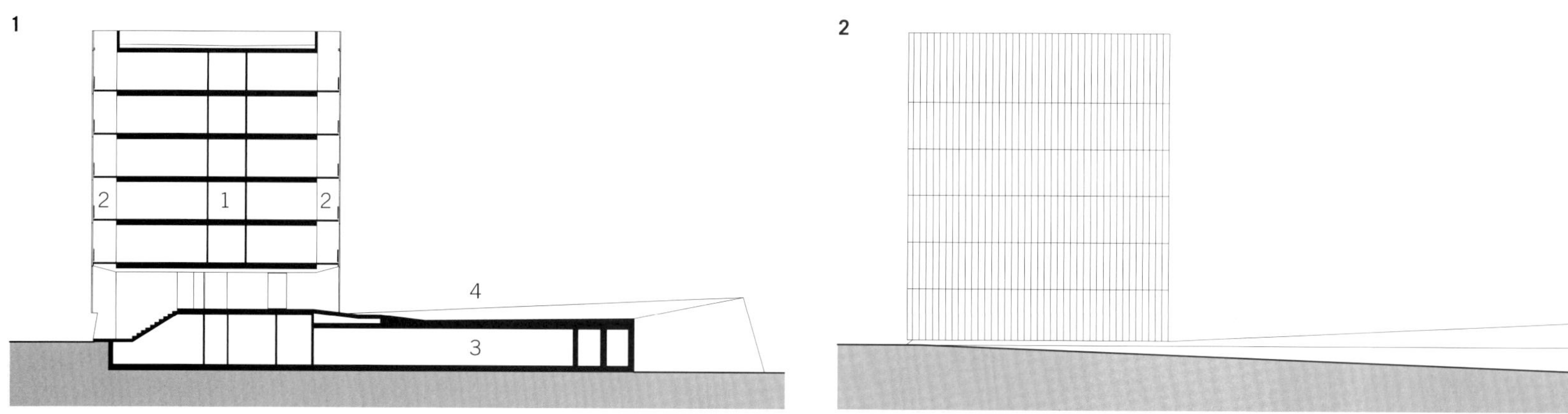

3

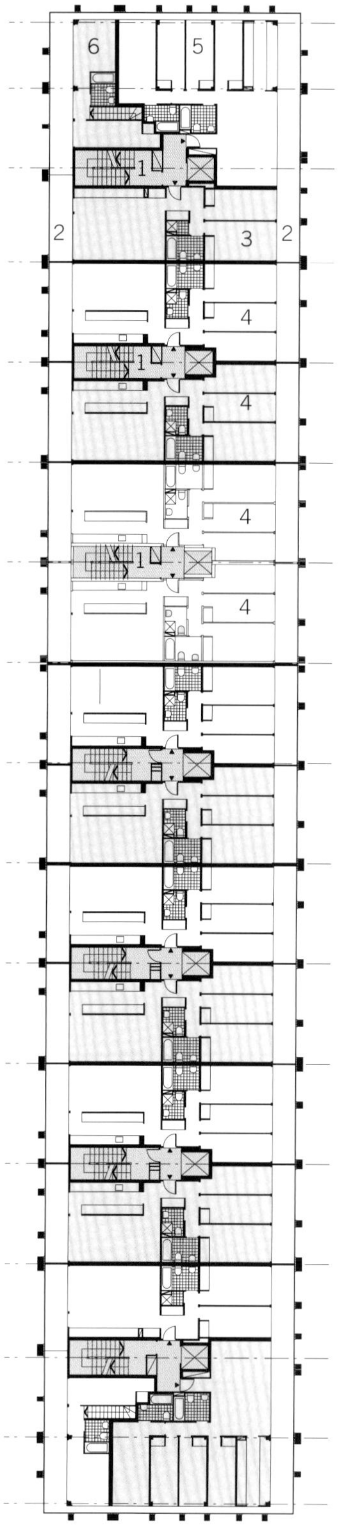

4

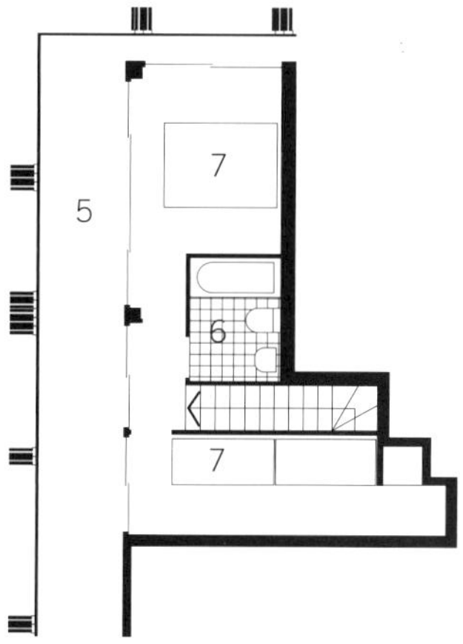

5

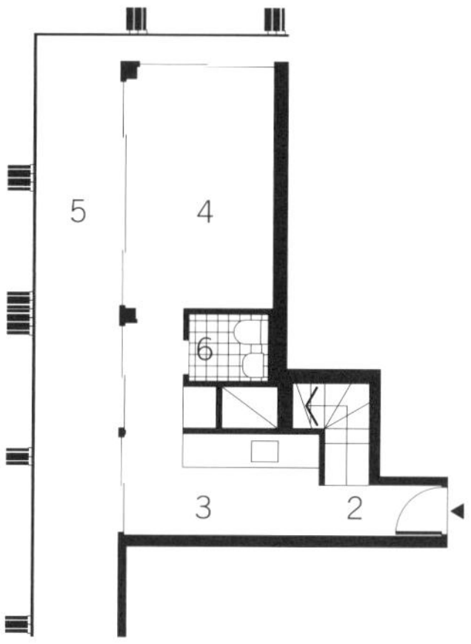

6

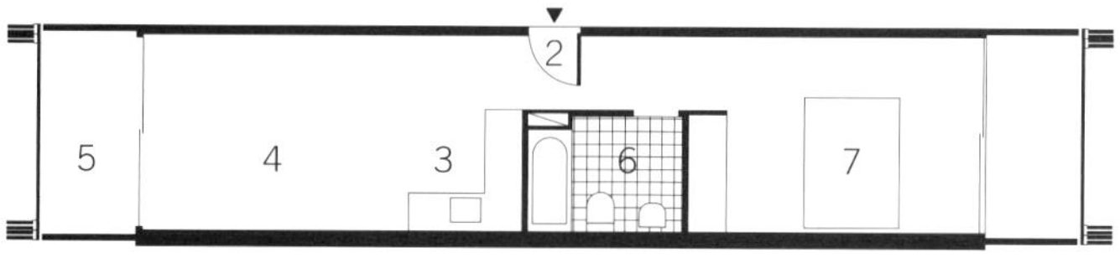

7

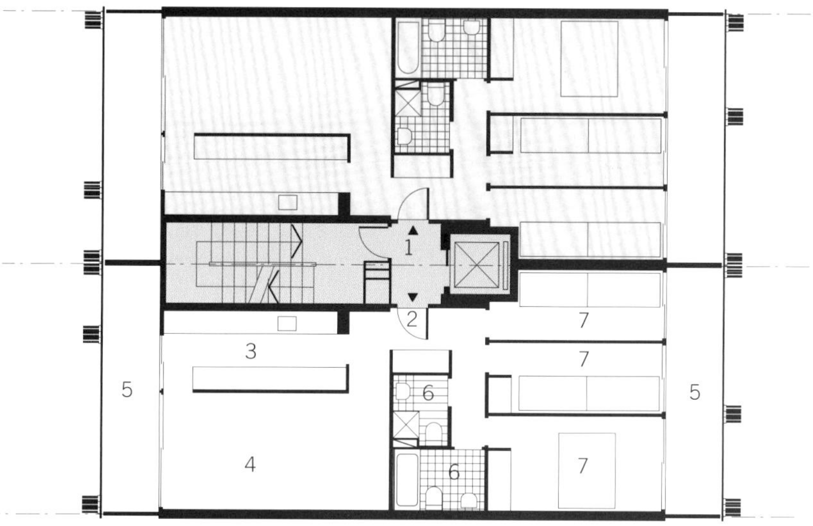

1 Cross-section 1:500

1 Access corridor
2 Terraces
3 Underground parking
4 Private garden

2 South elevation 1:500

3 Plan of typical floor level 1:500

1 Access stairs and lifts
2 Terraces
3 Two-bedroom flat
4 Three-bedroom flat
5 Four-bedroom flat
6 Corner maisonette

Plans of typical flats 1:200

4 Corner maisonette upper level

5 Corner maisonette lower level

6 One-bedroom flat

7 Three-bedroom flat

1 Stair and lifts
2 Entrance/hall
3 Kitchen
4 Living
5 Terrace
6 Bathroom/WC/ shower
7 Bedroom

Further Reading and References

General Histories, Monographs and Catalogues

Alpern, Andrew, *Apartments for the Affluent: A Historical Survey of Buildings in New York* (New York: McGraw-Hill Book Company, 1975)

Beattie, Susan, *A Revolution in London Housing* (London: Greater London Council/The Architectural Press, 1980)

Boyer, M. Christine, *Manhattan Manners* (New York: Rizzoli International Publications, Inc., 1985)

Brayer, Marie-Ange and Simonot, Beatrice, *Archilab's Futurehouse: Radical Experiments in Living Space* (London: Thames & Hudson, 2002)

Colquhoun, Ian, *RIBA Book of 20th-Century British Housing* (Oxford: Butterworth Heinemann, 1999)

Colquhoun, Ian, and Fauset, Peter G., *Housing Design: An International Perspective* (London: BT Batsford, 1991)

Cormes, James, *Modern Housing in Town and Country* (London: BT Batsford, 1905)

Craft Brumfield, W. and Ruble, Blair A., *Russian Housing in the Modern Age: Design and Social History* (Cambridge and New York: Cambridge University Press, 1993)

Cromley, Elizabeth C., *Alone Together: A History of New York's Early Apartments* (New York: Cornell University Press, 1990)

Darley, Gillian, *Villages of Vision* (London: The Architectural Press, 1975)

Esher, Lionel, *A Broken Wave: The Rebuilding of England 1940–1980* (London: Allen Lane, 1981)

Evans, Robin, 'Rookeries and Model Dwellings' in *Translations from Drawing to Building and Other Essays*, AA Documents 2 (London: Architectural Association, 1997)

Gausa, Manuel and Salazar, Jaime, eds, *Housing: New Alternatives, New Systems,* (Barcelona: Actar, 2002)

Glendinning, Miles and Muthesius, Stefan, *Tower Block: Modern Public Housing in England, Scotland, Wales and Northern Ireland* (New Haven and London: Yale University Press for the Paul Mellon Center for Studies in British Art, 1994)

Grinberg, Donald I., with forward by J. B. Bakema, *Housing in the Netherlands 1900–1940* (Delft: Delft University Press, 1977)

Howard, E. *Garden Cities of Tomorrow* (London: Faber, 1965)

Ibelings, Hans, *20th Century Urban Design in the Netherlands* (Rotterdam: NAi Publishers, 1999)

Kloos, Maarten and Wendt, Dave, eds, *Formats for Living: Contemporary Floor Plans in Amsterdam* (Amsterdam: Arcam, 2000)

Mozas, Javier, 'Collective Housing' ('Vivienda colectiva') in *a + t*, special issue: *Density III* (*Densidad III*), no. 21, Spring 2003

Muthesius, Stefan, *The English Terraced House* (New Haven and London: Yale University Press, 1982)

Paul, Samuel, *Apartments, their Design and Development* (New York: Reinhold Publishing, USA, 1967)

Ravetllat, Pere Joan, *Block Housing: A Contemporary Perspective* (Barcelona: Gustavo Gili, 1992)

Rossi, Aldo, *The Architecture of the City* (Cambridge, MA, and London: The MIT Press, 1982)

Rowe, Peter G., *Modernity and Housing* (Cambridge, MA, and London: The MIT Press, 1993)

Schittich, Christian, ed., *In Detail: High-density Housing* (Basel: Birkhauser, 2004)

Schneider, Friederike,ed., *Floor Plan Manual: Housing (Grundrißatlas: Wohnungsbau)* (Basel: Birkhauser, 1994)

Sherwood, Roger, *Modern Housing Prototypes* (Cambridge, MA, and London: Harvard University Press, 1978)

Smithson, Alison and Peter, *Changing the Art of Inhabitation* (London: Artemis, 1994)

Spier, Steven, ed., *Urban Visions, Experiencing and Envisioning the City* (Liverpool University Press and Tate Liverpool, 1993)

Tarn, J. N., *Working-class Housing in 19th Century Britain* (London: Architectural Association Paper No 7, 1971)

Yorke, F. R. S. and Gibberd, F., *The Modern Flat*, original edition, 1937 (London: The Architectural Press, 1948 edition)

Yorke, F. R. S. and Gibberd, F., *Modern Flats* (London: The Architectural Press, 1958 edition)

Journal special issues are listed with individual projects below

Websites

Architects' own websites are increasingly a source of accurate information on more recent projects, as are general sites such as greatbuildings.com, eng.archinform.net and galinsky.com. Roger Sherwood's continuously developing housingprototypes.org has become an invaluable source of information in this field.

References to Individual Projects

The following references, mainly to journals, are an indication only. Drawings and text describing many of these projects, especially the most well known, have been published in some detail in monographs and numerous other books, including those listed in the above general histories. Projects are listed in page number order.

Peabody Buildings ***page 18***

Cormes, James, *Modern Housing in Town and Country* (London: BT Batsford, 1905), pp9–12, 21–23

Rue Franklin Apartments ***page 20***

'Perret: 25bis rue Franklin' in *Rassegna* 28, 1979

Cheap Cottages Exhibition ***page 22***

Cormes, James, *op. cit.*

Miller, Mervyn, *Garden City Heritage Trails* (Letchworth: Letchworth Garden City Corporation), pp127–190

Van Beuningenstraat Housing ***page 26***

Grinberg, Donald I., with forward by J. B. Bakema, *Housing in the Netherlands 1900–1940* (Delft: Delft University Press, 1977), pp36–38

Gradins Vavin/Amiraux ***page 28***

Henri Sauvage 1873–1932 (Brussels: Editions des Archives d'architectures modernes, 1976)

Architecture + Urbanism, no. 9, September 1990, pp50–57

Ottagono, vol. 20, no. 77, June 1985, pp177–179

Hotel des Artistes ***page 30***

New York Times, July 25th, 1909

Architectural Digest, December 1984

Spangen Quarter ***page 34***

'Spangen: A Fragment of Rotterdam' in *Casabella*, vol. 49, no. 515, July/August 1985, pp42–53

El Pueblo Ribera Courtyard Houses ***page 36***

'Houses for Outdoor Life' in *Architectural Record*, July 1930, pp17–21

An Exhibition of the Architecture of R. M. Schindler, 1887–1953 (catalogue of exhibition organized by David Gebhard, Los Angeles: Los Angeles County Museum of Art, 1967)

Efficiency Apartments ***page 38***

Stanley Taylor, C., 'Efficiency Planning and Equipment' in *Architectural Forum*, special issue: *Apartment Hotels*, November 1924, pp204–268

Britz Hufeisensiedlung *page 40*
'Estates of the Twenties: Four Large Berlin Estates' in *Bauforum*, vol. 19, no. 113, 1986, pp41–45
AV Monografías, special issue: *European Housing*, no. 56, November/December 1995, pp2–110

Karl Marx-Hof *page 42*
Garden Cities & Town Planning, July/August 1931, pp173–182
L'Architecture d'aujourd'hui, October 1931, pp33–37
Perspektiven, no. 9, 1989, pp54–59

Weissenhofsiedlung Apartment Building *page 48*
Riley, T. and Bergdoll, B., *Mies in Berlin* (New York: Museum of Modern Art, 2001)

Weissenhofsiedlung Row Housing *page 50*
Deutsche Bauzeitung, vol. 111, no. 11, November 1977, pp27–35

Narkomfin *page 52*
Kopp, Anatole, *Ville et Revolution: Architecture et Urbanisme Sovietiques des Années Vingt* (Paris: Editions Anthropus, 1967), pp150–156
Kopp, Anatole, *Town and Revolution: Soviet Architecture and City Planning*, 1917–1935 (London: Thames & Hudson, 1970), pp115–159
Bliznakov, M., 'Soviet Housing During the Experimental Years 1918–1933' in Craft, Brumfield W. and Ruble, Blair A., eds, *Russian Housing in the Modern Age: Design and Social History* (Cambridge and New York: Cambridge University Press, 1993), pp85–148

Siemensstadt Housing *page 54*
Zodiac, no. 10, 1962, pp68–74
Casabella, no. 223, 1959, pp34–39

Lawn Road (now Isokon) Flats *page 56*
Cantacuzino, Sherban, *Wells Coates: A Monograph* (Gordon Fraser, 1978)
Article on the restoration by Avanti Architects in *The Architects' Journal*, vol. 223, no. 12, March 30, 2006, pp25–37

Vienna Werkbund Houses *pages 60 and 62*
L'Architecture d'aujourd'hui, no. 6, August/September 1932, pp40–49
Architectural Forum, vol. 57, October 1932, pp325–338

Bergpolder Building *page 64*
Roth, Alfred, *The New Architecture/La Nouvelle Architecture/Die Neue Architektur* (Zurich: Les Editions d'Architecture, 1938; second edition 1946)

25 and 42 Avenue de Versailles *page 66*
Monatshefte für Baukunst & Städtebau, December 1932, pp591–593
'Pages d'un journal du chantier/25 avenue de Versailles à Paris' in *Architectural Review*, October 1932, pp133–134

Highpoint I and II *page 68*
The Architects' Journal, special issue: *The Flat: Pride and Prejudice*, May 2, 1935, pp652–709
Architectural Review, October 1938, p161
Article by Toshiko Kinoshita and Kenji Watanabe in *Architecture + Urbanism*, no. 7 (322), July 1997, pp138–143

Kensal House *page 72*
Denby, Elizabeth, 'Kensal House, An Urban Village' and Maxwell Fry, E., 'Kensal House' in *Flats* (London: Ascot, 1938)
The Architects' Journal, March 18, 1937, pp466–467

Casa Rustici *page 74*
Rassegna di Architettura, vol 8, May 1936, pp141–147
Zevi, Bruno, *Giuseppe Terragni,* (Bologna: N. Zanichelli Editore SpA, 1980)

Bubeshko Apartments *page 76*
Gebhard, D., *Schindler* (San Francisco: Viking Press, 1972)
Sheine, Judith, *R. M. Schindler* (London: Phaidon, 2001)

Unité d'Habitation *page 82*
Jenkins, David, *Unité d'Habitation, Marseilles* (London: Phaidon, 1993)

Pedregulho Housing *page 86*
Bonduki, Nabil and Portinho, Carmen, *Affonso Eduardo Reidy 1909–1964* (Lisbon: Blau, 2000)

Churchill Gardens Estate *page 88*
The Architect and Building News, December 8, 1950, pp607–617, 628–629
Article by Henry Russell Hitchcock in *Architectural Review*, September 1953, pp177–184

Golden Lane Estate *page 90*
Architectural Review, June 1957, pp414–426
The Architect and Building News, August 29, 1957, pp271–289

Casa de la Marina *page 92*
etsav.upc.es/arxcoderch/
Arquitectura (Madrid), November 1967, pp1–37
Cuadernos de Arquitectura, no. 68–69, 1968, pp21–26

Workers' Housing *page 94*
Casabella, no. 218, 1958, pp40–49
McKean, John, *Giancarlo De Carlo: Layered Places* (Stuttgart and London: Menges, 2004)

860–880 Lake Shore Drive *page 96*
L'Architecture d'aujourd'hui, no. 79, 1958, pp60–65
The Architect and Building News, April 8, 1954, pp402–409

Price Tower *page 98*
Architectural Forum, May 1953, pp98–105
Architecture and Building, July 1956, pp268–270
Wright, Frank Lloyd, *The Story of the Tower* (New York: Horizon Press, 1956)

Keeling House *page 100*
Architectural Review, May 1960, pp304–312
Architectural Record, October 1960, pp212–213
Architectural Design, April 1956, pp125–126

Harumi Apartments *page 102*
Bauen & Wohnen (Munich), no. 1, 1960, pp39–41

Beacon Street Apartments *page 104*
Architectural Record, June 1959, p198

Hansaviertel Apartments *page 106*
Arkkitehti, no. IV, 1957, pp173–177

Hansaviertel Tower *page 108*
Forum (Amsterdam), no. 8, 1960–61, pp264–273
Architectural Design, December 1961, pp550–552

Bellevue Bay Flats and Houses *page 110*
Bauen & Wohnen (Munich), no. 3, 1962, pp99–104

Halen Housing
Architectural Design, February 1963, pp63–71
Werk, February 1963, pp58–71
Casabella, no. 258, 1961, pp27–31

Tapiola Housing *page 116*
Bauen & Wohnen (Munich), no. 4, 1969, pp126–127

Marina City ***page 122***
Architectural Record, September 1963, p215

Lafayette Park Apartments ***page 124***
Deutsche Bauzeitschrift, no. 1, 1964, pp19–24
Architectural Design, September 1960, pp353–354

Peabody Terrace ***page 126***
Dixon, John Morris, 'Yesterday's Paradigm, Today's Problem' in *Progressive Architecture*, vol. 75, no. 6, June 1994, pp100–107
Hale, Jonathan, 'Ten Years Past at Peabody Terrace' in *Progressive Architecture*, vol. 55, no. 10, October 1974, pp72–77

Blues Point Tower ***page 128***
'Australian Domestic Architecture' in *Architectural Review*, vol. 134, no. 797, July 1963, pp12–19, 55–56
Architecture & Arts, July 1962, pp46, 48–49

Bakkedraget Housing ***page 130***
Jørn Utzon: The Architect's Universe ([Humlebaek] Louisiana Museum of Modern Art [2004])
Prip-Buus, Mogens, ed., *The Courtyard Houses* (Hellerup: Blondal, 2004)

The Ryde ***page 132***
The Architects' Journal, Information Library, 12 October 1966
The Architects' Journal, Information Library, 16 August 1972

Habitat 67 ***page 134***
Architectural Review, special issue on Expo 67, vol. 142, no. 846, August 1967, pp143–150

Twin Parks Northwest Site 4 ***page 136***
Architectural Record, vol. 152, no. 3, September 1972, pp154–157
'Twin Parks as Typology' in *Architectural Forum*, vol. 138, no. 5, June 1973, pp56–61 (includes discussion of other Twin Parks sites by Richard Meier & Partners and Giovanni Pasanella & Associates)

Trellick Tower ***page 138***
The Architects' Journal, January 10, 1973, pp80–84
Dunnett, James, *Ernö Goldfinger: Works* (London: The Architectural Press, 1983)

Robin Hood Gardens ***page 140***
Architectural Design, vol. 42, no. 9, September 1972, pp557–573

Nagakin Capsule Tower ***page 142***
Domus, 520 (3), March 1973
Japan Architect, vol. 47, no. 190 (10), October 1972, pp17–38

University Centre Housing Urbino ***page 144***
McKean, John, *Giancarlo De Carlo: Layered Places* (Stuttgart and London: Menges, 2004)

Olympic Tower ***page 146***
Progressive Architecture, vol. 56, no. 12, December 1975, pp37–51
Architektur & Wohnwelt, vol. 83, no. 2, March 1975, pp114–116

Walden 7 ***page 148***
Cuadernos de Arquitectura y Urbanismo, no. 111 (6), November 1975, pp13–21
Architectural Design, vol. 45, no. 7, July 1975, pp402–417

Emmanuel Benaki Street Apartments ***page 150***
Frampton, Kenneth, ed., *Atelier 66: The Architecture of Dimitris and Suzanna Antonakakis* (New York: Rizzoli, 1985)

Housing on Calle Doña María Coronel ***page 152***
Cruz/Ortiz 1975–1995 (New York: Princeton Architectural Press, 1996)

Gallaratese Housing ***page 154***
Peereboom, Jan Dirk and Wintermans, Frank, 'Idealism Versus Dialectic in Social Housing of the 60s: Neave Brown in London and Aldo Rossi in Milan' in *Wonen-TA/BK*, no. 2, 1980, pp11–27
Casabella, vol. 38, no. 7 (391), July 1974, pp17–25

Quinta da Malagueira ***page 156***
El Croquis, vol. 13, no. 4 (68/69), 1994, pp76–81
Angelilo, Antonio, ed., *Siza: Architecture Writings* (Milan: Skira, 1997)

Corner Housing at Kochstrasse ***page 162***
El Croquis, vol. 8, no. 9 (83), September 1990, pp24–29
Architectural Review, vol. 181, no. 1082, April 1987, pp60–63
Nalbach, G. & Nalbach, N., eds, *Berlin Modern Architecture: The International Building Exhibition, Berlin 1987* (Berlin: Senatsverwaltung für Bau- und wohnungswesen, 1989)

Housing on Lützowplatz ***page 164***
GA Houses, no. 23, August 1988, pp152–157
Kleihues, Josef Paul and others, *Lotus International*, special issue: *Living in the City*, no. 41, 1984, pp18–93

St Mark's Road Housing ***page 166***
Building Design, no. 448, June 1, 1979, pp18–19

Rue des Hautes Formes ***page 168***
Lotus International, special issue: *Living in the City*, no. 41, 1984, pp94–127
GA Houses, no. 23, August 1988, pp68–77

Noisy II Housing ***page 170***
Galantino, Mauro, *Henri Ciriani: Architecture 1960–2000* (Milan: Skira, 2000)
Architectural Design, 7–8, 1982, pp92–99
GA Document, 3, 1981, pp68–79

Atlantis Condominium ***page 172***
'Rich and Famous: Two Apartment Buildings, Atlantis and Babylon, in Miami' in *Progressive Architecture*; vol. 64, no. 2, February 1983, pp99–107

Byker Wall ***page 174***
Architectural Design, vol. 45, no. 6, June 1975, pp333–338
Futagawa, Yukio, ed., *Global Architecture* 55, special issue: *Byker Development*, 1980

Housing for the Elderly ***page 176***
Deutsche Bauzeitung: special issue: *Growing Old*, vol. 119, no. 11, November 1985, pp10–42

Nemausus ***page 178***
Duroy, Lionel, *L'Architecture d'aujourd'hui*, special issue: *Le logement a l'aube d'une mutation radicale* (*Housing, at the dawn of a radical change*), no. 252, September 1987, pp1–49
Techniques et architecture, special issue: *Housing: Recent European Projects*, no. 375, December/January 1987/1988, pp62–151

Pence Place ***page 180***
GA Houses, no. 23, August 1988, pp194–197
L'Industria delle costruzioni, vol. 21, no. 192, October 1987, pp44–50

IJ-Plein ***page 182***
L'Industria delle costruzioni, vol. 24, no. 222, April 1990, pp20–25
'Housing Design as a Statement' in *Baumeister*, vol. 86, no. 4, April 1989, pp44–61 (IJ-Plein pp48–51)
'Low-income Housing: A Lesson from Amsterdam' in *Architectural Record*, vol. 173, no. 1, January 1985, pp134–143

Spiral House ***page 184***
Architectural Design, vol. 69, no. 9/10, 1999, p112
'The Tower and the Serpent' in *Techniques et architecture*, no. 394, February/March 1991, pp70–77

Nexus World Housing ***page 186***
Japan Architect, special issue: *Housing*, no. 4, 1991, pp92–103
Arquitectura Viva, no.23, March/April 1992, pp14–17

Rue de Meaux Housing ***page 188***
Techniques et architecture, no. 397, August/September 1991, pp38–47

Horizon Apartments ***page 190***
Construction Review, vol. 64, no. 2, May 1991, pp16–23

Kavel 25 ***page 196***
Archis, no. 1, January 1993, pp54–59
van der Burgh, Marja, *STRIP* (Rotterdam: Nai publications, 2003)

Carl-Spitzweg-Gasse Housing ***page 198***
Blundell Jones, Peter, 'The Rhetoric of Shelter' in *Architectural Review*, vol. 198, no. 1184, October 1995, pp66–69
GA Houses, no. 43, October 1994, pp114–116
Weiss, Klaus Dieter, *Deutsche Bauzeitschrift*, vol. 42, no. 6, June 1994, pp51–58

Schlesischestrasse Housing ***page 200***
Léon, H., Wohlhage, Konrad and Schneider, F., *Léonwohlhage: Bauten und Projekte: 1987–1997* (Basel: Birkhauser, 1997)

Silodam ***page 202***
Metz, Tracy, *Architectural Record*, vol. 191, no. 3, March 2003, pp114–121
'Ciutat Usada' in *Quaderns*, no. 234, July 2002, pp114–123

Sejima Wing, Kitagata Housing ***page 206***
Klauser, Wilhelm, *L'Architecture d'aujourd'hui*, no. 323, July 1999, pp90–91
'Cultural Hybrids' in *Archis*, no. 11, November 2000, pp50–57
Bauwelt, vol. 90, no. 20, May 21, 1999, pp1080–1103
Japan Architect, special issue: *Kazuyo Sejima (1987–1999) and Kazuyo Sejima & Ryue Nishizawa (1995–1999)*, no. 35, Autumn 1999, pp4–128

Courtyard Houses ***page 208***
Casabella, vol. 64, no. 678, May 2000, pp38–43
Baumeister, vol. 98, no.1, January 2001, pp53–90
2G, special issue: *Eduardo Souto de Moura: Recent Work*, no. 5 (1), 1998

Rue des Suisses ***page 210***
'Space and Identity' in *Architectural Review*, vol. 212, no. 1265, July 2002, pp42–49
'L'Heterotopie à Paris' in *L'Architecture d'aujourd'hui*, no. 337, November/December 2001, pp112–117

Schots 1 + 2 ***page 212***
Architecture + Technology, special issue: *Density IV*, no. 22, Autumn 2003, pp56–81

Yerba Buena Lofts ***page 216***
Praxis, special issue: *Housing Tactics*, vol. 1, no. 3, 2001, pp 5–128
GA Houses, no. 76, July 2003, pp130–139

The Whale ***page 218***
'Housing Differentiation' in *Lotus International*, no. 132, November 2007, pp2–129
L'Industria delle costruzioni, special issue: [*Experimental housing in the Netherlands*] no. 377, May/June 2004, pp4–75

Liverpool Street Housing ***page 220***
Casabella, vol. 69, no. 738, November 2005, pp54–57
Canizares, Anna G., *New Apartments* (New York: Harper Design International, 2005)

Mirador Apartments ***page 222***
Architecture + Technology, special issue: *Density I*, no. 19, Spring 2002, pp132–137
'Privacy and Publicity: Two New Social Housing Projects in Madrid Offer Rival Approaches to the Meaning of Home' in *Architecture* (New York), vol. 94, no. 11, November 2005, pp54–65

Consort Road Housing ***page 226***
Architecture Today, February 2008, pp36–45

Carabanchel 16 Housing ***page 228***
Blueprint, no. 259, October 2007, pp82–90
'Brits Abroad' in *RIBA Journal*, vol. 114, no. 7, July 2007, pp7–9, 16, 42–48

Index

Page numbers in *italics* refer to picture captions

Picture Credits

10 tl G.E. Kidder Smith, Courtesy of Kidder Smith Collection, Rotch Visual Collections, Massachusetts Institute of Technology
11t © Susan Carr/ESTO/VIEW
12 l & r Alexander Hartmann
13 Sérgio Padura/F.O.A.
15 tl & tr Hilary French
15 b Corbis/Bettmann
16 t bpk/Kunstbibliothek, SMB, Berlin
16 bl © Fredrika Lökholm
16 br Hilary French
17 tr The Mitchell Wolfson, Jr. Collection (Schultze & Weaver Collection), The Wolfsonian, Florida International University, Miami Beach
18 tl & tr Hilary French
20 tl Hilary French
20 tr Paul Raftery/VIEW
22 Hilary French
26 IISG, Collection Aedes
28 tl Artedia
28 tr Fondations Sauvage, Direction des Archives de France
30 © Matt Conte 2008
34 t Artedia
36 t © Michael-Leonard Creditor/Artifice Images
38 t *Architectural Forum* LI, no.6 (November 1924)
40 t Alexander Hartmann
42 t Hervé Champollion/akg-images
45 tl BPK, Berlin
46 tl Frank den Oudsten & Associates
46 tr © DACS 2008
46 bl Lucia Moholy/Bauhaus Archiv, Berlin © DACS 2008
46 br Alexander Hartmann
47 top010.nl
48 t Electa/akg-images
50 t Roland Halbe/RIBA Library Photographs Collection
50 b © DACS 2008
51 © DACS 2008
52 t RIA Novosti/TopFoto
54 tl Alexander Hartmann
54 tr Dieter Leistner/artur
56 tl Morley von Sternberg/Arcaid
56 tr RIBA Library Photographs Collection
60 t Keith Collie/RIBA Library Photographs Collection
62 tl & tr Hervé Champollion/akg-images
62 br © DACS 2008
63 © DACS 2008
64 top010.nl
66 tl & tr Hilary French
68 l Janet Hall/RIBA Library Photographs Collection
68 r Dell & Wainwright/RIBA Library Photographs Collection
72 l ©Annabel Craig/Architectural Association
72 r RIBA Library Photographs Collection
74 tl & tr Hilary French
76 t Grant Mudford
79 l © FLC/ADAGP, Paris and DACS, London 2008
79 r RIBA Library Photographs Collection
80 tl RIBA Library Photographs Collection
80 cr © Frank Lloyd Wright/ARS, New York and DACS, London 2008
80 br Jørgen Strüwing
81 l Alvar Aalto Museum
81 r Martin Bond/Alamy
82 l & r © FLC/ ADAGP, Paris and DACS, London 2008
86 t Marcel Gautherot/Acervo Instituto Moreira Salles
88 t © Fredrika Lökholm
90 tl Janet Hall/RIBA Library Photographs Collection
90 tr John Maltby/RIBA Library Photographs Collection
92 t Duccio Malagamba
94 t Aldo Ballo
96 t Ezra Stoller/ESTO
98 tl Alan Weintraub/Arcaid
98 tr Joe Price. © Frank Lloyd Wright/ARS, New York and DACS, London 2008
100 t Christopher Hope-Fitch/RIBA Library Photographs Collection
102 l & r photos: Maekawa Associates
104 t Stubbins Archive, Harvard University
106 t Alexander Hartmann
108 lt Alexander Hartmann
108 tr Broek en Bakema
110 t Jørgen Strüwing
112 t © Balthasar Burkhard
116 l Museum of Finnish Architecture/Kari Hakli
116 r Museum of Finnish Architecture/Ingervo
119 tl Peter Cook © Archigram 1964 (Photo © Archigram Archives 2008)
199 tr Philip Johnson Fund. Acc. No. 435.1967. 2008 © Dig. Image Museum of Modern Art, New York/Scala, Florence
120 tl Bill Tingey/Arcaid
120 bl Michael Harding/Arcaid
120 br Viennaslide
121 r Builder Group
122 tl Barry Edwards/Arcaid
122 tr © Ezra Stoller/ESTO
124 t © Wayne Andrews/ESTO/VIEW
126 G.E. Kidder Smith, Courtesy of Kidder Smith Collection, Rotch Visual Collections, Massachusetts Institute of Technology
128 tl & tr Harry Seidler & Associates
130 t Richard Weston
132 tl & tr Phippen Randall and Parkes
134 t Michael Freeman/Corbis
136 t © Ezra Stoller/ESTO
138 tl Alex Bartel/Arcaid
138 tr © Edmund Sumner/VIEW
140 tl & tr © Marjorie Morrison/Architectural Association
142 t Bill Tingey/Arcaid
144 tl & tr Archivio Progetti, Archivio Casali, Università IUAV di Venezia
146 t © Peter Aaron/ESTO/VIEW
148 t Viennaslide
150 tl & tr Antonakakis + Antonakakis
152 tl & tr Duccio Malagamba
154 t S. Brandolino/Architectural Association
156 t ©Alan Chandler/Architectural Association
159 l & r Alexander Hartmann
160 tl Viennaslide
160 tr Robin Hill/Danita Delimont Stock Photography
160 b © Sally-Ann Norman/VIEW
161 tl © Iwan Baan/Steven Holl Architects
161 tr © DACS 2008
162 t Alexander Hartmann
164 t Alexander Hartmann
166 t Martin Charles/Dixon Jones
168 t Nicolas Borel/Christian de Portzamparc
170 t P. Chair
172 t Robin Hill/Danita Delimont Stock Photography
174 tl & tr © Sally-Ann Norman/VIEW
176 tl & tr Alexander Hartmann
178 tl Georges Fessy
178 tr Philippe Ruault
178 b © ADAGP, Paris and DACS, London 2008
179 © ADAGP, Paris and DACS, London 2008
180 tl & tr Abby Sadin/Gwathmey Siegel & Associates
182 t © Peter Aaron/ESTO/VIEW
182 b © DACS 2008
183 © DACS 2008
184 t © Michael Krüger Architekturfotografie, Berlin
186 tl © Iwan Baan/Steven Holl Architects
186 tr Steven Holl Architects
188 tl & tr Hilary French
190 tl & tr Harry Seidler & Associates
193 tl KCAP
194 tl Shinkenchiku-sha/The Japan Architect Co., Ltd
194 tr © Rob 't Hart/MVRDV
194 b Tim Crocker/Proctor & Matthews
195 l&r Tim Griffith/Saitowitz
196 tl & tr KCAP
198 tl & tr © Paul Ott, Graz
200 tl & tr Alexander Hartmann
202 t © Rob 't Hart
206 t Shinkenchiku-sha/The Japan Architect Co., Ltd
208 t © Luis Ferreira Alves/Souto da Moura
210 tl & tr Hilary French
212 tl & tr Jan Bitter
216 tl & tr Tim Griffith/Saitowitz
218 tl Jeroen Musch/de Architekten Cie.
218 tr de Architekten Cie.
220 t Ross Honeysett/Ian Moore Architects
222 tl & tr © Rob 't Hart/MVRDV
226 tl & tr © Edmund Sumner/VIEW
228 t Francisco Andeyro García & Alejandro García González/FOA

Author’s acknowledgements

Thanks to Samson Adjei, Gregory Gibbon, Yan Ki Lee, Inka Hella and Kirsteen Mackay.

Thanks also to Philip Cooper, Liz Faber and Kim Sinclair at Laurence King, to picture researchers Claire Gouldstone and Cecilia Mackay, and to designer Anita Ruddell.

For Jessie

About the CD

The attached CD-ROM can be read on both Windows and Macintosh computers. All the material on the CD-ROM is copyright protected and is for private use only.

All drawings in the book and on the CD-ROM were specially created for this publication and are based on the architects' original drawings held in archives or supplied by the architects, or on previously published material either in professional journals or in the books listed in the Further Reading section. Every effort has been made to ensure accuracy in the drawings.

Drawings are by Hilary French, Samson Adjei, Yan Ki Lee and Gregory Gibbon.

The CD-ROM includes files for all the plans, sections and elevations featured in the case studies of the book. The drawings for each building are contained in a numbered folder as listed below. They are supplied in two versions: the files with the suffix '.eps' are vector Illustrator EPS files but can be opened using other graphics programs such as Photoshop; all the files with the suffix '.dwg' are generic CAD format files and can be opened in a variety of CAD programs.

The generic '.dwg' file format does not support 'solid fill' utilized by many architectural CAD programs. All the information is embedded within the file and can be reinstated within supporting CAD programs. Select the polygon required and change the 'Attributes' to 'Solid'; the colour information should automatically be retrieved. To reinstate the 'Walls'; select all objects within the 'Walls' layer/class and amend their 'Attributes' to 'Solid'.

All drawings are to the same scale as shown in the book. File names indicate project number, figure number and scale (for example, '01.2_200. eps/dwg' indicates the file is from project number 1, Peabody Buildings, is of drawing number 2 in that project, and is shown at 1:200).

The numbered folders correspond to the following buildings:

01. Peabody Buildings
02. Rue Franklin Apartments
03. Cheap Cottages Exhibition
04. Van Beuningenstraat Housing
05. Gradins Vavin/Amiraux
06. Hotel des Artistes
07. Spangen Quarter
08. El Pueblo Ribera Courtyard Houses
09. Efficiency Apartments
10. Britz Hufeisensiedlung
11. Karl Marx-Hof
12. Weissenhofsiedlung Apartment Building
13. Weissenhofsiedlung Row Housing
14. Narkomfin
15. Seimensstadt Housing
16. Lawn Road (now Isokon) Flats
17. Vienna Werkbund Houses (Loos)
18. Vienna Werkbund Houses (Lurçat)
19. Bergpolder Building
20. 25 and 42 Avenue de Versailles
21. Highpoint Flats
22. Kensal House
23. Casa Rustici
24. Bubeshko Apartments
25. Unité d'Habitation
26. Pedregulho Housing
27. Churchill Gardens Estate
28. Golden Lane Estate
29. Casa de la Marina
30. Workers' Housing
31. 860–880 Lake Shore Drive
32. Price Tower
33. Keeling House
34. Harumi Apartments
35. Beacon Street Apartments
36. Hansaviertel Apartments
37. Hansaviertel Tower
38. Bellevue Bay Flats and Houses
39. Halen Housing
40. Tapiola Housing
41. Marina City
42. Lafayette Park Apartments
43. Peabody Terrace
44. Blues Point Tower
45. Bakkedraget Housing
46. The Ryde
47. Habitat 67
48. Twin Parks Northwest Site 4
49. Balfron and Trellick Towers
50. Robin Hood Gardens
51. Nagakin Capsule Tower
52. University Centre Housing
53. Olympic Tower
54. Walden 7
55. Emmanuel Benaki Street Apartments
56. Housing on Calle Doña María Coronel
57. Gallaratese Housing
58. Quinta da Malagueira Housing
59. Corner Housing at Kochstrasse
60. Housing on Lützowplatz
61. St Mark's Road Housing
62. Rue des Hautes Formes
63. Noisy II Housing
64. Atlantis Condominium
65. Byker Wall
66. Housing for the Elderly
67. Nemausus
68. Pence Place
69. IJ-Plein Housing
70. Spiral House
71. Nexus World Housing
72. Rue de Meaux Housing
73. Horizon Apartments
74. Kavel 25
75. Carl-Spitzweg-Gasse Housing
76. Schlesischestrasse Housing
77. Silodam
78. Sejima Wing, Kitagata Housing
79. Courtyard Houses
80. Rue des Suisses Housing
81. Schots 1 + 2
82. Yerba Buena Lofts
83. The Whale
84. Liverpool Street Housing
85. Mirador Apartments
86. Consort Road Housing
87. Carabanchel 16 Housing